# EXILE, STATELESSNESS, AND MIGRATION

# Exile, Statelessness, and Migration

PLAYING CHESS WITH HISTORY FROM
HANNAH ARENDT TO ISAIAH BERLIN

SEYLA BENHABIB

PRINCETON UNIVERSITY PRESS
PRINCETON & OXFORD

Published by Princeton University Press,
41 William Street, Princeton, New Jersey 08540

In the United Kingdom: Princeton University Press,
6 Oxford Street, Woodstock, Oxfordshire OX20 1TR

press.princeton.edu

Cover image: Dani Karavan, *Passages, Homage to Walter Benjamin*, detail of
environmental sculpture, 1990–1994, Portbou, Spain. © Studio Karavan.

LCCN 2018930584

ISBN 978-0-691-16724-4

ISBN (pbk.) 978-0-691-16725-1

British Library Cataloging-in-Publication Data is available

This book has been composed in Arno Pro

Printed on acid-free paper. ∞

Printed in the United States of America

10  9  8  7  6  5  4  3  2  1

For Jim

After twenty years

# CONTENTS

# ACKNOWLEDGMENTS

THIS BOOK WOULD NOT HAVE BEEN POSSIBLE without the dedicated cooperation of many of my graduate students. *Stefan Eich* was there from the beginning when in 2012 I received the Leopold Lucas Prize of the Theological Faculty of the University of Tübingen that set me upon the path of autobiographical reflection on Jewish history and culture in Germany and Turkey. He helped identify sources, translated texts, and edited the prize lecture that has now been revised as chapter 2 of this volume.

Members of my Doctoral Colloquium that met Tuesday evenings for several years—Umur Basdas, Carmen Dege, Blake Emerson, Devin Goure, Anna Jurkevics, Elizabeth Krontiris, Paul Linden-Retek, and Clara Picker—have inspired me through their questions, writing, and conversations and have provided invaluable help for the research behind many of these chapters.

My thanks go to Nica Siegel, also a graduate student in the Yale political theory program, for her efficient and thorough work in the preparation of the bibliography in multiple languages.

A sabbatical leave from Yale University in spring 2016 and an invitation to the University of Cambridge as Diane Middlebrook and Carl Djerassi Visiting Professor of Gender Studies in spring 2017 enabled me to put the finishing touches on this volume. I would like to thank Professor Jude Brown of the Program in Gender Studies for her kind invitation. The time I spent in Cambridge, UK, proved particularly auspicious for my research. I arrived there with drafts of chapter 6—"From the 'Right to Have Rights' to the 'Critique of Humanitarian Reason'"—and chapter 7—"Legalism and Its Paradoxes in Judith Shklar's Work"—partially completed. I had some trepidation about basing my guest lecture as visiting professor on Hannah Arendt's work since she never seemed to have enjoyed much regard in the United Kingdom. I not only found that the broader public was now engaged with her work on statelessness and the refugee condition but that my predecessors as Diane Middlebrook and Carl Djerassi chairs—Gillian Rose and Judith Butler—had also discussed Arendt during their visits. On the occasion of this lecture, Jude Brown probed me to clarify what kind of political agency could reasonably be expected of human beings in refugee camps. In the course of several conversations, Duncan Bell and I shared exchanges on federalist and federationalist projects. Bell pointed me in the direction of some new research on Arendt and Berlin, which will be discussed in chapter 9.

Particularly helpful was a colloquium held on Judith Shklar's work on February 20, 2017, upon the invitation of Duncan Kelly within the context of his History of Political Thought seminars. Katrina Forrester's comments on this occasion were very important for clarifying Shklar's relation to realism. Thanks also to Duncan Kelly for bringing Peter Lassman's book on *Pluralism* to my attention.

William E. Scheuerman, on whose dissertation committee—chaired by Judith Shklar at Harvard—I had served as a second reader nearly three decades ago, provided me with very incisive comments on the full manuscript and was particularly helpful with comments on chapter 7.

During my Cambridge sojourn, I met Samuel Zeitlin, a graduate student from Berkeley working on his dissertation. Sam proofread and commented upon the first seven chapters of this manuscript and provided me with many valuable insights, some of which I tried to acknowledge in the text. He is a young scholar of immense erudition and is making his mark through his superbly annotated translations of Carl Schmitt's texts. Thanks are due to him for his outstanding help.

My interest in the themes of European, and in particular, German-Jewish intellectual history goes back to my first years in Germany when I arrived in 1979 as an Alexander von Humboldt Fellow. Upon settling in Frankfurt in the early 1980s, I met an extraordinary group of politically engaged Jewish intellectuals: Micha Brumlik, Dan Diner, Gertrud Koch, Cilly Kugelman, and Moishe Postone. We have remained friends for more than three decades and I learned a great deal from them about the European Jewish experience of the interwar and postwar years. They are my secret interlocutors in many chapters.

Conversations with Yirmiyahu Yovel during his tenure as professor of philosophy at the New School for Social Research have been extremely significant for me and chapter 2 is dedicated to him and his wife, Shoshana Yovel.

Over the years I have had dialogues on these issues with friends and colleagues, among them Asaf Angermann, Roger Berkowitz, Richard J. Bernstein, Susan Buck-Morss, Drucilla Cornell, Carolin Emcke, Rainer Forst, Peter Gordon, Jürgen Habermas, Dick Howard, Martin Jay, Karuna Mantena, and Jason Stanley. They have inspired me through their work and reflections.

Thanks also to Rob Tempio from Princeton University Press, in exchanges with whom the idea for this book emerged and for his patience in awaiting its completion.

This book is dedicated to James A. Sleeper with gratitude for two decades of conversations and insights that have probed with me the individual and collective Jewish experiences that shape thinkers' lives.

*Alford, Massachusetts*
New York City
October 2017

# CHAPTER ACKNOWLEDGMENTS

CHAPTER 2 IS BASED upon a lecture delivered when I was awarded the Leopold Lucas Prize of the Theological Faculty of the University of Tübingen in spring 2012. The revised lecture has appeared in a German-English edition as *Gleichheit und Differenz. Die Würde des Menschen und die Souveränitäsansprüche der Völker in Spiegel der politischen Moderne [Equality and Difference. Human Dignity and Popular Sovereignty in the Mirror of Political Modernity]* (Tübingen: Mohr Siebeck, 2013), 6–96. A shortened and revised version was previously published as "Judith Shklar's Dystopic Liberalism," in *Social Research* 61:2 (1994): 477–88. © 1994 The New School for Social Research. Reprinted with permission of Johns Hopkins University Press. Both versions have been significantly rewritten for inclusion in this volume.

Chapter 3 was first published as "Arendt and Adorno. The Elusiveness of the Particular and the Benjaminian Moment," in *Arendt and Adorno: Political and Philosophical Investigations*, edited by Lars Rensmann and Samir Gandesha (Stanford: Stanford University Press, 2012), 31–56. Copyright © 2012 by the Board of Trustees of the Leland Stanford Jr. University. All rights reserved, Reprinted by permission of the publisher, Stanford University Press, sup.org.

An earlier version of chapter 4 appeared as "Whose Trial? Adolf Eichmann's or Hannah Arendt's? The Eichmann Controversy Revisited," in *The Trial that Never Ends: Hannah Arendt's Eichmann in Jerusalem in Retrospect*, edited by Richard J. Golsan and Sarah M. Misemer (Toronto, Buffalo, and London: University of Toronto Press, 2017), 209–29. Copyright © 2017 by University of Toronto Press. Reprinted by permission.

Chapter 5 was first published in *Constellations*, vol. 20, no. 1 (2013): 150–63 as a review essay of Judith Butler, *Parting Ways. Jewishness and the Critique of Zionism.* Copyright © 2013 Blackwell Publishing Ltd. Reprinted by permission. It has been revised for inclusion in this volume.

Chapter 6 was first presented at the New School for Social Research upon the establishment of the Ari Zolberg Center for Migration Studies in spring 2015. It was delivered in Essen-Duisburg University's Center for Migrant Studies on January 28, 2016, and as my Diane Middlebrook and Carl Djerassi Visiting Professorship lecture in Cambridge University, UK, on February 13, 2017, and at Leeds University Law School on February 23, 2017. It is being published for the first time in this volume.

Earlier versions of chapter 7 were read at the Political Theory Conference organized by Tel-Aviv University on June 5, 2016; at the Minerva Center for Human Rights of the Hebrew University of Jerusalem on June 7, 2016; at the New School for Social Research on November 16, 2006; and at the Yale Political Theory Colloquium, November 30, 2016. Parts of it were also presented at the Cambridge Colloquium on the History of Political Thought on February 20, 2017. This is its first full publication.

A much shorter version of chapter 8 has previously appeared as "Oracle's Odyssey. Review of *Worldly Philosopher. The Odyssey of Albert O. Hirschman,* by Jeremy Adelman" in *Democracy Journal* (Fall 2013) No. 30.: 85–92. Copyright © 2013 by Democracy: A Journal of Ideas, Inc. Reprinted by permission.

Chapter 9 is based on a lecture I held during the Istanbul Seminars, organized by the RESET Foundation in May 2014 at Bilgi University. It appears in print for the first time.

# PREFACE

IN THE EARLY DECADES of the twenty-first century, exile, statelessness, and migration have emerged as universal experiences of humanity.
In 2000, there were 175 million migrants out of 6 billion of the world's
population. In 2015 the number of international migrants—persons living in a country other than where they were born—increased by 41% to
reach 244 million worldwide.[1] It is not the absolute number of migrants
or their proportion of the world's population that merits attention
(about 3.1% out of a world population estimated at about 7.5 billion are
international migrants) but the fact that their number has grown *faster*
than the world's population in this period. There has been an intensifica-
tion of migratory movements in the past fifteen years, with the condition of refugees reaching crisis proportions not encountered since
World War II. A report by the United Nations High Commissioner for
Refugees finds that 65.6 million, that is, one out of every 113 persons in
the world, was displaced by conflict, violence, or economic and ecologi-
cal disasters by the end of 2016.[2] Compared with today's suffering
masses of humanity from the Global South and East desperately trying
to reach the resource-rich countries of Europe, Canada, the USA, and
Australia, the intellectuals considered in this volume belonged to an
educated elite, even though they were predominantly Jewish refugees
persecuted on account of their religion and ethnicity. They had or
would receive a superb education, which enabled them to adapt quickly
to their host countries. In this book I explore the intertwinement of the
lives, careers, and thoughts of Theodor Adorno, Hannah Arendt, Walter
Benjamin, Judith Shklar, Albert Hirschman, and Isaiah Berlin among
others.

It has often been noted that the exodus of the Jewish intelligentsia from Europe produced one of the most brilliant and effervescent intellectual movements of the twentieth century. Indeed, these thinkers reflected upon their own experiences in a wrenching reckoning with the legacies of the European Enlightenment, Romanticism, and German Idealism. Many, among them Arendt, Adorno, and Berlin, saw in the tensions and conflicts developed by German Idealism—between reason and science, freedom and causality, the citizen and the individual—the sources of an intellectual collapse and malaise that would become particularly visible after the failure of Hegelian system-building.

Others, such as Shklar, Hirschman, and Berlin turned from German thought to the French and British Enlightenments and entertained a more skeptical habit of mind. Departing from the exaggerated ideals of human emancipation and reconciliation that dominated German thought, they searched for the rule of law in a decent society, and a social science that would illuminate the unrealized but intended consequences of human action. At least in one case, namely Albert Hirschman's, the exodus from Europe would lead to Latin America, India, and Africa. Nonetheless, the depth of their reckoning with the European legacy makes these thinkers indisputable interlocutors even for those who want to "provincialize Europe," in Dipesh Chakrabarty's famous phrase.

It is with the conviction of the universality of the human experiences addressed in their political philosophies as well as with the hope of retrieving the salutary plurality of their Jewish lives[3] that I approach these thinkers in this book. Four clusters of themes will guide my approach: Jewish identity and otherness; exile, voice, and loyalty; legality and legitimacy in liberal democracies; and pluralism and the problem of judgment. These themes will be refracted through each thinker's individual and collective experiences, but their significance transcends biographical detail and reengages us with the continuing dilemmas of our societies and politics in a new century.

# EXILE, STATELESSNESS,
# AND MIGRATION

# 1

# Intertwined Lives and Themes among Jewish Exiles

FEW IF ANY IMAGES capture the poignancy of the twentieth century better than that of Hannah Arendt and Walter Benjamin playing chess during their French exile from 1933 to 1940.[1] Benjamin and Arendt already knew each other from a distance in Berlin—she was married to his cousin Günther Anders (Stern)—but they grew closer during their time in Paris, and Arendt became part of a large circle of German émigrés alongside Benjamin in the cafes of the Latin Quarter. Arendt met her second husband, Heinrich Blücher, during evenings at Benjamin's apartment, and an affectionate friendship developed between the three of them. Benjamin and Arendt taught Blücher to play chess. "Yesterday I played chess with Benji for the first time, in a long and interesting game," Blücher wrote. Arendt responded playfully: "I am extremely proud you beat Benji. It reflects well on my teaching."[2]

As Arendt and Benjamin were playing chess, awaiting their fate as exiled Jewish intellectuals in Paris who were rendered stateless by Hitler's Germany, a young socialist from Berlin by the name of Otto Albert Hirschmann (later to be known as Albert Hirschman), was shuttling across four countries: France, Italy, Great Britain, and Spain. From July to October 1936, he fought in the Spanish Civil War near Barcelona with the Italian and German émigré battalions of volunteers, loosely under the leadership of the leftist but anti-Stalinist Workers' Party of Marxist Unification (Partido Obrero de Unificación Marxista (POUM)). When

France capitulated in the summer of 1940, Hirschman and his comrades convinced their commander to release them with fake military passes, and he made his way to the south of France. Soon he met a young Harvard-educated classicist, Varian Fry, who had come to Marseilles on behalf of the US Emergency Rescue Committee.

Fry and Hirschman spent the next five months preparing the departures of refugees whose names now read like a "Who's Who" of intellectual Europe: Hannah Arendt, André Breton, Marc Chagall, Marcel Duchamp, Max Ernst, Siegfried Kracauer, Alma Maria Mahler Gropius Werfel, and others (but not, alas, Walter Benjamin, who would commit suicide in September 1940 in the coastal Spanish town of Port Bou while waiting for papers to travel to Portugal).

Meanwhile, in the northeastern city of Riga Latvia, subject over the years to German as well as Russian influences, a Jewish family of doctors by the name of "Shklar" and their two young daughters fled in 1939 via Sweden to Siberia, then to Japan and finally settled in Montréal, Canada. Judith Shklar, the older of these two girls, would eventually come to study political theory at Harvard with another émigré intellectual from Weimar, Germany, Carl J. Friedrich. She would meet Hannah Arendt for the first time in one of the symposia organized by Friedrich on totalitarianism.

Also born in Riga, Latvia, in 1909, was Isaiah Berlin, who moved with his family to Petrograd, Russia, at the age of six, where he witnessed the revolutions of 1915 and 1917. In 1921 his family came to England, and he was educated at St. Paul's School in London, and at Corpus Christi College, obtaining a prestigious prize fellowship to All Soul's College in Oxford in 1932 (where he was the first Jewish person admitted). Berlin, a prodigious commentator, would have much to say about many of the other émigrés whose paths took them across the ocean to the United States.

This book traces the intertwinement of the lives and thought of these intellectuals and others as they confronted exile, migration, and, in some cases, statelessness. For Arendt and Shklar these questions were central and both wrote extensively about migration, exile, and citizenship. These themes are more attenuated and less central in the work of

Hirschman, although *Exit, Voice, and Loyalty*, while considered a contribution to the psychology of institutional behavior, is undoubtedly marked by Hirschman's own experiences of loss of political voice and loyalty.

These thinkers faced migration, exile, and statelessness because of their Jewish origins, regardless of whether they themselves identified as Jewish, whether they were believers, or whether they were practicing Jews or not. The "Jewish question" is never absent from their writings, although, with the exception of Arendt and Berlin, few take a public position in relation to Jewish identity or the establishment of the state of Israel. Nonetheless, as Yuri Slezkine observes, "The Modern Age was Jewish not only because everyone was now a stranger but also because strangers were organized—or reassembled—into groups based on common dissent and destiny. . . . [T]otal strangers became kinsmen on the basis of common languages, origins, ancestors, and rituals duly standardized and disseminated for the purposes. The nation was family writ large . . . Or perhaps it was Christianity writ small . . . In other words, the Jews were doomed to a new exile as a result of Judaizing their Apollonian hosts."[3] It is this condition of becoming a stranger in one's own land because one did not belong to a national "family writ large" (or "Christianity writ small"), that all thinkers considered in this volume were cognizant of and that is reflected in myriad ways in their writings.

For German Jews, the experience of belonging and not belonging, of being rendered migrants and internal exiles in their own country, began in the mid-nineteenth century, with the granting of certain civil rights to Jews residing in German territories. This led to questions such as: What does it mean for the individual to be an equal citizen and to wish to retain one's ethnic, cultural, and religious differences, or perhaps even to rid oneself of these differences altogether? What individual or collective forms would such expressions of difference take? The German-Jewish discussion carried on by these writers explored these paradoxes with honesty, ingenuity, and intensity. This is true not only for the towering figures of Hermann Cohen, Gershom Scholem, Hannah Arendt, Leo Strauss, Hans Kelsen, Walter Benjamin, Max

Horkheimer, and Theodor Adorno but also for other lesser-known figures, such as Rabbi Leopold Lucas and the cultural critic Moritz Goldstein, whose writings I explore in the second chapter of this volume.

Two of the most famous contributions reflecting on dilemmas of Jewish otherness in a modernizing Germany were: "The Science of Judaism and the Roadmap to Its Future Development" ("Die Wissenschaft des Judentums und die Wege zu ihrer Förderung"), by Rabbi Leopold Lucas, based on a lecture he gave on December 27, 1905, at the Society for the Promotion of the Science of Judaism, and a 1912 article by Moritz Goldstein, "The German-Jewish Parnassus" ("Deutsch-Jüdischer Parnass"), published in the German-nationalist weekly, the Kunstwart (see chapter 2 below). These essays are separated only by six years, yet the pride and hopes expressed by Rabbi Lucas, proud of his Judaism and Germanness at once, stand in stark contrast to the anxiety, disillusionment, and irony voiced by Moritz Goldstein about being unable to reconcile these two aspects of his identity. Goldstein coins the term the "eternally half-other" to express the predicament of Jewish intellectuals who know that they can never really be a part of German culture, and yet, in his words, "administer" the works of art, music, and literature of a people that denies them the right to do so.

The theme of the "eternally half-other" is a leitmotif in these essays. Arendt and Benjamin were very much aware of Moritz Goldstein's "The German-Jewish Parnassus," and they defended this legacy of half-otherness in their work by contrast to the official Judaism of Rabbi Lucas.

Arendt's writings on Judaism and, in particular, her critique of Zionism have found fresh and enthusiastic audiences in recent years, and most famously, Judith Butler in Parting Ways. Jewishness and the Critique of Zionism. Chapter 5 explores the synthesis that Butler seeks to establish between Arendt's views and Emmanuel Levinas's ontology of cohabitation. I show that Butler fails to appreciate Arendt's concepts of political action and plurality and seeks to derive an "ethic of cohabitation" from her work that is not to be found there. Butler's overall attempt is to retrieve ethical insights and motifs from non-Zionist and in some cases anti-Zionist Jewishness, in order to create a space for Arab-Jewish coexistence in Israel/Palestine—a political goal that I share, and that, interestingly enough, returns us to Moritz Goldstein's thesis of the Jew as the eternally half-other. What are the ethics and politics commensurate with such a project of fractured identity?

For Arendt, statelessness and totalitarianism were the principal evils of the last century, and both topics have hardly lost their relevance in our time. The fiftieth anniversary of *Eichmann in Jerusalem*, first published in 1963, rekindled the so-called "Hannah Arendt Wars" among New York intellectuals. The publication of Bettina Stangneth's monumental work, *Eichmann vor Jerusalem*,[4] along with the appearance of Margarethe von Trotta's acclaimed movie, *Hannah Arendt*,[5] forced many to reconsider Arendt's work. Some used Stangneth's book to argue that Arendt was duped by Eichmann's seeming lack of anti-Semitic sentiments and behavior in the trial and that she minimized his vicious and vindictive personality. Evil, they insisted, was not banal after all. Others repeated an objection, first made by Jewish historians, that Arendt's treatment of the Jewish Councils (Judenräte) was historically inaccurate, cruel, and judgmental. Neither claim is supported by Stangneth's book, which treats Arendt with great respect for what she was able to accomplish on the basis of the inadequate trial transcripts in her possession. (See chapter 4 below.)

Arendt not only experienced statelessness between 1933 and 1951 when she became an American citizen, but she also wrote theoretically about a condition that, until her famous discussion in *The Origins of Totalitarianism*, had been, at the most, a topic for international lawyers and historians of the European interwar period. The phrase through which she tried to capture the vulnerability of the stateless—"the right to have rights"—has reverberated in the twenty-first century as well. As the world has experienced a refugee crisis of proportions unknown since World War II, the asylum-seeker, the refugee, and the stateless have become prisms through which to explore the hypocrisies of contemporary liberal democracies and of the postwar state system, which, on the one hand, affirms the universality of human rights—including the right to asylum—and, on the other hand, gives nations the sovereign privilege to control their borders and engage in practices in defiance of their obligations under international law. Particularly irritating has been the transformation of "the right to have rights" into the right of "humanitarian intervention" through misguided administrative and political adventures. The protection of the right of the stateless has become a shield in order to hide the ideological pretensions of humanitarian reason, which reduces refugees to objects of pity and robs them of their political agency. These questions are discussed in chapter 6 in this volume.

During the controversy concerning Hannah Arendt's *Eichmann in Jerusalem* a little-known lecturer in the government department at Harvard University, Judith Nisse Shklar, published *Legalism. An Essay on Law, Morals and Politics* in 1964. What Shklar called her "bare bones liberalism" (*Legalism*, 5) carried the indelible marks of disbelief in the face of a world gone insane (see chapter 7 below). Yet what is distinctive about her voice as an émigré political theorist, and what sets her apart from Leo Strauss and Arendt (both approximately a generation older) is the lack of pathos with which she registered the destruction of her familial world and the end of her childhood. With the memory of the Nuremberg trials and the McCarthy hearings in the United States still very much alive, in *Legalism* she positioned herself against too much self-congratulation on the part of liberal democracies.

Like Albert Hirschman, Shklar had a skeptical view of human psychology, an emphasis on the passions, and a distrust of too much social engineering in political life. With her work we can retrieve a tradition within liberalism, in part Kantian in inspiration, but opposed to Kant in that it replaces the supreme moral law with the injunction against cruelty. If the Kantian moral law is the manifestation of our dignity, both because we can cognize it and because we can act in accordance with it, Shklar emphasizes that it is cruelty that destroys our dignity by subjecting us to arbitrary force as well as coercion.

Hirschman, by contrast, was more hopeful about political transformation and he was a Communist internationalist first and later, a socialist militant. Although raised in a German-Jewish bourgeois family in Berlin, early on he came under the influence of the French and British Enlightenments. He shared Shklar's admiration for Montaigne, and is reported to have carried an edition of Machiavelli's *The Prince* with him on his journeys through Europe. He had no particular inclinations toward German philosophy, though as a young political economist, he had studied both Hegel and Marx quite well. His life and work, as well as his times, are explored in chapter 8.

The final essay of this collection is devoted to Isaiah Berlin. Celebrated as a sage in recent years, Berlin made a systematic contribution to political thought by drawing a distinction between "pluralism" and "relativism." The plurality of incommensurable goods, be it in politics, morals, aesthetics, was a central tenet of Berlin's thinking. Yet equally crucial was his claim that incommensurability did not mean that "anything goes," because he believed that there were standards of judgment and conduct that ought to guide individuals and collectivities.

I explore this thesis through the prism of Max Weber's theory of the fragmentation and differentiation of value in modernity. I argue that Berlin is a Weberian, but one whose views are modulated by the experiences and expectations of living in a liberal civil society such as the British one to which he emigrated. I then discuss "the burdens of judgment" in John Rawls's work as one of the most sophisticated treatments of the question of value pluralism.

What is the relationship between the burdens of judgment and the answer to Carl Schmitt's decisionism? Carl Schmitt's challenge haunted Arendt no less than it did Leo Strauss, Berlin no less than Shklar. While Strauss showed that natural law thinking could not be so easily dismissed, Shklar turned to the rule of law and a robust conception of legality as the structures that would hold liberal societies together. Arendt, by contrast, argued that liberalism needed to be anchored in a civic-republican tradition that emphasized political participation and revived a sense for the res publica. In stressing the need for developing societies to make their own decisions and be rid of the grandiose "development projects" imposed upon them by experts, Hirschman also emphasized the virtues of self-governance and economic republicanism in overcoming poverty and dysfunctionality. The following chapters are dedicated to analyzing the answers provided by these thinkers to these puzzles— answers that are often arresting in their depth as well as brilliance.

Although Hannah Arendt is at the center of much of the following discussion, my goal is to situate her political thinking in a broader context of exchange both with her contemporaries such as Scholem, Strauss, Levinas, and Berlin, as well as to probe the limits of her political theory as revealed by contemporary reinterpretations. Hirschman's turn to the developing world in Asia, Africa, and Latin America is a sharp reminder of the Eurocentrism of Arendt's thought, while her reflections on law and revolution, as Shklar shows us, brilliant as they may be, are often capricious in interpretation and scholarship. My purpose is to situate her thinking as well as that of other émigré intellectuals in what Martin Jay once called "force-fields,"[6] which do not have a center but are rather a domain in which elements attract and repulse one another. It is through the attraction to as well as repulsion from one another of the many thinkers considered in this book that I have approached the force-field formed by these émigré intellectuals.

# 2

# Equality and Difference

## HUMAN DIGNITY AND POPULAR SOVEREIGNTY IN THE MIRROR OF POLITICAL MODERNITY

## An Autobiographical Introduction

At the start of the sixteenth century, after the Inquisition in Catholic Spain, many Jews escaped to neighboring Portugal, the Netherlands, and the United Kingdom. Our earliest known ancestor,[1] the rabbi Jacob Ibn-Habib, whose Arabic last name means "son of Habib," just as the "Ben" in my last name means "son" in Hebrew, was among the foremost members of the northwestern Spanish city of Zamora.[2] He tried to negotiate with the Spanish authorities to have the Jews of Zamora remain in exchange for land and money; when this failed, he fled to Portugal and from there to the provinces of the Ottoman Empire, first to Jerusalem and then Salonica. The Jews of Spain were offered hospitality by the Ottoman Empire.

Even after half a millennium, the story of the exile from Spain was not extinguished in the memory of Turkish Jewry, and in 1992 the five-hundredth anniversary of the beginning of Spanish Jewish life upon Ottoman shores was celebrated with great enthusiasm in contemporary Turkey. But still something remained of that melancholy induced by exile, and captured so beautifully by Yirmiyahu Yovel in the following passage:

When the Jews, crushed and subdued, were driven out of Spain in 1492, they had been living there for over a millennium, the greatest, most affluent and most civilized Jewish community in the world, and certainly the proudest. . . . Famous dates, such as 1492, are signposts for complex events. Their dry numerals are loaded with passionate human quality, and almost always conceal a longer story. In sailing out to sea, the exiles' memories were often heavier than their baggage: images of families split, homes abandoned, property hastily sold for almost no price at all . . . Beyond these recent personal memories, a veil of more distant, perhaps partly mythical reminiscences compounded the agony. . . . Many Jews had come to Sefarad—Hebrew for Spain—as their other Zion, a temporary new Jerusalem where God granted them relative repose in waiting for the Messiah. Now, instead of the Messiah, the grand inquisitor Torquemada was shattering their identity.[3]

It may not come as a surprise, therefore, that "hospitality" has played such a central role in my writings in the last decade. Certainly, it was article 3 of the "Definitive Articles" of Kant's "Perpetual Peace" essay that alerted me to the philosophical significance of defining "Weltbürgerrecht" in terms of *hospitality*. "Das Weltbürgerrecht soll auf Bedingungen der allgemeinen Hospitalität eingeschränkt sein." ("The law of world citizenship will be restricted to conditions of universal hospitality.")[4] Hospitality, however, is not full membership: the visitor remains an outsider. Or as Kant expresses it in his clear but harsh way, *Besuchsrecht* (right of visitation) and *Gastrecht* (right of residency) are not the same. Granting the former is a universal moral obligation, insofar as the purpose of the stranger in coming upon our lands is peaceful. The latter, by contrast, requires that the sovereign provide the stranger with a "wohltätiger Vertrag" (*beneficent agreement*). The permanent right of residency remains an act of sovereign beneficence and it is for this reason that the condition of the guest is always precarious. At any point in time, the sovereign can change the terms of the "contract of beneficence." Jacques Derrida, ever sensitive to the hidden meaning of terms, coined the term "hostipitality," pointing to the interlaced etymological origins of *hostis* and *hospis*, of *enmity* and *amity*, which the condition of being a guest always entails.[5]

For the Ottoman tradition, the Muslim teaching of protecting the *dhimmis* also played a role in their interaction with the Jews of Spain. The *dhimmis* are those who believe in a monotheistic God, and who are therefore protected by Muslims for being "people of the book," but who, in return for this protection, must pay a special tax. Protection implies inequality. Tolerance does not wash away the mark of difference borne by Jews and Christians in Muslim lands.[6]

Two other historical episodes in the collective memory of Sephardic Jews have deeply marked my own intellectual and political orientation: for most Jews of Turkey, the name of Sabbatai Zevi[7] conjures memories of humiliation, betrayal, and shame. The "false Messiah," whose reputation was saved from the dustbin of history by the magisterial work of Gershom Scholem, for the Jews of Turkey remains a reminder of their weakness and impotence when confronted with the sultan's might. In September 1666, Sabbatai Zevi was taken to the sultan's tent where he was put on trial for causing havoc among the sultan's Jewish subjects by pretending to be the Jewish king. He was given the option of apostasy or sure death. He converted to Islam and became Aziz Mehmed Efendi, and was appointed to be a keeper of the palace gates.[8] The "Dönmehs" of Salonica (literally in Turkish, those who "turned"),[9] the followers of Sabbatai Zevi, went on to play a very significant role in the administration of the Ottoman Empire—a role not unlike that of the "Schutzjuden" in Austro-Hungary and the German Kaiserreich. Together with Armenian and Greek Ottomans, they were among the first parliamentary representatives to the Ottoman Constitutional Assemblies in 1876 and 1908. Yet the memory transmitted by my family to me of this sad episode of Sabbatai Zevi and the Dönmehs is one of Jews' inability to stand up for themselves and to take their fortunes into their own hands.

This sense of vulnerability was even more intense when commingled with the gratitude toward Turkey that the Jews of my parents' generation felt in the face of Hitler's armies. My parents were married on September 1, 1939, as Hitler marched into Poland. Kemal Atatürk had died in 1938; the new republic was only fifteen years old. Was there to be a war of succession? Would Atatürk's legacy be honored? And above all, since the Ottoman Empire and the German Kaiserreich had been allies in the First World War, would Turkey enter or stay out of the war or would the Jews of Turkey survive or perish in the hands of the Nazis? İnönü, the new president of the Turkish Republic, kept his country out of the war by providing the German army in the Balkans with logistical assistance and food supplies. But the young Jewish men of Turkey were rounded up and sent to labor camps in Anatolia, where some were told that they were "digging their own graves."[10]

The Jews of Turkey were once more saved by their Turkish protectors; yet this rescue, if anything, heightened their sense of vulnerability, and perhaps also, resentment, toward their benefactors. The Turkish Republic had declared them equal citizens and had entitled them to equal rights, except that terms such as "Azinlik," the minorities, continued to circulate in official and unofficial language. Even in the young republic they were excluded from promotion to officers' ranks in the army. Compared with the enormous political and civic engagement of European Jewry in their respective governments, the proportion of Turkish-Jewish members of parliament, politicians, journalists, and even academics—a Jewish career all over the world—were minimal. We were equal yet different.

## The Dilemmas of German-Jewry

I offer these autobiographical observations as a preface to the larger themes of the paradoxes of equality and difference under conditions of Western modernity. What did it mean for the individual to be an equal citizen and to wish to retain one's ethnic, cultural, and religious differences, or maybe even rid oneself of these differences altogether? The German-Jewish tradition has explored these paradoxes with honesty, ingenuity, and intensity.[11]

Surely, there are contentions about the degree to which the story of German-Jewry has dominated Jewish historiography and philosophy, and whether in taking this narrative to be paradigmatic one does not do injustice to other Jewish experiences, including my own, originating in countries of the Middle East and former Arab lands (so-called Mizrahi Jews). Steven Aschheim quotes the philosopher Hugo Bergman, writing to his friend, Robert Weltsch: "When our European generation makes its exit, Jewry here will become like those today in Baghdad."[12] Being well aware of these legacies of Eurocentrism, this chapter will probe the universalizable kernel of the German-Jewish encounter with modernity while hoping to open up a space of reflection and action for a diasporic Jewish modernity beyond Eurocentrism.[13]

Two of the most famous essays by German Jews of the last century reflecting on Jewish cultural and religious otherness were: "Die Wissenschaft des Judentums und die Wege zu ihrer Förderung," ("The Science of Judaism and the Roadmap to Its Future Development") by Rabbi Leopold Lucas, based on a lecture he held on December 27, 1905, at the "Gesellschaft zur Förderung der Wissenschaft des Judentums,"[14] (Society for the Promotion of the Science of Judaism); and "Deutsch-Jüdischer Parnass," ("The German-Jewish Parnassus") by Moritz Goldstein of 1912,[15] published in the German-nationalist weekly called the *Kunstwart*. These essays are separated only by six years, yet the pride and hopes expressed in Rabbi Lucas's essay as a German Jew, proud of his Judaism and Germanness at once, stand in stark contrast to the anxiety, disillusionment, and irony voiced by Moritz Goldstein about being able to reconcile these two aspects of his identity.

In her historical research on Rabbi Lucas, Margret Heitmann explains that two important developments figured in the background of the establishment of the "Gesellschaft zur Förderung der Wissenschaft des Judentums." Already at the end of the nineteenth century strong anti-Semitic currents in Marburg led to the formation of the "Allgemeine Deutsch-Antisemitische Vereinigung" (The General German Association against Anti-Semitism). Similar developments took place in Silesia, where in 1893, five hundred people participated in the summer festivities of Silesian organizations against anti-Semitism. By the 1890s several associations against anti-Semitism, for the defense of Jewish history, literature, and the like, were established to counter these trends.[16]

For Rabbi Lucas there was another danger in addition to that of anti-Semitism, namely "religious indifference" (*religiösen Indifferentismus*).

Many German Jews were alienated from Judaism; many converted to Christianity; from his perspective there were no texts by Jewish authors that could refute theological anti-Judaism. Heitmann writes: "With the establishment of the 'Gesellschaft' [Society] Lucas pursued above all two goals: on the one hand the coming together of scientific-theoretical forces; on the other hand, the formation of a circle of members, who would be interested in Jewish scientific works and who would guarantee a large circle of readers and thereby the widest possible echo."[17]

In twenty-five years this society published one hundred volumes, among them the "Germania Judaica," in which, as Heitmann observes, "all important Jewish settlements of the Reich,"[18] and "those in which prominent Jews had lived from the earliest times till the Vienna accords would be listed in alphabetical order."[19] The *Germania Judaica* was to be accompanied by a "basic outline of the complete sciences of Judaism" and by a "Corpus Tannaiticum," which would encompass all texts from the Tannah. Rabbi Lucas went even further and demanded "great literary undertakings" (Lucas, 10) as well as a "Corpus Philosophicum" that would contain "the publication of the work of all significant Jewish philosophers" (Lucas, 11).

What was the concept of science—*Wissenschaft*—driving these attempts? Apart from testifying to the long history of Jewish existence within the borders of the Kaiserreich, what the rabbi and his colleagues undertook was a comprehensive overview of Jewish achievements in literature, philosophy, history, and theology. Yet this was not the business of science in the ordinary sense. Rabbi Lucas was quite conscious of the fact that this concept of "Wissenschaft" was revolutionary, since it meant documenting the history and achievement of the Jews *outside* the paradigms of the biblical history of the Jewish people. It was not just the history of the kingdoms and temples of ancient Israel, their destruction and the exile—the *galut*—of the Jewish people that was to be recorded. A *new* science of Judaism *redefined* the subject that it intended to study. This new science analyzed and documented Jews as a modern people, certainly with ancient roots, but residing not in biblical time but in a world-historical time, shared with other peoples.[20] How can such a science preserve the unique identity of this subject—the

Jewish people—without reducing its study to an ordinary scientific monograph, with an ordinary scientific title such as the "sociology of the Jews of Golgau," or "the anthropology of Jewish religious rites," or "the study of comparative religions of ancient Egypt, Greece, and Rome"? In fact, Rabbi Lucas's own doctoral work on Judaism during the Crusades was a contribution to such a study.[21] How then was the science of Judaism to be defined if it was to be distinct from ordinary historical, sociological, and anthropological research?

For Rabbi Lucas this science would be defined more by its goal than by its methodology. As he states it clearly: "It is no easy task to write the history of a people which is not happy, to list one disaster after another and then show where the seeds of the future are to be found in bitter times" (Lucas, 5). Add to this history of suffering, the works of theological anti-Judaism and cultural anti-Semitism, and "[I]t is easy to appreciate the practical uses of our science when one considers the harm that our opponents have caused against us through the scientific formulations of their presuppositions. Entire systems are used against us, a craftily woven net of observations and conclusions" (Lucas, 7). The tasks of a science of Judaism now become clear: to break with the traditional history of Judaism, narrated as if it were only one of persecution, destruction, and exile *and* to resist the denigrating and humiliating presentation of Jewish thought, life, and achievements in the works of other scholars. The science of Judaism is in the service of making an ancient people proud of itself and of its achievements in modern historical time. It is a form of redemptive history; a science that redeems the past in order to enable its continuity with the present so as to inspire the future.[22]

## Moritz Goldstein's Provocation

Six years later Moritz Goldstein published "Deutsch-Jüdischer Parnass," which brought its author the accusations of being a self-hating Jew, of allying himself with the Deutsch-Nationalen (German nationalists), some of whom at that point wanted nothing more than a clear acknowledgment of the impossibility of being a German *and* a Jew. Not only did Goldstein suffer the contempt of Zionists as well as anti-Semites; he also drew upon himself the wrath of the assimilated Jews, who considered themselves bearers of German culture as well as proud German citizens. Surprising as it may be, in his rejection of Zionism and assimilationism, Goldstein bears great kinship to Rabbi Lucas, because for both the burning issue was to build a Jewish public sphere and a Jewish way of speaking (*Sprechart*) through which to express one's unique historical, cultural, and scientific orientations and achievements. Aware of the firestorm that his essay was sure to cause, in its very early pages Goldstein writes: "I wished as well that we could wash our dirty laundry in our own home. However, we do not have a home. A Jewish public sphere does not exist; neither in Germany nor in Western Europe is it possible to address all Jews as Jews, even though we must accept that so much will be said about us by others."[23]

With great verve and irony Goldstein then narrates the enthusiasm with which the Jews of Europe, once the walls of their ghetto had been torn down, threw themselves upon the treasure of enlightened modernity. From journalism to art, from music to philosophy, European, and especially German, Jews made this new culture their own, they improved it creatively, and transformed it enthusiastically.[24] "Let us not deceive ourselves: we Jews, among ourselves, may have the impression that we are speaking to Germans as Germans—we *have* the impression. We may be named Max Reinhardt and may bring unimaginable excitement to the stage; we may be named Hugo von Hofmannsthal and introduce a new poetic style to replace the used up language of Schillerian images, or we may, as Max Liebermann, lead modern art. *We* may call that German; the others call it Jewish and they hear an 'Asiatic' tone in all of it. They miss the 'German sociability' [*germanische Gemüt*]; and even when they find themselves compelled to acknowledge our achievements (even if with some reservations), *they wish that we would achieve less*" (Goldstein, 286; emphasis in the text).

Goldstein then introduces a distinction between truth and science on the one hand and art on the other. There is no German, Chinese, or Jewish truth nor a national science, he argues; but there is national art— "Ja, es gibt *nur* nationale Kunst" (Goldstein, 289–90). ["Indeed, there is *only* national art."] It is not quite clear how this dualistic epistemology is justified. Certainly the national element is neither the goal nor the telos of art, but it is described as "the source of all achievement, from Homer and the Bible to Tolstoy and Ibsen" (Goldstein, 290). If this is the case, if for a people as well as for its art, the presupposition is that it must have a home (*eine Heimat*), then why not follow Zionism to Palestine and strive for the renewal of the Hebrew language and poetry? Why not follow Gershom Scholem, for whom the bitter truths of this essay only strengthened his youthful resolution to leave Germany for Palestine, where he would write the definitive history of Sabbati Şevi? Even those Jewish spirits of a more cosmopolitan disposition, such as Walter Benjamin and Hannah Arendt, acknowledged the force and truth of Goldstein's claims.[25]

Yet Goldstein was neither a Zionist, nor an assimilationist, nor a cosmopolitan, nor a religious Jew. "The rest of us, however, are in Moses's position," he writes, "who could see but not enter the promised land. We, who have escaped from the ghetto, we, the happy-unhappy children of West European culture, we the eternal-half ones, we the excluded and the homeless, we can't do anything with this new option. The young spring that has burst forth from the old roots of the Hebrew language does not bring us new green shoots; all we have is the grey phrase: make your peace with it! . . . In other words, no matter how much we may wish to distinguish culturally between the Jewish and the non-Jewish, in order to finally leave compromise behind us, this sense of only being half of something, this human and manly unworthiness one feels—this just seems to be impossible, at least in the near future" (Goldstein, 290–91).

Goldstein, who emigrated to the United States and wrote a retrospective called "German Jewry's Dilemma. The Story of a Provocative Essay,"[26] does not explain in 1912 why Zionism is not an option for him. This is all the more puzzling since he seems to share Herder's belief, also very widespread among Zionist pioneers, that true art and literature require that one should be at home among one's people and articulate its genius. Goldstein believes that art is different from science, and that art needs a home, or a ground from which it can "spring forth"—to use a Heideggerian locution. But for the "the eternal half-ones; the excluded and the homeless" ("die Ewig-Halben, Ausgeschlossenen und Heimat-losen,") who are the Jewish heirs of West European culture, this is not an option. Yet these outsiders are not really outsiders—and herein lies the irony—because they can no more get rid of German and West European culture than German and West European culture can get rid of them. The marginal, the excluded, and the eternal other, the Jew, belong to German culture, because "German culture is in no small measure also Jewish culture" (Goldstein, 291).

In these fast-moving and almost manifesto-like proclamations of the last pages of the essay, the project of forming a new cultural and political identity beyond assimilation and Jewish nationalism, in fact beyond all forms of nationalism, is anticipated. Writing as a European Jew, Gold-stein pleads for the radical hybridity of cultural identity and achieve-ment: he wants all to acknowledge the degree to which German culture since the Enlightenment is *also* Jewish culture. He calls upon the Jews to reflect upon their experiences of modernity and the Enlightenment *as* Europeans and *as* German Jews. Far from being a cultural aberration and a political misfit, this interpretation of the eternal half-other pro-jects a new identity that acknowledges this marginality to be a central source of creativity.

*Au fond,* all cultures are hybrid; it is only nationalist ideology that tries to freeze the living and self-contradictory flow that constitutes cul-tures by hierarchically organizing them into an official center, leaving an unofficial, homeless marginality to the so-called others.[27] The other that is constitutive of us is cast out and rendered alien, so that we do not have to face our own strangeness within ourselves, our own problematic multiplicity.

To tease these cultural reflections out of Goldstein's essay is not to engage in anachronism: like Rabbi Lucas, Goldstein pleads for the cre-ation of a Jewish public sphere for the *Jews of Europe,* whether as mod-ern participants in culture or as traditionally oriented believers who nevertheless wished to be respected in their practices and not be de-rided and discriminated against because of them. Whereas Rabbi Lucas attempts to found a science of Judaism in order to create a language through which an ancient people could rediscover itself in the modern European world without being ashamed of its history and achievement, Goldstein's essay is a *cri de coeur* of the European-Jewish intellectual. In both cases, one is attempting to negotiate the paradoxes of equality and difference, of being equal citizens in a modern republic and yet remaining the cultural, ethnic, or religious other. To assert one's identity as a European Jew means participating in the political experiences of modernity while creating one's own subaltern public, which would be distinct, but not cut off, from the mainstream. Nor are such reflections alien to our own times, even after the Holocaust and the establishment of the state of Israel.

Among contemporary cultural critics, it is George Steiner who can claim to carry Moritz Goldstein's mantle, and who has raised the status of the Jew as the half-other, as the "moral irritant and insomniac among men," into Judaism's great and continuing contribution to humanity.[28] Only when they are guests among nations, in the condition of perpetual exile, can Jews serve as the moral and cultural vanguard of nations. Steiner writes: "Stalin and Hitler made of the glorious noun 'cosmopolitan,' with its promise of the inalienable, a murderous sneer. But did not Rashi himself, acutest of Talmudic readers, tell of the everlasting need for Abraham to abandon his tent and rejoin the road? Did Rashi not instruct us that, when asking the way, a Jew should prove deaf to the right answer, that his mission lay with being errant, which is to say, in error and wandering?"[29]

Steiner's cosmopolitan Jewish vision irritates many, just as Goldstein's image of the Jews, as the eternal half-other, did. In a bitter article called, "George Steiner's Jewish Problem," Assaf Sagiv, an editor of the journal *Azure*, takes Steiner to task not only for his critique of Zionism and Israel but also for "his aloofness" from traditional Jewish religious writings.[30] Sagiv suggests that to demand of Jews that they remain eternal guests and wanderers among nations, acting as their moral conscience, may have more continuity with the anti-Semitic fantasy of the "wandering Jew" than with any kind of cultural or moral mission that ordinary Jewish human beings, who are not cultural aristocrats, can take upon themselves.[31]

Sagiv's commentary on Steiner reveals that old disputes, addressed by Rabbi Lucas and Moritz Goldstein at the beginning of the twentieth century, have not been resolved in the twenty-first either. They continue with passionate intensity, precisely because the German-Jewish encounter has a universal aspect that goes to the very heart of political modernity and the paradoxes of the nation-state. If anything, the establishment of the State of Israel has reproduced the dilemmas of European Jewry in another context—in the Middle East.

## Paradoxes of Political Modernity

In the German-Jewish encounter with political modernity the contradictory presuppositions constitutive of every nation-state are revealed. Now that the weaknesses of the Westphalian state-system are becoming increasingly apparent, whereas the alternative institutions that ought to transcend this system are still remote, we can identify some of these paradoxes more vividly. The dignity of equal citizenship for all and the sovereignty claims of the nation are the dual sources of legitimacy in the modern nation-state, and the tensions among them have accompanied and enframed our political experiences since the bourgeois democratic revolutions of the eighteenth century.

From Hannah Arendt to Hans Kelsen, from Leo Strauss to Hersch Lauterpacht, Jewish political and legal thinkers of the twentieth century have grappled with both dimensions of this paradox. While Kelsen, in his famous words, came to the conclusion that "the notion of sovereignty must be repressed" ("die Souveränitätsvorstellung freilich muß radikal verdrängt werden"),[32] Hannah Arendt translated the political paradoxes of modernity into the demand that "the right to have rights" ought to be respected for all humans. Yet it is also in her work that we encounter the deepest awareness that to be a right-bearing individual is to belong to a political commonwealth that defends and upholds one's right to have rights. The right to have rights does not presuppose a prepolitical natural individual, as conceived of fictionally in natural rights theories; rather, it refers to the civil condition of the legal person and the citizen who belong to a polity. (See chapter 6 below) But if the sovereignty of the nation is interpreted in such a way that those bearing certain identity-markers are precluded from belonging to it, popular sovereignty could lead to the denial to some of the right to have rights. For Hannah Arendt, the denationalization of the German-Jews and their loss of citizenship, their subsequent exile to other countries, and eventually their mass extermination became the lens through which to focus upon "The Decline of the Nation-State and the End of the Rights of Men" (*OT*, 267–302) in modernity.

Arendt carried on the Moritz Goldstein tradition in her own unique way. Just as Goldstein sought a middle ground between pure assimila-tionism and Zionism through his concept of the Jew as the "eternal half-other," Arendt praised the standpoint of the "self-conscious pariah." Contrasting "the pariah" and "the parvenu," terms that she inherited from the French Jewish journalist Bernard Lazare, Arendt argued that whereas the parvenu erases her otherness and engages in sycophantic imitations of the dominant culture, the pariah is cast into marginality by this culture. The "self-conscious pariah," by contrast, is the one who transforms the otherness of her identity into a moment of conscious opposition to the dominant culture, thereby gaining the self-respect that is denied to her by others through the very struggle to define her own identity.[33] Just as in Hegel's "master-slave dialectic," the pariah, like the slave, gains the right to say "I" when he/she refuses to be defined by the terms set by the master and struggles for self-definition.[34]

Reviving the moral and potential political resonances of the attitude of the "self-conscious pariah," and the "eternal half-other," to reflect on Jewish-Palestinian binationalism, Amnon Raz-Krakotzkin writes:

> Interestingly, Arendt's standpoint in this matter is quite similar to Gershom Scholem's, her "old friend" who became later her arch rival. Like him, she searched for a Jewish existence between orthodoxy (that, as such, remained closed upon itself) and assimilation. Like him, she searched for a distinctive Jewish politics. Her Pariah is obvi-ously drawn from the figures of the Jewish heretics such as were de-scribed by Scholem in his essays on Sabbatian subversive individuals since the seventeenth-century.[35]

Whereas the young Gershom Scholem condemned sharply the misuses of Sabbatian Messianism for Zionist and nationalist purposes and the denial of the rights of the Palestinian people, the older Scholem turned against the binational ideals that had animated him as well as Hannah Arendt, Judah Magnes, Martin Buber, and many others.[36] In the case of the establishment of the State of Israel as well, the triumph of national sovereigntism meant the denial of the right to have rights to another people, namely the Palestinians.[37] This is why in her clairvoyant and controversial articles on Zionism throughout the 1940s, Arendt kept warning against transporting to the Middle East legal paradigms and ideals of state formation emerging out of the European experience, and why, in particular, she criticized the illusion that only a sovereign nation-state could provide a homeland for the Jewish people.[38]

Controversy continues as to whether Arendt's objections to the establishment of the State of Israel have not been rendered irrelevant with the Holocaust of European Jewry as well as the Palestinian recalcitrance to accept the two-state solution (see chapter 5 below). Interestingly, although Arendt, like Hans Kelsen, was a critic of national sovereignty, she remained skeptical that international institutions established in the wake of World War II, such as the United Nations, the Universal Declaration of Human Rights (UDHR), or even legal instruments such as the Geneva Conventions on the Status of Refugees, could ever satisfactorily resolve these paradoxes of the modern nation-state.[39] Kelsen and Hersch Lauterpacht,[40] by contrast, as international jurists, insisted that unless the rights enumerated in the Universal Declaration of Human Rights were protected by an International Human Rights Court they would remain ineffectual. For Kelsen, in particular, sovereignty was not the actual or mystical expression of the will of a people, of an actual demos, but rather a *Grundnorm* of the international system of states, which accepted that national law would be based upon the authority of some institution or instance recognized as the final arbiter. But Kelsen insisted that the perspectives of international and national or domestic law were not exclusive but complementary: one could decide to choose one or the other.[41]

Kelsen's anxieties about sovereignty, like Arendt's own about the right to have rights are rooted in the modern Jewish-European experience.[42] What is the source of the authority of law: human will or reason? Or some more fundamental order that precedes human acts of law-giving? Does the law express principles of human justice, or is the law grounded in some other order that precedes but nevertheless constrains human justice? And if the law derives its authority from an act of will that is not to be bound by reason but expresses the decision of a mythical lawgiver or a collectivity called the nation, then how can the rights of the individual be secured? It is doubtful whether Kelsen himself could successfully resolve the "decisionist" challenge posed by Carl Schmitt.[43] Rather, Kelsen admits that the *Grundnorm* of the law must itself be posited and cannot be further justified; at its limits law encounters *the political.*

Unlike Hannah Arendt and Hans Kelsen, who built their political philosophies around the need to contain the tense structure of legitimation in the modern nation-state within the bounds of the rule of law and respect for human rights, Leo Strauss followed Scholem, Benjamin, and in particular Carl Schmitt in claiming that the aporetic structure of the modern nation remained caught in the political theology of sovereignty. In an early essay, commenting upon Carl Schmitt's "Concept of the Political," Strauss agreed with Schmitt that the ineliminable pluralism of value spheres, advocated by Max Weber and others, was insufficient to explain the "existential primacy of the political."[44] The political was not just one value sphere among others; for Schmitt, this primacy of the political was based on the ontological primacy of the "friend" and "foe" distinction. Strauss treads carefully here and argues that if, indeed, this antagonism is so fundamental, then what we are saying is that human nature itself is evil, eternally seeking to crush and annihilate the other. Strauss does not endorse this conclusion and like Thomas Hobbes, on whom both Strauss and Schmitt had written,[45] he argues that the avoidance of death and enabling the pursuit of the good life is the *summum bonum* of the political. But how can liberalism justify a vision of the good life, or even its adherence to the natural rights of the individual when liberalism itself remains caught up in the potential nihilism of acknowledging the irreconcilable pluralism of values in modernity? (See chapter 9 below on Isaiah Berlin.)

In his caustic commentary upon Weber in *Natural Right and History*,[46] Strauss writes: "Weber assumed as a matter of course that there is no hierarchy of values: all values are of the same rank" (Strauss, 66). "But," he continues, "is there no connection between justice and the good of society, and between the good of society and incentives to socially valuable activity?" (Strauss, 69). Such value pluralism cannot justify the vision of a liberal society and of individual rights. "Men cannot live without light, guidance, knowledge," concludes Leo Strauss, "only through knowledge of the good can he find the good that he needs. The fundamental question, therefore, is whether men can acquire the knowledge of the good without which they cannot guide their lives individually and collectively by the unaided efforts of their natural powers, or whether they are dependent for that knowledge on Divine Revelation" (Strauss, 74). For Strauss the struggle between philosophy and theology remains unresolved, and it is crucial that this be so if the liberal respect for the rule of law and the rights of the individual are to be protected.[47] Strauss is unique in reintroducing the relationship between philosophy and theology into the heart of modern political thought and also for searching for an alternative principle of political legitimacy in the experience of ancient Judaism—of Jerusalem—as distinct from that of Athens.[48]

## Democratic Legitimacy and Its Aporias: A Conceptual Model

The previous sections of this chapter have tried to illuminate some episodes in the cultural-historical experiences of German-speaking Jewry and have briefly portrayed the wealth and depth of responses developed by thinkers such as Arendt, Kelsen, and Strauss to the dilemmas of equality and difference within the modern nation-state. Upon a closer analysis, the aporia of political modernity shows the following structure: Ideally, democratic rule means that all members of a sovereign body are to be respected as bearers of human rights, and that the consociates of this sovereign freely associate with one another to establish a regime of self-governance under which each is to be considered both author of the laws and subject to them. This ideal of the original contract, in the version formulated by Jean-Jacques Rousseau and adopted by Kant, is a heuristically useful device for capturing the logic of modern democracies.

Modern democracies, unlike their ancient counterparts, conceive of their citizens as rights-bearing consociates. The rights of the citizens rest upon the rights of man. "Les droits de l'homme et du citoyen" do not contradict one another; quite to the contrary, they are coimplicated. This is the idealized logic of the modern democratic revolutions since the American and French examples, and in our days, it has been universalized into the modern state-form, respected by many, even if not the majority, of the 195 states in the world.

The democratic sovereign draws its legitimacy not merely from its act of constitution, but, equally significantly, from the conformity of this act to universal principles of human rights that are in some sense said to precede and antedate the will of the sovereign, and in accordance with which the sovereign undertakes to bind itself. "We, the people" refers to a particular human community, circumscribed in space and time, sharing a particular culture, history, and legacy; yet this people establishes itself as a democratic body by acting in the name of the universal. The tension between universal human rights claims and particularistic cultural and national identities is constitutive of democratic legitimacy. Modern democracies act in the name of universal principles that are then circumscribed within a particular civic community. This is the "Janus face of the modern nation," in the words of Jürgen Habermas.[49]

Since Rousseau, however, we also know that the will of the democratic people may be legitimate but unjust, unanimous but unwise. "The general will" and "the will of all" may not overlap either in theory or in practice. Democratic rule and the claims of justice may contradict one another. The democratic precommitments expressed in the idealized allegiance to universal human rights—life, liberty, property, and in our days, civil, political, and social rights—need to be reactualized and renegotiated within existing polities. Potentially, there is always a conflict between an interpretation of these rights claims that precedes the declared formulations of the sovereign and the actual enactments of the democratic people who could potentially violate such interpretations. We encounter this conflict in the history of political thought as the conflict between liberalism and democracy, and in a different form as the conflict between constitutionalism and popular sovereignty. In each case the logic of the conflict is the same: to assure that the democratic sovereign will uphold certain constraints upon its will in virtue of its precommitments to certain formal and substantive interpretations of rights. Liberal and democratic theorists disagree with one another as to the proper balance of this mix: while strong liberals want to bind the sovereign will through precommitments to a list of human rights, strong democrats reject such a pre-political understanding of rights and argue that they must be open to renegotiation and reinterpretation by the sovereign people—admittedly within certain limits.

Yet the paradox of democratic legitimacy has a corollary that has been little noted: every act of self-legislation is also an act of self-constitution. "We, the people" who agree to bind ourselves by these laws, are also defining ourselves as a "we" in the very act of self-legislation.[50] It is not only the general laws of self-government that are articulated in this process; the community that binds itself by these laws defines itself by drawing boundaries as well, and these boundaries are territorial as well as civic. The will of the democratic sovereign can only extend over the territory that is under its jurisdiction; democracies require borders. Empires have frontiers, while democracies have borders.[51] Democratic rule, unlike imperial dominion, is exercised in the name of some specific constituency and binds that constituency alone. Therefore, at the same time that the sovereign defines itself territorially, it also defines itself in civic terms. Those who are full members of the sovereign body are distinguished from those who fall under its protection, but who do not enjoy full membership rights. At the onset of political modernity, women, slaves, and servants (many of whom were women as well), propertyless white males, non-Christians, and non-white races were historically excluded from membership in the sovereign body and from the project of citizenship. They were, in Kant's famous words, "mere auxiliaries to the commonwealth."[52]

The boundaries of the civic community are of two kinds then: on the one hand, these boundaries define the status of those who enjoy second-class citizenship within the polity but who belong to the sovereign people in virtue of cultural, familial, and religious origins and affiliations. Women, as well as nonpropertied white males before the extension of universal suffrage, fell under this category; the status of these groups is distinct from that of other residents who not only have second-class status but who also do not belong to the sovereign people in virtue of the relevant identity-based criteria. Such was the condition of African-American slaves until after the Civil War and the declaration in 1865 of the 14th Amendment to the US Constitution, which conferred US citizenship upon black people; such was also the status of American Indians who were granted tribal sovereignty. The civil status of those of Jewish faith in the original thirteen colonies of the United States and throughout Europe until their emancipation after the Napoleonic wars can be described as one of transition from being "a mere auxiliary to the commonwealth" to becoming a full-fledged citizen, though never freed from the shadow of various forms of anti-Semitism.[53]

I have circumscribed in general theoretical terms the paradox of democratic legitimacy. The paradox is that the republican sovereign should undertake to bind its will by a series of precommitments[54] to a set of formal and substantive norms, usually referred to as human rights. Upon closer examination we see in fact that we are dealing with a dual paradoxical structure: on the one hand, between liberalism and democracy, that is between the will of democratic majorities to restrain themselves in terms of human rights (however defined);[55] on the other hand, with a paradox internal to democracies, namely that democracies cannot define *the boundaries* of their own membership democratically. Even if these aporias of the modern logic of the territorially circumscribed state-form can never be fully overcome, new developments have taken place since the UDHR of 1948 that have created a new framework for the international legal system. The most important aspect of these developments is the self-limitation of the sovereignty claims of nations according to the demands of multilateral human rights conventions.

## Jurisgenerativity: Between Nomos and Violence

To explore the relationship between this new international legal order and democratic sovereignty of peoples, I have introduced two concepts in my recent work. First is what I call the *jurisgenerative power* of cosmopolitan norms, and second, *democratic iterations*.

By "jurisgenerativity," a term originally suggested by Robert Cover,[56] I understand the law's capacity to create a normative universe of meaning, which can often escape the provenance of formal lawmaking. "The uncontrolled character of meaning exercises a destabilizing influence upon power," writes Cover. "Precepts must 'have meaning,' but they necessarily borrow it from materials created by social activity that is not subject to the strictures of provenance that characterize what we call formal lawmaking. Even when authoritative institutions try to create meaning for the precepts they articulate, they act, in that respect, in an unprivileged fashion" (Cover, 112). Laws acquire meaning in that they are interpreted within the context of significations that they themselves cannot control. There can be no rules *without* interpretation; rules can only be followed insofar as they are interpreted; but there are also no rules that can control the varieties of interpretation they can be subject to within all different hermeneutical contexts. It is in the nature of rules in general and law in particular that the horizon of interpretation transcends the fixity of meaning.[57]

To quote Cover again: "No set of legal institutions or prescriptions exist apart from the narratives that locate it and give it meaning. For every constitution there is an epic, for each decalogue a scripture" (Cover, 96). Law's normativity does not consist in its grounds of formal validity, that is its legality alone, though this is crucial. Law can also structure an extralegal normative universe by developing new vocabularies for public claim-making; by encouraging new forms of subjectiv-

ity to engage with the public sphere and by interjecting existing relations of power with anticipations of justice to come. Law anticipates
forms of justice to come, or in Cover's words, "Law may be viewed as a
system of tension or a bridge linking a concept of a reality to an imagined alternative—that is, as a connective between two states of affairs,
both of which can be represented in their normative significance only
through the device of narrative" (Cover, 101).

Law is not simply an instrument of domination and a method of
coercion, as theorists from Thomas Hobbes to Max Weber and Michel
Foucault have argued; "the force of law" (to use a phrase of Jacques
Derrida's)[58] involves anticipations of justice to come, which it can never
quite fulfill but which it always points toward. Law cannot displace the
political: it frames it, it enables it and yet is also altered by it.

It is important to note how much Cover's theory is rooted in his attempt to develop a conception of law that does justice both to the experience of paideic communities and the state. "Interpretation always
takes place in the shadow of coercion," writes Cover. "And from this fact
we may come to recognize a special role for courts. Courts, at least the
courts of the state, are characteristically 'jurispathic'" (Cover, 139).
Whether courts are always jurispathic is to be doubted since such a
sweeping statement questions the possibility that justice can ever be
rendered through the court system. But this is not the best way to
understand Cover. Cover is critical of the "statist" monopoly of jurisgenerative meaning and defends the value and integrity of "paideic"
communities (often religious in character). (See Cover, 107). Such communities of normativity always exist in the plural. "It is the problem of
the multiplicity of meaning," he writes, "the fact that never only one but
always many worlds are created by the too fertile forces of jurisgene-
sis—that leads at once to the imperial virtues and the imperial mode of
world-maintenance" (Cover, 109). "Imperial" for Cover also means a
form of world-maintenance—better still—the maintenance of the
world as ordered and predictable through the ever-present shadow of
violence. Cover's is a plea for Jewish self-governance in the liberal state,
deeply rooted in the recognition of the nomothetic force of the Torah
on the one hand and the norms of liberal constitutional democracies

on the other. For him, unlike for Kelsen, "insular communities often have their own, competing, unambiguous rules of recognition. They frequently inhabit a nomos in which their distinct *Grundnorm* is supreme from its own perspective" (Cover, 142). Cover is slow to acknowledge that paideic communities and imperial power are *both* necessary insofar as the imperial power of the state is needed to stave off the force of violence that paideic communities may unleash. He is in search of a "redemptive constitutionalism," which does not transfer to existing authority alone the force of declaring binding nomos, but which enables social movements as well as paideic communities to creatively appropriate and transform constitutional meaning through multiple iterations in the light of competing interpretive principles (Cover, 132). It is this aspect of Cover's work that is worth retrieving and not his hostility to state courts.[59]

Let us return to Moritz Goldstein's 1906 essay: What must be the features of a democratic public sphere if it is to offer the "eternally half-others; the marginalized and the homeless ones" voice and sanctuary? Democratic iterations can only lead to this goal, insofar as, in Kant's words, we can cultivate the "erweiterte Denkungsart"—"the enlarged mentality."[60] This cannot be achieved through law and politics alone. It requires the cultivation of moral and political judgment and of one's capacity to take the standpoint of the other(s).

## The Enlarged Mentality

Despite the Holocaust, and precisely because of the Holocaust, today more than ever since the end of World War II, Western societies once more face the problem of how to deal with the eternally half-other. For the Jews of Europe this project was destroyed, although remnants and even new offshoots of Jewish culture are thriving in contemporary Berlin, France, the UK, Poland, and Spain.

Nevertheless, there are forces in our world that consider themselves to be in the midst of a global civil war between Islamic Jihad, Europe, and the West. These sides play into each others' hands. The bombings in Madrid in 2004 and London in 2005; the Danish caricature controversy over the representation of the Prophet Mohammed (2005); the murder of Theo van Gogh in the Netherlands by a Moroccan militant (2004); the French "scarf affair" (1989–2004); the attacks on the office of *Charlie Hebdo* and Bataclan Music Hall in Paris in 2015; and the rise of ISIS or Daesh and the gruesome acts committed by it from Afghanistan to Brussels, from Istanbul to Paris, are some of the most contentious public confrontations of the last decades in which forces of political Islam and their opponents in Western democracies have faced each other. Viewed against this background, cosmopolitan ideals seem like pious wishes at best and naïve appeasements of dark forces of our civilization at worst.[61]

Tragically and ironically, reminding us once more of Moritz Goldstein's concept of the eternal half other, the murderer of Oslo, Anders Behring Breivik, who on July 22, 2011, massacred over seventy youth, both of migrant and Norwegian origin, named his manifesto on the emancipation of Europe "2083," referring thereby to the 400th anniversary of the conquest of Vienna by the Ottomans in 1683! Breivik's goal was to free Europe from its others, and neither he nor many others like him can accept that the guest is now a co-citizen, a neighbor, an associate, even a family member. Terms like "guest" and "hospitality" are today wholly inadequate to deal with the complexity of hyphenated identities in Europe. These terms, as Jacques Derrida has observed, cannot be easily disentangled from their origins in the Inquisition and European colonialism.[62] Europe today is the Europe of the "Mischmasch Deutschen,"[63] of the "Franco-Algériens" and "Franco-Maroquains." It is the Europe of Ethiopian and Albanian-Italians, of Pakistani and Hindu Brits. Is Moritz Goldstein's *cri de coeur* in 1912 so different than that of a Salman Rushdie, a Tahar Ben-Jelloun, a Zafer Şenocak, an Orhan Pamuk, a Deniz Utlu in our own days?[64] Echoing Goldstein, may we not say that just as German culture is "in no small measure" Turkish today that French culture is "in no small measure" Algerian, Moroccan, Tunisian? May we not say that contemporary literature in English is the literature of the diaspora of migrants, exiles, and the in-between? When will the Quixotic attempt to define "das echt Deutsche" (the authentically German) and "die Leitkultur" (the dominant cultur")—phrases that seek to perpetuate the marginality of the "half other"—come to an end?

The much-maligned term "multiculturalism" cannot capture the complexities of creating a culture in which those who are not at home can nonetheless find a home; a culture in which those who feel their otherness can nonetheless create a new vocabulary such as to extend the limits of our imagination by making us aware of the multiplicity within each of us. Such a culture enables us to take the standpoint of the other, not by eliminating the distance between us through some impossible expectations of full empathy, but rather, by helping us create that *negotiable in-betweenness,* through which I come to respect you as my equal, as the bearer of shared universal human dignity, all the while knowing you to be a concrete other, with an irreducibly different history, body, needs, and memory than mine. Kant, and following him Arendt,[65] called this *the enlarged mentality.* If the task of legal and political institutions is to protect the dignity of human beings and enable the legitimate exercise of popular sovereignty, surely one of the most important tasks of a democratic culture is to cultivate the enlarged mentality. Such cultivation, however, is never an act of passive contemplation but demands the unsettling encounter with the other, whose otherness compels us to turn inward and to reflect upon the stranger in ourselves.

The American literary critic Daniel Aaron has observed: "The process by which the 'minority' writer has passed from what I have called 'hyphenation' to 'dehyphenation' might be divided very roughly into three stages. . . . [I]n stage number one, the pioneer spokesman for a hitherto unspoken-for-minority—ethnic, racial, or cultural—writes about his Negro or Jewish compatriots in an effort to overcome—or better, to blur—the antiminority stereotype already stamped in the minds of the old-stock Americans. . . . [I]n stage number two, the hyphenate writer tends to be less conciliatory, less willing to please. . . . [F]inally, in the third stage, the minority writer passes from the periphery to the center of his society, viewing it no less critically, perhaps, but more knowingly. . . . Yet the dropping of the hyphen does not completely eliminate his marginal perspective. . . . Without renouncing his ethnic or racial past, he has translated his own and his minority's personal experiences ... into the service of the imagination. He has acquired, in short, *the 'double vision,'* as F. Scott Fitzgerald used this phrase" (my emphasis).[66]

The phrase "double vision" may be a more elegant and less demeaning way of expressing the condition of "the eternal half-other." It is the vision of the self-conscious pariah crystallized through the encounter with equality and difference in political modernity, yet retaining pride in otherness and cultivating it as a source of our shared humanity.

# 3

# The Elusiveness of the Particular

## HANNAH ARENDT, WALTER BENJAMIN, AND THEODOR ADORNO

### Benjamin and the Chess Master

Chess appears to have been not just a ~~pastime for~~ Walter Benjamin but a complex metaphor for thinking about history, progress, teleology, and the ironies of fate. The first thesis of Benjamin's "Theses on the Philosophy of History," composed in shock at the signing of the Hitler-Stalin pact, reads as follows: "The story is told of an automaton constructed in such a way that it could play a winning game of chess, answering each move of an opponent with a countermove. A puppet in Turkish attire and with a hookah in its mouth sat before a chessboard placed on a large table. A system of mirrors created the illusion this table was transparent on all sides. Actually, a little hunchback who was an expert chess player sat inside and guided the puppet's hand by means of strings."[1] The puppet, for Benjamin, was "historical materialism." Arendt had been entrusted to bring Benjamin's suitcase, which contained a version of this manuscript after his death, to the United States. Two decades later, she lovingly edited these and other texts of Benjamin's into a volume called *Illuminations. Essays and Reflections* in English.[2]

The ironic contempt towards the doctrine of "historical materialism" expressed by Benjamin via the metaphor of the chess-playing puppet was undoubtedly shared by Arendt and Blücher. Blücher, who had been a member of the Spartacist league in Berlin, founded by Rosa Luxemburg, broke with his faction after her death and escaped to Paris ahead of the German police. Yet neither he nor Arendt nor Benjamin gave up the hope that one would somehow beat the little mysterious hunchback dwarf, that is, the chess master who seemed to pull the strings of history. "To articulate the past historically," wrote Benjamin in Thesis 6, ". . . means to seize hold of a memory as it flashes up at a moment of danger. . . . In every era the attempt must be made anew to wrest tradition from the conformism that is about to overpower it."[3]

These few lines can serve as a guidepost for understanding Arendt's own practice of historical narrative, ranging from her discussions of anti-Semitism and imperialism in *The Origins of Totalitarianism* to her account of the French and American Revolutions in *On Revolution*, and even to *Eichmann in Jerusalem*. For Arendt, as for Benjamin, there was "redemptive power" in narrative.[4] The political philosopher, as narrator, had "to seize hold of a memory as it flashes up at a moment of danger," and undo the chess master's moves that always seemed to outwit historical actors by suffocating the new under the weight of historical conformism and false teleology.

It is the "Benjaminian moment" in their work that best reveals the subterranean affinities between Arendt and Adorno, two of the most famous exiles of the last century.[5] It is widely known that any consideration of Arendt and Adorno as thinkers who share intellectual affinities is likely to be thwarted from the start by the profound dislike that Arendt, in particular, seems to have borne towards Adorno.[6] In 1929 Adorno was among members of the faculty of the University of Frankfurt who would be evaluating the "Habilitation," essential to Günther Anders (Stern), Hannah Arendt's first husband, securing a teaching post in a German University. He found the work unsatisfactory, thus bringing to an end Stern's hopes for a university career. It was also in this period that Arendt's notorious statement regarding Adorno was uttered—"Der kommt mir nicht ins Haus"—meaning that Adorno was not to set foot in their apartment in Frankfurt.[7]

This hostility on Arendt's part never diminished, while Adorno endured it with a cultivated *politesse*. Arendt's temper flared up several more times at Adorno: first, when she was convinced that he and his colleagues were preventing the publication of Benjamin's posthumous manuscripts,[8] and secondly, when his critique of Heidegger—*The Jargon of Authenticity*—appeared.[9]

Of course, such psychological attitudes and personal animosities cannot guide our evaluations of a thinker's work, text, and legacy. And this is particularly true in the case of Arendt and Adorno, who not only reflected upon the "break in civilization" caused by the rise of fascism and Nazism, the Holocaust, and the defeat of the working classes in Europe and elsewhere, but also asked, "what does it mean to go on thinking?" after all that. They shared a profound sense that one must learn to *think anew*, beyond the traditional schools of philosophy and methodology. It is this attempt to think anew that I will refer to as their "Benjaminian moment." Put succinctly: Arendt as well as Adorno came to believe that thinking must free itself from the power of "false universals." This means not only refuting historical teleologies, but at a much-deeper level, it involves a categorical critique of all philosophical attempts at totalizing and system-building. For Arendt, honest thinking can only be accomplished in fragments; for Adorno, thinking must resist the temptation to overpower the object, letting it instead appear and assert itself over the epistemic imperialism of subjectivity. "Fragmentary constellations," which for Arendt illustrate the criss-crossings of tendencies, trends, and structures in culture, history, and society, all of which could have happened otherwise, and the "primacy of the object"[10] for Adorno, are central themes that reveal the legacy and influence of Walter Benjamin. This critique of false universals, shared by both, frees thought to face the "elusiveness of the particular" and leads to an eventual encounter with Kant's *Critique of Judgment*.[11] Arendt finds in Kant's doctrine of "reflective judgment" an epistemology for elucidating the particular without dismissing the intersubjective quality of all judgment. For Adorno, aesthetic judgment becomes a paradigm for thinking beyond the false harmonies of the "Naturschöne" (the naturally beautiful), on the one hand, and the awe caused by "das Erhabene" (the sublime) on the other. Can reflective judgment, whether moral, political, and aesthetic, restore the power of thought, then?

Adorno's 1934 essay on "The Actuality of Philosophy" and Arendt's 1946 essay on "What Is Existenz Philosophy?" will serve as my entry-points to this question.

## Adorno's Early Critique of Philosophy

On May 7, 1931, upon assuming a position in the Faculty of Philosophy of The University of Frankfurt, Adorno held a lecture with the title "Zur Aktualität der Philosophie" ("The Actuality of Philosophy").[12] The opening statement of this text already indicates the militant rigor with which the young professor is ready to take on the establishment of philosophy: "Whoever chooses philosophy as a profession today must first reject the illusion that earlier philosophical enterprises begin with: that the power of thought is sufficient to grasp the totality of the real. No justifying reason could rediscover itself in a reality whose order and form suppress every claim to reason; only polemically does reason present itself to the knower as total reality, *while only in traces and ruins is it prepared to hope that it will ever come across correct and just reality*" (*AP*, 120; my italics). Since the Left Hegelian critique (Feuerbach, Marx, Engels) of Hegel's phrase "that the actual is rational, and that the rational is actual" (*Was vernünftig ist, das ist wirklich; und was wirklich ist, das ist vernünftig*),[13] faith in the capacity of reason to "grasp the totality of the real" was shown to be a chimera at best and an ideology at worst. Following this tradition, Adorno is not only criticizing the hubris of philosophical thought but also indicating that "the real" itself "suppresses every claim to reason"; the failure of philosophy is not that of the thinker alone but also that of a reality that does not permit itself to be grasped as rational. "Only in traces and ruins," writes Adorno, introducing a Benjaminian phrase wholly unknown to philosophical discourse of the time, can a "correct and just reality" be encountered.

Adorno proceeds to survey the contemporary German philosophical scene. The question of Being, which calls itself the most "radical" (Heidegger), is according to Adorno "powerless . . . it is nothing more than an empty-form principle whose archaic dignity helps to cover any content whatsoever" (*AP*, 120). By contrast, the neo-Kantianism of the

Marburg School has preserved its "self-contained form as a system, but has thereby renounced every right over reality" (*AP*, 121). Georg Simmel's *Lebensphilosophie* is an attempt to reach beyond the categories to the real itself, but instead it "becomes resigned to the 'living' as a blind and unenlightened concept of nature" (*AP*, 121). Furthermore, the German Southwest School of Rickert tries to mediate between the extremes by producing "value" categories that set reality in relation to these values. But their locus and source remain undetermined: "they lie between logical necessity and psychological multiplicity somewhere" (*AP*, 121).

Adorno's greatest esteem in this essay is reserved for Husserl and his efforts at "transcendental phenomenology," aimed to gain "a trans-subjective binding order of being" (*AP*, 121). Even if he took as his beginning point the post-Cartesian "transcendental idealism," it was an "authentically productive and fruitful discovery of Husserl" that he recognized the meaning of "the non-deducible given" (*unableitbaren Gegebenheit*) as "the fundamental problem of the relationship between reason and reality" (*AP*, 121–22). But every Husserlian analysis of the given still rests on transcendental idealism, and it is proof of Husserl's "great and clear honesty" that "the jurisdiction of reason" (*Rechtsprechung der Vernunft*) remains "the court of final appeal" (*AP*, 122).

Adorno returns once more to Heidegger in this context: whereas Husserl, despite the origins of his phenomenology in transcendental idealism, acknowledges the problem of the "given" and the irreducibility of reality to the jurisdiction of reason, Heidegger transforms the ontology of being into "the existential analytic of Dasein."[14] "It is thus no accident," observes Adorno, "that Heidegger falls back precisely on the latest plan for a subjective ontology produced by Western thinking: the existentialist philosophy of Søren Kierkegaard" (*AP*, 123).

As I will show in the next section, there are astonishing parallels between Adorno's account of the collapse of objective idealism and the transition from Husserlian phenomenology to existential phenomenology and eventually to existentialism *tout court* and Arendt's own reconstruction of these same philosophical currents in "What Is Existenz philosophy?". Whereas Arendt will proceed from the failure of philosophy to restore a sense of being-at-home-in-the-world to the political implications of the analytic of *Dasein*, Adorno draws a suggestive parallel between Kierkegaard's leap into faith and the Heideggerian resolve unto death: "However, a leap and an undialectical negation of subjective being is also Heidegger's ultimate justification, with the sole difference that the analysis of the 'existing there' (*Vorfindlichen*—of the ready-to-hand), whereby Heidegger remains bound to phenomenology and breaks in principle with Kierkegaard's idealist speculation, avoids the transcendence of belief ... and instead recognizes solely the transcendence of a vitalist 'thus being' (*Sosein*) in death" (*AP*, 123).

Writing in 1931—before Heidegger joined the NSDAP and assumed the rectorship of the University of Freiburg, forever casting a shadow on his standing as a philosopher—Adorno, unlike Arendt in 1946, does not seek to uncover the possible links between Heidegger's existential ontology of death and anxiety and his Nazi politics. Instead, Adorno is still asking how "The claim to totality made by thought is thrown back upon thought itself, and it is finally shattered there too" (*AP*, 124). The categories of thrownness, anxiety, and death "are in fact not able to banish the fullness of what is living," but swinging between an irrational exuberance for the "pure concept of life," and feelings of dread and anxiety in view of the finitude of Dasein (*AP*, 124), the pendulum of phenomenology after Husserl disintegrates through these wild gyrations.

After the failure of these attempts at philosophical system-building, is philosophy itself actual? Adorno considers the efforts of the Vienna School to self-liquidate philosophy into science. Not denying "the extraordinary importance of this School," (*AP*, 125) he nevertheless argues that two problems cannot be mastered by the positivist turn to the sciences: first is the meaning of *the given* itself, which according to Adorno, "is not ahistorically identical and transcendental, but rather assumes changing and historically comprehensible forms" (*AP*, 125); the second is the problem of "the alien ego," accessible for empirio-criticism only "through analogy" (*AP*, 125). In singling out the problem of "the given" and that of "intersubjectivity" as the two problems to which empirio-criticism can provide no answers, Adorno may have been following Georg Lukács's *History and Class Consciousness*; Lukács, in the famous essay on "Reification and the Consciousness of the

Proletariat," highlighted these same two issues as being the pitfalls of bourgeois philosophy.[15] For Lukács, both problems had their roots in the inability of bourgeois thought, from Descartes to Kant and through Locke to Hume, to grasp the relation of the epistemic subject to the world not in terms of mere contemplation, but as a form of active, involved, material praxis of transforming nature in the process of socially laboring in cooperation with other human beings. Adorno does not take this materialist route of dissolving the problems of modern philosophy into a teaching of historically situated social labor.[16] Instead, he asserts that although "philosophy will not be transformed into science" under the positivist and empiricist attack, "philosophic problems will lie always, and in a certain sense irredeemably, locked within the most specific questions of the separate sciences" (AP, 125–26). He continues: "Plainly put: the idea of science (*Wissenschaft*) is research; that of philosophy is *interpretation* ... philosophy persistently, and with the claim of truth, must proceed interpretively without possessing a sure key to interpretation" (AP, 126; my emphasis).

Adorno's magisterial survey of the history and actuality of philosophy results in a rejection of "the power of thought to grasp the totality of the real" (AP, 120). Husserlian phenomenology confronts the non-deducible given; Heideggerian ontology leads to an existentialism of dread and death; Simmel's *Lebensphilosophie* results in an irrational exuberance toward an uncritical concept of life; the Marburg School of neo-Kantianism remains caught in a teaching of categories without any persuasive connection to the real; the Rickert School postulates values neither the origin nor the extent of which it can explain; the Vienna School, like Husserl, cannot resolve the problem of the given nor of "alter ego," nor of the constitution of intersubjectivity. How then is the concept of "interpretation" supposed to provide an answer to this formidable array of problems? And what does interpretation mean?

Interpretation is not to be confused with the problem of meaning; it is not the task of philosophy to present reality as if it were meaningful; nor should interpretation suggest a "second, secret world," behind the appearances. Referring now explicitly to Benjamin's *Ursprung des deutschen Trauerspiels,*[17] on which he had been teaching a seminar at that time, Adorno writes: "Authentic philosophic interpretation does not meet up with a fixed meaning which already lies behind the question; but lights it up suddenly and momentarily, and consumes it at the same time. Just as riddle-solving is constituted, in that the singular and dispersed elements of the question are brought into various groupings long enough for them to close together in a figure out of which the solution springs forth, while the question disappears—so philosophy has to bring its elements, which it receives from the sciences into changing constellations, or, to say it with less astrological and scientifically more current expression, into changing trial combinations, until they fall into a figure which can be read as an answer, while at the same time the question disappears. The task of philosophy is not to search for concealed and manifest intentions of reality, but to interpret unintentional reality, in that, by the power of constructing figures, or images [*Bilder*], out of the isolated elements of reality, it *negates [*aufhebt*] questions, the exact articulation of which is the task of science*" (*AP*, 127; my emphasis). Although Adorno concludes this passage with a gesture towards the "strange affinity between interpretive philosophy. . . . and the thinking of materialism," (*AP*, 127) his Frankfurt colleagues at that time, including Max Horkheimer, could not but have been astonished at this turn in Adorno's thinking towards this elusive concept of materialist interpretation.

In his 1937 essay on "Traditional and Critical Theory," Horkheimer would reverse Adorno's contentions: first, it is the task of philosophy to pose the questions, "the exact articulation" of which remains its (philosophy's) task. The sciences enable an answer, in that one can integrate their results into some kind of analysis of an "epoch approaching its end,"[18] but they do not supply philosophy with *its* questions. Second, Critical Theory rejects the problem of *the given*, by showing that, following Marx and Lukács, the given is constituted in and through a process of social labor and that nature is formed sociohistorically. Third, Critical Theory is critique in that it allies itself with the oppositional forces capable of transforming the false social totality.

Even if between the 1931 essay on "The Actuality of Philosophy" and the 1937 programmatic essay by Horkheimer on "Traditional and Critical Theory" Adorno's thinking underwent changes, he never accepted the program of social labor subscribed to by Horkheimer and Lukács, and insisted instead on the concept of "Naturgeschichte," with all its paradoxical implications. He defended the idea of the nature of history and of the historicality of nature, neither of which could be reduced to the intentional activities of empirical or transcendental subjects. Furthermore, Adorno resisted sociologizing philosophy. As Susan Buck-Morss (alias Benjamin Snow) observes, "Horkheimer believed as firmly as Adorno that bourgeois philosophy was in a state of decay, but he seems to have concluded that if metaphysics were no longer possible, then the philosopher had to look to the social sciences in order to find truth. For Horkheimer, the problem of "the object" tended to dissolve into (Marxian) sociology, the problem of "the subject" into (Freudian) psychology, and Critical Theory attempted to explain their interrelations. . . . Adorno . . . had an almost Hegelian faith in the immanent logic of philosophy."[19]

"A configuration of reality"; "changing constellations"; the "configuration of unintentional truth" through "historical images"—these are the Benjaminian phrases that tumble out of Adorno's pen in the last pages of this magisterial essay. In a grand dialectical move, however, at the end of the essay Adorno once more returns to the problem of Being and considers the following objection that could be raised against his own efforts as well. Could it not be objected, he asks, that "out of blind anxiety before the power of history . . . I bestowed upon historical facticity, or its arrangement, the power which actually belongs to the invariant, ontological first principles, practiced idolatry with historically produced being, destroyed in philosophy every permanent standard, sublimated it into an aesthetic picture game [*Bilderspiel*], and transformed the *prima philosophia* [first philosophy] into essayism"? (*AP*, 132). Adorno admits that these objections are legitimate, and that he will gladly accept the reproach of essayism. Essay-writing is a form of experimentation with the "power of freshly disclosed reality," (*AP*, 132) and if with the disintegration of philosophical certainties and pieties, the essay makes its reentry into philosophy, then Adorno welcomes this. "For the mind [*Geist*] is indeed not capable of producing or grasping the totality of the real, but it may be possible to penetrate the detail, to explode in miniature the mass of merely existing reality" (*AP*, 133). As we know, Adorno did not just practice the essay form, and in many of his writings he retained the urge towards the totality (and showed repeated failures to attain it) by making the dialectic "suffer violence in its own hands," to use a phrase of Hegel's.[20] Yet what I am calling the "Benjaminian moment," is not confined to this early essay but is deep and lasting in Adorno's philosophy, informing his well-known mature theses such as *the primacy of the object* and *the non-identical concept of the concept.*[21]

The next German thinker who uses concepts such as "configurations," "changing constellations," and "crystalline structures" in such prominent fashion is none other than Hannah Arendt in her preface to *The Origins of Totalitarianism*. The German title of this work— "Elemente und Ursprünge totaler Herrschaft"—"Elements and Origins of Totalitarian Domination," recalls Benjamin's "Ursprung des deutschen Trauerspiels" more explicitly.[22] In her first "Preface" in 1950, Arendt distinguished between "comprehension" and "deducing the unprecedented from precedents," which she rejected (*OT* [1950], viii). In the 1967 preface to part 1 of *The Origins of Totalitarianism*, around the time that she was editing Benjamin's writings in *Illuminations*, she wrote of totalitarianism versus "its elements and origins" (*OT* 1967, xv). Arendt is not concerned to establish some inevitable continuity between the past and present that would compel us to view what happened as what *had* to happen. She objects to this trap of historicist understanding and maintains that the future is radically underdetermined. If we recall Benjamin's chess-playing puppet, Arendt wants to show that the mysterious hunchback behind it does not pull the strings of history after all. Instead, she is searching for the elements of totalitarianism, for those currents of thought, political events, and outlook, which form a particular *configuration* and *crystallization of elements*, quite differently than they did in their original context. All historical writing is implicitly a history of the present. And it is the particular constellation and crystallization of elements into a whole at the present time that serve as methodological guides to their past meanings. Thus, none of the elements she assesses—anti-Semitism, the end of the rights of man, and the decline of the nation-state, the European scramble for Africa, race thinking, and bureaucracy—are sufficient by themselves alone to explain how a racially based Nazi exterminationist anti-Semitism, totally dependent upon a well-functioning bureaucracy, emerged. "The book, therefore," explains Arendt, "does not really deal with the 'origins' of totalitarianism—as its title unfortunately claims—but gives a historical account of the 'elements' which 'crystallized' into totalitarianism. This account is followed by an analysis of the 'elementary structure' of totalitarian movement and domination itself. The elementary structure of totalitarianism is the hidden structure of the book."[23] In view of the deep and lasting influence Benjamin had upon their thinking, the struggle that broke out between Adorno and Arendt (and also Scholem) over Benjamin's legacy may be more intelligible in retrospect. My goal in this chapter is to identify those Benjaminian elements in their thinking that go beyond matters of intellectual influence and personal entanglements to a much-deeper level of orientation in their thought. And for this, we need to turn to Arendt's own first properly philosophical essay after World War II, namely, "What Is Existenz Philosophy?" written in 1946 for *Partisan Review*.

## Hannah Arendt: Explaining European Philosophy to an American Audience

Adorno's "The Actuality of Philosophy" is a magisterial essay, astonishing in its self-confidence for one writing so early in his academic career. The same cannot be said of Arendt's "What Is Existenz Philosophy?".[24] It is written in a halting language, probably due to the fact that she had not yet gained fluency in English; it is pedagogical in tone, trying to introduce to an American audience, curious about trends in recent European thought, themes in German Idealism. There are a few too many "firsts" and assignments of periodicity: for example, that the word "existence" is used in the modern sense for the *first time* in Schelling's late work (*EP*, 167); "Modern existential philosophy *begins* with Kierke-gaard" (*EP*, 173); "Kant, who is *the real, though secret*, as it were, founder of modern philosophy" (*EP*, 168; My emphases). The reader has the sense that Arendt is trying very hard to render manageable for a general, and not necessarily philosophical, audience some of the deepest cur-rents of European philosophy since the death of Hegel.

Like Adorno, Arendt sees the collapse of the Hegelian system as the crucial point of entry into philosophical trends of the late nineteenth and twentieth centuries. She writes that "immediately after Hegel's death it became apparent that his system represented the last word of all western philosophy, at least to the extent that, since Parmenides, it had not ... ever dared call into question the unity of thought and Being" (*EP*, 164). But this questioning had already been accomplished by Kant; in that sense what culminated with Hegel was not an unbroken tradition but rather the illusion of restoring a tradition. It was Kant who had distinguished the concepts of our understanding from the sensory impressions that originate with the impact of the external world upon our sense organs—our intuitions (*Anschauungen*). The *that* of our con-ceptual apparatus can never explain the *what* of our sense perceptions. I may know from someone else's description what a lilac is and looks like, but I will never know what a lilac smells like until I have actually smelled one!

Arendt, however, draws from this two conclusions that diverge from Adorno's: first, "If Being and thinking are no longer the same, if think-ing no longer enables me to penetrate the true reality of things because the nature of things has nothing to do with their reality, then science can be whatever it likes; it no longer yields up any truth to man, no truth of any interest to man" (*EP*, 168). Arendt, unlike Adorno, does not envisage an intellectual division of labor between the sciences and philosophy. For her, even until her last work, *The Life of the Mind*, sci-entific knowledge accounts for factual reality and establishes truth, while the task of thinking, generally, and philosophy, more specifically, is to generate meaning (*LM*, vol. 1, *Thinking*, 14–15; 61). This concept of meaning in Arendt's mature work is quite close to Adorno's concept

of interpretation. Meaning searches for illumination via building constellations and via attempts to think the break in tradition such as to
reveal the emergence of the new and the unprecedented in all their
moral and political ambiguity. (See chapter 6 below for the legal and
political dimensions of the new and the unprecedented in history, pp.
107–9.) This feature of Arendt's thought is best exemplified through her
interpretations of the history of political philosophy, illustrated by her
essays such as those collected in *Between Past and Future. Eight Exercises
in Political Thought.*[25]

In her 1946 essay, unlike Adorno, Arendt turns to the disunity of
thought and being mainly for its implications for the human being as a
moral and political actor, as a "doer of deeds and a speaker of words,"
as she will later state in *The Human Condition* (*HC*, 176).[26] The Kantian
opposition of thought and Being, of concept and intuition, subjects
man himself to a set of untenable dualisms and antagonisms. As bodies
in space and time, human beings, like all matter, are subject to scientific
laws; they are determined, in ways that are obscure and unintelligible
to them, by forces in nature, including human nature. But they are also
creatures of reason who can act on the basis of moral principles that
they alone can formulate. Humans are creatures of freedom insofar as
they determine their actions in accordance with the moral law; yet, as
material bodies in space and time, they are subject to the laws of nature.
"At the same time that Kant made man the master and the measure of
man, he also made him the slave of Being" (*EP*, 171). "With this position, which followed directly from Kant," Arendt writes, "man was cut
off from the absolute, rationally accessible realm of ideas and universal
values and left in the midst of a world where he had nothing left to hold
onto" (*EP*, 169). Certainly, Arendt's reading of Kant here is not compatible with Kant's own self-understanding according to which human
dignity resides in admitting the limits of reason when confronted with
its antinomies. Existential despair about the human condition, despite
many pessimistic passages about the "crooked timber of humanity" is
not Kant's disposition. (See below chapter 9 on Isaiah Berlin's appropriation of this term.)

When Adorno himself reflects on these Kantian antinomies in his
other works,[27] it is to free the sensuous nature of humans as well as

*[handwritten margin note: contradiction of 2 laws]*

nature in general, from being the Other of reason—but also more radically, to rethink the relationship of concept and intuition, form and matter, reason and the impulses in such a way as to go beyond the metaphors of self-legislation and the hierarchical subjugation of impulses to reason. Here Arendt and Adorno agree: "Just as it was decisive for the historical development of the nineteenth century that nothing disappeared as quickly as did the revolutionary concept of the *citoyen*, so it was decisive for the development of post-Kantian philosophy that nothing disappeared as quickly as did this new concept of man that had just barely begun to emerge" (*EP*, 170). Adorno is not reluctant to bid this new concept of man a speedy farewell, whereas Arendt is more concerned with the damage done to the shared human world, when the *citoyen* disappears as quickly as the autonomous individual.

Into this rift caused by the disappearance of the rational subject and the *citoyen* enters Kierkegaard, who is seen by Arendt, as well as Adorno, as the one who has faced the abyss created by the antinomies of Kant no less than by the disappearance of Hegelian truths. "Kierkegaard set the 'individual,' the single human being, for whom there is neither place nor meaning in a totality controlled by the world spirit," against Hegel's system, writes Arendt (*EP*, 173). It follows, therefore, that "All essential questions of philosophy such as those concerning the immortality of the soul, the freedom of man, the unity of the world—which is to say, all the questions whose antinomical structure Kant demonstrated in the antinomies of pure reason, can be comprehended only as 'subjective truths,' not known as objective ones" (*EP*, 173). The universal is only significant in its relationship to the singular: this is Kierkegaard's deep insight. The *self* cannot be captured through abstractions such as the rational moral being; nor can "the knight of faith," in Kierkegaard's terms, be encountered via general sociological terms referring to the average bourgeois citizen. And the self is most singular in those limit situations (*Grenzsituationen*) when it encounters its own singularity most intensely. "Death is the event in which I am definitely alone, an individual cut off from everyday life" (*EP*, 174). Arendt, at this point in her reconstruction of these currents of thought, much like Adorno, moves from Kierkegaard to Heidegger's philosophy of Dasein to explore how existential ontology, following Kierkegaard's precedent, turns into a philosophy of dread, death, and anxiety.

Through their broad brush strokes that trace the dissolution of the unity of thought and being, and most importantly, in their singling out of the *emergence of the singular as opposed to the universal,* and in their acknowledgment of the absence of easy mediations and reconciliation between the universal and the singular, Arendt and Adorno come closer to each other in their diagnoses of philosophy after Hegel than either of them recognized or may have been willing to admit. In Arendt's exposé and critique of Heidegger in this essay—the first time after World War II that she expresses herself on his thought—we see the outlines of how she intends to think her way beyond false universals to a concept not of *the singularity of the self, but of the uniqueness of the person.* Where Adorno will resuscitate the dignity of the other of reason through his unique form of practicing dialectics without teleology, Arendt will go back to a move she first sees attempted by Husserl, namely the recovery of *the world* as an epistemological and even ontological category. Arendt actually begins this essay by considering phenomenology and pragmatism (she says nothing about the latter) as "the most recent and interesting epochal philosophical schools of the last hundred years" (*EP*, 164). Arendt views Husserl's attempt to "reestablish the ancient tie between Being and thought," through "the intentional structure of consciousness" (*EP*, 164) as a noble failure. Even if philosophical reconstruction can enable me to understand why there are chairs and tables at all, "it will never be able to make me understand why *this* table *is.* And it is the existence of *this* table, quite apart from tables in general, that evokes the philosophical shock" (*EP*, 165). Adorno saw a moment of honesty in Husserl's admission that the "non-deducible given" remains a problem for phenomenology; Arendt sees revealed in this an attempt "to evoke magically a home again out of a world which has become alien" (*EP*, 165; 36 in the original *Partisan Review* version which I use here). "Husserl's phrase 'to the things themselves' is no less a magic formula than Hofmannsthal's 'little things'" (*EP*, 165). "By transforming this alien Being into consciousness...," writes Arendt of Husserl, he "tries to give the world a human face again, just as Hofmannsthal, with the magic of little things, tries to reawaken in us the old tenderness toward the world"

(*EP*, 166). It is this "tenderness toward the world" that Arendt thought had collapsed around her with the events of the twentieth century, never to be quite restored. Nevertheless, it was the task of the thinker, as Benjamin wrote in Thesis 6 of his *Theses in the Philosophy of History*, "To articulate the past historically ... to seize hold of a memory as it flashes up at a moment of danger ... In every era the attempt must be made anew to wrest tradition from the conformism that is about to overpower it."

## How to Account for Heidegger?

The personal and philosophical drama[28] behind Arendt's essay cannot easily be captured in her reconstruction of the history of philosophy after Hegel up to the point when the existential analytic of Dasein emerges and the "world is well lost," to use Richard Rorty's famous phrase.[29] It is the first time after World War II that Arendt comments on Heidegger's political behavior during his rectorship of the University of Freiburg and establishes a philosophical, and not merely characterological, link between his actions and his philosophy. In a surprising move, Arendt turns to elements of Jaspers's philosophy—his concept of limit situations (*Grenzsituationen*) and communication—to move beyond the pitfalls of Heidegger's ontology toward a concept of the world.

The Arendt-Heidegger saga has been recounted many times and this is not the place to revisit it.[30] Arendt is just as skeptical in her evaluation of the Heideggerian analytic of Dasein as Adorno was in 1931. After crediting Heidegger with "picking up the question that Kant had broached," (*EP*, 177) she writes that "Heidegger claims to have found a being in whom essence and existence are identical, and that being is man. His essence is his existence" (*EP*, 177). Yet, far from recovering a sense of being-at-home-in-the-world, when Heidegger argues that Dasein has an "ontically-ontologically pre-eminent rank," he "puts man in the exact same place that God had occupied in traditional ontology" (*EP*, 178).

We may want to contest this interpretation, which hardly does justice to the principles of "thrownness," "temporality," and "care," all of which have their sources in a more traditional philosophical theology with

Augustinian roots. We also know that Heidegger, after his turn (*die Kehre*), much like Adorno, forfeited the epistemic priority of the subject and insisted on a receptivity and openness to Being with bucolic phrases such as "Man is the shepherd of Being."[31]

Arendt is not unaware of these other dimensions in Heidegger's thought and gives very careful reconstructions of being-unto-death and resoluteness. But she insists that "the crucial element of man's being-in-the-world, and what is at stake for his being-in-the-world is quite simply survival in the world. That is the very thing that is denied man, and consequently the basic mode of being-in-the-world is alienation, which is felt both as homelessness and anxiety. In anxiety, which is fundamental fear of death, is reflected the not-being-at-home in the world" (*EP*, 179). The *who* of Dasein is the unique, singular self who can only face her death as hers. But a "Self, taken in isolation, is meaningless," observes Arendt (*EP*, 180). The only thing that this Self can do is to resolutely take its singularity into account, and this "taking into account" has no determinate moral and political content. In fact, it can only be filled with a political content that is either naïve in its lack of judgment concerning the political world or is mendacious in its willingness to jump resolutely into the flow of events after hearing history's call.[32]

Arendt, as well as Adorno, sees in Heidegger's attempt to restore the unity of thought and being via the analytic of Dasein a colossal philosophical failure that moves towards a vacuous subjectivism and that cannot recapture being-in-the-world. It is at this point that Arendt locates the intrinsic, and not merely accidental, link between Heidegger's philosophy and his politics. "Later, and after the fact, as it were," she writes, "Heidegger has drawn on many and muddled concepts like 'folk' and 'earth' in an effort to supply his isolated selves with a shared, common ground to stand on . . . *But if it does not belong to the concept of man that he inhabits the earth together with others of his kind, then all that remains for him is a mechanical reconciliation by which the atomized selves are provided with a common ground that is essentially alien to their nature. All that can result from that is the organization of these selves intent only on themselves into an Over-self in order somehow to affect a transition from resolutely accepted guilt to action*" (*EP*, 181–82; my emphasis).[33]

With this comment Arendt is not only diagnosing Heidegger's political *parti pris* (siding with) for the Nazis, the full extent of which she still did not know in 1946, but she is stumbling upon one of the leading insights of her mature thought, namely, that Heidegger's existential analytic of Dasein as Self makes it impossible to think the *site of the political*, which is always that of Being-in-the-world with others. Heidegger himself had already written: "By reason of this with-like-Being-in-the-world, the world is always the one that I share with Others. The world of *Dasein* is a with-world. Being-in is Being-with-Others. This Being-in-themselves within-the-world is *Dasein-with*."[34] However, concepts such as *Self* and *Dasein* are singularly inappropriate to disclose the dimension of "*Mitsein*" (Being-with). This is the case because "existence itself is, by its very nature, never isolated. It exists only in communication and in awareness of others' existence. Our fellowmen are not (as in Heidegger) an element of existence that is structurally necessary but at the same time an impediment to the Being of the Self... In the concept of communication lies a concept of humanity new in its approach though not yet fully developed that postulates communication as the premise for the existence of man" (*EP*, 186). Arendt's programmatic path is now clearer to see: from here on, she will reinterpret Heidegger's concept of "being-in-the-world-with" through a concept of communication, the outlines of which are not given here, but wherein she sees herself indebted to Jaspers.

It is in *The Human Condition* that the new category of "plurality," which brings these dimensions together, will be articulated (*HC*, 175 *ff.*). Humans inhabit a space with others who are both their equal and yet distinct from them. Plurality is expressed through speech. "If action as beginning corresponds to the fact of birth, if it is the actualization of the human condition of natality, then speech corresponds to the fact of distinctness and is the actualization of the human condition of plurality, that is, of living as a distinct and unique human being among equals" (*HC*, 178). But this is precisely the step that Heidegger does not take: although the world is always a world shared with others, although Mitsein is a fundamental condition of Dasein, all forms of Mitsein other than being-unto-death are dismissed as inauthentic. They represent the fallenness of Dasein into the chatter (*Gerede*) of the everyday and into the "light of the public that darkens all"—(*Das Licht der Öffentlichkeit verdunkelt alles*). Although I cannot develop the point here, it is noteworthy that with the category of *plurality*, and her insistence on the unity of speech and action, Arendt, along with Wittgenstein, becomes one of the few twentieth-century thinkers to note the significance of language as speech, as the give-and-take among human beings. Admittedly, this concept of speech is not much developed in her thought, and is interpreted instead through metaphors such as "the web of human relationships" (*HC*, 181–84).

Arendt's 1946 critique formulates an insight that is crucial to her analysis of totalitarianism: that societal atomization—the breakdown of civic, political, and cultural associations—and the loneliness of the atomized masses make them susceptible to the influence of totalitarian movements. Atomized existence in a mass society creates worldlessness. The world is constituted by our common and shared experiences of it to the degree that we can trust that the orientations and significations we follow are more or less those shared by others as well. This commonness of the world is the background against which the plurality of perspectives that constitute the political can emerge. Politics requires a background of commonality as well as the recognition of plurality and perspectival character of judgment of those who share this common space. Although Heidegger, through his analysis of Dasein's worldliness as a form of Mitsein, made "being-with" constitutive of the human condition, his analytic of Dasein, rather than illuminating human plurality, testified to the progressing atomization, loneliness, and worldlessness of the individual in the concluding years of the Weimar Republic.

Departing from what I have called "Western philosophy's love affair with death,"[35] Arendt in *The Human Condition* turned to natality, plurality, speech, and human action to open up a categorical realm for thinking the political. It is only through this form of being-with-others as talking and acting selves that the singular can be recaptured and can free itself from the dominance of the universal. Whereas Adorno's mature thinking formulates a novel interpretation of the "concept" such as to reclaim the singular and the particular against false universals, Arendt sees in narrative in general, and Kant's theory of judgment in particular, a move beyond the defunct ontological unity of thought and being. The Benjaminian moment returns for her.

## Totalitarianism and the Question of Ethico-Political Judgment

With the rise of European fascism and Nazism, for Arendt as well as for Adorno, the critique of false universals and ontological certainties through the exercise of good judgment assumed an urgent moral and political dimension. Although little-noted, the "authoritarian personality" type theorized by the Frankfurt School and other social scientists of the period is one who singularly lacks the capacity for good judgment and this was an issue that greatly preoccupied Arendt as well. For Adorno and his coworkers, the authoritarian personality was incapable of evaluating individuals and circumstances without being imprisoned by rigid categories. These types of personalities submitted their will as well as their judgment to those higher than themselves while demeaning those who stood in a position of social inferiority to them.[36] Such personalities were prone to paranoia in that they projected their own aggressive feelings towards individuals whom they then claimed to be hostile to themselves, who wanted their destruction and the like. Anti-Semitism, argued Adorno and Horkheimer, was based on complex processes of projection and paranoia. As the *Dialectic of Enlightenment* expresses it, "If mimesis makes itself like the surrounding world, so false projection makes the surrounding world like itself. If for the former the exterior is the model which the interior has to approximate, if for it the stranger becomes familiar, the latter transforms the tense inside ready to snap into exteriority and stamps even the familiar as the enemy."[37] The result of such psychic processes of projection is loss of judgment, of the capacity to assess and properly evaluate both the circumstances around oneself as well as the consequences of one's actions.

Whereas Adorno uses the language of psychoanalysis and social psychology to characterize this general loss of capacity for judgment,

Arendt asks repeatedly what the relationship is between "Thinking and Moral Considerations."[38] "Might the problem of good and evil, our faculty for telling right from wrong, be connected with our faculty of thought?," she asks.[39] This is why she claims that the most striking quality of Eichmann was not stupidity, wickedness, or moral depravity but what she describes as "thoughtlessness." This claim leads to the further puzzle that Martin Heidegger, the one who thought in a fashion that no other could, and Adolf Eichmann, the one who could not think at all, both were complicit in the Nazi regime. Could the power of thought alone not only prevent one from doing evil, but also enable one to judge the moral and political salience of particular circumstances?

It was the Eichmann affair that showed the centrality of judgment for human affairs in many and varied ways: there was the *retrospective judgment* that every historian and narrator of past events exercised; there was the *moral judgment* of the contemporaries who conducted the trial against Eichmann and judged his actions; and there was also the *lack of a faculty of judgment* on Eichmann's own part. (See chapter 4 below.) Prompted by the urgency of these problems, Arendt turned to Kant's *Critique of Judgment*.[40]

Arendt's unusual and somewhat idiosyncratic reading of Kant's moral philosophy in relation to the problem of judgment has been discussed widely. As Richard Bernstein has remarked: "Arendt well knew that, even though she invokes the name of Kant, she was radically departing from Kant. There is no question in Kant that the 'ability to tell right from wrong' is a matter of practical reason and not the faculty of reflective judgment which ascends from particulars to generals or universals."[41] Judgment, for Kant, "as the ability to think the particular as contained under the universal," is *determinative* when the universal is given and the particular is merely subsumed under it. It is *reflective*, if only the particular is given and the appropriate universal has to be found for it (*CJ*, 18–19). Although Kant thought that the faculty of judgment was most needed with respect to teleological judgments concerning nature and with respect to aesthetic judgments to ascertain the beautiful, Arendt insisted that judgment was a faculty of "telling right from wrong,"[42] and not just the beautiful from the ugly.

In view of our analysis of Arendt's 1946 "What Is Existenz Philosophy?" essay, we can now see that for Arendt the problem of judgment, although it was of prime importance in the moral and political realm, originated early on with her critique of the search for false universals in the history of philosophy. Her attempt to move beyond the crises of philosophy by discovering a way of thinking the new and the unprecedented in all their particularity points precisely to that conceptual problem that Kant's "reflective judgment" was supposed to tackle. The evidence for this interpretation of Arendt's interest in the problem of judgment is provided by the fact that already in 1961, before the Eichmann trial, in an essay on "The Crisis in Culture" Arendt explicitly discusses Kant's doctrine of reflective judgment and the role of *sensus communis*. The latter, she writes, is "the idea of a sense shared by all of us ... that in reflecting takes account (a priori), in our thought, of everyone else's mode of presenting [something], in order as it were to compare our own judgment with human reason in general" (*CJ*, 160).[43] Furthermore, "the power of judgment rests on a potential agreement with others, and the thinking process which is active in judging something is not, like the thought process of pure reasoning, a dialogue between me and myself ... And this enlarged way of thinking, which as judgment knows how to transcend its individual limitations, cannot function in strict isolation or solitude: it needs the presence of others 'in whose place' it must think, whose perspective it must take into consideration and without whom it never has the opportunity to operate at all."[44]

Enlarged thought (*erweiterte Denkungsart*) is not empathy, for it does not mean assuming the standpoint of the other. It means making present to oneself the perspective of others involved, and it means asking whether I could "woo their consent." Enlarged thought displays the qualities of judgment necessary to retrieve and to do justice to the perspectival and plural quality of the shared world. Judgment requires the moral and cognitive capacities for worldliness, that is, an interest in the world and the human beings who form the world; it also requires a firm grasp of where one's own boundaries lie and where those of others begin. Whereas thinking requires autonomy, consistency, tenacity, independence, and steadfastness, judging requires worldliness, an interest in one's fellow human beings, and the capacity to appreciate the standpoint of others without projection, idealization, and distortion. There are certainly tensions between the faculties of thinking and judging. Tenacity of thought may lead one to ignore the others' claims upon oneself and to deny their perspectives as valid. Often, philosophical thought suffers from a certain worldlessness, precisely because it seeks consistency, not perspectivality. But it is the task of judgment to restore the commonality of the world in its full plurality. May we say then that judgment is needed to establish "configurations" and "crystallization of elements" in their singularity as well as commonality? How can we capture these configurations? Can we do so by building metaphors? "In other words," observes Arendt, "the chief difficulty here seems to be that for thinking itself—whose language is entirely metaphorical and whose conceptual framework depends entirely on the gift of metaphor, which bridges the gulf between the visible and the invisible, the world of appearance and the thinking ego—there exists no metaphor that could plausibly illuminate this special activity of the mind, in which something invisible within us deals with the invisibles of the world" (LM, 123). Thinking dwells in the language of metaphors and tries to bridge the gap between the visible and invisible realms. The political thinker, as opposed to the speculative philosopher, must have the capacity to *share* the power of metaphor with her fellow-human beings such as to nourish and sustain the fragile plurality of the shared world, which, at any moment, can disintegrate and be overwhelmed by propaganda, kitsch, and the loss of common sense.

What I have been calling Arendt's "Benjaminian moment" is caught up in this tension between the universal and the particular, metaphor and reality, the faculties of thinking and judging. Metaphor provides abstract, imageless thought with an image drawn from the world of appearances and "whose function is 'to establish the reality of our concepts'; it thus undoes, as it were, the withdrawal from the world of appearances that is the precondition of mental activities" (LM, 103). Arendt is referring once more to Kant's *Critique of Judgment*, paragraph 59, "On Beauty as the Symbol of Morality." "Now," writes Kant, "I maintain that the beautiful is the symbol of the morally good; and only because we refer the beautiful to the morally good (we all do so naturally and require all others to do so, as a duty) does our liking for it include a claim to everyone else's assent, while the mind is also conscious of being ennobled" (*CJ*, 228). Arendt herself does not explore this connection between beauty and the morally good. It is Adorno who, through his concept of the *Naturschöne*, will explore this link and introduce another mode for retrieving the particular from being swallowed by false universals.

## Judgment in Adorno's Aesthetic Theory

Whereas Arendt sees in Kant's theory of reflective judgment and *sensus communis* a categorical strategy for retrieving the specificity of the particular, Adorno engages in a dialectical struggle with Kant's moral theory for some eighty pages in *Negative Dialectics* (*ND*, 268ff.). Freely deploying psychoanalytic categories against Kant's theory of the self and of the Categorical Imperative, Adorno writes: "According to the Kantian model, the subjects are free, insofar as, conscious of themselves, they are identical with themselves; and in such identity they are once more unfree, insofar as they stand under its compulsion and perpetrate it. They are unfree as non-identical, as diffuse nature, and as such free, because in the stimulations that overcome them—the non-identity of the subject with itself is nothing else—they will also overcome the compulsive character of identity" (*ND*, 295ff.). Adorno repeats a charge brought against Kantian moral philosophy since the young Hegel's critique that the Kantian moral law, formulated through the principle of the Categorical Imperative, amounts to a principle of tautology. "Act only in such a way that the maxim of your actions can be a universal law for all," is translated into the principle: "Act in such a way that the maxim of your actions does not contradict itself."[45] This translation of the universalizability principle in ethics into tautological identity is a rhetorical tour de force. What Adorno adds to this is that the compulsion towards identity, displayed through the search for a moral principle that does not contradict itself, actually is not autonomy but unfreedom. The epistemic and moral subject of Kantian philosophy—"the I that must accompany all my apperceptions"—reveals this rigid search for an identity that can only be achieved at the cost of denying not only otherness but the otherness within the self as well. The Kantian moral law is a perfect instance of rigid identity-formation through repression within and without.

"Utopia," writes Adorno, "would be the non-identity of the subject that would not be sacrificed" ("Utopie wäre die opferlose Nichtidentität des Subjekts," *ND*, 277). This non-sacrificial non-identity, however, must not be understood as reconciliation," as "being-by-oneself-in-otherness." In Hegel's understanding of freedom "as being-by-oneself-in-otherness," otherness simply becomes the narcissistic mirror in which Spirit can contemplate itself. To be by-oneself-in-otherness can only be achieved through the aesthetic experience of the Naturschöne—the "naturally beautiful."[46] To be sure, one cannot interpret the Naturschöne as if it were an eternally given and unchanging substratum of beauty. Rather, the "naturally beautiful" is antithesis, the antithesis of society (*AT*, 101–3) and as undetermined, the antithesis of determination (*AT*, 113). It is an "allegory," a "cipher," a "sign" (*Zeichen*) of reconciliation. It is a mode in which the mediation between humans and nature, between subject and object, can be thought of; it is not a state of affairs, a final condition, but an aporetic longing that can only be captured as "allegory" and as "cipher." In terms that unmistakenly remind us once more of Benjamin, Adorno writes, "The naturally beautiful is the cipher [*Spur*] of the non-identical in things set upon their course of universal identity" (*AT*, 114).[47] From the standpoint of conceptual thought, the naturally beautiful, precisely because it can only be intimated but not stated, is deficient. But the utopia of a non-sacrificial non-identity of the subject is intimated in that noncompulsory relation to otherness that forces the subject to forget him- or herself and thus to catch a glimpse of the moment of reconciliation. As Albrecht Wellmer observes, "Adorno sees in natural beauty a cipher of nature that does not yet exist, of nature in a state of reconciliation, which has thus developed beyond the splitting of life into mind and its object . . . The work of art, as an imitation of natural beauty, thus becomes the image of a nature which has found its speech, a nature redeemed and liberated from its muteness, just as it becomes the image of a reconciled humanity."[48]

Yet this image requires *philosophical interpretation* (*AT*, 193). It is important to properly capture the interpretive complementarity as well as dissonance between art and philosophy: To quote Wellmer again: "Philosophy, whose utopia is 'to unseal the nonconceptual' by means of concepts, but without reducing it to conceptual categories . . . remains tied to conceptual language (what Adorno calls 'die meinende Sprache') in which the immediacy of the aesthetic presentation of truth cannot be reconstituted. Just as a moment of blindness adheres to the immediacy of aesthetic perception, so does a moment of emptiness adhere to the 'mediacy' of philosophical thought. Only in combination are they capable of circumscribing a truth which neither alone is able to articulate."[49] Undoubtedly, for Adorno the naturally beautiful was not an aesthetic paradigm alone but a moral ideal as well: the "non-sacrificial nonidentity" of the subject suggests a life-form and a form of conduct that we can only capture in moments of intimation.

In contrast with Arendt, and above all with Kant, there is one dimension in this experience of the naturally beautiful that is missing in Adorno: the *communicability* of this experience, the necessity that our judgments of the beautiful be communicable and shareable with others. Kant's theory of aesthetic judgment for Arendt accomplishes both the revelation of particularity and a model of communication that is not based on coercion, but upon "wooing the consent of others" in whose place we must think. Following a similar line of thinking, Albrecht Wellmer has juxtaposed a Wittgensteinian theory of the concept to what he names "the rationalistic fiction" to which Adorno subscribes, and writes that "there is a mimetic force at work in the life of linguistic meaning, a force which enables what is non-identical in reality—as Adorno would say—to be reflected as something non-identical in linguistic meanings."[50] Arendt herself saw this "non-identical in linguistic meaning," to be revealed through the web of relationships, embedded in narratives that are constitutive of the "who" of the self and the "what" of our actions (*HC*, 181–85). It was in this constant and inevitable tension between the standpoint of the I and the other, between what my actions mean for me and how they are understood by others, that the perspectivality of the world was lodged. And because action is speech, this perspectivality does not just shatter into so many shards of a broken glass, but can be woven, undone, and rewoven just like a web. Arendt, in this sense, anticipated Habermas's critique of Adorno, which signaled the transition from the critique of instrumental reason to communicative rationality in the history of the Critical Theory of the Frankfurt School.

In his 1969 article, "Theodore Adorno—The Primal History of Subjectivity—Self-Affirmation Gone Wild," Habermas writes with reference to the utopia of the non-identical: "Whoever meditates on this assertion will become aware that the condition described, although never real, is still most intimate and familiar to us. It has the structure of a life together in communication that is free from coercion. We necessarily anticipate such a reality, at least formally, each time we want to speak what is true ... Adorno might just as well have not assented to this consequence and insisted that the metaphor of reconciliation is the only one that can be spoken ... The wholly other may only be indicated via determinate negation; it cannot be known."[51]

In her critique of the false universals in the history of philosophy, Arendt herself already made this communication-theoretic turn with means derived from Kant's aesthetic theory and her not fully developed concepts of speech, action, and narrativity.

Exploring the intellectual affinities and dissonances between Adorno and Arendt, as I have tried to do in this chapter, not only permits us to reconstruct what still remains one of the most impressive traditions of philosophical flourishing in the history of Western thought, it also permits us to see that beyond all schisms among schools and personal hostilities among persons lies the vast horizon of philosophical moves and countermoves of the German-Jewish tradition, which is breathtaking in its conceptual configurations.

# 4

# Whose Trial? Adolf Eichmann's or Hannah Arendt's?

## THE EICHMANN CONTROVERSY REVISITED

### The Never Ending Controversy

It is rare to encounter a work of twentieth-century philosophy that has reached as wide an audience and caused as much furor as Hannah Arendt's 1963 volume on *Eichmann in Jerusalem. A Report on the Banality of Evil*.[1] Based on her coverage of the trial of Adolf Eichmann in Jerusalem from April 11 to December 15, 1961, for the *New Yorker*, this acrimonious and tangled controversy cast a long shadow on her otherwise illustrious career as a public intellectual and academic.

Although she was and continues to be severely attacked by the Jewish community,[2] ironically this book is Arendt's most intensely Jewish work, in which some of the deepest paradoxes of retaining a Jewish identity under conditions of modernity came to the fore in her search for the moral, political, and jurisprudential bases on which the trial and sentencing of Adolf Eichmann could take place.[3] Gershom Scholem's phrase that Hannah Arendt "lacked Ahabath Israel,"[4] "loving belonging to the Jewish people," is indeed cruel. Arendt never denied her Jewishness; if anything, for her it was so much a part of the order of the given that she was puzzled by Scholem's claim that "I regard you wholly as a daughter of our people."[5] To which she replied: "The truth is that I have never pretended to be anything else or to be in any way other than I am, and I have never even felt tempted in that direction. . . . To be a Jew belongs for me to the indisputable facts of my life . . . There is such a thing as a basic gratitude for everything that is as it is; for what has been *given* and not *made*; for what is *physei* and not *nomō*. To be sure such an attitude is prepolitical, but in exceptional circumstances—such as the circumstances of Jewish politics—it is bound to have also political consequence, though, as it were, in a negative way."[6] But Arendt did not "merely belong to them," as Judith Butler entitled her review of *The Jewish Writings*.[7] In the interwar years, she was a political activist, a left Zionist who pleaded for a binational state in Palestine; after immigrating to the United States in 1941 she advocated for a Jewish army to fight against the Nazis in the name of the Jewish people. After Judah Magnes's death and the extinction of the dreams of a "bi-national state that would be a part of the Mediterranean comity of peoples,"[8] Arendt lost the platform from which she could speak. The State of Israel was busy building and consolidating a new nation and was beleaguered by constant threats of war. World Jewry, aghast at the horrors of the Holocaust, was in no position to criticize Israel but expressed almost unconditional solidarity with it. By 1961, the generation of German-Jewish intellectuals such as Judah Magnes, Martin Buber, and even Scholem himself, who had occasionally envisaged some kind of binational polity in Israel-Palestine, was disappearing as were many Holocaust survivors. In Israel, the trial was used by the Ben-Gurion government as a form of political education, mobilizing sentiment for the project of nation-building and the triumph of the Zionist ideal.[9]

Equally important, the Eichmann trial was the first time since the Holocaust that the pretense of normality about these events that had begun to reign in Israel, Germany, and the rest of the world was shattered and the painful task of recollection and rearticulation begun. As many historians have noted about this period, for us who have the benefit of more than half a century of discussion, research, and publicity about Nazi atrocities and the Holocaust, it is even hard to imagine how scanty such public knowledge and scholarship were in the early 1960s.[10]

Psychoanalysis teaches us that recollection and the narration of trauma have their own temporality: uncovering why trauma is remembered at specific moments and repressed at others, what triggers human memory at certain points such that the crust of the past can be penetrated by articulations in the present, is crucial to the process of therapeutic analysis. It is odd that despite all the ink that has been spilled by Jewish and Israeli historians over Arendt's *Eichmann in Jerusalem* (and in the continuing attempts to refute Arendt in recent works by David Cesarani and Deborah Lipstadt),[11] it is hardly taken into account that Arendt herself was a survivor, and her "Olympian distance"—as Ralph Ellison once named it[12]—may also have been a defense against the traumatic possibility of falling into the hands of the Gestapo. After she fled from the women's internment camp in Gurs, in the South of France, had she been caught, Arendt faced sure death by deportation to Auschwitz. She was fortunate enough that unlike her close and unlucky friend, Walter Benjamin, she and her husband, Heinrich Blücher, were able to reach the United States in 1941. Arendt, who rejected psychoanalysis,[13] would most likely be offended by this interpretation, yet there is so much evidence in her language and in the construction of narrative voice in *Eichmann in Jerusalem* that reveals a storm raging within her, that this reading is hard to resist. Arendt's much-misunderstood sarcasm as well as her thinly veiled contempt for Eichmann himself were like layers of additional skin in which she had to clothe herself so as to permit her to provide one of the first and most dramatic accounts of the destruction of European Jewry.[14]

Just as memory and the process of recollection (*Erinnerung*) have their own temporality, so do the reading and reception of texts. It is by now possible to construct the historiography of successive readings of *Eichmann in Jerusalem*. In the mid to late 1960s, Arendt's book was interpreted in the light of Stanley Milgram's famous experiments about the facility with which cruelty and torture could be exercised by seemingly ordinary individuals who obeyed authority and silenced their own conscience. Milgram, in fact, began carrying out these experiments in 1961 during the time that the Eichmann trial was proceeding in Jerusalem and published his own results in 1963, thinking that references to

Arendt's study would increase his credibility.[15] Three decades later, Christopher Browning's famous analysis of the Reserve Police Battalion 101 in his book *Ordinary Men. Reserve Police Battalion 101 and the Final Solution in Poland* (1992), and Daniel Goldhagen's *Hitler's Willing Executioners* (1996), largely written as a refutation of Browning's claims, would define the hermeneutic horizon against the background of which Arendt's thesis about "the banality of evil" would be reread.[16]

Browning and Goldhagen are identified with different schools of interpreting the centrality of anti-Semitism and the Holocaust to the Third Reich. The "functionalist" historical school started by Hans Mommsen emphasizes that the "final solution" and the extermination of European Jewry were not the driving forces behind many developments in the Third Reich.[17] Goldhagen, and more recently, Saul Friedländer,[18] claim that "apocalyptic anti-Semitism" was indeed the central impetus for the National Socialist ideology of the Reich. Richard Wolin as well has characterized Arendt's position as belonging with the "functionalist historians."[19] Yet a cursory examination shows that Arendt's own writings contain elements of both approaches, with the emphasis on ideology predominating in her early work, while the latter work focuses more on institutional and systemic factors in the functioning of national socialism. It is simplistic therefore to reduce her reflections to one or another school of interpretation.[20]

The latest installment in this controversy, which once more refocuses the debate on the matter of Eichmann's personality and his anti-Semitism, is the impressive work by Bettina Stangneth called *Eichmann vor Jerusalem*.[21] A closer analysis of Stangneth's findings will also help shed further light on the thesis of "the banality of evil."

## Eichmann *before* Jerusalem

Discussions of the German edition of Stangneth's book (2011) had centered around the neo-Nazi circle of sympathizers who gathered in Argentina, their connections to postwar Germany, their hopes to influence political events there, and the claim that successive German governments resisted bringing Adolf Eichmann to trial. "Many who were caught in the network of the criminal state from which so many had profited, felt themselves as accomplices," Stangneth writes, "even if the time after 1945 had not been a period of painful questions for them personally. In this atmosphere of collective silence even the resurgence of a name which had become a symbol disturbed one" (*EvJ*, 530–31).

Eichmann himself wanted to be tried in Germany, knowing that he would not be condemned to death because statutes considering Nazi crimes to be "crimes of state" forbade the imposition of capital punishment upon individuals for obeying laws that were legal at the time of the Third Reich (*EvJ*, 263). Fritz Bauer, the state attorney general of Hessen, who was on Eichmann's trail, may have been the first to tip Israelis to Eichmann's whereabouts since his own attempts to bring war criminals to trial had been thwarted by the Adenauer government (*EvJ*, 163).[22] Stangneth notes that more than 2,425 pages of documentation are still held in a dossier by the German Central Intelligence Service, which refuses to make them public (*EvJ*, 533). As late as September 10, 2009, a decision was made by the office of the German Chancellor not to release this material on the grounds that "the abstract . . . interest in the discovery of truth" had to be balanced against "the good of the State; the protection of informants and the personal (privacy) rights of concerned third parties" (*EvJ*, 524). These aspects of Stangneth's book, which directly address the culture of silence and repression in postwar Germany's failing "to work through the past" (*Vergangenheitsbewälti-gung*)[23] have all been neglected by American commentators. Instead the trial of Adolf Eichmann has been turned once more into the trial of Hannah Arendt. It is as if not Adolf Eichmann but Hannah Arendt needed to stand trial before the judges of Jerusalem!

For example, the historian Deborah Lipstadt avers that "if previous researchers have seriously dented Arendt's case, Ms. Stangneth 'shatters it.'"[24] The intellectual historian Richard Wolin, heralding "the demise of a legend," announces that Arendt, "perhaps out of her misplaced loyalty to her former mentor and lover Martin Heidegger . . . insisted on applying the Freiburg philosopher's concept of 'thoughtlessness' (*Gedankenlosigkeit*) to Eichmann. In doing so, she drastically underestimated the fanatical conviction that infused his actions."[25]

But can Eichmann not be a convinced Nazi anti-Semite and also banal? In what sense did Arendt mean that Eichmann "was not stupid. It was sheer thoughtlessness—something by no means identical with stupidity—that predisposed him to become one of the greatest criminals of that period"? (*EiJ*, 287–88.) Stangneth does not address such questions nor does her book throw much light on the larger philosophical issues underlying Arendt's analysis, but she is respectful of Arendt's work: "Arendt read the protocols of the interrogation and the trial unlike anyone else. And with this she fell into a trap, because Eichmann in Jerusalem was no more than a mask. She did not recognize this, but impressively it was clear to her that she had not understood the phenomenon as well as she wanted to" (Stangneth, *EvJ*, 21). What, then, was this phenomenon?

Stangneth brings to light new evidence about Eichmann's persona and thinking based mainly on the so-called "Argentina papers." After 1979 large chunks of interviews conducted with Eichmann more than twenty years earlier in 1957 by Willem S. Sassen, a Dutch Nazi journalist who had become a German citizen, became available. It took nearly twenty years for this material to emerge more or less complete because, with the death of his lawyer Servatius, Eichmann's posthumous papers were deposited in the national German archives in Koblenz. Sassen himself had also given everything in his possession back to the Eichmann family by then (*EvJ*, 514–15). These included over one thousand pages of typed conversation with handwritten comments, as well as taped recordings (the originals of which would emerge only in 1998), and an additional five hundred pages of handwritten material and commentary, some by Eichmann and some by Sassen (*EvJ*, 471). The interviews and Eichmann's own notes were in preparation for a book to be published by the Argentine-based neo-Nazi Press, *Dürer Verlag*, run by Eberhard Ludwig Ceasar Fritsch (*EvJ*, 151). Since the late 1950s the goal of this publishing house, and of the circle of old Nazis and Nazi sympathizers assembled around it, was to influence events in Germany, and especially to counter the charges of the mass murder of the European Jews. Eichmann was composing a book with the title, *Others Have Spo-*

*ken, Now I Will* (*Die anderen sprachen, jetzt will ich sprechen*). He had asked Sassen to publish these documents if he were to die or fall into the hand of the Israelis (*EvJ*, 473). After Eichmann's arrest, Sassen prepared a photographic film of the convolute of a thousand pages but decided to sell only about one hundred pages. Eichmann's wife, Vera, who was now destitute financially and alone with her four sons in Argentina approved of the sale. Eventually only 150 pages of handwritten material and six hundred pages of typescript, which amounted to no more than 60% of the interviews and 40% of the handwritten documents, were sold to *Life* magazine. This did not include additional papers and archives, which had been buried rapidly by Eichmann's son in the family's garden upon his arrest. Only after thirty years would they be made available to the British historian and Holocaust denier, David Irving, in October 1991 (*EvJ*, 517).

Sassen, who quickly came under the suspicion of having betrayed Eichmann, proceeded to sell some additional material to the German magazine *Der Stern* and two other Dutch publications. With the publication of the *Life* magazine series, Eichmann, who was by then in an Israeli jail, suffered a nervous breakdown, but he and his lawyer, Servatius, managed to come up with a defense to cast doubt on the veracity of the Sassen interviews.

Arendt was able to read neither the entirety nor even a significant portion of this material but was quite familiar with the interview in *Life*. She knew that "Eichmann had made copious notes for the interview, which was tape recorded and then rewritten by Sassen with considerable embellishments," and she also knew that although the notes were admitted to the trial as evidence, "the statement as a whole was not" (*EiJ*, 238). Israel's state prosecutor, Gideon Hausner, had a bad copy of the more complete material, yet he and the Court continued to assume that the *Life* magazine materials and the transcripts were the same. They were not (*EvJ*, 496–97). Stangneth further explains that of the 713 typed and eighty-three handwritten pages in Israel's possession, Hausner could only use eighty-three pages. Eichmann and Servatius had managed to convince the Court that this was inadmissible evidence, supposedly because the recorded statements were uttered under the influence of alcohol and with Sassen's encouragement to induce Eichmann to make sensationalist pronouncements for publicity purposes. Stangneth concludes that both had lied successfully: Eichmann by pretending to be a down-and-out exile, given to drunken exaggerations of his role in the murder of European Jews, and Sassen, an ambitious journalist out to make money and fond of journalistic confabulations.

## Was Arendt Wrong about Eichmann?

The Argentine Papers give us new insights into the intensity of Eichmann's anti-Semitic worldview, insights that Arendt missed. Stangneth cites a statement by Eichmann's former friend and colleague, Dieter Wisliceny, during the Nuremberg trials: "[Eichmann] said: He would jump laughing into the grave because the feeling that he had five million people on his conscience would please him extra-ordinarily" (EvJ, 93).[26] This then led Göring to comment: "This Wisliceny is a small pig, who only appears big, because Eichmann is not here" (EvJ, 93).

Would full access to this material have led Arendt to change her assessment that Eichmann was banal and "thoughtless"? Not if one understands and uses German as she did, and not if one understands the philosophical contexts within which she meant precisely what she said.

Consider the following: Commenting on Eichmann's claim that he was not a "mass murderer," Stangneth writes that his "inner morality is not [based on] an idea of what is right or a universal moral category, not even a form of self-examination, [but on] the recognition of a dogma which is uncontested by National Socialists, namely that each *Volk* has the right to defend itself with all possible means and one's own people has the most right to do so" (EvJ, 264). Conscience is nothing other than this "morality of the Fatherland that lives in every human being," which Eichmann also calls "the voice of the blood" (EvJ, 264).

In a farewell message to sympathizers in Argentina, Eichmann also "threw caution to the winds" and declaimed: "I say to you honestly . . . I was the 'conscientious bureaucrat.' I was that indeed. . . . [but] within the soul of this conscientious bureaucrat lay a fanatical warrior for the freedom of the race from which I stem ... what my Volk requires ... is for me a holy commandment and a holy law" (*EvJ*, 391).

It is this strange mixture of bravado and cruelty, of patriotic idealism and the shallowness of racialist thinking that Arendt sensed because she was so well attuned to Eichmann's use of language. As Stangneth puts it, "With her sense of language and concepts educated through classical German literature, Hannah Arendt describes how Eichmann's language is like a changing torrent of thoughtless greyness, cynically violent thoughts, internalized self-pity, unintended comedy and in part incomprehensible human pitifulness" (*EvJ*, 259).

Precisely because Eichmann's worldview was a self-immunizing mixture of anti-Semitic clichés circulating since *The Protocols of the Wise Men of the Elders of Zion* (which Eichmann knew to be a forgery), of an antiquated idiom of German patriotism, and even of a craving for the warrior's honor and dignity, Arendt concluded that Eichmann could not "think," not because he was incapable of rational, calculating intelligence but because he could not think for himself beyond clichés. He was banal precisely because he was a fanatical anti-Semite, not despite it.

Although Arendt was wrong about the depth of Eichmann's anti-Semitism, she was not wrong about these crucial features of his persona and mentality. She saw in him an all-too familiar syndrome of rigid self-righteousness; extreme defensiveness fueled by exaggerated metaphysical and world-historical theories; fervent patriotism based on the supposed purity of one's Volk; paranoid projections about the power of Jews and envy of them for their achievements in science, literature, and philosophy; and contempt for Jews' supposed deviousness, cowardice, and pretensions to be the "chosen people."[27]

This syndrome was banal in that it was widespread among National Socialists. Nevertheless, by coining the phrase "the banality of evil" and by declining to ascribe Eichmann's deeds to the daemonic or monstrous nature of the doer, Arendt knew that she was going against a tradition of Western thought that saw evil in terms of ultimate sinfulness, depravity, and corruption. Emphasizing the fanaticism of Eichmann's anti-Semitism cannot discredit her challenge to the tradition of philosophical thinking; it only avoids coming to terms with it.

## Thoughtlessness—Kant or Heidegger?

There is a famous exchange between Judge Raveh—one of the presiding Israeli judges in the trial—and Eichmann about Kant's moral philosophy that Arendt cites in *Eichmann in Jerusalem*. Eichmann says: "I meant by my remark about Kant that the principle of my will must always be such that it can become the principle of general laws" (*EiJ*, 136). Arendt notes that Eichmann's meaning perverts Kant's Categorical Imperative: Whereas in Kant's philosophy the source of the Categorical Imperative is practical reason, "in Eichmann's household use of [Kant], it was the will of the Führer" (*EiJ*, 137).

When Arendt uses the phrase "the inability to think" to characterize critically Eichmann's reduction of conscience to the *voice of blood*, and of the Categorical Imperative to the command of the Führer, she is taking as given the Kantian terminology, in which to think means to think for oneself, to think consistently, but also from the standpoint of everyone else.[28] These preoccupations antedate the Eichmann trial. In 1961 Arendt had published an essay called "The Crisis in Culture: Its Social and Political Significance," in her collection *Between Past and Future*.[29] Portions of this essay had appeared as "Society and Culture" in *Daedalus* (82/2, Spring 1960) earlier, and there are significant passages in her posthumous *Denktagebuch* from the late 1950s as well on the relationships between thinking, judging, and thinking from the standpoint of others.[30]

These reflections on Kant's moral philosophy, as remote as they may seem at first to the case of Eichmann, are especially relevant to understanding Arendt's use of "thoughtlessness." As already discussed in chapter 3 above, after writing that Kant's *Critique of Judgment* contains "perhaps the greatest and most original aspect of Kant's political philosophy," Arendt continues: "In the *Critique of Judgment*, however, Kant insisted upon a different way of thinking, for which it would not be enough to be in agreement with one's own self, but which consisted of being able to 'think in the place of everybody else' and which he there-fore called an 'enlarged mentality'" (emphasis in the text).[31] Further-more she added: "That the capacity to judge is a specifically *political* ability in exactly the sense denoted by Kant, namely, the ability to see things not only from one's own point of view but in the perspective of all those who happen to be present . . . these are insights that are virtu-ally as old as articulated political experience" (my emphasis).[32]

Not only Eichmann but all those who wore the ideological blinkers of totalitarianism were incapable of thinking in this Kantian and Arend-tian sense. Ideological thinking immunizes itself against the world by fitting all evidence into a coherent scheme that cannot be falsified, and renders one blind to differences and perspectives that do not fit into one's *Weltanschauung*. It was this ideologically conditioned thoughtless-ness that permitted Eichmann to sit days on end with an Israeli officer, Captain Less, and tell him the sad story of his own life and the wrongs he believed had been done to him. Arendt comments: "The longer one listened to him, the more obvious it became that his inability to speak was closely connected with his inability to *think*, namely, to think from the standpoint of someone else" (*EiJ*, 49).

Commentators, such as Richard Wolin, stress not the Kantian but the Heideggerian sources of Arendt's use of "thoughtlessness." "It is on the basis of Heidegger's fatalistic critique of modern technology as an unalterable condition of modern life that Arendt derives her view of Eichmann as a human automaton, or, following Eichmann's own self-description during the trial, as a mere 'cog' in the Nazi machinery of extermination," Wolin writes.[33] Arendt actually believed none of the cog in the machine theories and considered Eichmann quite responsible for his actions (*EiJ*, 91–93; 114; 140; 145). Wolin's eagerness to prove that Arendt's views of Eichmann's thoughtlessness and her theory of Nazi totalitarianism at large are indebted to Heidegger, drive him to a factual blunder, namely, to his claim that it was only after 1970, almost a decade after the trial that Arendt turned to the Kantian categories of thinking, judging, and in particular thinking from the standpoint of others. As we have seen, however, Arendt was preoccupied with these themes before, during, and after the trial.

In 1954 Heidegger had published an essay, "What Is Thinking?," in which he indeed writes that "most thought-provoking in our thought-provoking time is that we are still not thinking."[34] The German text explicitly says: "überall herrsche nur die *Gedankenlosigkeit*," using the same term that Arendt would later deploy in the Eichmann case.[35] Yet for Heidegger that we are still not thinking stems from the fact that "the thing itself that must be thought about turns away from man, has turned away long ago,"[36] meaning that the inability to think is a form of "the forgetting of Being." For Heidegger, the thoughtlessness of modern man is not the inability to think from the standpoint of others; quite to the contrary, such thoughtlessness stems from being all too beholden to what others may think and turning away from Being itself.

Undoubtedly, Arendt knew this text but, far from following Heidegger, she ascribed to the category of thinking quite a different meaning than he did.[37] This is because she never changed her mind about the fact that with the concentration camps and the Holocaust something unique had taken place in human history that had fundamentally altered the essence of politics and perhaps even human nature itself. It was not *this* evil that was banal, but the quality of mind and character of the perpetrators. Even though she did not know of the full depth of Eichmann's Nazi fanaticism, Arendt never thought of him as a mere "cog in the machine," (which as Bettina Stangneth shows Eichmann invented as a way of defending himself),[38] nor, however, did she honor him by ascribing to him diabolical dimensions.

Her preoccupation with the Kantian as opposed to the Heideggerian meanings of thinking stems from her attempt to understand the connections between thinking, judging, and acting morally. Writing in the postscript to *Eichmann in Jerusalem* that she would have welcomed a discussion of the concept of the "banality of evil," she continues: "Eichmann was not Iago and not Macbeth, and nothing would have been farther from his mind than to determine with Richard III 'to prove a villain.' . . . [T]hat such remoteness from reality and such thoughtlessness can wreak more havoc than all the evil instincts taken together, which, perhaps are inherent in man—that was, in fact, the lesson one could learn in Jerusalem" (*EiJ*, 287–88). In using the phrase "the banality of evil" and in explaining the moral quality of Eichmann's deeds not in terms of the monstrous or demonic nature of the doer, Arendt became aware of going counter to the tradition of Western thought, which saw evil in metaphysical terms as ultimate depravity, corruption, or sinfulness. She asked again: "Might the problem of good and evil, our faculty of telling right from wrong, be connected with the faculty of thought? ... Could the activity of thinking as such, the habit of examining whatever comes to pass or attract attention, regardless of results and specific contents, could this activity be among the conditions that make men abstain from evil-doing or even actually 'condition' them against it?"[39] Further she pondered: "Do the inability to think and a disastrous failure of what we commonly call conscience coincide?"[40] Arendt's reflections on these issues are anything but conclusive.

It is one of the perplexities of her "exercises in political thought" that although Arendt emphasized the relevance of *enlarged thought* and *taking the standpoint of others* as being crucial for political and public judgments, in her 1971 essay on "Thinking and Moral Considerations," written a decade after the Eichmann trial, she reverted to a Platonic model of the unity of the soul with itself. In this essay, following Socrates in the *Gorgias,* she described conscience as the harmony or oneness of the soul with itself.[41] But as Mary McCarthy observed, Arendt was too quick in assuming that out of the self's desire for unity and consistency alone a principle moral stance would emerge.

Already over a decade earlier, McCarthy had asked Hannah Arendt: She had been pondering Raskolnikov's old problem in Dostoevsky's *Crime and Punishment.*[42] "Why shouldn't I murder my grandmother if I wanted to? Give me one good reason." Arendt responded with a professorial gesture that acknowledged the depth as well as difficulty of McCarthy's question: "The philosophic answer would be the answer of Socrates: Since I have got to live with myself, am in fact the only person from whom I shall never be able to part, whose company I shall have to bear forever, I don't want to be a murderer; I don't want to spend the rest of my life in the company of a murderer."[43] McCarthy is not convinced: "The modern person I posit would say to Socrates, with a shrug,

'Why not? What's wrong with a murderer?' And Socrates would be back where he started."[44]

As if to prove McCarthy's point that one could well live with oneself even as a murderer, Adolf Eichmann admitted during the trial that he would have killed his own father if he were ordered to do so—but only if his father had actually been a traitor to the cause. In Eichmann's case, unlike Socrates, there was a voice that supervened over his conscience; in fact a voice that altogether replaced individual conscience: this was the voice of the party and the movement. Eichmann never considered himself a mere murderer of innocent Jewish women and children; he called himself an "idealist" and was at pains to emphasize that he fought a war against the "enemies" of the Reich—no matter how far from reality it seemed to describe helpless, vulnerable, and destitute Jewish masses, now huddled in ghettoes and camps throughout East-Central Europe, as the "enemies" of the Reich. Eichmann was shrewd and he certainly thought for himself when it came to his own benefit and advantage; but he did not think for himself in that he did not have a moral compass that was independent of the party and the movement.

Nor could Eichmann think from the standpoint of others, since they were already defined and categorized for him as "the other." They had ceased to be moral beings worthy of equal respect and consideration. They had become dehumanized. But the trial transcripts also reveal how difficult and surreal this process of dehumanization was as if to document that the other is always also in our midst, even when not one of us. Repeatedly, Eichmann is at pains to emphasize his proper and dignified conduct, and even friendly dealings, with officials of the Jewish community in Vienna and Budapest.[45]

It would seem then that the capacity to take the standpoint of the other is not just a cognitive ability at which some are better than others. It is true that some people project so much of themselves onto others that they cannot distinguish between "me" and "you"; whereas others are so empathetic and have such weak ego-boundaries that they cannot tell where the "I" ends and "you" begin. Eichmann's dehumanization of the Jews and his inability to take the standpoint of others was a case of extreme paranoid projection through which the other became merely a blank screen for the fears and delusions of the self. Taking the stand-point of the other then is not simply a cognitive capacity but one that involves complex psychological and motivational dimensions as well.

Under what conditions do individuals lose such capacities? Under what conditions does thoughtlessness of such magnitude emerge that individuals wash away the boundaries between self and other, demon-ize the other, become immune to reality, seek for a kind of coherence that the facts do not permit, and get lost in self-justifications that cannot be falsified?

Certainly these psychological syndromes are more common than we would like to think but it is also clear that they alone, without the mas-sive sociocultural upheavals and economic dislocations in social and political life, do not lead to mass murder and genocide. Arendt did not believe that modernity or modern technology alone had given rise to totalitarianism. This is why *The Origins of Totalitarianism*, in which she deals with the rise of Nazism and Soviet totalitarianism historically, is an unwieldy work. It is not a mono-causal account but a rich exploration of many elements and their configurations in modern societies—such as the collapse of the rule of law in the nation-state, the rise of anti-Semitism, race thinking in the encounter with Africa, and the practice of administrative massacres in Western colonies—all of which come together in some fashion to enable totalitarian politics (*OT*, xxi-xl). There is no teleology to Arendt's account just as there are no easy an-swers to her characterization of Eichmann's banality.

The trauma of the Holocaust of European Jewry is so deep in us that like a wound that one scratches before it has healed, it will keep bleeding. Hannah Arendt's *Eichmann in Jerusalem* scratches where it has not healed and probably never will. This is why the controversy will "die down, simmer," but "erupt" again and again, in Irving Howe's wise words.[46]

## Postscript

In an extraordinarily perceptive account of the controversy occasioned by the Stangneth book and called "The Trials of Hannah Arendt," Corey Robin notes that indeed the fate of Arendt's book is closely tied to the

evolving political and historical sensibilities of diasporic—and particularly—American Judaism.[47] He observes that the generation of survivors and witnesses to the Holocaust "is nearly gone, and the question
of Jewish Councils, of collaboration and war, has receded. And while
the controversy over *Eichmann* remains, the controversialists have
moved on. Now the focus is on Arendt's treatment of Eichmann's anti-
Semitism. That issue was always lurking in the antechamber of discussion, but in the last decade it has entered the main room—and with it,
the fate of the state of Israel."[48] Robin notes how Arendt's long and
complicated relationship to Zionism has become center-stage in recent
years (see chapter 5 below), but rather than wade into these waters
again, he explains how unusual Arendt's moral and legal philosophy is
by exploring its origins in a form of Jewish ethic.

Reflecting on George Steiner's phrase, "the blackmail of transcendence," the Jewish insistence that "the world take a leap into the void in
the name of a God who cannot be named," Robin links Arendt's attempt
to create a "new political morals" to this source.[49] Robin notes how Judaism imposes "a mindfulness about material life," and argues that not
the Athens of the Greeks nor the spirit of Kant but Jerusalem may be
the site but also the spirit of Arendt's text. "The intransigence of her
ethic of everyday life, her insistence that every action matters, that we
attend to the minutes of our practice—not the purity of our souls but
the justness of our moral conduct and how it will affect things . . ."[50]
reminds her readers, claims Robin, and particularly Arendt's Jewish
readers, "of a strenuous ethic, an ethic that reminded the Jews of their
peculiar obligations to their God."[51] But if this is so, who was she, Hannah Arendt, to judge so vehemently not only the executioners but also
the victims? Wasn't this strenuousness a sign of her hubris, of her utter
arrogance in the name of a certain moral intransigence to which she
seemed to lay monopoly?

Robin ends his essay by commenting on the criticisms of Arendt's
book by New York intellectuals, such as Norman Podhoretz, Lionel
Abel, and Irving Howe, and asks whether the creation of Israel has not
only liberated the Jew from his Judaism but perhaps has enabled him

finally to be able to say to himself: "Now that we have a state, now that we have a home, may we not give up the burdens of judging and being judged, may we not enjoy our ease in Zion, may we not give up this bloody-minded mindfulness, may we not at long last be like other nations?"[52] In contrast to this desire for normalization and for getting rid of the strenuousness of the "ethics of transcendence," Arendt seems to cloak herself in the mantel of the prophets of Israel who predict brimstone and fire should Israel forsake its God and its covenant!

Perhaps no other passage captures this spirit of the prophetic search for justice better than the much-quoted exchange with Scholem where Arendt writes: "Let me tell you of a conversation I had in Israel with a prominent political personality who was defending the—in my opinion disastrous—nonseparation of religion and state in Israel. What he said—I am not sure of the exact words anymore—ran something like this: 'You will understand that, as a Socialist, I, of course do not believe in God: I believe in the Jewish people.' I found this a shocking statement and, being too shocked, I did not reply at the time. But I could have answered: The greatness of this people was once that it believed in God, and believed in him in such a way that its trust and love toward Him was greater than its fear. And now this people believes only in itself? What good can come of that?"[53]

Commenting on this passage, Ned Curthoys writes that "Arendt, like [Hermann] Cohen in 1916, [Martin] Buber in 1934, and [Ernst] Cassirer in 1944, rejects an insular Jewish politics that retains confidence only in its own historically derived *ethnos*."[54] Curthoys sees here a turning point in which Arendt's "Zionist influenced critique of the Enlightenment as an era of assimilation corrosive of Jewish politics is gradually supplanted by a liberal Jewish affirmation of the Enlightenment as a living resource for reflection on ethical and intellectual virtues."[55]

It is ironic that whereas Corey Robin sees passages such as this as harkening to an old Jewish prophetic ethics, Ned Curthoys reads these same passages as a reaffirmation of an Enlightenment Jewish liberalism in the tradition of Hermann Cohen and Ernst Cassirer. And of course, for Cohen as well as for his student Cassirer, Kantian ethics, which they considered the pinnacle of the Enlightenment and the spirit of Judaism were, when not identical, deeply kindred. In that sense, Robin is exaggerating that Jerusalem and Kŏnigsberg were that far apart; at least for the Jewish neo-Kantians this was by no means the case.

Yet as fascinating as it is to pursue these trails in Arendt's thought or in that of her kindred neo-Kantians such as Cohen and Cassirer, we still have to contend with the fact that, as opposed to the moral gesture displayed in the spirit of her writings, Arendt wrote *no* systematic moral philosophy, and when she reflected on moral questions her sources were always Socrates, Aristotle, Kant, Machiavelli, and Nietzsche.[56] Let us also not forget the philosophical oddity that it is not in the Kantian Categorical Imperative but rather in Kant's doctrine of judgment that Arendt finds the true sources of Kantian ethics. Like many of her contemporaries she shared with young Hegel and Schiller the critique of the Kantian moral law as being an exemplar of "legalism" in ethics (see chapter 7 below). This is a position that puts her deeply at odds with the unforgivingly law-abiding mind-set of prophetic Judaism as interpreted by Hermann Cohen.[57]

In conclusion let me observe that appeals to the enlarged mentality and taking the standpoint of the other are by themselves insufficient bases for a philosophical ethics. They presuppose rather than justify what a universalist ethics must establish, namely, the obligation that I owe to respect you as one whose standpoint matters and must be taken into consideration. Every universalist ethics must establish rational and reasonable grounds as to why such an obligation is justifiable. Arendt had no faith in such justificatory discourses though she kept presupposing a universalist ethics as the basis for the enlarged mentality.[58] She was much more interested in those instances when "the chips are down," and the individual must exercise her own powers of judgment.

Arendt's work on the Eichmann affair, however, also shows that taking the standpoint of the other is not just a moral but also a political matter. "Thoughtlessness" is the privilege of the master and the dominator who can project his own sense of power such as to crush the subjectivity of others precisely because they have no power to resist him. Resistance and struggle by the other are necessary to put an end to the narcissism of the master and to force a reversibility of perspectives. "Taking the standpoint of the other" does not mean just anticipating in thought what the other may think and feel, but it also obliges us to hear the voice of the other through dialogue and in shared practices. Hegel was right: the master does not know that the slave has a mind of his own until the slave manifests his own subjectivity through his labor on inert matter.[59] In Hegel's account, the master still does not grant the slave the respect he is owed as an equal human being. For Hegel such reciprocal recognition and respect for each other could only be achieved through centuries of struggle and the advent of modernity. Arendt had little patience for such philosophies of history but at least she would have to agree with Hegel that attaining such reciprocal respect and the ability to overcome thoughtlessness were not just moral qualities of the individual but required the political task of world-building through practices and institutions.

# 5

# Ethics without Normativity and Politics without Historicity

ON JUDITH BUTLER'S *PARTING WAYS.*
*JEWISHNESS AND THE CRITIQUE OF ZIONISM*[1]

THE ANNOUNCEMENT early in the summer of 2012 that Judith Butler was awarded the Adorno Prize of the city of Frankfurt led to an intense controversy that engulfed officials of the German-Jewish and Israeli communities, members of academia, journalists, and public intellectuals. At issue was whether, given her support of the Israel Global Boycott, Divestment and Sanctions Movement (BDS), and statements she allegedly made during a meeting at Berkeley in 2006 that Hamas and Hezbollah were parts of the "global left" (statements she has not retracted to this day),[2] Butler should have been honored in the name of a Jewish-German refugee and one of the revered founders of the Critical Theory of the Frankfurt School.

The official representative of the Jewish community in Berlin charged Butler as being a "well-known anti-Semite and enemy of Israel." Progressive intellectuals with strong ties to the Critical Theory of the Frankfurt School signed a petition in support of the award, praising Butler's achievements yet distancing themselves both from her boycott of Israel and her statements regarding Hamas and Hezbollah. I was a signatory to this petition and still stand by my support for Butler in receiving this prize.

Yet this controversy hardly focused on Butler's major statement about Israeli politics and the ethical-spiritual legacy of Jewishness in *Parting Ways. Jewishness and the Critique of Zionism.* In eight penetrating essays, Butler outlines a vision of politics for Israel-Palestine that she summarizes with the odd term of "cohabitation" (*PW*, 176). This is a vision inspired by a radical democratic politics of binationalism, not in the narrow sense of "one state, two peoples," but in the much-deeper sense of acknowledging the ethical interdependence of the narratives of Jewish, Arab, and Palestinian peoples. Unfortunately, "cohabitation" is a misleading term that suffers from Victorian connotations of living or residing together out of wedlock. A more felicitous term would have been preferable. Nonetheless, Butler's achievement is to retrieve ethical imperatives towards a vision of cohabitation by reviving Jewish memories of exile and persecution, in that she reexamines long-forgotten distinctions between cultural and political Zionism by considering, Primo Levi, Walter Benjamin, Martin Buber, Hannah Arendt, Gershom Sholem, Edward Said, and above all, Emmanuel Levinas, to whom Butler is deeply indebted, and against whose Zionist politics she finds herself struggling throughout this book.

These essays continue the ethical turn that has been evident in Butler's work since *Antigone's Claim. Kinship between Life and Death* and *Precarious Life. The Powers of Mourning and Violence.*[3] Much like the evolution in Jacques Derrida's work, from a wholly ambivalent relationship to ethical subjectivity and the legacy of democratic revolutions toward a more open embrace of the ethical—and, at least in Derrida's case, of radical democracy[4]—Butler too distances herself from her earlier critiques of subjectivity and her skepticism toward the project of democracy. Yet her ethics still remain without normativity and her politics without historicity. Let me state clearly that I see *no* necessary connection between her ethical and political philosophy and her *parti pris* for Hamas, Hezbollah, and the Israel BDS movement. These remain matters of political judgment, and, in my view, hers are deeply mistaken. Yet there is more than an accidental connection between her vision of an ethics without normativity and politics without historicity, and her blaming political Zionism for all the miseries and injustices that befell the Palestinian and Jewish peoples since 1948. While I welcome the discursive space that Butler is trying to create by reengaging the critical dialogue about Israel and Middle Eastern politics, I do not believe that we will get very far by repeating the formula that "Zionism is a form of settler colonialism," (*PW*, 4) or that the struggle for Palestinian rights and self-determination is part of the struggle of the Global Left—whoever that may refer to. These are not instances of "thinking without banisters," which Hannah Arendt recommended to us when facing the political challenges of our times,[5] but of thinking within banisters. Philosophically, the most innovative aspects of Butler's work are her reading of Levinas against Levinas, and her interpellation of Arendt for her own theory of cohabitation.

## Levinasian Ethics

"Levinas remarked on multiple occasions, that 'the face is what one cannot kill,'" writes Butler. "This remark is, indeed, remarkable," she continues, "if only because we know quite literally that the face can be killed, and with it a face of a certain kind. But if Levinas is right . . . then it would seem to follow that although the body can be killed, the face is not killed along with the body . . . Rather, the face carries an interdiction against killing that cannot but bind the one who encounters the face and becomes subject to the interdiction the face conveys" (*PW*, 54). At first blush, Levinas's claim is historically, anthropologically, culturally, and even psychologically wholly counterintuitive: when has the face of the other ever prevented the killing, the slaughter, and the murder of the other?[6] Yet for Levinas the face is not simply the physical appearance of the other, but a certain mode of being-with-the-other. Butler observes, "there is no way to separate the face from that precise encounter with the face to which we are subject, to which we cannot help but be subject, in the face of which we have, in effect, no choice, bound as we are by the interdiction imposed upon us" (*PW*, 54). The face of the other, then, subjects us to itself; this moment of *beholding* the other is also when the interdiction not to kill is imposed upon us.

Widely considered one of Levinas's central philosophical insights, this puzzling phrase contains a devastating critique of all philosophies based on the primacy of the autonomous subject or of the lonely Dasein. Because the face of the other speaks to us, calls to us, and because we are beholden to it, first philosophy—*prima philosophia*—is fundamentally ethics. It is not through my death that the authenticity of my Dasien is revealed; rather, it is the realization of my own vulnerability in the face of the other and of the other's vulnerability vis-à-vis me that is fundamental. Whether this vulnerable being-face-to-face is understood literally as the urge of the self to kill or destroy the other, as in Hegel's master-slave dialectic, or whether it is interpreted more psychoanalytically as the wish that the other may disappear and let the sovereign ego reign supreme without vulnerabilities is inconsequential. Levinas's philosophical struggle with the rationalist tradition from Descartes to Kant and Husserl on the one hand, and his continuous wrangles with Heidegger on the other, are all rolled up into this pithy phrase—"the face is what one cannot kill."

This is important for Butler precisely because she accepts many of Levinas's insights. "Once ethics is no longer understood exclusively as disposition or action grounded in a ready-made subject, but rather as a relational practice that responds to an obligation that originates outside the subject, *then ethics contests sovereign notions of the subject and ontological claims of self-identity.* Indeed, ethics comes to signify the act by which place is established for those who are "not-me," comporting me beyond a sovereign claim in the direction of a challenge to selfhood that I receive from elsewhere" (*PW*, 9; my emphasis). Butler uses the phrase "ec-static relationality" in this context (*PW*, 9).

There is something deeply compelling about these insights. Following similar intuitions, I had named this dimension of the ethical that of the "concrete other" in contrast to the "generalized other."[7] All ethical relations involve this moment of responsiveness and *respons-ibility*, in the sense of being able to *respond* to the suffering as well as joy, pain as well as ecstasy of the other. To learn to *read* faces is part of how we become human beings. Yet surely, this alone cannot be the essence of the ethical, even though it may well be its origin, both philosophically and psychogenetically.

Consider how this "ec-static relational practice" can go normatively wrong: the circle of those toward whom I feel such responsiveness and responsibility will inevitably be narrow. How can I extend natural human sympathies beyond those to whose claims I am subject in some special way and toward whom I feel special responsiveness? Furthermore, what does radical relationality entail? Do you and I share a common understanding of moral responsibility? Do we need to debate it among ourselves or do we simply know what it entails? And if I get caught up in "ec-static relationality" and cannot judge for myself whether this is indeed the correct way to act or the proper responsibility to assume, will I not be subject to the myriad demands and wishes of others and lose my own ethical individuality in the process? This vision of ethics dissolves into three alternatives: ethical particularism, including various forms of familialism and tribalism; ethical intuitionism; and/or loss of ethical agency.

As with the injunction to take the standpoint of the other, unless it is emphatically stated that the other is, in the first place, all human beings to whom I owe respect and concern, "ec-static relationality" leaves the circles of its addressees undefined and can thus be interpreted as a form of ethical particularism.

Ethics is not social ontology.[8] Social ontology, even one that is as sophisticated and psychoanalytically inspired as Butler's is, can help disclose the permutations of self-other relations as well as uncover the necessary bases for the formation of receptivity so as to enable the self to become an ethical person, but it cannot lead us to normativity. In the course of the development of a child's moral experience, a decentering occurs, such that the self-other relationship is subjected to more and more abstract criteria of rightness and wrongness. Leaving behind the "good boy, good girl" orientation, the adolescent begins to experience conflict both with proximate others and within herself. Such ethical conflict can only be resolved by moving to a more abstract level at which society's own moral injunctions are subject to a critical perspective in the light of more general moral precepts. Moral autonomy emerges out of such attempts to resolve the conflicting claims of relationality by learning how to balance abstract moral injunctions with the concrete situations and obligations that one faces.[9]

For some time now, much discussion around an ethics of autonomy as distinguished from an ethics of relationality has been caught in false binarisms: if moral universalists insist on the necessity of a normativity that goes beyond familalism, tribalism, and intuitionism, they are accused of accepting a false view of a sovereign subject, supposedly guided only by formalistic constraints and unaware of the real substance of the ethical. Universalists, in turn, are deeply suspicious of the language of "ec-static relationality," and see such a concept as paving the way for moral particularism, and perhaps even political conservativism.[10] Butler is aware of these binarisms but she leaves her own position tantalizingly unclear: "The face of the Other thus disrupts all formalisms, since a formalism would have me treat each and every other of *equal* concern and thus no other would ever have a singular claim upon me. But can we, really, do without all formalisms? And if we cannot do without all formalisms—including the principle of radical equality—then how do we think about the face in relation to such political norms? Must the face always be singular, or can it extend to plurality?" (*PW*, 57).

The force of this rhetorical question is clear: no, we cannot do without all formalism even though there are limits to formalism. Indeed, a good ethical theory or a good account of the ethical must be able to do justice to the singular as well as the universal, or in my terms, to the standpoint of the concrete as well as generalized other. Yet Butler does not tell us how.

Why would Butler resort to Levinas to think critically about "Jewishness" and "Zionism" then, even while citing Levinas's acknowledgment that "the ethical relation required by the face is not the same as the domain of the political" (*PW*, 55)? In Levinas's work, Jewishness and/or Judaism (they are not so clearly distinguished), emerges as a *philosophical* category and forms the basis of his critique of European thought as such. For Levinas, Judaism is not in the first place a political but an ontological project.

# Levinas and Jewishness

In an illuminating essay, "Levinas and Judaism," Hilary Putnam throws light on the tensions between universalism and particularism in Levinas's work by pointing out that for Levinas, "one has to understand the paradoxical claim implicit in his writing that, in essence, all human beings are Jews."[11] Putnam parses this puzzling claim through an etymology of the Hebrew word *hineni. Hine* is often translated as "behold" and it "performs the speech-act of calling attention to, or presenting, not describing" (*LJ*, 38). *Ni* is a contraction of the pronoun, *ani*, I. Thus, *hineni* means, "Here I am." Putnam then observes that, "when Levinas speaks of saying *me voici*, what he means is virtually unintelligible if one is not aware of the Biblical resonance. The fundamental obligation we have, Levinas is telling us, is the obligation to make ourselves available to the neediness (and especially the suffering) of the other person ... This does *not* presuppose that I sympathize with the other, and certainly does not presuppose (what Levinas regards as the self-aggrandizing gesture) a claim to 'understand' the other ... this fundamental obligation is a 'perfectionist' obligation, not a code of behavior or a theory of justice. But Levinas believes that if the taking on of this obligation is not present, then the best code of behavior or the best theory of justice will not help" (*LJ*, 38).

Putnam's intervention is illuminating on several counts: first, like Butler, he agrees that for Levinas the core of Judaism is this infinite responsibility in the face of the other; second, unlike Butler, he is sensitive to the distinction between what he calls—following Stanley Cavell— "legislators" versus "perfectionists" in moral theory. Emmanuel Levinas, he maintains, is a "moral perfectionist" (*LJ*, 36). By contrast, legislators provide moral and political rules and try to solve moral dilemmas by devising ideal constitutions. "Moral perfectionists believe that the ancient questions—'Am I living as I am supposed to live?' 'Is my life something more than vanity, or worse, "mere conformity!",' writes Levinas. Purnam and Cavell agree that Emerson, Nietzsche, and Mill are outstanding examples of moral perfectionists; for Putnam the great Jewish philosophers, "particularly Buber, Cohen, Levinas and Rosenzweig are moral perfectionists" (*LJ*, 37).

This distinction is illuminating, less because the characterization of the legislators is either accurate or particularly original—it is not—but because it helps us highlight the question of how ethics and politics are or ought to be related to one another according to the perfectionists.

What about the politics of Judaism in Levinas's view? Butler is both attracted to and troubled by the following statement from Levinas: "Of course, we do not owe Judaism to anti-Semitism, no matter what Sartre may say. But perhaps the ultimate essence of Israel . . . derives from its innate predisposition to involuntary sacrifice, as exposure to persecution . . . To be persecuted . . . is not an original sin, but the obverse of universal responsibility—a responsibility to the Other—that is more ancient than any sin."[12] Many Jews, whether Zionist or not, could not or would not want to live up to this formulation of the historical Jewish experience. Zionists would argue that precisely this ethics of sacrifice had condemned Jews to passivity and victimhood throughout their history, and just as Arendt contended, precisely for this reason, Jews had to assume historical and political responsibility and act for themselves. Other thinkers such as George Steiner, for example, see in the exilic condition of the Jews not a history of victimhood but rather a cosmopolitan spirit. (See chapter 2 above on Steiner.)

Levinas himself, by contrast, upon the founding of the State of Israel, agreed with the Zionist position and defended the Jewish State all his life with very little criticism. In an important interview conducted in 1982, after the Sabra and Shatilla massacres in the Palestinian refugee camps that were then supposedly under the protection of the Israeli army with Ariel Sharon at its helm, and which resulted in the death of several hundred innocent women, children, and the elderly in the hands of the Christian Lebanese Phalangists, Levinas acknowledges the responsibility, not the guilt, he feels for these massacres and continues:

> I think there's a direct contradiction between ethics and politics, if both these demands are taken to the extreme . . . The Zionist idea, as

I now see it, all mysticism or false immediate messianism aside, is nevertheless a political idea which has an ethical justification. It has an ethical justification insofar as a political solution imposes itself as a way of putting an end to the arbitrariness which marked the Jewish condition, and all the spilt blood which for centuries has flowed with impunity across the world. *The solution can be summed up as the existence, in conditions which are not purely abstract, that is, not just anywhere, of a political unity with a Jewish majority.* For me, this is the essence of Zionism. It signifies a State in the full sense of the term, a State with an army and arms which can have a deterrent and if necessary a defensive significance. Its necessity is ethical . . . My people and my kin are still my neighbors. When you defend the Jewish people, you defend your neighbor (emphasis mine).[13]

Levinas goes on to admit that there may be a contradiction between ethics and politics even for the Jews, "a people with a long ethical tradition."[14] When pressed by the journalist Shlomo Malka, if, he Levinas, as a philosopher of "the other," would not admit that for the Israeli the other is above all the Palestinian, Levinas answers: "My definition of the other is completely different. The other is the neighbor, who is not necessarily kin, but who can be . . . But if your neighbor attacks another neighbor or treats him unjustly, what can you do? Then alterity takes on another character, in alterity we can find an enemy, or at least then we are faced with the problem of knowing who is right and who is wrong, who is just and who is unjust. There are people who are wrong."[15]

Levinas implies, while not stating it in so many words, that the Palestinian people are not really the neighbor of Israel because they engage in hostilities towards Israel; they are thus in the existential condition of alterity vis-a-vis the Jews.[16] And in this condition, the neighbor can become my enemy.

Butler clearly rejects this political position, but because she shares so much of Levinas's philosophy of the ethical, she provides her own rather original interpellation of the condition of infinite responsibility and of being a neighbor: "I am always possessed by an elsewhere, held hostage, persecuted, impinged upon against my will, and yet there is still this 'I,' or rather 'me,' who is being persecuted. To say that my 'place' is already the place of another is to say that place itself is never singularly possessed and this question of cohabitation in the same place is unavoidable. It is in light of this question of cohabitation that the question of violence emerges. Indeed, if I am persecuted, that is the sign that I am bound to the other. If I were not persecuted by this claim upon me, then I would not know responsibility at all" (PW, 62). Yet is this true? Why should I not be equally bound to the other if I refuse to be persecuted, and instead fight, resist, escape, and organize against the other? We see Levinas himself rather surprisingly oscillating between the language of infinite responsibility and Zionist militancy. Walking a difficult tightrope, Butler wishes to hold on to Levinasian ethics as social ontology while at the same time distancing herself from his political views. *For Butler, the Levinasian ethics of infinite responsibility becomes a politics of neighborly cohabitation,* whereas Levinas himself concedes to the Zionists the upper hand of *raison d'etat,* and is content with pleading for a responsible mediation of the ethical and the political.[17] Nowhere do the convolutions that Butler is led to as a result of this appropriation of Levinas become more evident than in her reading of Hannah Arendt.

## Butler on Arendt

Butler admits that she came to Hannah Arendt's writings rather late (PW, 23). She reviewed *Hannah Arendt's Jewish Writings* in the *London Review of Books* in 2007, under the title "I merely belong to them." Deconstructing distinctions between Halachic,[18] that is, religious versus ethnic definitions of Judaism, between what one is born into and what one chooses to be or is forced to be by the society around one, Butler's tone towards Arendt was skeptical. This has changed. The two chapters on Arendt in *Parting Ways*—"Is Judaism Zionism? Or, Arendt and the Critique of the Nation-State" and "Quandaries of the Plural. Cohabitation and Sovereignty in Arendt," take up nearly seventy pages in a 240-page work. Clearly, Arendt is challenging.

It is not hard to see why. In the last two decades, Arendt's writings on Zionism and Jewish topics have been rediscovered by revisionist Israeli scholars, who see in her reflections on Zionism throughout the 1940s a forewarning of the tragedies that would befall the Israeli and Palestinian peoples in subsequent years.[19] Butler is aware of this revisionist Israeli historiography and writes, "but if it is historically and politically incumbent to understand that history as a founding catastrophe, and to locate the sites of its contingent emergence as that particular state formation and not some others, we might be able to think outside this narrative lockdown" (*PW*, 25). What fascinates Butler most are Arendt's last words against Eichmann in the epilogue to *Eichmann in Jerusalem*. "In her view," writes Butler, "cohabitation is not a choice, but a condition of our political life" (*PW*, 23). This is a strange attempt to interpellate Arendt for her own social ontology via the use of terms, such as "cohabitation," that are not Arendt's at all.

In that much-cited epilogue, Arendt wrote: "And just as you supported and carried out a policy of not wanting to share the earth with the Jewish people and the people of a number of other nations—*as though you and your superiors had any right to determine who should and who should not inhabit the world*—we find that no one, that is, no member of the human race, can be expected to share the earth with you. This is the reason, and the only reason, you must hang" (*EiJ*, 277–79).[20] Butler asks: "Is the final verdict that Arendt delivers something other than vengeance?" (*PW*, 162). And given that Arendt herself rejects vengeance as "barbaric," what else is going on in this passage?

The epilogue to *Eichmann in Jerusalem*, and indeed, the tone of the entire book, has been the subject of discussion among Arendt scholars for some time now.[21] Butler is a careful and provocative reader of texts. Her reading of this passage not only examines Arendt's distinctions between mass murder, administrative massacres, and genocide, but tries to tease out what she calls a "principle" (*PW*, 163) out of Arendt's text. "If Arendt is right, then it is not only that we may not choose with whom to cohabitate, but that we must actively preserve the unchosen character of inclusive and plural cohabitation; we not only live with those we never chose and to whom we may feel no social sense of belonging, but we are also obligated to preserve their lives and the plurality of which they form a part. *In this sense, concrete political norms and ethical prescriptions emerge from the unchosen character of these modes of cohabi-tation"* (PW, 151; my emphasis).[22] This may be Butler, but it is certainly not Arendt. Arendt writes of "plurality" and not of "plural cohabita-tion." Let me recall some of the most distinctive features of Arendt's understanding of plurality, so that these differences may become clearer.

Plurality for Arendt, along with worldliness and action, constitute "the human condition," that is, "the basic conditions under which life on earth has been given to man" (HC, 7). Plurality is the *fact* that cor-responds to our irreducible sameness as members of the same species and yet at the same time expresses our irreducible difference from one another. "Plurality is the condition of human action because we are all the same, that is, human, in such a way that nobody is ever the same as anyone else who ever lived, lives, or will live" (HC, 8). This plurality is the precondition of the possibility of all political life: because we are members of the same species who have speech and reasoning and who are thus capable of *logos*—reasoned speech—we can communicate with one another, build a world together, as well as destroy one another. And since we are all subject to similar bodily needs and confront like-wise the struggle with nature, we face the "circumstances of justice," how to establish just institutions under conditions of rough human equality of needs, talents, capacities, vulnerability, and scarcity.

Plurality is also what enables diversity and perspectivality. "In acting and speaking, men show who they are, reveal actively their unique per-sonal identities and thus make their appearance in the human worlds, while their physical identities appear without any activity of their own in the unique shape of the body and sound of the voice. The disclosure of 'who' in contradistinction to 'what' somebody is—his qualities, gifts, talents and shortcoming, which he may display or hide—is implicit in everything somebody says and does" (HC, 179). We live in a world con-stituted by narratives about the *who* as well as the *what* of action; this web of narratives is the medium through which the multiplicity and diversity of perspectives on human affairs converge and conflict, are woven together and torn apart.

No passage better captures the relationship between the concept of plurality and the problem of genocide than the following:

If it is true that a thing *is* real . . . only if it can show itself and be perceived from all sides, then there must always be a plurality of individuals or peoples . . . to make reality even possible and to guarantee its continuation. In other words, the world comes into being only if there are perspectives . . . If a people or a nation, or even just some specific human group, which offers a unique view of the world arising from its particular vision of the world . . . is annihilated, it is not merely that a people or a nation or a given number of individuals perishes, but rather that a portion of our common world is destroyed, an aspect of the world that has revealed itself to us until now but can never reveal itself again. Annihilation is therefore not just tantamount to the end of the world; it also takes its annihilator with it.[23]

As Patricia Owens observes about this passage, "Wars of annihilation that aim to wipe out a particular group attack the basic fact of human plurality and violate the 'limits inherent in violent action.' With genocide we are not 'just' talking about large numbers of dead but something that is potentially immortal. The public, political world, the political constitution of a people, the outcome of people's living together, and debating their common affairs is also destroyed with genocide."[24] Genocide violates "an altogether different order," writes Arendt in *Eichmann in Jerusalem* (*EiJ*, 272).

The crucial distinction between Arendt's concept of plurality and Butler's concept of cohabitation is that, for Arendt, plurality emerges for human beings through their interaction with one another via speech and action. It is only because we are members of the same species, who are more or less equal and equally vulnerable, that speech and action can constitute a world of individuation and differentiation against this background of givenness. The web of narratives is the medium through which the multiplicity and diversity of perspectives on human affairs is knitted together. We tell of who we are and of what we do through a narrative.

By contrast, in Butler's account of cohabitation there is no emphasis either on speech or on action. Often cohabitation in her text sounds more like a Heideggerian condition of "thrownness," *Geworfenheit* (of being-thrown-into-the-world with others whom one has not chosen to be with) than an Arendtian condition of plurality. "[A]s embodied creatures," writes Butler, "we would have to think about questions of need, hunger, and shelter as crucial to this plurality; in other words, plurality would have to be thought of as a certain kind of material interdependency such that being able to live and being exposed to death are also, in part at stake in this social condition. We find the idea of precarious life here" (*PW*, 176–77).[25] This interpretation de-emphasizes speech and action with others that are the sine qua non of the political for Arendt in favor of "precarity." Why does Butler avoid or elude these concepts? Principally because she is suspicious of Arendtian concepts of action and the self as harboring an indefensible vision of the sovereignty of the autonomous subject. Butler is also uncomfortable with the possible essentialism that seems suggested by some passages of Arendt's, which emphasize "the revelation of the self through speech and action," as if there were a stable self behind such deeds and words. Once more, we are back to the problem of performativity and whether "there is a doer behind the deed?" (Nietzsche).[26]

Butler does not recapitulate the debates between essentialism and performativity that dominated feminism in past years. Rather, she sees a misguided concept of the sovereign self as being evident in Arendt's insistence that, following Kant, one ought to exercise "reflective judgment." "If Arendt," she writes, "is only figuring sovereign decision here, showing what good decision is, or performatively enacting good decision on the model of the just sovereign, she has certainly taken distance from the notions of equality and the processes of pluralization and universalization that characterize both her social ontology and the benefits of her theory for democratic politics. My point is neither that she subscribes to a notion of sovereign action at the expense of collective making nor that she subscribes to social forms of deliberation at the expense of sovereign action and decision. Rather, I am saying that she vacillates between the two and that this tension seems to form a recurring and irresolvable dimension of her thought" (*PW*, 175).

Yet why not see this vacillation as a source of strength in Arendt's thought rather than as a problem and a confusion?[27] Isn't it precisely because Arendt is a thinker of *the political* that she emphasizes the moment of individual action and decision *as well as* of collective resolve and deliberation? And what exactly does the qualifier "sovereign" really add to the argument? In her reflections on thinking and moral considerations, which is what Butler is commenting upon here, Arendt stresses the need to be able to exercise individual judgment precisely during those moments when the chips are down and the political world, through the fabrication of lies and ideologies, is lost to us. Precisely during moments such as those, we have to rely on some individuals as well as groups of individuals who defy dangerous odds, exercise judgment, and engage in political action. All this is too individualistic for Butler and contradicts her emphasis on precariousness and vulnerability. She recognizes this: "It is for this reason that *I think that the recourse to the sovereign mind, its faculty of judgment, its individual exercise of freedom, is in some quite strong tension with the idea of cohabitation* that seems to follow both from Arendt's accusation against Eichmann and her own explicit reflections on plurality" (*PW*, 177, my emphasis). Is Butler reading Arendt's concepts of action and freedom correctly?[28]

## On Action and Tragedy

Arendt recounts that when she was arrested by the Gestapo in the spring of 1933 and was forced to flee to Paris through Prague with her mother, she had been carrying out research in the Prussian State Library at the request of the Zionist leader Kurt Blumenfeld on the extent of anti-Semitic measures undertaken by nongovernmental organizations, business associations, professional clubs, and others.[29] Arendt had met Kurt Blumenfeld in 1926 at a student event in Heidelberg. Blumenfeld in turn was preparing to present this material at the eighteenth Zionist Congress. The two formed a lifelong friendship, only to be interrupted by the publication of *Eichmann in Jerusalem* in 1963.

Arendt's interest in Jewish matters has been amply documented, but what remains perhaps unexplained is why this involvement was so acute on the part of the daughter of a German middle-class assimilated Jewish family. Undoubtedly, as Elisabeth Young-Bruehl has argued, part of the answer lies in the familial background.[30] Arendt's paternal grandfather, Max Arendt, was a staunch leader of the Jewish community in Koenigsberg (Kaliningrad), and although an anti-Zionist, he was a man who explicitly identified himself as a Jew. Her mother, an early sympathizer of Rosa Luxemburg, was a fiercely proud woman, who instructed her daughter to report to her immediately every word or gesture of anti-Semitism in school. Also not insignificant is Arendt's deep awareness of the contrast between the experience of German Jewry, to whom she belonged, and East European Jewish refugees who flocked to the city of Kőnigsberg, where Arendt grew up, as permanent and temporary workers. This contrast between the affluent and emancipated German Jewry, who enjoyed civil and political rights, and their Eastern brethren, who only enjoyed limited civil rights or none at all under Tsarist Russia, affected Arendt deeply and gave her a sense of the contrast among the experiences of various Jewish communities, which was unusual for its time.[31]

Butler misses these nuances in Arendt's views about the collective dimensions of Judaism, and places Arendt all too easily in the company of thinkers such as Hermann Cohen, the great Kantian Jewish thinker and a German nationalist.[32] Butler's affiliation of Arendt with Cohen, for which there is very little historical and textual support, then permits Butler to level charges of Eurocentrism and rationalism against Arendt.[33] In such passages, Butler does injustice to her own admirable hermeneutical skills and creates simple equivalences between rationalism, the sovereign subject, Eurocentrism, and Zionist colonialism.[34] Butler seems beholden to an anti-imperialist jargon of the politics of purity. In this respect, she not only misses the significance of acting without guarantees and thinking without banisters, but also ignores the moment of great truth about the Palestinian movement that the late Edward Said noted.

## Edward Said and the First Gulf War

During the First Gulf War (1990–91), when Saddam Hussein invaded and tried to annex Kuwait and George H. W. Bush started raining missiles on the Iraqi capital, many in the Arab world saw Saddam's invasion as a power-grab by a murderous and dictatorial regime but were equally dismayed by the pyrotechnics of the US superpower, flexing its muscles for the first time after the end of the Cold War. The Palestinian Liberation Movement, under the leadership of the late Yasser Arafat, proclaimed its solidarity with the Iraqi regime to whose financial munificence it was beholden. Edward Said criticized the Palestinian resistance movement for its naive anticolonial, third-world rhetoric, as well as for accepting the Oslo I Accords. [35] With the end of the Iraqi regime, Iran replaced Iraq as the patron of the Palestinian Hamas wing, while a more moderate Palestinian leadership emerged in the ensuing years in the West Bank under the leadership of Mahmood Abbas, which some consider—unjustly in my view—as being a sell-out to the Israelis and the USA. The age of innocence for the Palestinian resistance movement has ended, just as it has ended for the idealist visions of early Zionism. Each of two ideologies—the third-world nationalist liberation rhetoric of the Palestinians and the "holier than thou" idealism of the early Zionist settlers—are well past their prime and have been embroiled in tragedies as well as triumphs, lies as well as truths. They now face one another in an increasingly multipolar Middle East. Politics is often the site of the tragic. I mean "tragedy" here in the sense developed by the young Hegel who saw tragedy, not as in the Greek plays to be a product of "hamartia," of a certain kind of arrogance or blindness on the part of the hero or heroine, but rather as the clash of two rights, of two moral principles with equal claim upon our allegiance facing each other in struggle. [36]

In passages such as the following Butler ignores this tragic history: "The reason why," she writes, "the Global Boycott, Divestment and Sanctions Movement includes among its goals the rights of Palestinians dispossessed in 1948 as well as the damaged rights of Palestinian Israelis is that it is not possible to restrict the problem of Palestinian subjugation to the occupation alone . . . We fail to see the structural link between the Zionist demand for demographic advantage and the multivalent forms of dispossession that affect Palestinians who have become diasporic . . . *Perhaps coexistence projects would fare better if they had as their single and guiding aim the undoing of Israeli colonial power and mili-*

*tary force*" (*PW*, 217; my emphasis). I am not sure what Butler has in mind with this last sentence. It sounds as if it is a call for the dismantling of Israel as a state and of its military. Is Butler advocating all-out-war instead of cohabitation then? She ends this paragraph by invoking "promising forms of bi-nationalism," (*PW*, 217) presumably a binationalism to be established after the end of the State of Israel?

Unlike Butler, I do not believe that Zionism was a colonial-settler project from the start, intending to dispossess the Palestinian people and to rob them of their land. Hatched in the minds of a Viennese journalist (Theodor Herzl), and adhered to by idealists with the vision of creating a new Jewish people who would not suffer under the yokes of inequality, insult, and oppression that had been their lot in Christian Europe in particular (Ahad Ha'am's vision, for example), this community in the Yishuv would not have become a state had it not been for two historical events: the Balfour declaration, which showed the same blindnesses that all nationalist self-determination movements of the early twentieth-century held towards the claims of others,[37] and, more importantly, the Holocaust of European Jewry. Had it not been for the Holocaust, the small community of idealistic dreamers in Palestine would certainly have held the sympathy of the world Jewish community, but sooner or later they would have disappeared as a separate political entity.

As psychoanalytically astute as Butler is, she seems to turn a blind eye to the lingering collective psychosis of many Jews, whether in Israel or not, namely, their fear of annihilation in the hands of a hostile world as well as the post-1945 persecution of the Jews of the Middle East, such as in Iraq and Yemen. The tragedy of Israel is that the stronger Israel has become militarily, the more paranoid and bullyish it has become.[38] The volatility of shifting political alliances in the Middle East as well as the new weapons technologies, which can easily threaten Jerusalem and Tel-Aviv in minutes, have contributed to this growing paranoia. Add to this admixture the seemingly permanent conservative majority that has now emerged in Israel as a result of the growing influence of religious parties and the migration of more than one million Russian Jews with rather right-wing views, and the future of Israeli politics is quite blocked.

These two developments have disrupted the fragile coalition of alliances between centrist, left-center, and right-of-center parties that had dominated Israeli politics since its founding in 1948. The result has been the election of right-wing governments in the last fifteen years, the general weakness of the Left, and even the collapse of the centrist Kadima party. Israeli society is now witness to horrendous eruptions of racism not only against Palestinian and Arab youth but also against African guest workers and African refugees.

Is there any hope then? I believe there is but not through the BDS movements, which are based upon a false analogy between the Israeli-Palestinian conflict and the South African anti-apartheid struggle, but through continued, sustained, and deep engagement with all countries in the region. Even if the Arab Spring in Egypt was crushed and the Egyptian military under Al-Sisi returned to power, it was a new generation of Egyptians who first put their lives on the line and who showed one more time that the legacy of revolutions, as Hannah Arendt would say, appears in unexpected ways and creates those "elementary republics" in the public square, which come into contradiction with established institutions (*OR*, 254–63). This young literate generation of men and women are present everywhere in the Arab world; they are networked throughout Europe and the USA and in many other countries as well via migratory nets of kin and family. Today this new generation has not found its political voice; and it has become demoralized by the military victories of ISIS or Daesh in the region.

Israelis, who for a long time considered themselves as the sole democratic people in the Middle East, were taken aback by the Arab Spring and the uprisings in Tunisia as well as Syria and Yemen. But many have rejoiced in it as well. Protests against Israeli government policies, inspired by Tahrir Square erupted in the summer of 2011 in Tel-Aviv, with thousands of young people chanting for social justice, housing, and jobs. Hundreds of Arab citizens of Israel participated in these protests. The number of Arab youth who are now perfectly bilingual is growing and, along with it, their political capacity to engage Israeli society directly. Many Palestinian Arabs living in occupied East Jerusalem would much rather become Israeli citizens in an open and gender-egalitarian society than live under the rule of Hamas or ISIS or Daesh.

Any call for cohabitation between the Israeli and Palestinian peoples that does not balance the continuing and justifiable fear of extinction on the part of Israeli Jews with the legitimate claims and aspirations of the Palestinian people is a nonstarter. This means that Israelis themselves will need to think hard and fast about the impossible situation they have created in aspiring to maintain a Jewish state on the one hand and continuing to occupy the territories of the West Bank on the other. But the facts on the ground are moving in a different direction and much to the chagrin of liberal Zionists who still advocate a two-state solution: given the military and economic dependence of the West Bank territories upon Israel, maybe the time has come to call for a "confederation of Israeli and Palestinian peoples," with two parliaments and two separate electoral systems but a common defense and security policy over territory and air space, and sharing water and other natural resources. Under such a scenario, the considerable achievements of the Israeli state and society in economic, technological, medical, and intellectual areas would not need to be dismantled but Israeli sovereignty would be disaggregated and nested into a joint confederal model.

This idea of a confederation of peoples of the Middle East is not new. Arendt first proposed it in the 1940s.[39] What makes this model so attractive is that we see an example of a successful disassembling of national sovereignty together with respect for the democratic exercise of collective and individual rights in the case of the European Union—and this despite all the economic and political woes of the last two decades! It is unlikely that such a model can simply be transplanted to the Middle East, but what is important about this first truly novel legal and political formation since the end of World War II is the transcendence of militarized nationalisms in the name of a new understanding of legal and political sovereignty.

Could this vision also offer an aspirational alternative for resolving the Israeli-Palestinian conflict and in time for all the peoples of the

Middle East? Maybe one way to think past the current stalemate is to leave behind the tired formulae of "two states for two peoples" or "one state and two peoples" and to have the courage to envisage a new modality of political togetherness beyond the murderous politics of nation-statism and nationalism.

# 6

# From the "Right to Have Rights" to the "Critique of Humanitarian Reason"

IN THE FIRST TWO DECADES of the twenty-first century it is astonishing that the fate of refugees and asylum seekers would emerge as a worldwide problem. In an age when the movement of everything across borders, from capital to fashion, from information to news, from germs to money has intensified human mobility continues to be criminalized. The refugee is increasingly treated not only as an alien body but as the enemy who is interned in detention camps, held in deportation sites, or in absurd Euro-bureaucratic parlance, gathered in "hotspots."

It is surely a supreme historical irony that the European Union, emerging as it did out of the ashes of the Holocaust and with the bitter memory of two world wars behind it, should find itself at the point of unraveling in recent years because of the desired entry into Europe—among other factors to be sure—of 2 to 2.5 million Syrians and refugees from other countries. Admittedly, no one is being sent to labor or extermination camps as in the 1930s although the number of detention camps is increasing. Furthermore, the European Union has failed to live up to its own human rights commitments by stamping refugees' arms with indelible ink (as the Czech and Hungarian police did); by having them chased by police dogs and water cannons (as the Macedonians, Slovenians, and Hungarians did), by subjecting them to excruciating limbo about their future lives, which Greece still does with the nearly fifty thousand unprocessed refugees housed on the islands, and which France and the United Kingdom have done shamelessly by creating the now-dismantled "jungle" in Calais.[1]

Although the refugee crisis is affecting the European Union in specific ways because of the special architecture of the European Union, which has eliminated internal borders in some cases while sharing a common external border,[2] it is not only the European continent that faces this challenge. As discussed in the preface, the number of worldwide refugees at the end of 2016 stood at 65.6 million, with one in every 113 persons *displaced* the world over.[3]

As the number of refugees has increased worldwide, not only has the number of camps grown but camps have ceased to be places where one held people temporarily; rather, they have become semipermanent. The largest refugee camp in the world, Kenya's Dadaab, is twenty years old and houses 420,000 refugees. The Palestinian refugee camps in Southern Lebanon are in many cases seventy to fifty years old, depending on whether the refugee population was created in 1948 or 1967. The refugees who live in these camps, and in some cases who have spent their entire lives there, become PRSs, i.e., those in "protracted refugee situations."[4]

Refugees, asylees, IDPs—internally displaced persons—PRSs, and stateless persons are new categories of human beings created by an international state-system in turmoil and are subject to a special kind of precarious existence. As Arendt had already noted: "The post-war expression of 'displaced persons' has been expressly invented in order to make disappear from the world the disturbing fact of 'statelessness' by ignoring it."[5] Their plight reveals the most fateful disjunction between so-called "human rights"—or "the rights of man" in the older locution—and "the rights of the citizen"; between the universal claims to human dignity and the specificities of indignity suffered by those who possess only human rights. From Arendt's justly famous discussion of the "right to have rights" to Giorgio Agamben's *Homo Sacer*, to Judith Butler's "precarious lives" and Jacques Rancière's call to "the enactment of rights," the asylum seeker, the stateless, and the refugee have become *metaphors* as well as *symptoms* of a much-deeper malaise in the politics of late modernity.[6]

In this chapter, after briefly recalling Hannah Arendt's discussion of the right to have rights, I will consider Jacques Rancière's trenchant critique of Arendt. Rancière not only misreads Arendt, but much of what he defends as the necessary enactment of rights is quite compatible with an Arendtian understanding of political agency. I will then turn to the quandaries of "humanitarian reason," in Didier Fassin's felicitous phrase. To address them, we need a new conceptualization of the relationship between international law and emancipatory politics; a new way of understanding how to negotiate *the facticity* and *the validity* of the law (Habermas), including international humanitarian law, such as to create new vistas for the political.

## The Right to Have Rights and Its Many Puzzles

From 1933 to 1951, when she became a naturalized American citizen, Arendt was a stateless person.[7] Following her arrest by the Gestapo in Berlin, she fled to Paris, where she started helping refugees, overseeing Baroness Germaine de Rothschild's donations to Jewish charities. As German troops began to roll across the French border, all German men between the ages of seventeen and fifty-five, as well as women without children, were ordered to report to internment camps. After a week spent in the notorious "Velodrome d'Hiver" (now named "Place des Martyrs Juifs"), Arendt and others boarded at Paris for Gurs, a camp where Spanish refugees of the Civil War and International Brigade fighters had been imprisoned.

When France fell to the Nazis six weeks later and rumors spread that the internees would be turned over to the Gestapo, in the ensuing confusion Arendt found a way to escape the camp at Gurs. She rode a bike, walked, and hitchhiked in the chaos of those early days to a friend's house in Montauban, not far from Toulouse. One day she ran into Heinrich Blücher on the street who was looking for her and the two found a house, awaiting passage across France. Eventually, they made their way to Marseilles and then to Lisbon via Spain,[8] where they boarded the ship to the shores of New York. It was during that time that *The Origins of Totalitarianism* (1951) took shape.

In an article written for the journal *Die Wandlung* in 1949, edited by Karl Jaspers, and in part later reproduced in *The Origins*, Arendt argued that there was only one *human* right, and that was "the right to have rights," to be recognized as a member of an organized political community.[9] As she would write two years later: "We become aware of the existence of a right to have rights (and that means to live in a framework where one is judged by one's actions and opinions) and a right to belong to some kind of organized community, only when millions of people emerge who had lost and could not regain these rights because of the new global political situation ... The right that corresponds to this loss and that was never even mentioned among the human rights cannot be expressed in the categories of the eighteenth-century because they presume that rights spring immediately from the 'nature' of man ... the right to have rights, or the right of every individual to belong to humanity, should be guaranteed by humanity itself. *It is by no means certain whether this is possible*" (*OT*, 296–97. My emphases). Since then the "right to have rights" has become the well-known phrase through which to capture the plight of the stateless, the refugee, the asylum seeker, and the displaced person, that is, the plight of those who have been cast out of the framework "where one is judged by one's actions and opinions."

Arendt's famous lines raise several philosophical issues that need to be disentangled from one another, and the first of these is the normative justification of rights. Throughout this discussion, Arendt polemicizes against the grounding of human rights upon any conception of human nature or history. For her, conceptions of human nature commit the mistake of treating humans as if they were mere substance like entities found in nature. Following Augustine and Heidegger, she argues that humans are the ones for whom the question of being has become a question. She quotes Augustine: "Quid ergo sum, Deus meus? Quae natura sum? ("What then am I, my God? What is my nature?") The answer simply is, "quaestio mihi factus sum," "I have become a question for myself" (*HC*, fn. 2, 11). This capacity for self-questioning is also the source of one's freedom. Although human freedom is not limitless and

is subject to the facticity of the "human condition"—namely worldliness, plurality, natality and labor, work, and action—it is with reference
to this condition alone and not in the light of a fixed concept of human
nature that we must try to justify the right to have rights.

Arendt's rejection of any justificatory role that the concept of history
may play is complex. Since the late 1950s she was engaged in a conversation with Karl Marx, whom she accused of having brought the tradition
of Western political thought to an end by substituting a philosophy of
history for a political philosophy proper.[10] Arendt's reading of Marx is
often dismissive and inaccurate, attributing to Marx some of the least
defensible concepts of historical causation and teleology. As discussed
in chapter 3, in this respect she was much influenced by Walter Benjamin's "Theses on the Philosophy of History."[11] Polemicizing against the
German social democrats of his time, who were still too stunned by the
German-Soviet Non-Aggression Pact signed in August 1939 to engage
in resistance to the onslaught of fascism, Benjamin had argued against
their deterministic accounts of history. He claimed that privileging impersonal social forces—the so-called "forces of production"—to act as
if they would be the engines of inevitable political change was no less
deluded than a teleological account of history that attributed to it an
end goal, a *telos*. Such accounts were morally reprehensible because they
made humans into passive "instruments of a world-spirit" (Hegel) or
of the forces of production (Marx) and robbed them of oppositional
agency. One had to brush "history against the grain," to use a Benjaminian locution.[12]

What then is Arendt's own philosophical justification of the right to
have rights? [13] Many passages such as the following have been read as
displaying Arendt's *decisionism* and/or *political existentialism*: "We are
not born equal; we become equal as members of a group on the strength
of our decision to guarantee ourselves mutually equal rights. . . . Our
political life rests on the assumption that we can produce equality
through organization, because man can act and change and build a common world, together with his equals and only with his equals" (*OT*,
301). Some have interpreted these passages not only as displaying
Arendt's *existential decisionism* but also for accepting the "English" as

opposed to the "French" interpretation of rights. In "The Aporias of Human Rights and the 'One' Human Right. Regarding the Coherence of Hannah Arendt's Argument," Christoph Menke considers Arendt's "belated" and "ironic" appeal to Edmund Burke's critique of the rights of man (*OT*, 299–301). He writes, "thus, rights 'as such' do not exist, because laws 'as such' do not exist. For Arendt, this double insight—first that all rights depend upon laws, and second that all political legislation is inescapably tied to a certain 'locale'—is the true essence of Burke's famous statement that he preferred 'the rights of an Englishman' over those of the human being."[14] This so-called "English interpretation" of rights reduces Arendt's position to a form of social conventionalism according to which human rights would be viewed as "entitlements" or "entailments," which accrue to one in virtue of one's status as a subject of a commonwealth. Whatever we can infer from Arendt's "ironic" endorsement of Edmund Burke's reflections on the follies of the revolution in France, her entire discussion of the right to have rights, unlike Burke's, is a critique of the status quo and a plea to transform the sovereign privileges of the state system. Arendt, unlike Jeremy Bentham then and Alasdair MacIntyre in our times, does not consider human rights to be "nonsense upon stilts."[15]

Menke admits that this cannot be Arendt's sole intention and on the basis of Arendt's reflections in *On Revolution* he distinguishes between a *Déclaration de Droits de l'Homme* and a *Bill of Rights*. Bills of Rights always apply to a specific human community while a "Declaration of the Rights of Man and Citizen" is supposed to hold for the universal rights claims of everyone. The *right* to have rights cannot be of the same order as the rights possessed by those who are already members of a polity; so a Bill of Rights cannot capture its meaning. This right is a right to membership; it is "the one right without which no other can materialize."[16] Menke reinterprets this right to membership, however, not as a right to citizenship and nationality but in view of Arendt's concept of human dignity. The dignity of man consists in having rights as a member of political community.[17] Menke then reaches a rather surprising conclusion: "Human dignity as a concept only offers a way out of the crisis of human rights if, first, it introduces an entirely different anthropology than that of modern natural law, namely, an anthropology of a politico-linguistic form of life as opposed to an anthropology of quasi-natural human 'needs' or 'interests;' and if, second, the concept of human dignity introduces an entirely different fundamental concept of right: a concept that grounds subjective rights in the experience of what is the right thing for human beings."[18]

Certainly, we can agree that Arendt develops quite a different philosophical anthropology than that of modern natural law theorists. Her distinction between *human essence* and *the human condition* is based on this rejection of human nature theories. Yet even if human dignity is rooted in the anthropology of a politico-linguistic life-form, this claim is so general as to be vacuous. That same human condition can also give rise to totalitarianism and statelessness, which seek to negate and destroy conditions of human belonging. For this reason, Menke's quasi-objectivist appeal to ground "subjective rights in the experience of what is the *right thing* for human beings" is unconvincing, since the whole question is to define what "*the right thing* for human beings" is. Menke's answer to Arendt's aporia of human rights ultimately has recourse to an ontological founding of human dignity in the human condition now interpreted as a new philosophical anthropology. Readings of Arendt that emphasize the "abyss of freedom" and the unexpected and contingent dimensions of the political in her work seem to me closer to her intentions.

Ayten Gündogdu addresses these issues in a novel way in *Rightlessness in an Age of Rights. Hannah Arendt and the Contemporary Struggles of Migrants.* Her starting point is not "a foundation derived through justificatory procedures but instead ... *political practices of founding human rights* ... A right to have rights, in its striking groundlessness, urges us to understand new rights claims such as the ones raised by undocumented immigrants as *declarations* that involve the invention and disclosure of a new political and normative world."[19] Rather than seeing declarations, as Menke does, as attempts to *ground* universal rights Gündogdu resorts to Arendt's analysis of new beginnings created by the revolutionary "abyss of freedom" (Arendt, *The Life of the Mind,* vol. 2, *Willing,* 207). Such beginnings "rupture the linear continuity of time"[20] and initiate a new political practice calling for the founding of new rules and institutions. In this respect, "what is at stake is not only justification or reason-giving but instead the *political invention and disclosure of a new world*" (emphasis in the text).[21]

New beginnings are animated by "principles," even if their emergence cannot be grounded in them in the sense of being deductively predictable or deducible from these principles. Arendt, following Montesquieu, understands principle as an animating spirit.[22] What then is the principle that animates the call for a right to have rights? Gündogdu agrees with Étienne Balibar[23] that the principle animating the call for a right to have rights is *equaliberty*, which denotes "an equal claim to political activity, and it highlights the inextricably intertwined nature of equality and freedom."[24] Equaliberty as a principle is animated in and through reenactments that are "not fully authorized by the instituted configurations of rights, citizenship, and humanity. Such iterative practices change the boundaries of our political and normative universe, as they introduce us to new subjects who were formerly not recognized as human beings entitled to rights."[25]

As Gündogdu herself notes, this reading of Arendt is quite akin to my concepts of democratic iterations and jurisgenerative politics.[26] But she takes issue with my claim that the validity of universalist and cosmopolitan human rights norms do not derive from the act of democratic iteration alone but from context-transcendent norms that are immanent in speech acts. My recourse to the context-transcendent norms presupposed by speech acts that raise validity claims simply means that, in any conversation aiming at redeeming such validity claims, *equaliberty*—that is, the equality of speech partners and their equal freedom to say "yes" or "nay"—is counterfactually presupposed. Insofar as political authority is rationally justifiable and is not just based on force, coercion, violence, and deceit,[27] we enact *equaliberty* counterfactually every time we address one another and seek to give reciprocally acceptable justifications.

This view is not at all incompatible with those moments when a new principle erupts unto our political life, new subjects make their entry into the public sphere such as to reconfigure the meaning of rights, citizenship, and humanity. To recognize such newness, however, we must present the universal and the particular in a novel constellation since the new is only new against a recognizable background of the old, of what has been taken for granted. New constellations rearrange terms, practices, institutions, and subject positions in such a way that the shape of a different world emerges. But we must be careful not to romanticize the new by neglecting that what is new can also be loathesome, unimaginable, or open an "abyss under our feet," as Arendt thought the unprecedented aspect of extermination camps had done.[28] All that is new is not salutary; it is the reconfiguration of existing elements so as to create a *better* and *more just* world that is defensible.

The principle of *equaliberty* animating the right to have rights draws its force precisely from the fact that philosophy cannot deny *the other* the right to seek grounds as to why he or she is excluded from being recognized as a rights bearing person. There are no such good reasons that would deny any human being the right to be an addressee of a validity claim that must eventually be justified with reasons.[29] This slim but crucial insight is essential for understanding the force of the right to have rights. Arendt, at one and the same time, by invoking this claim shows that there are *no* good reasons for denying such rights to all human beings, while exposing the difficulty of reconfiguring the existing trinity of "state-people-territory" (*OT*, 282) such as to accommodate such rights. The aporetic nature of her phrase transcends existing configurations of rights without prescribing what a new configuration might look like. It is thus important not to mistake her position for a form of legal positivism or a pseudo-ontology of human dignity but to insist on the radicalness of the right to have rights.

## The Right to Have Rights as a Right to Place

In a recent study called, *The Right to Have Rights. Citizenship, Humanity and International Law,* Alison Kesby has parsed the right to have rights into five topoi: the right to have rights as a "right to place in the world"; as a right to nationality; as a right to citizenship; as a right to humanity; and as a right to political agency.[30] Arendt's discussion of having a "place in the world" is crucial because it moves across several dimensions at once and thus needs careful analysis.

Arendt herself writes on two registers and often shifts from one to the other without pause or clarification. I will call these the *phenomenological* and the *institutional* analysis of place. "The fundamental deprivation of human rights is manifested first and above all in the deprivation *of a place in the world* which makes opinions significant and actions effective" writes Arendt (*OT*, 376) and continues, "This extremity, and nothing else, is the situation of people deprived of human rights. They are deprived, not of the right to freedom but of the right to action; not of the right to think whatever they please, but of the right to opinion" (*OT*, 376; my emphasis). For Arendt, a place in the world is always the space within which human behavior and interaction take place and thought and opinion are communicated because humans cannot exist but by appearing to each other (*HC*, 179).[31] The human condition unfolds in a space of appearances, in which we act, speak, and interact. This space of appearances is not always institutionalized as a public, political sphere—only under certain conditions does the space of appearance become a public sphere with its own institutions, laws, and demarcations from other realms. For Arendt, who now shifts from a phenomenological to an institutional register in one and the same passage, the stateless, the refugee, and the displaced person are said to be deprived "not of the right to freedom but of the right to action; not of the right to think whatever they please, but of the right to opinion." Strictly speaking, such individuals, particularly under conditions of internment in camps, are of course deprived of the freedom to act in certain ways. But they are deprived of "the right to action" and "the right to opinion" in the sense that they lack an institutional and interactional framework through which what they say and do can be recognized and responded to by others. They have ceased to be the source of recognized validity claims, which can only be parsed with respect to a shared public framework in the world. Their capacities for responsibility and agency are increasingly diminished. They face the threat of becoming *worldless*, precisely because they have no demonstrable, institutional, and interactional framework within which they can be situated.

This diminution of the person and the increasing sense of unreality that grows with the passage of time in detention and concentration camps have been explored primarily in works of literature by Elie Wiesel, Primo Levi, Imre Kertesz, and others.[32] Well aware of the findings of social psychologists such as Bruno Bettelheim who had studied these phenomena in the camps,[33] Arendt's discussion moves between a *phenomenology of worldlessness* and *the loss of the public sphere by the stateless.* What kind of moral and political agency can we attribute to human beings who are in the process of losing their place in the world? It is clear that in camps the space of appearances of human action and words does not just cease and humans have not really lost all their capacity of action and opinion. Nevertheless, the oft-noted phenomena of depression, listlessness, staring into the void, and dissociation among such camp inmates proves that Arendt's phenomenology of worldlessness was quite apt (*OT,* 439).

## The Right to Have Rights and Post-World War II Legal Developments

Since Arendt penned her discussion of the right to have rights, international institutions and international law have changed the landscape against the background of which she wrote. The Universal Human Rights Declaration of 1948 in Articles 13, 14, and 15 addressed some of these questions. Article 13 reads: "Everyone has the right to freedom of movement and residence within the borders of each state." The second clause of this Article states: "Everyone has the right to leave any country, including his own, and to return to his country." Article 14 encodes "the right to asylum": "Everyone has the right to seek and to enjoy in other countries asylum from persecution." The second clause places certain limitations by stipulating that "this right may not be invoked in the case of prosecutions genuinely arising from non-political crimes or from acts contrary to the purposes and principles of the United Nations." Article 15 seeks guarantees against "denaturalization" or "loss of citizenship," by stating that "everyone has the right to a nationality," and further declaims, "no one shall be arbitrarily deprived of his nationality nor denied the right to change his nationality."[34]

Together with the United Nations Convention on the Prevention and Punishment of the Crime of Genocide of 1948, the 1951 Geneva Conventions on the Status of Refugees, and in particular the two international human rights covenants, namely the International Covenant on Civil and Political Rights [(ICCPR); signed in 1966 and entered into force in 1976, with 168 state parties as of 2016] and the International Covenant on Economic, Social, and Cultural Rights [(ICESCR); entered into force the same year with 164 state parties as of 2016], these documents, and the institutions of compliance and monitoring they have created, have altered the legal landscape for the entitlement to and exercise of international human rights.[35]

International human rights theory and practice have implications for Arendt's considerations. In the first place, Article 15 of the UDHR that "denaturalization" and rendering human beings "stateless" is a violation of international human rights is in complete agreement with Arendt's intention. The obverse side of denaturalization is "naturalization" or gaining access to citizenship or to some kind of permanent membership or residency in a polity. There is *no* such human right in any of the international covenants although there are many provisions against denaturalization. Granting citizenship and the conditions in accordance with which it can be granted remain sovereign state privileges, as the ten million stateless in our current world still testify. In *The Rights of Others* I have suggested how such a human right to membership and citizenship can be formulated.[36]

Arendt was acutely aware that although developments in international human rights law were absolutely necessary to address the plight of the stateless and the displaced, at the time of the composition of *The Origins,* she believed that international law "is only concerned with laws and treaties, which regulate the relations of sovereign nations in peace and war" (my translation).[37] She endorsed the concept of "crimes against humanity," proposed by Chief Justice Jackson in the Nuremberg trials as anticipating a form of legality that would stand "over the nations," but claimed that under the then-existing understanding of state sovereignty this was impossible.[38]

Nonetheless, nowhere is this continuing tension between sovereignty-transcending rights claims and sovereignty norms more apparent than in the case of the major legal instruments of the postwar period that still regulate refugee and asylum movements. The 1951 Refugee Conventions and their 1967 Protocol generate a series of distinctions between convention refugees and other persons displaced on account of civil war, generalized violence, and natural catastrophes. On the one hand, it is stated that "the principle of *nonrefoulement* is so fundamental that no reservations or derogations may be made to it. It provides that no one shall expel or return (*refouler*) a refugee against his or her will, in any manner whatsoever, to a territory where he or she fears threats to life or freedom."[39] On the other hand, the five protected categories are: race, religion, nationality, membership of a particular social group, or political opinion. With the leadership of Canada and then the United States, these categories have been expanded recently to cover gender-based and gender-related crimes such as female genital mutilation and practices of child marriages as well.[40] The convention refugee was principally modeled after the dissident, the prisoner of conscience, and the resistance fighter. The convention requires proof of individual persecution, imposing on refugees themselves and the receiving states quite a heavy administrative procedure of examination and verification.

In an age of increasing generalized violence, ethnic cleansing, civil wars, and armed confrontations among non-state groups, in what sense is the 1951 Convention adequate to deal with the rights of the most vulnerable? In response to such concerns, the heads of state of the Organization of African Unity (now African Union) formulated the *Convention Governing the Specific Aspects of Refugee Problems in Africa*, adopted in Addis Ababa on September 10, 1969, and entered into force in June 20, 1974.[41] A similar document, *The Cartagena Declaration on Refugees*, was adopted at a colloquium held at Cartagena, Colombia, November 19–22, 1984. This document, while nonbinding, set out regional standards for refugee processing and resettlement in Central America, Mexico, and Panama.

The Cartagena Declaration states that "among refugees [are included] persons who have fled their country because their lives, safety or freedom have been threatened by generalized violence, foreign aggression, internal conflicts, massive violation of human rights or other circumstances which have seriously disturbed public order."[42]

Neither the 1951 Refugee Convention nor other legal instruments recognize conditions of extreme poverty and material deprivation as grounds for legitimate asylum. Economic migrants are considered individuals who raise spurious claims to protection and refuge. But why are extreme poverty and material deprivation not a legitimate ground for seeking opportunities to escape from them? Particularly under conditions of global economic interdependence when the policies of advanced capitalist economies that cause damage to the environment all over the globe have far-reaching consequences, what sense does it make to turn so-called economic migrants away at the door, or better still, to douse them with water cannons or set police dogs upon them as was done in the so-called "jungle" in Calais? Isn't redressing extreme poverty just as fundamental a human right as the right not to be tortured?

Furthermore, the subject of human rights law is the *individual person,* even if the circumstances and causes leading individuals to seek refuge and asylum are always collective; in centering on the individual, the law is forced to neglect the *interdependence of economic, climate-related, military, and other factors in the society of states,* which give rise to these collective circumstances. Laws and legal regimes create further differentiations and distinctions that trap individuals in conditions *of administrative dependency.* This aspect of *legal governmentality,* which generates such distinctions as among displaced persons, refugees in protracted situations, and stateless persons, is a double-edged sword, often robbing individuals of the autonomy, dignity, and initiative that their protection of human rights was intended to guaranteed in the first place. Refugee camps, whether in cities or in the desert, are sites of indignity and humiliation. The elaborate game of head counting, status granting, and legal classification in the meantime has spawned a transnational set of institutions, treaties, and litigations, as well as creating armies of aid-workers, humanitarians, camp directors, and international lawyers in addition to hundreds of NGOs and INGOs. These limitations of legal instruments together with the apparatus of legal governmentality they have given rise to result in the pitfalls of "humanitarian reason."

## The Critique of Humanitarian Reason

Didier Fassin, to whom we owe this term, defines it as follows: "Humanitarian reason governs precarious lives: the lives of the unemployed and the asylum seeker, the lives of sick immigrants and people with AIDS, the lives of disaster victims and victims of conflict—threatened and forgotten lives that humanitarian government brings into existence by protecting and revealing them."[43] Fassin, who for many years worked with Médècins Sans Frontières (Doctors without Borders) in a high capacity, is brutally honest about the shortcomings of "humanitarian reason," which is certainly one of the offshoots of the politics of international human rights. He writes, "I have tried to grasp what humanitarian reason means and what it hides, to take it neither as the best of all possible governments nor as an illusion that misleads us. It seems to me that by viewing it from various angles . . . we can render the global logic of humanitarian reason more intelligible."[44]

An earlier and influential critique of humanitarian reason that linked it to Arendt's right to have rights was formulated by Jacques Rancière in "Who Is the Subject of the Rights of Man?."[45] Composed in 2004, after the US invasion of Iraq had taken place and the wars in Afghanistan and Iraq were at their height, Rancière begins by noting how the Rights of Man, or in more contemporary language, Human Rights, which were rejuvenated by the dissident movements of Eastern Europe and the Soviet Union in the 1970s and '80s, were transformed in the first decade of the twenty-first century into "the rights of the rightless, of the populations hunted out of their homes and land and threatened by ethnic slaughter. They appeared more and more as the rights of the victims, the rights of those who were unable to enact any rights or even any claims in their name, so that eventually their rights had to be upheld by others, at the cost of shattering the edifice of International Rights, in the name of a new right to 'humanitarian interference'—which ultimately boiled down to the right to invasion."[46] Human rights, the rights of the rightless, became the ideological scaffolding for humanitarian reason at best and for humanitarian intervention at worst.

Rancière's essay is rich in polemic and sweeping in its generalizations. Often it is hard to distinguish between his understanding of what Arendt said and the way Arendt's words have been deployed by others such as Giorgio Agamben. Commenting on Agamben's claim that "the camp can be put as the 'nomos' of modernity,"[47] Rancière notes that refugee camps, the zones where illegal migrants are parked by national authorities such as Meluia in Spain or Lampedusa in Italy, or the Nazi death camps of the last century,[48] are thereby subsumed under the sweeping logic of a sovereignty exercising "bio-power." This is indeed the "night in which all cows are black," to use a Hegelian locution,[49] that is, a mode of thinking for which all relevant distinctions disappear. Unlike Arendt, who separated carefully the unique logic of totalitarianism from that of modern mass democracies and many other regime forms such as tyranny and despotism, the camps appear here as the culmination of a sweeping logic of bio-power intrinsic to modernity.

Rancière takes Arendt to be arguing that the Rights of Man are the rights "of those who have no rights, the mere derision of right."[50] For her this equation is made possible because, having lost their place in the world and having been ejected out of the public framework of membership in a polity, these individuals are entrapped in *mere life*, which for Arendt means the life of the *idiotes*- from the Greek etymology for "private life," i.e., those who live an apolitical life. I suggested above that Arendt herself does not distinguish clearly between *the phenomenology of the space of appearances* and *the public sphere*, with the consequence that she claims that the stateless are deprived of the right to action and to opinion, thereby suggesting that the loss of a public framework of membership is somehow equivalent to the end of the space of appearances altogether. It is not. The space of appearances for the individual ceases only at death.

Rancière's main disagreement with Arendt centers around the question of democracy; he claims that Arendt's diagnosis of the paradoxes of the rights of man amounts "actually [to] a critique of democracy."[51] Having identified "the rights of man" with the "rights of the *idiotes*" or private individual alone, Arendt, on Rancière's reading, cannot see that the essence of democracy is challenging the boundary between the public and the private. Instead she essentializes the public/private distinction. And in a critical slight of hand, the "stateless, the refugee and the asylee" are identified with the "private, poor, unpoliticized individual." Yet Arendt's point is *precisely* that the poor, the private, and unpoliticized individuals *belong* to a polity; they are members of some human community and their condition cannot be compared to that of the stateless whose plight is that *no* human community seems to want them. Recall her ironical comment that even slaves had more rights than the stateless! [52]

Why is Rancière so obviously misreading Arendt? Primarily because he wants to fit Arendt's position into his scheme of the "archipolitical," which he understands as a "depoliticizing [of] matters of power and repression and setting them in a sphere of exceptionality that is no longer political, in an anthropological sphere of sacrality situated beyond the reach of political dissensus." [53] This then develops into a critique of Arendt's distinction between the private and the public realms and ultimately of her separation of technological and economic matters from political ones. Arendt's admittedly faulty views on this matter have little to do either with a sphere of sacrality or with that of a state of exception, and many who believe in the art of careful reading, and particularly feminist theorists, have subjected these aspects of her thought to a clearer critique than Rancière has.[54]

Nonetheless, it is worth singling out Rancière's striking restating of the paradox of human rights, namely, that one seems least in possession of them when one is "merely" human. He writes: "The Rights of Man are the rights of those who have not the rights that they have and have the rights that they have not."[55] The subject of rights are those who engage in a process of subjectivization, or enactment of rights, such as to bridge the two sides of this equation. The first half of this paradox, "The Rights of Man are the rights of those who have not the rights that they have," is concretized by Rancière with respect to Olympe de Gouges, the aristocratic woman who sided with the revolution but who was guillotined by the Jacobins for participating in the male sphere of citizenship and questioning the place of the women-mother-citizen that the revolutionaries were devising under the influence of Rousseau's regressive theory of gender roles. Olympe de Gouges exercised the human rights that the declaration proclaimed she had but that she was not entitled to exercise because she was a woman. And when she did so she became the subject of rights that she did not have, i.e. that of participation in the public sphere, and was guillotined for her transgressions![56]

There is something powerful in Rancière's formula and it is indeed a helpful way of thinking through the disjunction, the *décalage*, between human rights and the rights of citizen. To do so, however, we have to move back from text to context, from conceptual analysis to an outline of institutional and legal developments since 1948 as they bear on the rights of those without rights. The second half of Rancière's formula, "The Rights of Man are the rights of those who . . . have the rights they have not," can be parsed in the light of contemporary human rights law, which entitles the rightless to rights they can make their own only by claiming them, and which, in some cases as I will explore below, ironically also curtails these rights on the basis of arbitrary distinctions.

## Refugees' and Migrants' Political Agency

Arendt's description of the condition of the stateless at times seems to render them as abject subjects, as for example in this moving and powerful passage from "We, Refugees": "We lost our home which means the familiarity of daily life. We lost our occupation, which means the confidence that we are of some use in this world. We lost our language, which means the naturalness of reactions, the simplicity of gestures, the unaffected expression of feelings."[57] Ironically, Arendt herself was a fascinating counterexample to the sense of loss of confidence and worldliness described here: as a refugee, she was neither without initiative nor autonomy and this was true for many others as well.

Still, some things have changed in our world, and the refugee, the asylee, and the stateless person are increasingly political actors who claim the "rights that they do not (supposedly) have," that is, the rights that are denied to them. "Les Sans Papiers" in France; the "Dreamers" and DACA recipients (Deferred Action Childhood Arrivals) in the United States, and "Los Indignados" in Spain, many of whom are migrant workers, are demanding the rights that they may not be acknowledged as having according to the constitutions of states in which they may be residing but which they do have as human beings *simpliciter* under various international human rights conventions. These are the rights to equal conditions of work, to schooling for their children, to health care, to representation via counsel in their own language during intake interviews,[58] and much more. Today's refugees and asylum seekers are aware of these rights under international law[59] also because of the remarkable solidarity exercised by many civil society groups and organizations. Because of such solidarity, they do not hesitate to invoke these rights in the face of recalcitrant and hostile border guards and policemen.

Alison Kesby points out that as attractive as such a conception of political agency may be, there are still serious objections to be raised against Rancière's doctrine of the *entitlement* to rights as the *enactment* of rights, precisely because there may be limitations to people's *ability* to assert such rights. "Is it feasible, for example," she asks, "for a politics of dissensus to take place within the confines of social isolation of an immigration detention centre and the enervating predicament of the indefinite detention? . . . Is a collective subject to emerge from isolated individuals in immigration detention; that is in a detention centre operating according to what has been termed a logic of 'halting the ability to enact rights' and of 'strategies of silencing such as geographical and social isolation'?"[60]

Kesby's astute remarks send us back to a key issue in the construction of the figure of the migrant and the refugee in contemporary political thought: they are either abject subjects, the new *homini sacri* of the systems of sovereignty, or they are the oppositional subjects of *dissensus* (Rancière) who seem to have rights only insofar as they can assert them. While Rancière's emphasis on the agency of refugees, migrants, and asylum seekers is salutary, it also runs the risk of burdening the most vulnerable with their own defense as well as being voluntaristic in making the entitlement to rights dependent upon the capacity to assert them as well as to have them recognized. Surely the claim to rights cannot rest on the *ability* to make others recognize them who may or may not be inclined to do so. How can we rethink the interdependence between politics and international human rights and humanitarian law beyond voluntarism and cynicism?

International human rights law since 1948 has created norms, instruments, and institutions through which states' treatments of nonnationals, documented and undocumented migrants, refugees, asylum seekers, and displaced persons and the violation of their international rights can be contested and litigated. With the advent of international human rights law, individuals are recognized as holding human rights directly under international law. What does this mean concretely? It means in the first place that the civil and political rights of citizens as codified in various constitutions and bills of rights can themselves be criticized in the light of internationally acknowledged human rights standards. Particularly the transnational women's movements across the globe have used CEDAW (The Convention Against the Elimination of All Forms of Discrimination Against Women) to force their governments and public institutions to comply with the Convention's standards for equal pay for equal work, against sexual harassment, against sexual discrimination, and for consideration of women's special health and physical needs. Other examples can be drawn from social struggles and litigations made possible by the ICESC in enabling indigenous groups' claims to their own territories and cultural patrimony in the Global South. An intense debate had raged in the United Kingdom with its accession to the European Convention for Human Rights and Fundamental Freedoms about prisoners' disenfranchisement or loss of voting rights. On several occasions the British government was criticized by the European Court of Human Rights for violating prisoners' human rights under the Convention.[61] In all these instances, international human rights instruments have created a conceptual and normative space within which a jurisgenerative struggle could take place between international human rights norms and legally institutionalized civil and political rights. The dialectic between humanitarian reason and jurisgenerativity has thus created possibilities for the stateless, the refugee, and the asylum seeker to negotiate the line between being an abject subject of compassion and administrative logic *versus* being a legal person as well as a political activist claiming the recognition of his or her international human rights.

As discussed in chapter 2 above, by *jurisgenerativity* I mean that law can also structure an extralegal normative universe by developing new vocabularies for public claim-making—by encouraging new forms of subjectivity to engage with the public sphere and by interjecting existing relations of power with anticipations of justice to come (see pp. 28–30 above). Yet particularly with respect to the status of the undocumented migrant, the stateless person, and the unrecognized asylum seeker, jurisgenerativity is curtailed by state sovereignty breeding new forms of *jurispathy*. This is when the power of the state to transform law into violence is most felt. Kesby observes that "the assumption of the international human rights system is that the rights contained in the various international human rights treaties are to be enjoyed by *all* who are within a state's jurisdiction," and that "a fundamental principle of international human rights law is the principle of equality and non-discrimination" (my emphasis).[62] Nonetheless, although in most treaties, such as the *International Convention on the Protection of the Rights of All Migrant Workers and Members of Their Families* (New York, December 1990. Entered into force July 2003), nationality is a prohibited ground of discrimination (Art. 1(1)), "immigration status" is not listed as a category that is prohibited to discriminate against,[63] thus leaving the undocumented and the stateless migrant vulnerable and unprotected against state violence. The disciplinary state apparatuses have exploited this "silence" of the law vis-a-vis the status of the undocumented and irregular migrants and have resorted increasingly to their detention and forced deportation.

It is a paradox of humanitarian reason and jurisgenerative developments that they also create new distinctions, divisions, and thresholds among various categories of persons. Particularly because these developments in human rights law are dependent upon respect for the territorial sovereignty of states, ironically they end up encouraging states to use detention and deportation tactics to avoid their responsibilities under international law. With the worldwide development of the security state and the spread of the ideology of the permanent state of emergency to fight against terrorism, even the principle of non-refoulement has been compromised. Gündogdu reports, "From 2000 to 2012, the number of 'camps' used for immigration detention in Europe has increased from 324 to 473,"[64] giving rise to a regime, also common in the United States, which scholars call have named "crimmigration."[65]

In addition to the growing use of practices of internment and detention in dealing with irregular migrants, the nature of state borders has also changed. In recent decades borders have been transnationalized and internationalized. They have been expanded through the use of military vessels to intercept refugees at sea for example;[66] they have also been extraterritorialized by giving airline personnel or private security firms the authority to check and determine immigrations status, deny admission, and even detain those they deem illegal migrants.[67] Under these circumstances, can the stateless refugee and undocumented migrant be equated with one another? "Whereas nation-state borders enclosed a specific territory and were institutions designed to regulate cross-border movements and transactions, today's borders enclose certain persons. Undocumented migrants offer a counterexample to the oft-cited disappearance of borders ... migrants encounter this border zone everywhere. The undocumented migrant is therefore a figure of the border like no other, represents the border and is its special subject."[68] Of course, *some* undocumented migrants, but not all, are *stateless* refugees or internally displaced persons. For Julia Schulze Wessel, it is the initiative, enterprising spirit, fluidity, and resistance of today's undocumented migrants when compared to the lack of agency of the stateless described by Hannah Arendt that makes the difference between these two groups. This leads her to question the usefulness of

Arendt's analysis for our own days. But from the standpoint of having rights, no matter what the ingenuity of undocumented migrants as borderless subjects may be, they are still confronted with the same *jurispathic* logic of territoriality and sovereignty, even if it is now in the form of extraterritorial jurisdiction and shared sovereignty entrusted to non-state actors. For that reason, I do not see an analytical displacement of the refugee by the undocumented migrant.

## Conclusion

What makes Arendt's reflections on the right to have rights so compelling are the philosophical, moral, and legal dimensions it addresses at once. For the philosophical purists, her non-foundationalism and lack of clarity concerning rights will present a problem; nevertheless the phrase "the right to have rights" evokes so much and can be dealt with at so many levels at once that it will continue to resonate and enlighten us even as we continue to face the same political conundrums in our own days. It is through the interrelationship of these various dimensions that we can also recognize the complexities of the Arendtian conception of freedom. For Arendt, freedom is world-building with others and requires a place in the world within which we are situated in networks of action and interaction. It is only because we are bodies in space that we also need a place in the world. Although Arendt has frequently been misread as if she wanted to dispense with embodiment, by Rancière as well as Butler, this is not right. The human condition is deeply *embodied* and *embedded* in webs of narratives that can only be housed in a material world constituted through the "labor of our body and the work of our hands" (*HC*, 79).

This conception of embodied agency is not only fundamental to contemporary feminist theories' insights about the body, but we should also not forget that Arendt is the theorist of "natality," which she explicitly juxtaposed to what I have called the "western philosophical tradition's love affair with death."[69] Natality for her does not only mean dependency and precarity of human beings but also underscores the ontological fact that no human child who is ever born will be like any other in their actions and speech. This embodied capacity for human agency requires a place in the world in and through which it can unfold. The world's refugee camps are housed by women and children who are more vulnerable because of their bodily needs and more dependent upon a stable place in the world than their male counterparts. More children than adults perish in refugee camps and women in camps are subject to sexual assault and abuse. Analyzing the gender politics of the right to have rights and addressing the gender complexities of humanitarian reason is a task ahead.

I have tried to argue in this chapter that the sea change from the right to have rights to the critique of humanitarian reason should neither lead us to the defense of the sovereigntist nation-state system nor should it produce a flippant dismissal of the realm of international law and international institutions as being products of an imaginary consensus. Rather, one has to recognize the unending tension between the facticity and validity of the law and of institutions in general as they produce those cracks and fissures into which a politics of jurisgenerativity can intervene.

# 7

# Legalism and Its Paradoxes in Judith Shklar's Work

## A Skeptical Émigré

During the controversy that erupted around Hannah Arendt's *Eichmann in Jerusalem*, a little-known lecturer in the Government Department at Harvard University by the name of Judith Nisse Shklar published *Legalism. An Essay on Law, Morals and Politics* in 1964.[1] Written in the direct and acerbic style that would become her mark, Shklar states: "This is, then, a polemical and opinionated book. It is, however, not meant to be destructive . . . The object here is to stir up controversy by a clear confrontation of incompatible positions, not just to upset the genteel academic applecart" (*Legalism*, viii). Shklar's wish to stir up controversy was not fulfilled. At the time the book was largely ignored by legal theorists[2] as well as political philosophers, but it did signal the emergence of the singular voice of one younger than German-Jewish luminaries such as Hannah Arendt and Leo Strauss who dominated American academia in political theory during those years.

Shklar belonged to the generation of European Jewish émigrés whose world was shattered—and whose childhood had been brought to an end by Hitler, as she expressed it in one of her most poignant and, to my knowledge, only piece of autobiographical writing.[3] Born in 1928 to a German-speaking family of doctors living in Riga, Latvia, that also included Russian Jewish relatives, she escaped with her parents and sister, via Sweden to Siberia, and then to Japan and finally to Canada. At McGill, Shklar studied political theory with Frederick M. Watkins, before doing doctoral work at Harvard with Carl Friedrich, who had also been Watkins's advisor. What Shklar called her "bare bones liberalism" (*Legalism*, 5) carried the indelible marks of disbelief in the face of a world gone insane. Yet what is distinctive about her voice as an émigré political theorist, and what sets her apart from Strauss and Arendt, both half a generation older than she, is the lack of pathos with which she registered the destruction of her familial world and the end of her childhood. Although brought up in a German-speaking Jewish household, Judith Shklar was not a German-Jewish philosopher. Her skeptical and restrained temperament put her rather in the company of East European ironists like Franz Kafka, Milan Kundera, or György Konrad.[4]

In contemporary thought Shklar is being celebrated as a precursor of "realists" who, in the words of William Galston, are critical of what they regard as the "moralism, legalism, and parochialism of American liberal theory."[5] I will argue that characteristic of Shklar's thinking is psychological realism about human nature but a rejection of realism as a theory of state behavior and international relations, whose proponents Shklar called "disappointed liberals" at one point.[6] Furthermore, for Shklar, the relationship of law to politics is contentious, but the rule of law in the domestic sphere and the legitimacy of international criminal law are crucial to democratic liberalism and to what she would later name the "liberalism of fear."[7]

In this chapter I first consider Shklar's early book, *Legalism. An Essay on Law, Morals and Politics,* in which she distinguishes among aspects of legalism as ideology, as creative policy, and as an ethos of the law. Shklar was unable to explain how these various dimensions of legalism could be reconciled plausibly with one another. In her work, "the facticity" and "the validity" of the law (Habermas) face each other as unreconciled dimensions[8]. Furthermore, while her critique of criminal international law is being revived today in the name of a certain skepticism toward institutions of international law, this critique needs to be balanced against her full-throated defense of the legitimacy of the Nuremberg trials. Shklar's discussion of the Nuremberg trials merits consideration along with Hannah Arendt's *Eichmann in Jerusalem*. The contentious and complicated relationship of law and politics in Arendt's and Shklar's works will be considered in the final sections of this chapter.

## Legalism: An Essay on Mentalité

With the memory of the Nuremberg trials and the McCarthy hearings in the United States still very much alive, Shklar positioned herself in *Legalism* against too much self-congratulation on the part of liberal democracies. Drawing a rather sharp line between ideologies of free market capitalism and the political essence of liberalism, she wrote of her contribution:

> It is, at its simplest, a defense of social diversity, inspired by that bare bones liberalism which, having abandoned the theory of progress and every specific scheme of economics, is committed only to the belief that tolerance is a primary virtue and that a diversity of opinions and habits is not only to be endured but to be cherished and encouraged. The assumption throughout is that social diversity is the prevailing condition of modern nation-states and that it ought to be promoted (*Legalism*, 5).

For her, European fascism and the Holocaust were not to be interpreted as phenomena proving the "end of Western rationality," as Adorno and Horkheimer had argued,[9] or as Arendt formulated it, "a break in the continuity of Occidental history" (*BPF*, 26). Shklar was unsure that there had ever been a *single* tradition of Western reason, and she disliked the self-congratulatory emphases on the West. She wrote: "There is no one Western tradition. It is a tradition of traditions. Moreover, political freedom," she added against Cold War apologists, "has been the exception, a rarity, in Europe's past, remote and recent" (*Legalism*, 22).

But what is legalism? "It is the ethical attitude that holds moral conduct to be a matter of rule following, and moral relationships to consist of duties and rights determined by rules" (*Legalism*, 1). This claim at first suggests that Shklar's concern is with moral philosophy of a certain kind. Shklar, who was to write a book on Hegel's *Phenomenology of Spirit*,[10] could have been thinking of Hegel's critique of the legalism and of the abstract rigor of Kant's moral philosophy. In a famous discussion in the *Phenomenology of Spirit*, called "gesetz-prüfende" (law-testing) and "gesetz-gebende Vernunft" (law-giving reason), Hegel dissected the antinomies of Kantian moral theory.[11] If moral reason was to test the maxims of human action, would the operation of non-contradiction alone be sufficient to distinguish among them?[12] But if practical reason was to legislate such maxims, how could it derive more concrete maxims out of the pure form of the Categorical Imperative alone? Kantian moral reason was either empty or, if it generated content, it did so because it smuggled in presuppositions about human beings or society into the content of the Categorical Imperative.

Although she devotes a few pages to a critique of Kantian morality (*Legalism*, 47–49; 57), Shklar was not really concerned with moral theory but rather with legalism as a way of thinking that tries to insulate law from morals as well as from politics. The first part of the book deals with a critique of analytical positivism—including the views of Hans Kelsen and H.L.A. Hart—as well as of natural law theories. Whereas analytical positivism attempts to distinguish law from both politics and morals by professing ideological neutrality and formalism, natural law approaches set a premium on law and moral agreement—which, in turn, is incompatible with diversity and tolerance (*Legalism*, 5). Shklar thinks that her critique of legalism applies equally well to both perspectives, but this is not convincing. The difficulty with natural law theories is not the *separation* but rather the *conflation* of law and morals (*Legalism*, 8), and even of law and politics. The real target of her critique is the legal positivist tradition, and in particular, the relationship of legalism to liberalism. And here she makes a number of distinctions concerning legalism that begin to blur the crispness of her original assertions.

Legalism is said to be the "ideology" of its practitioners, in that they believe that the legal system consists of the rule of law, and that the law rests on formally correct rationality in the sense specified by Max Weber

(*Legalism*, 21). Shklar calls this an "ideology" because the coercive power as well as the fact that it is obeyed by those it addresses are far from evident in legal systems (*Legalism*, 35);[13] rather, these aspects of the law accomplish their goals because the legal system is "part of a social continuum" (*Legalism*, 3). This critique of legal formalism and her insistence that law must be seen in a social context have led some to call Shklar a "postmodernist,"[14] or more plausibly, to classify her as a precursor of the "critical legal studies movement."[15] Neither classification can do justice to Shklar's own conflictual account of the relation of legalism to liberalism. Shklar herself tried to capture this relationship in a paradoxical formula: "The great paradox revealed here is that legalism as an *ideology* is too inflexible to recognize the enormous potential of legalism as a *creative policy* but exhausts itself in intoning traditional pieties and principles which are incapable of realization. This is, of course, the perennial character of ideologies. It should not, however, in this case, lead one to forget the greatness of legalism as an *ethos* when it expresses itself in the characteristic institutions of the law" (*Legalism*, 112; my emphases).

This statement comes from the opening section of part 2 of the book, devoted to law and politics and in particular to international law and the trials in Nuremberg and Tokyo. Legalism has at least three dimensions: it is an *ideology*; it is a *creative policy*; and it is an *ethos of the law*. It is indeed paradoxical that, if legalism is an ideology, it would also be accepted as creative policy as well as admired as an ethos. Practitioners prefer one policy to another and adopt one ethos rather than another precisely because they believe they have good and justified reasons to do so. If they thought that such policy or ethos were *merely* ideological, they would be less sanguine in accepting them. Yet by "ideology" Shklar does not mean "false consciousness" or "distortion" in the Marxian sense but rather "a series of personal responses to social experiences which come to color, often quite insensibly, all our categories of thought" (*Legalism*, 41). Viewed as such, for the "historian of ideas," as she also calls herself (*Legalism*, preface, vii), legalism is ideological not because it is a form of false consciousness but because it reflects the inevitable perspective of the practitioner of "mature legal systems,"[16] such as articulated in the theories of J. L. Austin, Kelsen, and Hart. We may say that in this context ideology seems to mean something like the *inevitable presuppositions without which a practice may not make sense*. To use the language of the late Wittgenstein, some rules are constitutive of what it means to play poker or to do algebra, and for the poker player, as well as the one who solves algebra problems, a certain perspective is inevitable. Yet this is not what Shklar has in mind, either, since she denies that what is called the "inevitable perspective of the mature legal system" amounts to *the constitutive rules and practices* of a system without which one cannot be a player or a problem solver; rather, she suggests that to separate law radically from morals and politics is a *choice* not an *epistemic inevitability*.

Shklar's historical contextualization of Kelsen's pure science of law, which she names "a homeless ghost," (*Legalism*, 34) is vivid and accurate and exemplifies her mode of thinking about these various dimensions of legalism: "In fact," she writes, "it is clear enough to an historian that it is not fortuitous that Kelsen's 'pure theory' has its origins in the Vienna in which psychoanalysis and logical positivism also had their home. All these concentrated attacks on traditional myths and irrationalities of every sort arose in the midst of a veritable caldron of religious, social and ideological conflict. All are negative responses to the fanaticized consciousness and the distortions which it engenders . . . Here liberalism is bound to identify itself with the ideal of a strong but neutral state that stands above and aloof from the wars of ideology and thus morality. . . . The pure science of law is a vision of the law of such a state" (*Legalism*, 41).[17] Written a decade before the intellectual historians Allan Janik's and Steven Toulmin's felicitous *Wittgenstein's Vienna*[18] instructed Anglo-American readers about the subtleties of the milieu out of which Kelsen's theory grew, Shklar was ahead of her time in contextualizing Kelsen's theory in this fashion.

In an essay called "In Defense of Legalism," written shortly after her book was published, Shklar introduced yet a fourth dimension to this concept without, however, clearly delineating it as such. "Legalism" refers here to a *theoretical* way of looking at the law by moral philosophers, jurists, and others. It is not so much the perspective of the insider, the practitioner, that is emphasized, but that of the outsider who is trying to *understand* legal systems. For example, she asks: "What mature moral attitudes and political ideologies are and are not compatible with 'mature' legal systems? What are the social limits of legalistic mores?"[19] Shklar observes that Max Weber had already discussed these questions but that legal theorists have not paid him enough attention, and she quotes Weber: "For the lawyer an order is either valid or not, but no such alternative exists for the sociologist. Fluid transitions exist between validity and non-validity."[20]

Nonetheless, as inevitable as contextualization and a sociological attitude may be in order to demystify legalist theories of law, can we whole-heartedly recommend that legalism be adopted by the legal practitioner, even while we know it to be a historically contingent perspective reflecting the preferences of a certain social milieu? Shklar's intellectual honesty leads her to confront this question head-on. "Anyone who asserts that justice is a policy and that the judicial process is not the antithesis of politics, but just one form of political action among others, must expect to meet certain outraged accusations" (*Legalism*, 143). But the answer, she says, is that "there is politics and politics" (*Legalism*, 143).

As opposed to victor's justice and sham political trials, "there are occasions when political trials may actually serve liberal ends, where they promote legalistic values in such a way as to contribute to constitutional politics and to a decent legal system. The Trial of the Major War Criminals by the International Military Tribunal at Nuremberg probably had that effect" (*Legalism*, 145). Is this answer satisfactory? Can Shklar really put to rest accusations of "victor's justice" (*Siegerjustiz*) about the Nuremberg trials? Before turning to her account of those trials, let us stress the conceptual conundrums, and even impossibilities, of reconciling legalism as ideology, policy, and ethos. Even in the non-pejorative sense of ideology, it is hard to defend legalism as a *policy* and to recommend it as an *ethos* once it is demystified by the contextual work of the intellectual historian. Shklar's principal objective of reconciling liberalism and legalism remains remote and paradoxical. It is unclear whether the perception of the judicial process as only one form of political action among others can be reconciled with the ideals of equality and impartiality to which liberalism is committed. [21]

Samuel Moyn contends that "legalism . . . not only does work but must work as a noble lie: philosophers, and perhaps associated guardians, know it is false but allow its many votaries to proceed as if it were true because only the myth makes their conduct possible." [22] Moyn radically disagrees with Shklar's somewhat cheery assessment of the influence of Nuremberg on postwar Germany and legal developments. He is skeptical that, having suffered the excessive politicization of law under the Nazi regime, the German people would be ready to switch to a more humane and liberal politics "by adopting a legalism they simultaneously knew was a myth but adopted purely and self-consciously as a matter of political utility."[23] Obviously, Moyn argues, "One difficulty with legalist myths—whether it is fatal or not is a matter of dispute—is that the people will get wind of the truth."[24]

We have to tread carefully here. For Shklar, legalism is not a lie—whether noble or not. She insists that her considerations "do not imply a criticism of legalism as an ethos or of law as an institution. It must be repeated the hope is that a greater degree of social self-awareness will make legalism a more effective *social force*, a more intelligible and defensible *political ideology* and a more useful concept in *social theory*."[25] Shklar may have been too sanguine in thinking that a "greater degree of social self-awareness" would not instead lead to a dismissive attitude toward legalism in all its dimensions.[26] Despite her intentions, we have to conclude that the various dimensions of legalism as ideology, policy, ethos, and legal sociology remain unreconciled in her work. Furthermore, the work of contextual demystification practiced by the political theorist in her vocation as "an historian of ideas" (*Legalism*, "preface," vii) does not clarify the normative relationship between legalism and liberalism,[27] or that between the rule of law and moral and political autonomy.

## The Significance and Puzzles of the Nuremberg Trials

In 1962–63 the young Judith Shklar sat in the Harvard University Library reading the transcript of the Nuremberg trials, just as Hannah Arendt, who had traveled to Jerusalem to attend the opening sessions of the Eichmann trial, would pore over the thousands of pages of trial transcripts she had brought with her. Shklar is one of the first to address the philosophical puzzles of international criminal law in the post-World War II period. "There was and is no system of international criminal law," she wrote, "just as there are no international community and international political institutions to formulate or regularly enforce criminal laws" (*Legalism*, 157).[28] Despite this almost-militant dismissal of international criminal law, she reaches the surprising conclusion that "what makes the Nuremberg Trial so remarkable is that, in the absence of strict legal justification, it was a great legalistic act, the most legalistic of all possible policies, and, as such, a powerful inspiration to legalistic ethos" (*Legalism*, 170).[29] While the trial was a political one in that it aimed to eliminate a political enemy and its ideology, "it need have given offense neither to legalistic nor to liberal values." And it was "only because the crimes against humanity were the moral center of the case that all this was possible" (*Legalism*, 170).

It is surprising that of the three charges considered in the trial—crimes against the peace or waging aggressive war; war crimes; and crimes against humanity—Shklar should focus insistently on crimes against humanity. Her reasons were as follows: she thought that the first charge against the Nazis was justifiably subject to the argument *tu quoque* (*Legalism*, 161), that is, that the leaders of states judging the Nazis had committed no less criminal acts against the peace than the Nazis had.

Regarding the charge that the Nazis had committed war crimes, Shklar's riposte is that, of course they had, but they had also engaged in acts that went far beyond the Hague Convention of 1907, which the French representative on the Tribunal wanted to consider as the binding document. Shklar, like Arendt, is convinced that what justifies the charge of crimes against humanity is the *novelty* of the acts in which the Nazis had engaged: "To say that the charge of crimes against humanity was unknown is therefore no argument against it" (*Legalism*, 163).

In *Eichmann in Jerusalem* Arendt had argued that the Jerusalem Court erred in condemning Eichmann for "crimes against the Jewish people" in the first instance and by naming "crimes against humanity" only as the third and separate charge (*EiJ*, 244–45).[30] In the dramatic epilogue to *Eichmann* (*EiJ*, 277), speaking in the voice of the Judges of Jerusalem, Arendt explained what crimes against humanity means for her. Genocide, the highest of the crimes against humanity, is an attack upon the human status and human plurality, which is the condition "under which life on earth has been given to man" (*HC*, 7). For Arendt, nothing less than a full-fledged ontological defense of human plurality could justify the significance of crimes against humanity and its pinnacle, genocide.

Shklar says nothing about the justification of crimes against humanity. Undoubtedly, she would dismiss Arendt's ontological anchoring of this concept in the human condition of plurality as a variant of natural law thinking. Can we rest satisfied though with the simple positing of a new criminal statute to deal with new and unprecedented acts? As is well known, the German defense lawyers, both in Nuremberg and during the Eichmann trial, kept raising the objection of "nulla crimen, nulla poene sine lege" ("no crime, no punishment without the law"), although none went so far as to claim that the mass slaughter of innocent civilians, women, and children was a justifiable act of war. Rather, they maintained that the overall criminality of the regime left no choice but to consider the will of the Führer as the law of the land. In that sense, legality in the Third Reich meant criminality.[31]

This form of perverted legalistic consciousness, exercised by the likes of Eichmann, clearly was what Shklar herself also had in mind by "legalism," that is, blind obedience to orders and the law of the land, no matter how perverse and criminal. Yet by leaving the concept of crimes against humanity so unelaborated and philosophically unjustified, she left her own argument open to the charge of *Siegerjustiz*. "As for the Eichmann case it, too, does not really create new problems for legal theory," she writes. "Eichmann, alas, was always a Jewish problem" (*Legalism*, 155). According to her, from the nonlegal point of view, the trial had to be judged in terms of its political value for the various Jewish communities involved, but from a theoretical point of view, the problems being the same in Nuremberg and in the Eichmann trial, there was no need to consider them separately (*Legalism*, 155). This is not so however. Without the evidence concerning the Nazi genocide of the Jews, which was not all that central to the Nuremberg trials, the category of crimes against humanity hangs in midair. In this sense, the Eichmann trial contributed far more to the project of international criminal law than Shklar may have been willing to admit. Was this a case of the possible "anxiety of influence" on her part vis-a-vis Arendt's towering contribution, or was it indicative of deeper differences between the two thinkers? Or possibly of both?

## The Anxiety of Influence? Shklar on Arendt

Between 1963 and 1984 Judith Shklar wrote about Hannah Arendt on five occasions.[32] From her elegiac and deeply appreciative essay in *The New Republic*, written shortly after Arendt's death on December 4, 1975, and called "Hannah Arendt's Triumph," to her brief review of Arendt's *Lectures on Kant's Political Philosophy* in 1984, Shklar's tone changes from reverence to impatience and even dismissiveness. In "Hannah Arendt's Triumph," Arendt is eulogized as "the very last and finest voices" of a shattered culture. "Now there is no one left who can speak about and out of the depth of the experience of German Jewry. She was one of the last survivors of a spiritual republic whose social history was as terrible and brief as it was intellectually radiant and enduring."[33] But only eight years later in 1983, in "Hannah Arendt as Pariah" Shklar chides Arendt for her use of the distinction between "pariah" and "parvenu," arguing that to condemn Jewish assimilation "not as false and foolish, but as vulgar" is a sign of ultimate snobbery.[34] Arendt is said to have clung "to a bizarre notion" that being Jewish was "an act of personal defiance and not a matter of actively maintaining a cultural and religious tradition with its own rites and patterns of speech."[35] Arendt did not even know

Yiddish or Hebrew (Shklar knew both), but she did receive superb German *Bildung*, including Greek, Latin, and philosophy! Perhaps the most intemperate words are Shklar's concluding observations that "American Jewry is a flourishing community, while German-Jewish culture died with Hannah Arendt."[36]

The Eichmann trial occupies a large place in Shklar's "Hannah Arendt as Pariah" piece from the *Partisan Review* in 1983 but it is barely mentioned in earlier articles.[37] It is as if, twenty years after the Eichmann controversy, there was still some settling of accounts that Shklar had to do. After asserting that Arendt had nothing very new to say about how one should assign responsibility for acts committed by public agents in their capacity as government functionaries or those who should try them, she concludes that in *Eichmann in Jerusalem*, "they are discussed in a derivative and amateurish way. Legal theory was not her forté."[38] Shklar then goes on to marvel at the arrogance and "extraordinary ignorance" (*EiJ*, 372) with which Arendt "generalized wildly about the infinitely complex and diverse communities of Eastern Europe, about whose history and structure she knew exactly nothing" (*EiJ*, 373). "Extraordinary ignorance" is not a charge that Arendt's work is often confronted with. Arendt's heavy reliance on Raoul Hilberg's *The Destruction of East-European Jewry* is well documented; this may have been inadequate, but it was hardly "extraordinarily ignorant."[39]

Even "more than ignorance and dissociation," which, according to Shklar, Arendt had displayed in *Eichmann in Jerusalem*, she had also "caused pain and justified rage. She meant to inflict the first and need not have been astonished at the latter."[40] To inflict pain willingly and with intent is cruelty, and for Shklar cruelty is a principal moral vice. A year later in *Ordinary Vices* (1984), she would ask: "How can we be expected to endure the humiliations inflicted by an uncontained snobbery? Our only consolation may well be that without moral aspirations there would be no moral hypocrisy, and that without trust there would be no betrayals. But there is nothing to redeem cruelty and humiliation."[41] By accusing Arendt of harbouring at least two of four cardinal vices, namely hypocrisy and snobbery—the others being betrayal and misanthropy—Shklar delivered her own version of Scholem's judgment on Arendt. (See chapter 4 above.) Arendt was again charged with lacking love of the Jewish people in that she would go so far as willingly inflicting cruelty on them.

This certainly is not right. Shklar was unable to assess sympathetically the degree of pain and self-implication that Arendt's text also evinced. We can only speculate about what caused Shklar's outburst twenty years after the publication of *Eichmann in Jerusalem*, [42] and what prompted the change of heart between the elegiac tone of affection displayed in "Hannah Arendt's Triumph" and the strange glee with which the end of German-Jewry is announced in "Hannah Arendt as Pariah."

## Arendt and Shklar on Law, Constitution, and Revolution

While Shklar's reflections on *Eichmann in Jerusalem* did not throw much light on the problems of international law and international jurisdiction, her considerations of Arendt's *On Revolution* are both apt and further illuminate the nexus of law and politics for both thinkers. Unlike most commentators, Shklar had a very precise sense that the kind of historical writing Arendt engaged in was not a mere exercise in nostalgia, but a form of what Nietzsche had called "monumental history." She wrote: "At its best, monumental history is addressed to political actors, to remind them that great deeds were performed by notable men and that what was once feasible is at least possible again. The past is presented as a storehouse of politically useful knowledge which one ignores at one's peril."[43] Shklar proposed to read Arendt's *On Revolution* as an exercise in monumental history, as a search for the lost treasure of revolutions. Every act of founding contains within itself the danger that future generations will cease to respect it and act by it. The arbitrariness of the founding has two dimensions: first, "it does not depend on any prior rules for justification. Its principle is its own justification ... It is, second, arbitrary not only normatively, it is also an unforeseeable and irregular interruption of the ordinary course of history and political life."[44]

This fear of arbitrariness is at the source of Arendt's much-disputed contrast between the American and the French Revolutions: the French revolutionaries, who thought they were establishing a new Rome, were caught in the destructive dynamic of the *assemblé constituant* (constituting) and *assemblé constitué* (constituted assemblies). When the will of the nation, as the constitut*ing* assembly, was seen as the source of all power and of the legitimacy of law, there were no ropes to bind Ulysses to the mast and to resist the call of the sirens—to recall here Jon Elster's famous argument about Ulysses and the sirens.[45] Instead, an unstoppable set of challenges would unfold as a consequence of which the authority of each constituting moment would be destabilized by the search for a yet more originary and foundational moment that preceded it. How could the will of the people be most sincerely and authentically represented? Arendt's condemnation of Robespierre's appeal to the suffering masses and his claim to be the only one to truly represent them are well known.[46] She thought that it was a matter of historical contingency and the good luck of the American revolutionaries that they were not, in the first place, representatives of the "nation" as such but of the thirteen colonies in whose name they first signed the Declaration of Independence. This institutional contingency was one factor that permitted them to avoid the destructive "ricorso" of founding and refounding that the French revolutionaries got caught in.[47] Shklar was less sanguine that the tension between tradition and revolution, founding and authority could ever be resolved.

Aspects of Arendt's reading of revolutions, particularly her interpretation of the American political experience, baffled Shklar, whose last book on *American Citizenship. The Quest for Inclusion*[48] is in many ways a belated answer to Arendt's *On Revolution*. Instead of marginalizing the plight of African American slaves in the new republic, as Arendt had done, Shklar places the injustice of slavery and the wounds it has inflicted on the meaning of American citizenship at the very center of her analysis. By arguing that the status of being a wage-earner and a job holder is just as fundamental to the public identity of Americans as their participation in the public happiness of political life, she shows that, as the first modern civil society in the bourgeois period, the American republic from its inception combined the socioeconomic question with the political one.[49] Against Arendt, Shklar is claiming that economic justice and economic equality, political independence and participation cannot and should not be separated.

Whereas for Shklar the law was irretrievably and thoroughly political, Arendt operated with two models of law in her work, one of which sought to shield the law from the destructive dynamics of the political, and the other, which acknowledged their intertwinement. This distinction is often summarized with the terms *nomos* and *lex*. In *The Human Condition* she likened the law (*nomos*) to the fences and the walls drawn around the city that first made politics at all possible.[50] The purpose of the law was to unite as well as to separate the members of the demos by defining the boundaries that demarcated the private from the public, the *oikos* from the *polis*. Arendt's strict separation in this work between the "private sphere of the household" and the "public sphere of the polis" is beset with tremendous conceptual difficulties—not the least of which are the consequences it has for the status of women.[51] Granted this, it would be a mistake to think that Arendt naturalized law's relation to politics, whereas Shklar thought that law was political all the way down. Arendt well knew that the founding act of the polity was a human act full of peril, and that the lawgivers of antiquity no less than the revolutionaries of the modern age had to encounter the risk that their authority would be rejected. Certainly with modernity and the "break in tradition," authority and tradition could no longer blend as they once had in Rome.[52] For Arendt as well as for Shklar, the law, on the one hand, framed the political and thus had to stand outside it, and on the other hand, the law was made possible by the political acts of humans joining together in contract, association, and promise.

Arendt and Shklar then do not disagree about the political character of law, but whereas Shklar is convinced that legalism and liberalism need to be reconnected in a disenchanted universe that has demystified the sources of law, Arendt searches for some element in the Western tradition, for some aspect of political experience, to give law solidity without ontologizing it. This is her *second* model of law that she finds in the Roman concept of *lex*, as distinguished from *nomos*, and originating with the word *ligare*, meaning "an intimate connection or relationship"; it later comes to mean contract. "Roman *lex*, makes intersubjective relationships among citizens and peoples the basis of law. . . . Through *lex*, political relationships are extended."[53] But *lex* is boundless; it does not set limits to the multiplicity of human associations that can be formed. If Carl Schmitt's concept of *nomos* is caught in the pseudo-concreteness of suggesting that law emerges from an original relation to the land, *lex* suggests a dizzying possibility of alliances, misalliances, promise-keeping and breaking, harmony and strife. For Arendt, what stabilizes the boundlessness of action is the creation of institutions, the binding of the will toward the future, that is, the project of *constitutio libertatis*. Successful revolutions initiate a *novus ordo saeclorum*; they make possible a new world of human affairs within which action can now unfold. For her, as for Shklar, neither nature nor historical development can guarantee such success. The stability of good institutions is always fragile. Political philosophy, either as the retrieval of past treasures, which Arendt considered herself to be engaged in, or as the practice of a historian of ideas bent on demystification, as Shklar thought herself to be doing, can offer no future guarantees.

Arendt and Shklar distance themselves from the natural law tradition as well as from legal positivism. Whereas Arendt attempts to place the law in the context of her theory of the human condition—plurality, action and the need to build lasting institutions—Shklar does not entrench the law in any broader understanding of human capabilities. For both, good law and sound legal institutions are the preconditions of decent politics. Although she leaves the relationship of liberalism to legalism somewhat tenuous, and remarks that legalism has also been used by authoritarian systems as an instrument of control (*Legalism*, 57; 119–21), Shklar insists that justice and equality go hand in hand—though not without conflict.[54] Arendt's concern is with containing or binding the originary violence inherent in the founding moment of polities such that the *demos* as a new *polis* can sublimate this violence through a promise to bind its will into the future.[55]

Judith Shklar was too much of a skeptic to extend her "liberalism of fear" into a civic-republican understanding of public autonomy, although she greatly respected the refounding of political liberalism, which John Rawls's work signified.[56] Arendt, on the other hand, defended civic republican autonomy, but never analyzed why law was a central medium through which public reason had to be articulated in modern constitutional democracies. Shklar had a clear and unblinkered sense of how and why sheer legalism could go wrong and of how and why it could never be a substitute for democratic engagement. These themes would emerge in her later books such as *The Faces of Injustice* and *American Citizenship*. Her early book, *Legalism*, however, remains exemplary to the extent that she would outline sharply the illusions of the rule of law, when understood as if it were a neutral and self-standing system, removed from politics. Yet she never doubted that the integrity of the rule of law must be upheld and that its practitioners must fight for the values internal to its meticulous exercise, as she believed to have been the case in the Nuremberg trials, for example.

A passage from Robert Post captures in pithy terms the interdependence of law and politics that Shklar may have been aiming at.

> Politics and law are thus two distinct ways of managing the inevitable social facts of agreement and disagreement. As social practices, politics and law are both independent and interdependent. They are independent in the sense that they are incompatible. To submit a political controversy to legal resolution is to remove it from the political domain; to submit a legal controversy to political resolution is to undermine the law. Yet they are interdependent in the sense that law requires politics to produce the shared norms that law enforces, whereas politics requires law to stabilize and entrench the shared values the politics strives to achieve.[57]

## Obligation, Loyalty, and Exile

In the last years of her life, Shklar was preparing a course on obligation and exile to be offered under the rubric of "Moral Reasoning" in Harvard's core curriculum.[58] She had given lectures on this topic at various American universities and was gearing up for a series of lectures to be

offered in Cambridge, England, in fall 1992 before her wholly unexpected death on September 17. It is, of course, fascinating that at this
point in her life Shklar would return to themes that had such autobiographical resonance for her. The two essays she published on these topics do not deal with the personal dimension explicitly.[59] Shklar begins
by expressing her dissatisfaction with two kinds of approaches to political obligation that had dominated contemporary discussion in political
theory: the one discussion parsed distinctions between universalistic
morality and legal attachments; the second was a spin-off of discussions
concerning the Civil Rights Movement and the Vietnam War and focused on conscientious objection ("OLE," 39). Neither approach satisfied Shklar because it was the conflict of loyalties that was of most interest to her. She proceeded to differentiate between obligation,
commitment, loyalty, allegiance, and fidelity ("OLE," 40).

Obligation is "rule-governed conduct" referring to laws and law-like
demands made by public authorities ("OLE," 40). Moral and political
quandaries, however, do not arise at this level: it is only when one's
"chosen obligations," that is one's commitments, begin to come into
conflict with other unchosen attachments that significant conflicts
emerge. Loyalty is understood as "attachment to a social group," in
which membership may or may not be chosen. "And when it comes to
race, ethnicity, caste, and class, choice is not obvious. The emotional
character of loyalty sets it apart from obligation" ("OLE," 41). Fidelity,
like loyalty, has an affective dimension and is owed to individuals such
as family members, friends, and lovers. While commitment is the
most general category to describe these attachments, "allegiance"
stands between fidelity and loyalty; it can be owed to abstract symbols
such as a flag ("OLE," 43). There are not only conflicts between these
various types of human attachments, but there may be contradictions
embedded within each of them, such as when family and friends to
whom one is loyal may have their own conflicts and one is caught
in-between.

Conflict between loyalty and obligation is most characteristic of the
age of nationalism, when state and nationality do not coincide, as they
rarely do ("OLE," 44). Since it is hardly to be expected that modern

states would ever be so homogeneous ethnically, linguistically, or in terms of religion or ideology, such conflicts of attachments were bound to increase in the age of modern nation-states. By examining the fate of exiles, one may gain some understanding of the conflicts inherent in such multiple loyalties. Admitting that she despairs ever of "completing her list" of what makes an exile, Shklar nonetheless ventures to define an "exile as someone who involuntarily leaves the country of which he or she is citizen. Usually it is thanks to political force, but extreme poverty may be regarded as a form of coercive expulsion" ("OLE," 45). Two of the most famous exiles of antiquity were Themistocles and Aristides; coming to the modern period, one needs to recall Captain Dreyfus ("OLE," 48), Willie Brandt ("OLE," 51), Japanese Americans ("OLE," 49), and German Jews ("OLE," 50).

It is fascinating that in her discussion of modern exiles, Shklar confirms the grounds for being entitled to refugee status as defined by the Geneva Conventions. As noted above, the five designated categories in the Convention are race, religion, nationality, membership of a particular social group, or political opinion.[60] The convention refugee, much as in Shklar's analysis of the exile, was principally modeled after the political dissident, the prisoner of conscience, and the resistance fighter. Clearly, the vast majority of German Jews and Japanese Americans, who were persecuted on the basis of ascriptive grounds rather than consciously chosen allegiances or political opposition, would not fit this model; yet, the line between exile and refugee is often porous. Acknowledging this, Shklar writes, "The dreadful reality of our world is that no one wants to accept this huge exiled population. What they need is a place to go, and these are increasingly hard to find" ("OLE," 51). Noting that the "pieds noirs"[61] from North Africa can return home, much like the Jews the world over who may go to Israel if they so choose, Shklar observes that this is not the case for the vast majority of the world's exiled populations ("OLE," 52). After more than a quarter of century of exposure to the worldwide refugee problem and a better understanding (so one hopes) of its causes, Shklar's words strike us in their lack of the right tonality: "The dwellers in refugee camps can best be compared to America's African slaves. And as we look on helplessly at the *ever-growing number of human refuse heaps,* we might perhaps listen to the voice of conscience" ("OLE," 52; my emphasis).

Shklar was too astute a student of history not to recognize that this analogy between African American slaves and contemporary refugees was wrong as discussed in chapter 6 above, but she, like Arendt, whom she invokes once more in these last pages, believes that refusing human beings membership in a polity because they speak a different language, practice a different language, or belong to a different race or ethnicity perpetrates gross injustice. "Offering citizenship to exiles may prove the most significant means of taming political loyalty" ("OLE," 54), she observes. And while it is hard to believe that the world can ever reach a modus vivendi such that many will not have to seek refuge in other lands, "nevertheless, the less injustice there is, the less likely it is that refugees will populate the world and bring with them their *terrible misery and mischief*" ("OLE," 55; my emphasis).[62] Shklar's language about exiles and refugees vacillates between moral compassion for their lot and hardheaded realism about the sheer vulnerability of the refugee condition in a world of recalcitrant politics.

Andreas Hess concludes that, "Shklar's academic career and work can indeed be explained by Shklar's self-image and interpretation of having been a particular kind of refugee. Furthermore, the suggestion here is that Shklar developed and actively promoted a certain habitus of and view that have their roots in her experience of exile and emigration. Her self-perception as being self-made and searching for intellectual independence and impartiality clearly had their roots in that early experience."[63]

Having arrived at Harvard at the age of twenty-one and staying until her death, Shklar enjoyed great stability and academic eminence; yet it is as if that long and perilous journey from Riga to Sweden, then across Siberia to Japan, on to New York and finally to Montréal, Canada, left its traces in her writings, which continued to ponder the human conditions of fear and cruelty, exile and marginalization.

# 8

# Exile and Social Science

## ON ALBERT HIRSCHMAN

IT IS OFTEN NOTED that in natural as well as the social sciences certain explanatory paradigms win out over their rivals because of their simplicity and elegance. Surely, "exit" and "voice" belong among the most elegant pairs of concepts in the social sciences along with "Gemeinschaft and Gesellschaft" (Tönnies); "mechanical" and "organic" solidarity (Durkheim); "instrumental" and "value" rational action (Weber); and "honor" versus "respect" (Bernard Williams). As with any binarism, they can easily be scrambled and their contrasting lines can be erased. Yet once they are formulated, their force in enabling us to grasp the social world remains. The real work of conceptual analysis must then focus on the third term that has been omitted or repressed. It is to Hirschman's credit that he complicated the exit versus voice binarism with the third—"loyalty." If "exit" falls to the domain of the economist and "voice" is more in the purview of the political scientist, "loyalty" flows into cultural sociology, anthropology, religious studies, and psychoanalysis. Together with Clifford Geertz, Quentin Skinner, and other colleagues who were gathered in the Institute for Advanced Studies in the late 1970s and 1980s, Albert Hirschman came to call this approach "interpretive social science."[1]

In *Exit, Voice, and Loyalty* Albert Hirschman wrote: "the image of the economy as a fully competitive system where changes in the fortunes of individual firms are *exclusively* caused by basic shifts of comparative advantage is surely a defective representation of the real world" (my emphasis).[2] He was being polite: the real world is not populated by rational actors in the marketplace alone seeking to increase their marginal utility or competitive advantage, as neoclassical models of economics would have us believe. In associations such as the family, the state, and religious, civic, and professional institutions, loyalty dominates and often trumps exit in favor of voice; in many cases of economic behavior, as well, "[the] voice option is the only way in which dissatisfied customers or members can react whenever the exit option is unavailable" (EVL, 33). "Exit" means leaving behind a product, a service, a firm, or a country to seek others, whereas "voice" refers to the choice to seek influence and have a say in determining the future quality of products or institutions. Often loyalty tips the balance in favor of staying and seeking a voice rather than exiting.

Exit for Hirschman is rational behavior and closely parallels what Judith Shklar had called "obligation" in her essay on "Obligation, Loyalty, and Exile." Obligation is rule-governed conduct, referring to compliance with laws and law-like demands ("OLE," 40). Moral and political quandaries arise when one's chosen obligations, that is one's commitments, come into conflict with other, unchosen, attachments. Loyalty, for both Shklar and Hirschman, signifies affective attachment, but whereas Shklar understands it as "attachment to a social group," in which membership may or may not be chosen ("OLE," 41), for Hirschman loyalty is a more abstract form of attachment that may involve commitment to a product or even a brand name.

Albert Hirschman knew about exit, the search for voice, and the conflicts of loyalties first-hand through his eventful life and travels. As he wrote: "Crossing boundaries is not only characteristic of the physical moves I have undertaken (or had to undertake) in the course of my life; it is also distinctive of the interdisciplinary travels I have engaged in ever since I started to write."[3] Indeed, "Hirschman's life was a personal history of the twentieth century," observes Jeremy Adelman,[4] but it was also a life of intense political commitment and activism that transmuted itself into relentless reformism with the passage of time. Hirschman was interested in social science as a form of moral inquiry, or in his words, he dreamt of "a 'social science for our grandchildren,'" a social science that would be worth bequeathing to future generations.[5]

## Crossing Borders, Crossing Boundaries

Otto Albert Hirschmann was born to a well-to-do Jewish family in Berlin in 1915 and was named after Otto von Bismarck, when the nationalist euphoria over the German Reich's military triumphs had not yet been dimmed by its defeat in 1918. His family thoroughly shared in the illusions of Germany's assimilated Jewry, some of them converting to Christianity to enable their social mobility and professional acceptance. In Amos Elon's touching phrase, they had not yet experienced "The Pity of It All."[6] The young Albert refused Christian confirmation and became politicized as an adolescent through the influence of his older sister Ursula, who had already declared herself a communist. His sister married the Italian socialist Eugenio Colorni (1909–44), of the *Socialismo liberale* movement, who become one of the greatest intellectual influences upon Hirschman's life. *Exit, Voice, and Loyalty* is dedicated to the memory of Colorni, who was killed in Rome by a Nazi ambush in 1944.

Not only his sister, but many of his teachers in Berlin's distinguished "Französisches Gymnasium," which he attended for nine years in the 1920s, were dedicated socialists and communists, soon introducing Hirschman to the works of Hegel, Marx, and Lenin. His immersion in French language and education gave him quite a different orientation than that of Arendt, Horkheimer, and Adorno. Unlike Arendt, who defended her attachment to the German language with the phrase "Die Sprache ist ja nicht verrückt geworden" ("language has not become insane"),[7] and as distinguished from Adorno and Horkheimer, whose unique philosophical idiom remained that of German idealism, Hirschman felt that "the German language may have been his mother tongue (*Muttersprache*), but it was not his home (*Heimat*)."[8] In April 1933, after his father's death and after Berlin was rocked by anti-Semitic violence, the eighteen-year-old Hirschman left for France with his sister, not to return until decades later.[9]

Paris in the interwar years was teeming with refugees, militants, and expatriates of all political stripes. Arendt and Walter Benjamin were there; as were white Russians such as Alexander Kojève, whose lectures on Hegel electrified a generation of French intellectuals, including Jean-Paul Sartre, Simone de Beauvoir, and Maurice Merleau-Ponty. They were soon joined by others fleeing Mussolini's fascism. Still others, such as Rafael Abramovitch Rein, who had been a leader of the Russian Workers Social Democratic Party in exile, had escaped Stalin's henchmen. Subsequently employed as a journalist for the American *Jewish Daily Forward*, Rein acted as a surrogate father figure for Hirschman for some years. These groups formed that "other Europe" of the antifascist resistance, which remained "uprooted from country but loyal to cause," in Adelman's words.[10]

Between 1935 and 1938, Hirschman shuttled across four countries, crossing borders in and out of France, Italy, Great Britain, and Spain. From July to October 1936 he fought in the Spanish Civil War near Barcelona, an experience that left him not only with physical but also with deep psychological wounds; to the very end of his life, he refused to talk about this even with his wife Sarah Chapiro, a Lithuanian-Jewish and French-educated refugee. While others reacted to the pain and losses suffered by the European Left after the defeat of the Spanish Civil War, with phrases such as "darkness at noon" (Arthur Koestler) or "like a tear in the Ocean" ("Wie eine Träne im Ozean" by Manès Sperber"), the twenty-three-year-old Hirschman would simply say "Lascia perdere" ("let it go"), presaging that mixture of pragmatism and principle that was to characterize his entire life.[11]

The last episode of Hirschman's dramatic life on the European continent came when, after returning from Spain in 1938, he was drafted the following year into the French army to fight for a short period against Germany before France surrendered to Hitler in the summer of 1940. Assuming the pseudonym of Albert Herman upon being discharged from the French army on August 14, 1940, Hirschman met the young Harvard-educated classicist, Varian Fry, who had come to Europe on behalf of the Emergency Rescue Committee.[12] Walter Benjamin had just committed suicide in the coastal Spanish town of Port Bou while waiting for papers to transit to Portugal. Together, Fry and Hirschman spent a year preparing the departures of famous refugees. Hirschman himself was not among the luminaries, but eventually the Rockefeller Foundation gave him a passage on the SS *Excalibur* and a travel allowance to reach the University of California at Berkeley, where he was to study on a fellowship under Jack Condliffe. This was his fourth or fifth emigration; even he was not sure anymore. The passage to America ended with his name change: Otto Albert Hirschmann became Albert O. Hirschman.

Hirschman left Europe with formidable intellectual skills: Not only was he fluent in German, French, English, Italian, and Spanish but he had studied some law in Germany, administrative sciences and statistics in France's College of Commercial Studies in Paris (HEC), and economics at the London School of Economics in 1936, where he became familiar with the works of Keynes and Hayek. He also had a lifelong fascination with Flaubert, Dostoevsky, Montaigne, Montesquieu, and Machiavelli. This cross-disciplinary erudition and orientation makes it understandable why Hirschman never felt comfortable with the self-congratulatory inanities of so-called "post-ideological" American social science and its facile search for grand paradigms and models. In an article called "The Search for Paradigms as a Hindrance to Understanding,"[13] he criticized in strong language a certain cognitive style in the social sciences. "I believe that the countries of the Third World," he wrote, "have become fair game for the model-builders and paradigm-molders, to an intolerable degree" ("The Search for Paradigms," 335). He accused such social science not only of intellectual vacuity but also of presenting those countries as "constantly impaled on the horns of some fateful and unescapable dilemma" ("The Search for Paradigms," 336). Before he set out of "provincialized" European[14] and American thinking about the developing world, and emigrated with his family in 1952 to Colombia for a number of years, Hirschman participated in one of the great utopian projects of European socialism, which was to bear fruit only after the devastations of World War II.

## The Dreams of European Federalism

Hirschman entered "that neglected, ravaged space between the romance of revolution and the firmament of reaction,"[15] in Adelman's elegant words, with his first book, *National Power and the Structure of Foreign Trade*.[16] Reflecting on Germany's imperial economic designs toward Central and Eastern Europe and Italy's toward Ethiopia, he examined how strong states manipulated trade to bolster state power at the expense of weak states; "the breakdown of the world system and the clash between big blocs was hardly an irrational, nationalist pathology,"[17] and greater global integration did not check such behavior by making countries more interdependent. Hirschman then advanced an idea far ahead of its time—and this would not be the only occasion when he displayed a seer-like capacity to anticipate what was necessary in the future while resisting facile predictions. The only way to achieve peace and welfare in Europe and beyond, he argued, was "by a frontal attack upon the institution which is at the root of the possible use of international economic relations for national power aims—the institution of national economic sovereignty."[18] He advocated that "the exclusive power to organize, regulate, and interfere with trade must be taken away from the bonds of single nations," and turned over to "consular services," "chambers of commerce," and "export-import banks."[19]

In establishing clear connections between military aggression and foreign trade that went far beyond the standard leftist belief that capitalism necessarily led to imperialism, Hirschman argued for a new model of national sovereignty. His interest was in making European currencies transferable among one another and he began "drafting a project for a European central bank and currency."[20] Only after the devastation of the European continent through World War II would Europeans take a first step in this direction in April 1948 with the establishment of the OEEC (Organization for European Economic Co-operation.)

For Hirschman, working on the reconstruction of postwar Europe was a moral as well as political debt he owed to his Italian socialist friends from his Paris days. That unique blend of political liberalism and socialism first articulated by the Italian theorist Carlo Rossi, inspired

Eugenio Colorni, Altiero Spinelli (Hirschman's sister Ursula's second husband), and Ernesto Rossi to work together on a manifesto for a post-bellum Europe while some were still in prison in fascist Italy. Smuggled out of the prison on Ventotene Island by Rossi's wife, the Ventotene Manifesto envisaged a postwar Europe that would be not just a league of states but also a supra-national federation of European peoples.

The Ventotene Manifesto (Manifesto di Ventotene), entitled "For a Free and United Europe. A Draft Manifesto" ("Per un'Europa libera e unita. Progetto d'un manifesto"), soon became the official statement of the European Federalist Movement (Movimento Federalista Europeo) and called for a break with Europe's nationalist past through a restruc-turing of its political and economic institutions.[21]

The Manifesto begins by declaring that freedom is the principle of modern civilization and that the "equal right of all nations to organize themselves into independent states" (Article I, subsection a), was for a while "a powerful stimulus to progress." The formation of nation-states enabled freedom from foreign oppression, the consolidation of demo-cratic institutions, and the growth of solidarity among citizens. In the current situation of Europe, however, the Manifesto declares, "the na-tion has become a divine entity, an organism which must only consider its own existence, its own development, without the least regards for the damage that others may suffer from this. The absolute sovereignty of national States has led to the desire of each of them to dominate, since each feels threatened by the strength of the others, and considers that its 'living space'[22] should include increasingly vast territories that give it the right to free movement and provide self-sustenance without needing to rely on others." Under these circumstances, the state has turned from being "the guardian of the citizen's freedom" into "a master of vassals bound in servitude." Totalitarian states have succeeded in cen-tralizing all social and economic forces to pursue their dreams of domi-nation and autarky. The Manifesto condemns the "privileged classes" of Europe for aiding and abetting the rise of dictatorships after WWI, and ridicules the belief in "race" as a scientifically bogus concept. The au-thors claim that the Nazi "pseudo-science of geopolitics" was created to prove the soundness of imperialist theories about living space, but they observe that "because of the economic interdependence of the entire world, the living space required by any people which wants to maintain a living standard consistent with modern civilization can only be the entire world" (Article I, subsection c).

Looking ahead to the defeat of Nazi Germany and its allies after the war, the authors begin part 2 of the Manifesto with the observation that "the defeat of Germany would not automatically lead to the reorganization of Europe in accordance with our ideal of civilization" (part 2, "Post-War Tasks. European Unity"). The privileged classes of the old national systems will dampen feelings and passions of internationalism, while the British leaders, probably in agreement with the Americans, will advocate a "balance-of-power" politics, while anarchists and some socialists will call for "a constituent assembly," and communists will pursue the dream of the triumph of the proletariat, exhibiting various degrees of loyalty or distance from Russia. Revealing their own technocratic and antipopulist biases, at one point the authors write with reference to the ideals of constituent assemblies: "During revolutionary times, when institutions are not simply to be administered but created, democratic procedures fail miserably. The pitiful impotence of democrats in the Russian, German, Spanish revolutions are the three most recent examples" (part 2).

What is to be done then? The Manifesto lists a number of measures that Hirschman, working for the American government for the reconstruction of postwar Europe, would find thoroughly congenial: i. the definitive abolition of Europe into national, sovereign states; ii. the recognition that it is impossible to maintain a balance of power among European states while militarist Germany is on an equal footing with other countries; nor, however, can Germany be broken up into pieces; iii. German dominance in Europe; the fears of smaller countries of losing their independence (the Balkan question, the Irish problem, etc.) are "matters which would find easy solutions in the European federation"; iv. the United States of Europe "can only be based on the republican constitution of federated countries";[23] v. in order to constitute a steady federal state, this Europe must have at its disposal a "European armed service instead of national armies"; vi. nonetheless, "each state will retain the autonomy it needs for a plastic articulation[24] and development of political life according to the particular characteristics of various peoples."

We know now, with the privilege of more than seventy years of hindsight, that none of this was as easy as the authors had imagined it to be. The European Union is still poised in an uneasy tension between the idea of a federal state of Europe and a "post-national" sovereign entity, in which aspects of national sovereignty have been disaggregated but also reassembled in novel ways.[25] There is no "European army"; instead there is a European border guard, operating through FRONTEX, whose main purpose is to control and prevent migrants and refugees from crossing into Europe's borders. (See chapter 6 above.)

Nonetheless, the authors of the Ventotene Manifesto were right that some form of post-national European federalism was the only way to guarantee peace and prosperity, respect for human rights and dignity, social justice and solidarity in post-World War II Europe. They may have been wrong in the details, but their general vision is quite consistent with the principles of today's European Union.[26]

## Between Reform and Revolution: Out of Europe

Given his continuing, intense engagement with Europe, where he was even stationed as an American soldier and interpreter from 1944 to 1945, it is surprising that Hirschman's life would pivot so radically at one point and take him and his young family away from Europe and North America to Colombia where they would spend the next ten years. Ironically, Hirschman turned to Latin America because his leftist European past shadowed his Washington career and scuttled his desires to move from the Federal Reserve to the Treasury Department. Gripped by growing anticommunist hysteria, the Treasury's Enforcement Agency was unable to clear him for security, and eventually it came to light that he had fought on the side of the socialists and against communists in Spain. Yet these shadings of red and pink in young Hirschman's life as a member of the European left were too subtle for bureaucrats in Washington to untangle, so in 1952 the Hirschmans left for Colombia.

His engagement with Central America, and then all of Latin America, and eventually India and Africa, inspired Hirschman's major theoretical contributions not only to development economics, but also to political sociology, social psychology, and cultural anthropology. *The Strategy of Economic Development*, first published in 1958 and translated into ten languages, took issue with the dominant orthodoxies of his day by arguing against "pathologizing backwardness."[27] At the time, "balanced growth" perspectives prevailed among economists as well as think-tank specialists and development entrepreneurs, who had a strong preference for investments in mega-projects such as ports, roads, and power grids. Hirschman, by contrast, was interested in investments in those sectors of a country's economy that seemed at first invisible or even insignificant. He favored investments that would promote people's capacity to solve problems in a capitalist world, and the ability to make development decisions. He wrote: "Development theory and practice therefore face the task of examining under what conditions development decisions can be called forth in spite of these imperfections, through pacing devices or inducement mechanisms."[28]

In his 1994 preface to *Development Projects Observed*, he described the intellectual atmosphere in the US Department of Defense, under the leadership of Robert McNamara and his "Whiz Kids," who by defining the allocation of funds for various purposes by the use of an acronym, PPBS (Planning, Programming, and Budgeting System), tried to create a "technocratic aura." [29] He called his book something of a "spoilsport" ("Hidden Ambition," 128). He also admitted that the chapter in "The Principle of the Hiding Hand," in *Development Projects Observed*, was "close to a provocation,"[30] because it seemed so operationally useless. Yet he had a hidden agenda: "to endow and surround the development story with a sense of wonder and mystery that would reveal it to have much in common with the highest quests ever undertaken by humankind" ("Hidden Ambition," 129).

This sense of "wonder and mystery" about development projects never left Hirschman. Revisiting the idea of development economics in a later essay, he observed how the orthodoxies of neoclassical economics and neo-Marxist theories mirrored each other.[31] The neoclassical approach claimed that economics consisted of simple yet universally valid theorems under which participation in a market economy would benefit all participants, be they individuals or countries, and that trade and increased exchange between developed and underdeveloped economies would be to the advantage of the latter.

Neo-Marxist economics, by contrast, claimed that exploitation and "unequal exchange" were an essential and permanent feature of relations between the developed center and the underdeveloped periphery; consequently, the economic structure of these countries and their path to development could not follow the same pattern of industrialization under capitalist auspices.[32] Hirschman notes that Marx's own thoughts "on this latter topic are notoriously complex," in that some of them seem to endorse a single evolutionary pattern of development where the industrially developed countries present to the less developed ones the image of their own future. At other times, Marx admits that different paths of the emergence of market relations and industrialization are possible, and that in fact the path to socialism for some countries may be that of avoiding the capitalist commodity market altogether.[33]

Hirschman observes that orthodox economics were deeply challenged by the Keynesian revolution, which showed that neoclassical models held only when there was full employment but not when there was substantial unemployment or underemployment of human and material resources. One consequence of Keynesianism was that the gulf between underdeveloped economies, which suffered from *rural underemployment*, and developed economies, which created *industrial unemployment*, was not as radical as it seemed. There were inefficiencies in both cases.

Hirschman argued that "underdeveloped countries did have hidden reserves, not only of labor, savings, entrepreneurship, and maybe other resources as well. But to activate them, Keynesian remedies would be inadequate. What was needed were 'pacing devices' and 'pressure mechanisms'; whence my strategy of unbalanced growth."[34] A consequence of this manner of considering development and underdevelopment would be that "our understanding of the economic structures of the West will have been modified and enriched by the foray into other economies" ("Rise and Decline," 9). In this evolution of scientific ideas and models, there would be a "dialectical reversal" in that the *otherness* of the *other* would be reversed through the discovery that our own group was not all that different. Reflecting on the emergence of murderous fascist and authoritarian regimes in Latin America in the 1970s, Hirschman noted how in this respect they were not all that different from developments that had devastated Europe throughout the 1930s. He concluded cannily: "Given what was seen as their overwhelming problem of poverty, the underdeveloped countries were expected to perform like wind-up toys and to 'lumber through' the various stages of development single-mindedly, their reactions to change were not to be nearly as traumatic or aberrant as those of the Europeans. . . . [O]nce again, we have learned otherwise."[35]

Hirschman's seminal ideas, such as the principle of the "Hidden Hand," began to emerge through these encounters. It is not easy to distinguish this principle clearly from Adam Smith's "Invisible Hand" or from Hayek's concept of the "unintended consequences of social action." Undoubtedly, Hirschman felt affinities to both. Yet what preoccupied him, explains Amartya Sen in his foreword to the twentieth anniversary edition of *The Passions and the Interests*, were not "unintended but realized effects," but rather the importance of "intended but *unrealized* effects" (my emphasis).[36]

The origins of this insight went back to a question that had haunted him since his travels in Nigeria: why did Nigerian railways perform so poorly in the face of competition from trucks, even for the transport of peanuts grown some eight hundred miles away from the ports?[37] Hirschman made the counterintuitive observation that the presence of competition in this case meant that the weaknesses of the railroad system would lead many to exit rather than fight against it through voicing grievances. The *intended effect* of the construction of the railroad system was to attain *efficiency* by shifting away from the trucking system; instead, the *unintended* effect was the continuing presence of trucking and the overlooking and indulgence of the railroad's inefficiencies by government managers. The explanatory paradigm of the "Hidden Hand" needed to focus on the *intended but unrealized* effects in many development projects, which, it would turn out, were not always as detrimental as in the particular case of the Nigerian railroad system!

Hirschman explains: "In Nigeria, then, I had encountered a situation where the combination of exit and voice was particularly noxious for any recovery: exit did not have its usual attention-focusing effect because the loss of revenue was not a matter of the utmost gravity for management, while voice did not work as long as the most aroused and therefore the potentially most vocal customers were the first ones to abandon the railroads for the trucks" (EVL, 45).

In a later work, Hirschman clarifies that his own principle of the "Hidden Hand," while sharing with many theorists of conservative and liberal thought an emphasis on the "unintended consequences of social action," distinguishes between "the unintended" and "the undesirable."[38] Not all unintended consequences of social action are undesirable; quite the opposite, some are quite welcome, such as the spread of male literacy through universal military service or women's chances of employment outside the home that were made possible by compulsory public education.[39]

## Exit, Voice, and the State: Confronting the Fate of the German Democratic Republic

Among the most impressive characteristics of Hirschman as a social and political thinker, besides his graceful capacity to cross the boundaries of the various social sciences, was his penchant for self-subversion.[40] He did not tire of questioning his own assumptions. It may have been an irony of fate that the most significant challenge to the exit versus voice binarism that complicated it considerably came from the fall of the Berlin Wall and the revolution in East Germany in 1989. "The events of 1989," he wrote, "were not experienced as stemming from an enigmatic turnabout in the functioning of social processes ... A problem arises only for the social scientist who seeks a deeper understanding and who, in the course of this attempt, fashions a conceptual framework that initially makes it easier, but subsequently can make it more complicated, to understand what is going on. In that case, of course, our analyst may still come out on top by showing how instructive it is that events should have diverged from the original scheme!"[41] Hirschman was referring to the fact that the exit option to West Germany by East German dissidents and opponents considerably complicated the exercise of voice, in that the Communist regime of East Germany had used exit as a safety valve to relieve pressure for changes on their system and regularly deported oppositional intellectuals to West Germany. But at one point, East German citizens themselves refused to leave—although they could—and started to build up an oppositional movement united around the slogan "Wir bleiben hier." ("We stay here.") The old socialist revolutionary, who had left Berlin as an adolescent, was clearly fascinated by these events in his partitioned homeland and even more by the way in which German scholars claimed that his exit/voice theory was being tested "experimentally on a large scale" by the upheaval in East Germany.[42]

The East German case complicated Hirschman's binarism not only politically but theoretically as well, because Hirschman himself had acknowledged in an earlier essay that he had paid more attention to economic activities and had dealt with the state only briefly in his famous book. Hence, "Exit, Voice, and Loyalty" needed to morph into "Exit, Voice, and the State,"[43] precisely because the state as an association was very different from the market or the firm. Two features of the modern state in particular stood out: territoriality and legitimacy. The modern state-form emerged with the "territorialization" of space, that is with the division of the face of the globe into domains of discrete political and jurisdictional authority. According to this so-called "Westphalian" model, the state is the highest authority with the jurisdiction to control all that is living and dead upon its territory. Historically, very few state forms reached the degree of centralization, coherence, and control that this model seemed to presuppose. In Stephen Krasner's famous words, "sovereignty is hypocrisy."[44] Nonetheless, unless we are dealing with completely failed states or states in conditions of civil war, such as in today's Iraq, Syria, and Afghanistan, exit from one state invariably implies entry into another. In the territorialized globe *emigration* and *im-*

*migration* are two sides of the same coin. One cannot *emigrate* from one country without *immigrating* into another. *Exit, voice, and loyalty* in the modern state are intricately linked with movement across borders.

*Legitimacy* signifies that the inhabitants of a state recognize the rightness of the central jurisdictional authority to demand their obedience and compliance. Such recognition may or may not imply loyalty: ethnic minorities may show such recognition, not because they are loyal, but because they have no other possibilities of exit into a state of their own. And if they see such options, they may engage in secessionist movements.[45]

In "Exit, Voice, and the State," Hirschman approaches these issues through his own unique and almost counterintuitive lens (at least to this reader). In the first part of the essay, he focuses on the "fissiparous politics" of societies without the state, also known in the anthropological literature as "acephalous," "segmentary lineage systems, "fission and fusion." Hirschman notes: "A large part of that literature deals with what in modern politics is known as 'secession' rather than as 'emigration.' In other words, the tendency toward fission frequently takes the form of a group detaching itself from a larger one while staying (or moving about, in the case of nomadic tribes) in the same area as before. The exit concept could, of course, be extended to cover cases of this sort."[46] Where such an exit option exists, "centralized societies with specialized state organs" cannot come into being. But what would be the relevance of this observation in a world with divided territories? How do the international laws, norms, and agencies regulating cross-boundary movements across states in the modern period affect the exit-voice-loyalty triad?

Hirschman's perspective on these issues is not that of the international lawyer or human rights theorist but has implications for both. With regards to the period of the absolutist European state system in the seventeenth and eighteenth centuries, he observes that monarchs, statesmen, and political philosophers from James Harrington to Sir James Steuart, to Montesquieu and Hume, were less obsessed by the emigration of their subjects than by capital flight or the flight of "moveable wealth." They generally perceived capital's mobility as a salutary restraint on arbitrary government (*EVS*, 99). "Today," observes Hirschman, "the mobility of capital is infinitely greater (within the capitalist world) than at the time of Montesquieu and Adam Smith" (*EVS*, 100). Not only can transnational corporations move their subsidiaries from one country to another; they can refuse to roll over the loans of countries they consider "out of line" (or in World Bank language, countries that may not accept "structural adjustment" programs) or they can engage in massive capital flight.

Politically, in the largest and most central countries of the capitalist center, flight occurs in response to threats of reforms in taxation and redistribution, but for these major players, observes Hirschman, "voice will be activated by the impossibility of exit" (*EVS*, 100). His examples are Victorian England and the United States of the twentieth century, where capitalism has acted as an "active problem-solver" (*EVS*, 101). In the more peripheral states, the absence of strong support for capitalism coexists with "difficulties at effective reform" (*EVS*, 101).

Certainly, it is hard to assess the extent to which these observations still hold in the age of neoliberal globalization, when the worldwide movement of financial assets and the dominance of financial over manufacturing capital are in the ascendancy. European and Canadian social democracies, along with the United Kingdom and other commonwealth countries such as Australia and New Zealand, seem to fit Hirschman's model better than the United States, where offshore investments and capital mobility have increased in the last decades to the detriment of investment in labor and resources at home. Could it be that not only the movability of capital but also that of labor needs to be taken into account in explaining some of these differences?

The final sections of "Exit, Voice, and the State" are devoted to problems of "outmigration," first in the nineteenth and later (and much more briefly) in the twentieth century. Emigration in the nineteenth century, unlike capital flight, was freely permitted since it alleviated economic as well as political problems. Hirschman observes: "the ships carrying the migrants contained many actual or potential anarchists and socialists, reformers and revolutionaries" (*EVS*, 102). Mass migration thus reduced social protest in the sender countries. But it also had a more counterintuitive consequence: "because a number of disaffected people had departed, it became comparatively safe to open up the system to a larger number of those who stayed on. In this manner, exit-emigration may have made it possible for democratization and liberalization to proceed in several countries prior to World War I without political stability being seriously imperiled" (*EVS*, 102). Bringing this observation to the realities of the mid-1970s in Europe, Hirschman notes himself how counterintuitive it is that "the likelihood that opening the gates and permitting outmigration may allow a regime to liberalize itself" (*EVS*, 103). Still he wonders whether the emigration of Greek, Portuguese, and Spanish workers to France and Germany during the 1960s and 1970s may not have had made it easier for these countries to negotiate a passage to democracy.[47]

## Hirschman as a Political Theorist

Fortuitous and unpredictable constellations of events and human actions continued to fascinate Hirschman. Turning to the history of ideas about the emergence of capitalism, he produced *The Passions and the Interests. Political Arguments for Capitalism before Its Triumph*.[48] An elegant essay in the history of ideas of seventeenth- and eighteenth-century thought, it sought to throw light on how the passions for monetary and commercial pursuits, once condemned as "cupidity," "avarice," and "ambition," were transformed into the ubiquitous concept of "interest" and freed from the language of moral opprobrium. When viewed as an inescapable aspect of human nature, these interests could not be eradicated; they could only be countered by other affects and interests. The idea of divided government and the separation of powers gained acceptance by "being presented as an application of the widely accepted and thoroughly familiar principle of countervailing passion" (*PI*, 30).

In his deep appreciation of Enlightenment ideals and through his subtle focus on the role that emotions and passions play in politics, Hirschman is closely allied with Judith Shklar. Like her, he shares a deep sense of irony and contingency about human affairs and, like her, remains committed to social progressive causes and is quite bemused by the follies of American politics. The rise of neoconservativism and continuing attacks on the welfare state in the United States led him to compose *The Rhetoric of Reaction: Perversity, Futility and Jeopardy*.[49] An unusual blend of intellectual history, social scientific observation, and political analysis, this book traces the origins of conservative thought back to the reactions of Edmund Burke, Joseph de Maistre, Gustav le Bon, Adam Muller, and others to the French Revolution. Hirschman deftly connects these reactions to Charles Murray's, Milton Friedman's, and the *Commentary* crowd's recent critique of the American welfare state. *Perversity* means that any action to improve socioeconomic and political life only worsens the conditions it seeks to remedy (*RR*, 7). The literature on the "dependency of the poor" created by the welfare state would be one such example. The conservative *futility* thesis holds that all such attempts are unavailing; they will change nothing. Those who consider the causes of poverty to be rooted in racial or genetic features of intelligence or group pathologies are likely to advocate the futility thesis. The *jeopardy* thesis argues that the cost of the proposed change or reform is too high as it endangers some previous accomplishment. Minimum wage laws, for example, may exacerbate unemployment pre-cisely among those groups that these laws most intended to protect.

Hirschman's goal was not simply to analyze the anatomy of conser-vativism, but to illuminate the "rhetorics of intransigence" (*RR*, 168). The jeopardy, futility, and perversity theses have their counterparts (and in many cases these forms of thought generated each other *as* counter-parts) in progressive thinking: To the *jeopardy* thesis, progressives jux-tapose belief in "synergy" and "mutual support" of reform proposals. Progressive thought espouses a world in which "all good things go to-gether" (*RR*, 151), and tragic trade-offs are not required. The conserva-tive *futility* thesis, based on belief in deep structures or immutable laws of motion of society, is mirrored precisely in Marxism, which also claims to have uncovered the "laws of motion of capitalist society" (*RR*, 157). The interplay between the progressive and conservative versions of the *perversity* thesis is even more subtle: If all human action to change social conditions results in making them worse, then future action is necessary precisely because of the desperate predicament that we find ourselves in: for the Left "the old order must be smashed and a new one rebuilt from scratch *regardless* of any counterproductive consequences that might ensue" (RR, 163; emphasis in the text). So the perversity thesis actually encourages an equally perverse politics of the apocalypse! Hirschman concludes on a coy note, hoping that his diagnosis of the weaknesses of progressive thought will not lose him many friends (RR, 164), who, he adds, are "long on moral indignation and short on irony" (RR, 165).

Hirschman died in 2012. By then his reputation was global and he had been showered with many accolades and awards as well as honored by conferences dedicated to his thought. His nobility of commitment as well as sobriety of vision are rare today: Our politics is mired in a sphere beyond "the rhetoric of intransigence," and in "murderous and rancorous contempt," to use his words, while many of our social science departments are bent on educating our students to be specialists and number crunchers, or "paradigm wielders," as he would have called them. The story of his life and work is edifying by showing not only how deep his political principles and moral dedication ran, but also by reminding us that political life, at its best, is based on summoning the "better angels of our nature," even though we must never lose that sense of irony about the unforeseen and the unexpected consequences that may defeat our efforts.

# 9

# Isaiah Berlin

## A JUDAISM BETWEEN DECISIONISM
## AND PLURALISM

UPON SIR ISAIAH BERLIN'S DEATH on November 5, 1997, Leon Wieseltier, one of the most influential editors of *The New Republic*, wrote an
encomium titled with the Talmudic saying, "When a Sage Dies, All Are
His Kin."[1] Wieseltier wrote elegiacally: "The pluralists are his kin, and
they must mourn"; "The rationalists are his kin, and they must mourn";
"The democrats are his kin, and they must mourn"; The nationalists are
his kin, and they must mourn"; finally, "The Jews were his kin, and they
must mourn."[2]

Commentators on Berlin's work—even those most sympathetic to
his best-known theses such as the inescapable plurality of human values, two kinds of liberty, and the hedgehog and the fox as styles of
thought—have not been quite so sanguine: Whether Berlin can reconcile all his kin despite his Talmudic skills remains a vexing question.[3]
The relationship of liberalism to Berlin's value pluralism remains
fraught, as does the question whether value pluralism can avoid
relativism.

Although his family migrated from Latvia to Russia in 1915, when he
was six years old and then to the United Kingdom in 1921, unlike "the
eternally half-others" (*der ewig halb-anderen*) discussed in this collection (see chapter 2 above) Isaiah Berlin was a migrant, but was neither
stateless nor an exile. If anything, he represents a superb example of

successful migration and integration. As Wieseltier observes, "Berlin was a creature of loyalties, and he expounded a critical philosophy of loyalty. He lived a dutiful, polycentric, generous, and unidolatrous life. 'I remain totally loyal to Britain, to Oxford, to liberalism, to Israel,' he remarked. He was, you might say, a rootful Jewish cosmopolitan, and so the most blessed of man."[4] Judith Shklar was closer to the truth when she wrote that conflict between loyalties is endemic and that if anything they would increase in the age of nation-states. (See chapter 7 above.) A seamless reconciliation of all these dimensions of one's identity was an illusion. In a review of Berlin's work Shklar stated: "If one cares, as Berlin so obviously does, about how one behaves as part of a group, about such values as loyalty and personal honour, then one must accept the fact that in actual life our moral choices are not un-limited and that we more often have to select nuances rather than bold aims."[5] She admits, however, that this "seems to have been implied [rather] than said" in Berlin's work ("Review of *Against the Current*," 35). Contrary to what Shklar recommended, Isaiah Berlin's views on value pluralism led him to articulate bold aims rather than nuances nor did he attain the reconciliation among his conflicting commitments that Wieseltier praised.

Shklar and Berlin admired each other and shared a skeptical tempera-ment as well as a dedication to the study of the history of ideas as the indispensable method of pursuing political philosophy in their time.[6] Both were haunted by political upheavals. The memory of the Social Democratic and Bolshevik revolutions in Russia never left Berlin, and Shklar returned time and again to the predicament of Weimar and the fragility of the legal and constitutional institutions of liberalism. Nei-ther shared Hannah Arendt's conviction that the legacy of failed revolu-tions could only be countered by the activist civic republicanism of self-governing communities. Shklar retained a respectful admiration for Arendt that appears to have worn thin with time, whereas, for reasons that still need to be fully explored, Berlin intensely disliked Arendt's work and persona and even seemed to hold her in contempt.[7]

Let me contextualize these conflicting views of Berlin's work and persona through the prism of Max Weber's doctrine of value pluralism.

I will distinguish Weber's "existentialist pluralism" from the "liberal value pluralism" of Berlin, and both from the "epistemic pluralism" of John Rawls, whose analysis of "the burdens of judgment" proposes some solutions to the puzzles of value pluralism and perspectival plurality that escaped both Arendt and Berlin.

## Max Weber on Disenchantment and Value Pluralism

The influence on Isaiah Berlin's thought of Max Weber's diagnosis of modernity as a process of disenchantment or *Entzauberung*, characterized by "warring gods" and an "inevitable polytheism," has been discussed by Steven Lukes as well as Peter Lassman. In "Isaiah Berlin in Conversation with Steven Lukes," Lukes asks: "There are other writers than yourself whom I could think of—for example Max Weber, or Nietzsche or Carl Schmitt, who have observed this clash between values but have drawn conclusions that are rather different than yours."[8] To which Berlin replies: "Let me tell you that I first have to admit to you something very shaming. When I first formulated this idea, which is a long time ago, I'd never read a page of Weber. I had no idea that he said these things. People often ask me, but surely Weber is the first person to say this. I answer that I am sure he is, but I had no idea of it" ("Conversations," 102). Peter Lassman remarks on this exchange with Lukes that, "One can excuse Berlin's lapse of memory here, but he seems on other occasions to have shown more awareness of Weber's work than he was prepared to admit."[9] Lassman recalls that in his 1969 introduction to his *Four Essays on Liberty* Berlin had remarked that "the classical—and still, it seems to me, the best—exposition of this state of mind [i.e. pluralism] is to be found in Max Weber's distinction between the ethics of conscience and the ethics of responsibility in 'Politics as a Vocation.'"[10]

It is interesting to note that Weber gave his lecture on January 28, 1919, "thirteen days after the murder of Karl Liebknecht and Rosa Luxemburg in Berlin and nine days after the election for the Constituent Assembly of the Weimar Republic, to an audience of liberal, patriotic students in Munich."[11] According to Eich and Tooze, with this lecture

"Weber did his best to deny any real historic significance to either the Russian or the German Revolutions, including the radical socialist government that still ruled in Munich itself."[12] Given this political and historical background, it is surely no coincidence that Berlin, who despised the Bolshevik and other revolutionaries as much as Max Weber did, would quote from this essay.

Regardless how much of Weber's work Berlin admitted to being familiar with, Weber's theory of disenchantment and polytheism is important as a heuristic device by which to explore Berlin's own views. By "disenchantment," Weber primarily meant the loss of magic, first achieved through the rise of the mathematical natural sciences in the sixteenth and seventeenth centuries.[13] As a result of these developments, our explanations of nature no longer needed recourse to mythological, cosmological, religious, or other doctrines. The loss of magic signified not only a change in methods and theories for explaining natural phenomena; it also signified the loss of the socially integrative power of worldviews based on religion, mythology, or cosmology, which had functioned as the legitimating glue of premodern societies. *Entzauberung* for Weber was a process of rationalization and differentiation; in fact, he often used the terms "rationalization" and "loss of magic" in the same breath.[14]

What did Weber mean by characterizing modernity not only as *Entzauberung* but also as a process of *Ausdifferenzierung*—differentiation?[15] Differentiation refers to *societal differentiation* as well as to *value differentiation*. Modernity brings about differentiation processes at the societal level, through the "disembedding"[16] of the economy from the household and the polity, occasioned with the shift from an agricultural peasant-based economy to a market-based and eventually industrialized commodity economy, including the sale and purchase of labor power as a commodity. Furthermore, with the separation of the economy from the polity comes the rise of an independent administrative staff in charge of affairs of state. The state bureaucracy is no longer compensated through the performances of personal services or via donations of land, labor, and other commodities such as grain, game, and agricultural products as tributes or tithes. The gradual monetization of relations of political authority and domination (*Herrschaft*) changes the nature of political legitimacy as well. There ensues a shift from personalistic to impersonal and bureaucratic modes of rule, which Weber names "legal-rational authority."[17]

For Weber, such developments only designated "ideal types" drawn with broad brushstrokes.[18] Historically, not even West European societies followed a single pattern of societal differentiation as outlined in this ideal type model. The United States, with its protestant and Calvinist-inspired capitalism and state-formation developing subsequent to markets and civil society, rather than preceding them as in Western Europe, exhibited an altogether different path to societal differentiation than Catholic Spain and even Germany in which market and civil society would take much longer to emancipate themselves from the power of the state.[19]

The path to value-differentiation is different from, though not unrelated to, societal differentiation. The intellectual developments of modernity not only bring about the rise of the mathematical sciences of nature, but with the spread of the prestige of this dominant intellectual paradigm, other fields of inquiry such as religion, ethics, aesthetics, and jurisprudence are obliged to question their own methods of inquiry and criteria of validation. Weber is an antipositivist to the extent that he does not believe that the new sciences of nature supply the only model of rational inquiry. He follows Kant and the neo-Kantian school of epistemology in arguing that every sphere of knowledge has certain presuppositions in accordance with which it is constituted.[20] For example, in the natural sciences we presuppose that—using Kant's phrase—"nature is the existence of things under laws," and that our explanations have the form of law-governed regularities. In the social sciences, according to Weber, no matter how distant from us in time and space they may be, we have to presuppose that we can understand the *meaningful course of human* action through the ideal reconstruction of a means-end relationship.[21] Even if a pattern of human action seems very strange and alien to us, as social scientists we have to assume that we can create a model for the explanation of such actions by imaginatively reconstructing what human agents seek to achieve through them, what their purposes and the means to attain such purposes are. Weber called this method *Verstehen* (explanatory understanding) as opposed to deductive and inductive reasoning and "nomothetic" explanations.[22]

Weber distinguished the cultural or human sciences (*die Geisteswissenschaften*)—what we would today call "the humanities," such as philosophy, history, and the history of art, music, theatre, and film—from the natural as well as social sciences. In these fields our object of inquiry is not social action alone; rather, we presuppose that culture *as such* is valuable and that any aspect of the universe can become interesting and culturally significant as long as human beings attribute some meaning and value to it. As Weber writes: "The concept of culture is a *value-concept*. Empirical reality becomes "culture" to us because and insofar as we relate it to value-ideals ... We cannot discover, however, what is meaningful to us by means of 'presuppositionless' investigation of empirical data."[23]

These Kantian assumptions about the constitution of separate value spheres led Weber to argue that under conditions of modernity, differentiation would result in a polytheism of values; or, in the dramatic terms of "Science as a Vocation," the war of "competing gods": "Many old gods ascend from their graves; they are disenchanted and hence take the form of impersonal forces. They strive to gain power over our lives and again they resume their eternal struggle with one another." [24]

It is appropriate to characterize Weber's form of value pluralism as "existentialist" for the following reasons: not only do these values compete with one another, that is, something can be true without being good and be good without being beautiful, but also because we don't possess overarching and commensurate criteria for choosing among these competing values. It is up to the individual to decide what her ultimate goals in life will be, and as he states it dramatically in one of his methodological essays: "It is really a question not only of alternatives between values but of an irreconcilable death-struggle like that between 'God' and the 'Devil.' Between these, neither relativization nor compromise is possible."[25] And rising to a poetic crescendo, he continues: "The fruit of the tree of knowledge, which is distasteful to the complacent but which is, nonetheless, inescapable, consists in the insight that every single important activity and ultimately life as a whole, if it is not to be permitted to run on as an event in nature but is instead to be consciously guided, is a series of ultimate decisions through which the soul—as in Plato—chooses its own fate, i.e. the meaning of its activity and existence" (Weber, "Ethical Neutrality," 18).

Weber's rather dramatic formulations and the existential darkness of his views have led many thinkers, from Leo Strauss onward, to accuse him of nihilism (see chapter 2 above). Yet this is not accurate. There is a nonnegligible rationalist kernel to Weber's vocation as a sociologist. He emphasizes that although social science cannot tell us which goals to choose, it can enlighten us about the consequences of our actions and policies once such a choice is made. The social scientist cannot dictate whether we ought to pursue equality for all through full employment or instead opt for market competition, which will exacerbate inequalities. These values, goals, and policies are for politicians and citizens to determine. What the social scientist can provide are generalizations to the effect that if you want to pursue full employment, you are likely to end up with a certain amount of inflation. If you want to pursue social solidarity, you may face challenges such as capital flight and increased class resentment. Unlike Albert Hirschman, who was interested in social science as a form of moral inquiry and who dreamt of "a 'social science for our grandchildren,'" a social science that would be worth bequeathing to future generations,[26] Weber had no such illusions. His was a social science for those who could bear the "fate of the times like a man"; the rest could seek solace in the arms of "the old Church."[27]

This function of social science to enlighten and inform us about the consequences of social action has implications for Weber's ideal type of the two ethical orientations—the ethics of conscience (*Gesinnungsethik*) versus the ethics of responsibility (*Verantwortungsethik*). Berlin, as we saw above, cites these two ethical orientations as the exemplary case of value pluralism. The one who pursues the ethics of conscience says, "let the world be damned, I will pursue my principles and my goals. My conscience alone is what matters; the consequences of my actions do not matter. I will act according to my principles, whatever may be the consequences. *Pareat mundus, fiat justitia.* Let justice be done and the earth perish!" The ethics of responsibility, however, tries to mediate between the costs and the consequences of the *foreseeable* results of one's actions and one's principles and values. Although Weber admires those who stand firmly on principle, it is clear that only those who have a sense of the balance between means and ends, that is, statesmen and the charismatic politicians who have a sense of the ethics of responsibility, should put their hands "on the wheel of history" (Weber, "Politics as a Vocation," 115). The rest are saints and adventurers, but they are not statesmen!

Despite his confidence in the capacity of social science to throw some light on the social world, Weber admitted that whether or not to pursue science, any science, was a question that could not be answered rationally. He sensed that modern individuals would be tempted to escape the iron cage of modernity by reintroducing some magic into the world and predicted that they would be tempted to act willfully and irrationally in order to reenchant the world. One option was to take flight in religion, another would be to seek transcendence in the aesthetic and the sensual realms. But in the realm of politics, such efforts to escape the iron cage of modernity, rationalization, and bureaucracy would lead into the arms of a charismatic leader and/or to plebiscitarian democracy, both of which would challenge the legal-rational paradigm of legitimacy by weakening formal, institutional rationality. Weber's pluralism did not lead him to place much faith in liberalism. He considered liberal institutions too weak to withstand the tides of the times and praised strong, nationalist statesmen who would be able to sail the ship of state.[28]

## Berlin's Value Pluralism

Berlin shares Weber's tragic sense of choice among competing values, but he does not believe that this has been a problem in modernity alone. He often refers to the thought of Machiavelli to show that even in fifteenth- and sixteenth-century Florence there were conflicting values: the values of Christianity, which advocated humility, honesty, and service, stood in contrast to the virtues of the ancient republics', with their search for glory, civic courage, and placing the good of the city above one's own.[29] Berlin also reminds us that most Greek tragedies are about the clash of incompatible values: Antigone is forbidden by Creon, the king of the city, from burying her brother Polynices, because he has revolted against the city. The burial of her brother is dictated for Antigone by the laws of piety and the religious demands of family obligations; if her brother is not given the proper burial, then his soul will wander forever in front of the gates of the netherworld and will never come to peace. Creon, by contrast, is there to defend the integrity of the state against those who take up arms against it, as Polynices had done. Yet, despite this clash of values, Creon's dogmatism and inability to forgive Polynices is his tragic flaw: the play calls for a reconciliation of the values of the city and the hearth, since the identity of the city itself is based upon respect for the gods of the tribes, the *Demei*, to whom families belonged.[30]

For Berlin such clash of values is a fundamental aspect of the human condition throughout human history.[31] Forms of life differ across time and space, and even within our own societies different forms of life coexist, and strongly differing values are advocated by different groups. Values clash, and as he puts it, as dramatically as Weber: "These collisions of values are of the essence of what they are and what we are. If we are told that these contradictions will be solved in some perfect world in which all good things can be harmonised in principle, then we must answer, to those who say this, that the meanings they attach to the names which for us denote conflicting values are not ours" (Berlin, "The Pursuit of the Ideal," 11). Not only can there be no harmony among these values, there is also no hierarchy among them: again in words that do not fail to remind us of Weber, Berlin declaims: "Some among the Great Goods cannot live together. . . . We are doomed to choose, and every choice may entail an irreparable loss" (Berlin, "The Pursuit of the Ideal," 11).

Whereas Weber's existentialism of values is well suited to the "allure of the dark times" in which he lived,[32] Berlin's kind of value pluralism sits uncomfortably with his defense of liberalism and appears to undermine rational commitment to it. As is well documented, the origin of Berlin's thesis of value pluralism is his critique of *monistic* views of human freedom and history that aim at the realization of a single goal— be it the classless society; the establishment of an aristocracy of talent; the ideal of "from each according to his abilities to each according to his needs." Such visions of positive liberty will entitle public authority to coerce ordinary human beings to live up to the force of the ideal. "On les forcera d'être libre," in Rousseau's famous words.[33] Only an acknowledgment of the *plurality* of values in human life and tolerance toward the diversity of goals that can be pursued by human beings is compatible with the ideals of a free society.

What Berlin names "monism" is akin to the antitotalitarianism critique of Cold War thinkers such as Karl Popper, Raymond Aron and Friedrich Hayek. The postmodernist critique of the ideal of totality and of Marxist "meta-narratives" is also not unrelated to this perspective.[34] But how then does one justify the value of individual liberty of choice, or of liberalism on the basis of value pluralism? Couldn't a Schmittian decisionist argue that the choice of a vision of the political as the most intense and supreme value is the right one? Such a commitment would necessarily be accompanied by distinctions between friend and foe. What would Berlin's answer be? From a Weberian perspective, there is no compelling answer against a Schmittian vision of politics, and this is why Schmitt considers himself a student of Weber's and cites him approvingly in his *Concept of the Political*.[35]

Yet Berlin is neither a relativist nor a nihilist. More importantly, he does not accept the positivist distinction between descriptive versus value judgments or the ascription of rationality only to the first. In a brief essay on "The Rationality of Value Judgments," first published in 1964, he gives the example of a man who was in the habit of pushing pins into other people. He engages in an imaginary conversation with this man and asks him whether he "should do to others what he would try to prevent them from doing to him. He says that he does not understand: pins driven into him cause him pain and he wishes to prevent this; pins driven by him into others do not cause him pain, but on the contrary, positive pleasure, and he therefore wishes to continue to do it."[36] Upon being pressed by the imaginary interlocutor to explain whether it makes a difference to him whether he presses pins into tennis balls or human persons, the man answers that he cannot respond to the interlocutor's strange concern. "At this point," writes Berlin, "I begin to suspect that he is in some way deranged. I do not say (with Hume), 'Here is a man with a very different scale of moral values from my own. Values are not susceptible to argument. I can disagree but not reason with him,' as I should be inclined to say of a man who believes in hara-kira or genocide. I rather incline to the belief that the pin-pusher who is puzzled by my question is to be classified with homicidal lunatics and should be confined in an asylum and not in an ordinary prison" ("Rationality of Value Judgments," 317).

One should balk at Berlin's concession that a man "who believes in genocide" is more intelligible than one "who cannot see that the suffering of pain is an issue of major importance in human life" ("Rationality of Value Judgments," 317) since genocide is the annihilation of the way of life of a people as bearers of certain identity-markers and as certain kinds of human beings. Surely pathological sadism is no more extreme than the behavior of the *génocidaires*. Berlin's whole discussion is painfully reminiscent of some of the psychological explanations put forward regarding the behavior of Nazi officers as well as doctors (see chapter 4 above), whose normality was likewise questioned and to whom sadism of various kinds had been attributed. But Berlin is strangely silent about this issue and instead he concludes that: "This seems to me to show that the recognition of some values—however general and however few—enters into the normal definition of what constitutes a sane human being . . . In this sense, then, pursuit of, or failure to pursue, certain ends can be regarded as evidence of—and in extreme cases part of the definition of—irrationality" ("Rationality of Value Judgments," 317). Is this a fall back upon a conception of human nature or human essence? Berlin admits that he "owes much to Aristotle and Kant" but says no more than that ("Rationality of Value Judgments," 317).

It is not human nature nor human essence nor even the human condition that Berlin has recourse to but the concept of the "human horizon." In *The Pursuit of the Ideal*, he tries to elucidate again why his concept of pluralism is different from relativism: "'I prefer coffee, you prefer Champaign, we have different tastes. There is no more to be said.' That is relativism. But what I should describe as pluralism is different. But Herder's view, and Vico's, is not that: it is what I should describe as pluralism—that is, the conception that there are many different ends that men may seek and still be fully rational, fully men, capable of understanding each other and sympathizing and deriving delight from each other, as we derive it from reading Plato or the novels of medieval Japan—worlds, outlooks, very remote from our own. Of course, if we did not have any values in common with these distant figures, each civilization would be enclosed in its own impenetrable bubble, and we could not understand them at all."[37]

Like Weber, Berlin insists on the possibility of transhistorical human understanding, and emphasizes not only the likelihood but also the actuality of *Verstehen*. Weber does not appeal to a common humanity in arguing that such understanding is possible; he only asserts that, as social scientists, we find such human action and conduct meaningful and interesting and search to comprehend it. Just as sociological inquiry enlightens about the limits of possibility in the social world, so too, for Berlin, inquiry into fundamental human values educates us about our shared world. This is the enlightenment function of political theory and why the study of human values, pace logical positivists, is worthwhile in itself.

In "Does Political Theory Still Exist?," Berlin traces the development of modern sciences and their impact on political thought in terms quite similar to Weber's model of the differentiation of value spheres. He insists that "the basic categories in terms of which we define men . . . are not matters of induction and hypothesis."[38] Society, freedom, sense of time, suffering, productivity, happiness, truth, illusion, and the like are constitutive of what it is to be human. Political philosophy provides us with models, paradigms, and conceptual structures in the light of which such categories are rearranged and a sense of what is a human being and a member of a polity. Such "doctrines are not concerned with specific facts, but with ways of looking at them, they do not consist of first-order propositions concerning the world. They are second- or higher-order statements about whole classes of descriptions of, or responses to, the world and man's activities in it" ("Does Political Theory Still Exist," 220). Such models, paradigms, and conceptual structures preserve "a considerable degree of continuity and similarity from one age to another," and political theory is an exercise of rational curiosity that seeks to understand these differing and often competing models, paradigms, and structures and subjects them to a "desire for justification and explanation in terms of motives and reasons, and not only of causes of functional correlations or statistical probabilities" ("Does Political Theory Still Exist," 224).

What is to be done then? First and foremost, in all our actions we must avoid inflicting extremes of suffering even if the study of political philosophy may provide neither deductive nor inductive proof for this proposition. This is the principal obligation of a decent society. Furthermore, in such a society one can engage in an experimental politics of balance, compromise, and trade-off. In a phrase reminiscent of Kierkegaard, on whom both Arendt and Adorno had focused (see chapter 3 above), Berlin concludes: "There is no escape: we must decide as we decide; moral risk, cannot, at times, be avoided. All we can ask for is that none of the relevant factors be ignored, that the purposes we seek to realize should be seen as elements in a total form of life, which can be enhanced or damaged by decisions."[39]

For Berlin himself such a moment of decision came while serving in Washington, DC, as a British official. He got wind that the US and British government would issue a joint statement condemning Zionist agitation. According to David Caute, Berlin leaked "the story to a Zionist publisher, who informed Henry Morgenthau, secretary of the US Treasury. Having thus tipped off the Jewish lobby, Berlin managed to disguise his own role from the last British Ambassador, Lord Halifax."[40] Thus when the chips were down and the time came to act on behalf of one set of values rather than other, Berlin did not hesitate to choose: his loyalty to Israel and to the Jewish people, although he was not a religious

Jew, trumped his loyalty to the British Crown. Nor was he a universalist or binationalist like Arendt, the young Scholem, and Judah Magnes. He "tended to refer to the Arabs cursorily, as 'the Arabs,' not differentiating between the Palestinian population and the neighbouring Arab states. His prism was that of Western politics and personalities, and he did not publicly challenge the refusal of the USA and the UK to welcome Jewish refugees and Holocaust survivors in the required numbers,"[41] even though privately, he was willing to risk his reputation and career for the sake of the establishment of the State of Israel.

During these years, Hannah Arendt was writing for the Yiddish newspaper in New York, *Der Aufbau*, criticizing the Biltmore declaration that demanded the whole of Palestine for a Jewish State. And in 1945, she would pen one of the most important and far-reaching essays on the Israel-Palestine question under the title, "Zionism Reconsidered."[42] As the wheel of history turned, Berlin and Arendt each decided to put their hands on it: Berlin gambled for the creation of a Jewish state in Palestine that would be both liberal and nationalist; Arendt attempted to do justice to the national aspirations of the Palestinian people and opted for a binational homeland integrated into a federation of Mediterranean peoples. Neither wager was wrong: Berlin was right in demanding that immigration to Palestine be permitted for the Jews of Europe escaping the Holocaust, and Arendt was right in believing that it was imperative to find a polity and a state-form that could do justice to all people of Palestine. These are the dilemmas facing Israel in Palestine still today.

Philosophically Berlin left much too much unclear. In what sense were values objective? Can those who live under certain values be deceived by them? What are the limits and constituents of the human horizon? What and who belongs to the "human horizon" and who or what doesn't and why? Can a decent society and the experimental liberalism of trade-offs and give-and-take be justified without appealing to more robust moral and political principles? Despite his essayistic brilliance and great insights into the history of ideas, Berlin's writings leave the relationship of value pluralism to liberal democracies fundamentally tenuous.[43]

# A Brief Epilogue on John Rawls and
# the Burdens of Judgment

The dilemmas of liberalism haunted Judith Shklar no less than Isaiah Berlin, Leo Strauss no less than Hans Kelsen. Max Weber and Hannah Arendt viewed liberalism's crisis through a broader lens, as being embedded in the institutional as well as value dilemmas generated by modernity. While Weber was troubled by the weaknesses of parliamentary institutions in post-World War I Germany, Arendt mourned the passing of the spirit of freedom that had flickered, even if briefly, in the revolutionary experiments of the Räterepublike of Munich and Berlin (the revolutionary councils of workers, soldiers, and students). With the murder of Karl Liebknecht and Rosa Luxemburg in Berlin on January 15, 1919, Heinrich Blücher left the Spartacist League, of which Luxemburg and Liebknecht had been the leaders. Arendt herself, after meeting Kurt Blumenfeld at a student gathering in Heidelberg in 1926,[44] turned increasingly to Jewish and Zionist politics. For these émigrés we may say that a "Weimar syndrome" haunted their work: How to defend modern constitutional republics intellectually and institutionally in an age of value pluralism as well as class conflict? Strauss and Berlin would opt for free markets after World War II, whereas Arendt as well as Shklar would prove more sympathetic to various social measures for ensuring some form of socioeconomic equality among citizens.

The most courageous and comprehensive attempt in the second half of the twentieth century to reformulate liberalism such as to counter his own version of the "Weimar syndrome" has been John Rawls's. His contribution provides a fitting conclusion to this discussion of the intractability of the challenges of value pluralism.

By Rawls's own version of the "Weimar syndrome," I mean his attempt to reformulate value pluralism as a problem of "reasonable disagreement" in constitutional liberal democracies. In "The Priority of Right and the Ideas of the Good," (1998) written nearly a quarter of a century after *A Theory of Justice* (1971), Rawls observes that: "As Sir Isaiah Berlin has long maintained (it is one his fundamental themes), there is no social world without loss—that is no social world that does not exclude some ways of life to realize in special ways certain fundamental values. By virtue of its culture and institutions, any society will prove uncongenial to some ways of life."[45] In the footnote that accompanies this passage, Rawls adds:

[I] believe that Weber's views rest on a form of value skepticism and voluntarism; political tragedy arises from the conflicts of subjective commitments and resolute wills. For Berlin, on the other hand, the realm of values may be fully objective; the point is rather that the full range of values is too extensive to fit into any one social worlds; not only are they incompatible with one another, imposing conflicting requirements on institutions, but there exists no family of workable institutions with sufficient spaces for them all. That there is no social world without loss is rooted in the nature of values and the world; and much human tragedy reflects that; a just liberal society may have far more space than other worlds, but it can never be without loss.[46]

This passage throws a rather unusual light on how to frame Rawls's own project of political liberalism. It is also a moving acknowledgment of the *tragedy of the political*, a point of view deeply shared by Weber, Arendt, Strauss, Schmitt, and Berlin.

For Rawls, "reasonable pluralism," as opposed to pluralism of *any* kind, is what liberal constitutional democracies must accept as a baseline. Enduring disagreement about the good life and the different and incompatible values that we pursue to attain our visions of the good are an aspect of our condition as late moderns. We must resist the temptation to avoid this condition by trying to impose upon one another a uniform understanding of the good life, whether in religion, ethics, aesthetics, or science.

However, it is not only disagreement but also *cooperation* that characterizes human existence. Whereas Weber and Berlin emphasize the inevitable conflict of values, Rawls is emphatic that no human society can endure over time if it does not enable *human cooperation*. From a philosophical point of view, the fundamental clash of values may be insoluble; but a defense of political liberalism to realize the principles of a just society cannot be based on a metaphysical doctrine about values alone. Rather, it accepts that "there exists no family of workable institutions with sufficient space" for all values (Rawls, "Priority of Right," 462–63). A just society is one in which citizens can view the terms of their cooperation as being chosen by themselves as free and equal persons, who are capable both of rationality and reasonableness. "As reasonable and rational we have to make different kinds of judgments. As rational we have to balance our various ends and estimate their appropriate place in our way of life; and doing this confronts us with grave difficulties in making correct judgments of rationality. On the other hand, as reasonable we must assess the strength of peoples' claims, not only against our claims, but against one another, or on our common practices and institutions, all this giving rise to difficulties in our making sound and reasonable judgments."[47] We must try not only to balance rationally the various goals and ends of our own conceptions of the good life, but, because we live in a society where other individuals pursue conceptions that are radically different from ours, we must also evaluate their conceptions as well as judge their impact on our way of life together; and this is when it is incumbent upon us to act as *reasonable* beings and accept reasonable limits upon the conduct of our own lives.

Rawls's work enables us to see that value pluralism alone cannot establish conditions for a just and decent society. We need stronger premises about who we are as moral beings and as citizens of a polity. In order to endure over time, social cooperation must be based on the *reciprocity* of fair terms of cooperation through which persons can address one another. Such cooperation is guided "by publicly recognized rules and procedures that those cooperating accept and regard as properly regulating their conduct."[48] The reconstruction of such fair terms of cooperation in order to assure a just society over time is what political liberalism aims at. "Public reason" articulates those "constitutional essentials" that are an aspect of the basic institutional structure of liberal societies.

In the nearly half a century since he articulated his project, Rawls has subjected it to many revisions. Moving away from the conceits of *A Theory of Justice*, which claimed to formulate principles of justice "*sub specie aeternitatis*, he settled on a more post-metaphysical view of political liberalism as a contextual articulation of the values and principles immanent in liberal constitutional democracies. These issues are well known, and there is no need to recapitulate them here. But as Rawls's theory has become more contextual, the distinction between "reasonable" and "unreasonable" forms of pluralism has become more contested. Many have questioned whether Rawls's theory of "reasonable pluralism" does not amount to a colossal *petitio principii* in that it redefines pluralism itself to make it compatible with reasonableness, thus blunting its critical edge. Many worldviews, ideologies, and doctrines, deemed "unreasonable," are thereby left out of the purview of Rawls's framework.[49]

Yet it is important to note that reasonable pluralism for Rawls is not just a political but an epistemic condition, that forms an integral part of a scientifically enlightened culture. Rawls goes farther than his critics to acknowledge that in constitutional liberal democracies, the "burdens of judgment" never cease, and citizens' task in providing each other with reciprocal reasons is interminable.

Whereas Weber assumed that science could provide definitive answers that we are free to accept or not, Rawls's epistemology is much more tentative, and it is tempered by the fallibilism of the American pragmatist tradition from Willard Van Orman Quine to Richard Rorty and beyond. In his remarkable discussion of the "burdens of judgment," Rawls lists six sources of epistemic pluralism: (Rawls, *Political Liberalism*, 56–57)

i. The evidence: how can we judge that it bears on a case—in law, in medicine, in science?

ii. Even when we agree about the evidence, we may assess its weight and import differently. In courts of law and in medicine, once we establish something as evidence, we still have to reach a common judgment about the proper weight to give it.

iii. All our concepts, not only moral and political ones are general, and are subject to *indeterminacy*, and we must rely on judgment and interpretation about their applicability as well as their range.

iv. How we interpret our concepts, the way we assess evidence and weigh moral and political values, is shaped by the totality of our lived experiences.

v. Often there are different kinds of normative considerations on both sides of an issue, and reasonable people may disagree.

vi. Finally, we may each bring to bear very different normative considerations to the same body of evidence.

And at this point Rawls once more cites Berlin: "[as] Berlin reminds us, any system of institutions has limited social space and only some values can be realized and many hard choices seem to have no clear answer" (Rawls, *Political Liberalism*, 57, fn. 10). Rawls accepts that other forms of prejudice and bias besides those listed above, such as self- and group-interest, blindness, and willfulness, can also play a role in coloring our judgments. Even conscientious and well-intentioned citizens, while exercising judgment, "even after free discussion," may not all arrive at the same conclusion (Rawls, *Political Liberalism*, 58).

These conditions of reasonable pluralism lead Rawls to articulate an ideal of democratic toleration. Some have wondered whether these epistemic conditions of disagreement are not so radical as to throw into question a lot of what Rawls has proposed in *Political Liberalism*. Peter Lassman writes: "The attempt to separate pluralism from reasonable disagreement is not compelling. If we point to Rawls's 'burdens of reason' [*sic*] argument in order to identify the sources of disagreement, then it would appear that this clean separation of the two principles cannot be made as easily as he implies."[50] I am more sympathetic than Lassman to Rawls's attempt to distinguish the "burdens of judgment" from the principles of public reason and I endorse a constructivist account of the principles of cooperation in a just society.[51] In this chapter I am only concerned to emphasize that in response to his own version of the Weimar syndrome, Rawls's work returns us to the problem of the indeterminacies of judgment, which we had already encountered when discussing Arendt and Adorno on the mediation of the universal and the particular in chapter 3.

———

As we can see from this brief discussion, pluralism is not relativism. Each thinker considered in this chapter acknowledges the multiplicity and incommensurability of values, while also setting some limits on "anything goes": anything does not go, everything is not defensible. For Weber, those limits are set by a rational, scientific mindset that ought to inform an ethics of responsibility. Though science itself can never answer the question about the value of science itself, there is little question in Weber's mind that for the politician and the statesman to ignore the evidence of the sciences would be an act of irrationality and irresponsibility.

For Berlin, the boundaries to value pluralism are constituted by what he calls "the human horizon," which enables us to recognize each other across time and space; at the same time, Berlin urges us to seek the reduction of human suffering and strive for the creation of a decent society. Although he does not justify these values any further, he seems to take for granted that most, if not all, human beings will seek to live by them.

For Rawls, constitutional democracies have to accept the reasonable pluralism of values and the inevitable burdens of judgment. Nevertheless such reasonable pluralism can be practiced only as long as we recognize each other as free and equal citizens to whom we can attribute both rationality and reasonableness. Only thus can we defend democratic toleration.

The problem of judgment is not one that permits clear-cut theoretical solutions. As we already saw in chapter 3, Adorno as well as Arendt return to Kant's distinction between "determinative" and "reflective" judgment. It is reflective judgment that challenges and fascinates them: that is, the capacity for exercising "enlarged mentality" in situations when the principles that should guide us are either not readily available or have been discredited. Berlin appears to feel no particular metaphysical *angst* in view of this question, whereas Weber is completely preoccupied with it. For Berlin, there is a horizon of shared human understandings and certainties, whereas for Weber, who saw the collapse of Kaiser's Germany and experienced the emergence of an uncertain future, there is no such certainty.

Rawls's dilemma is different than that of Weber or Berlin: Rawls does not believe that principles of moral and political thought do not hold; he gives the most vivid, and to my mind, still unsurpassed, defense of the principles of political liberalism. However, the question that haunts him is whether the burdens of judgment that even these principles have to bear can assure that a common civic point of view will endure over time. How far can the divergence in burdens of judgment go without diremptive forces pushing us so far afield that a common conversation is no longer possible? Not only in this chapter but throughout this book I have returned to this anxiety, at times referring to it as the "Weimar syndrome," and have probed the various answers offered to quiet it by an extraordinary group of émigré intellectuals.

# Conclusion

## THE UNIVERSAL AND THE PARTICULAR.
## THEN AND NOW

IT HAS OFTEN BEEN REMARKED that the rivalries of émigré politics are of the most intense kind. Certainly the preceding chapters have provided enough evidence for this truism: the struggle that broke out among Arendt on the one side and Scholem and Adorno on the other in curating the posthumous work of Walter Benjamin; Isaiah Berlin's bitter comments about Arendt and his attempts to discredit her work; Strauss's cutting dismissal of Berlin's value pluralism; and, of course, the Eichmann controversy. We have seen skirmishes and outright intellectual wars among these intellectuals. Yet beyond personal animosities and rivalries four themes link the work of these thinkers : Jewish identity and otherness; exile, voice, and loyalty; legality and legitimacy in liberal democracies; and pluralism and the problem of judgment.

*Jewish Identity and Otherness.* The rise of modern liberal societies in Western Europe enabled emancipation via the extension of civil and political rights to Jewish populations. But this circumstance also posed special challenges to retaining Jewish identity while embracing equality in predominantly Christian societies. As has been told well by authors such as Amos Elon, George Steiner, Yuri Slezkine, and others, the German-Jewish experience yielded an intellectual and spiritual response of unparalleled brilliance and depth to this tension between identity and equality. This outburst was accompanied from the start by the suspicion that all was not well within putative emancipation, and that, in Moritz Goldstein's words, "the German-Jewish Parnassus" was an illusion, because the larger German society had never believed and would not accept that the Jews were true heirs of German culture and philosophy. Even while recognizing this attitude, Goldstein denies it and asks what a Jewish idiom (*Sprechart*) and public sphere would look like for the Jews of Europe. He introduces the locution of the Jews as "the eternal half-other."

I have argued that this search for ways and reasons to preserve aspects of one's individual and collective identity as a form of equality-in-difference continued in the work of Hannah Arendt (who knew and admired Goldstein's essay) in her invocation of the persona of the "self-conscious pariah," who has no desire to assimilate wholly into the larger society and to become a *parvenu*. Nor does Arendt accept the standpoint of the pariah, who is pushed or pushes herself to the outer edges of respectable society. The self-conscious pariah cultivates an attitude of critical distance and searches for the universal in the particular.

Shklar, deeply aware of this dimension in Arendt's work, named her most extensive commentary on her, "Hannah Arendt as Pariah." She claimed that Arendt clung "to a bizarre notion" that being Jewish was "an act of personal defiance and not a matter of actively maintaining a cultural and religious tradition with its own rites and patterns of speech."[1] Shklar was not reluctant to declare the German-Jewish tradition dead after Arendt's passing away.

Despite this final reckoning with Arendt's life and work, which she had admired and valued at other points, Shklar, like Arendt herself, and like nearly everyone else discussed in this volume, was a secular Jew. The only exceptions are Emmanuel Levinas and Robert Cover, who were religiously observant. While Leo Strauss's reflections on Athens and Jerusalem and his thesis that modernity had to grapple with political-theology are well known, less attention has been paid to the Jewish sources of Cover's theory of law as *jurisgenerativity*. As discussed in chapter 2, Cover claims that all *nomos* requires narratives that cannot be supplied by the secular state with its *jurispathic* apparatus of the courts and enforcement. *Paideic* communities of meaning (often religious in character) always exist in the plural, and they challenge the monopoly of narrative by the secular state.

Cover's reflections on paideic communities have gained a new relevance in our age in which the nation-state's monopoly on the meaning of public lives has waned but not disappeared. The much-used and abused term "multiculturalism" cannot begin to address the dilemmas of maintaining equality and difference in the global era and of the legal as well as cultural challenges this poses.[2] I have suggested that in today's political discourse, Islam and Islamism have become the principal signifier of otherness in the affluent democracies of the West. How to maintain one's otherness and idiom in a democratic public sphere that recognizes both plurality in the Arendtian sense and pluralism in Berlin's sense continues as a principal challenge for us today.

*Exile, Voice, and Loyalty.* The Hebrew term "galut," according to the Jewish Virtual Library, "expresses the Jewish conception of the conditions and feeling of a nation uprooted from its homeland and subject to alien rule."[3] The secular Zionist project since Theodor Herzl sought to put an end to this condition by creating a homeland for the Jewish people in Palestine.[4] For religious Zionists and religious Jews in general the return to Zion is not just a project of creating a homeland but it is returning to the "promised lands of Eretz Israel," to the land promised by God to the Jewish people.

Of the thinkers considered in this book, Berlin and Levinas were most sympathetic to and endorsed the idea of a return to Palestine as the historical homeland of the Jewish people. Having analyzed the significance and rise of nationalism out of the spirit of European romanticism in many of his writings, Berlin thought that the Zionist goal, whether in its secular or religious form, was a legitimate aspiration of the Jewish people, although he himself chose to make a home in a liberal, democratic, and increasingly multicultural Britain.

It was Levinas who transmuted the longing to put an end to the pain of galut into the ethical imperative that comes from being "faced" with the other. Yet we can never fulfil this imperative, and, as Judith Butler notes in her insightful reconstruction of the Levinasian imperative, to be confronted with the "face" of the other also means never to be at home, since the other can unsettle me, grab hold of me, and subject me to herself. (See chapter 5 above.)

Yet galut can persist without becoming an ethical imperative. One can be in exile without feeling exiled and homeless. Although Shklar, Hirschman, and Berlin lost the countries of their birth and were exiled from them, they ceased to be exiles in the sense that they found a new home in their adoptive countries. Arendt as well, despite her support of political as opposed to religious Zionism in the 1930s and 1940s, found a home in the United States. In her work, the exilic consciousness was never quite stilled, and it led her from one controversy to another.

The most famous analysis of exit, voice, and loyalty is that of Albert Hirschman. As discussed in chapter 8, for Hirschman, "exit" is a broader concept than "exile" in that it can signify not only the end of allegiance to country, kin, and tribe, but also, more prosaically, quitting a firm or even merely abandoning a brand. Hirschman's contribution not just to economic but democratic political theory lies in his analysis of the interplay between exit and voice. This is not a simple dynamic: the absence of exit need not always mean the presence of voice, just as the availability of exit need not mean the absence of voice. It is fascinating that Hirschman himself modified this aspect of his formula when he encountered the political condition of his divided birth-city of Berlin and the East German dissident movement. He added "loyalty" to his famous dichotomy of exit versus voice to explain those conditions when individuals chose to remain even in the absence of voice because they felt loyalty and attachment.

Shklar was more interested in the endemic conflict of loyalties between exile, voice, and obligation. For her such multiple loyalties were an aspect of the modern condition, and she distrusted nationalisms that sought to reduce conflicts of loyalty by monopolizing one form of obligation among others. A liberal society in a minimal sense was based on the avoidance of cruelty, but a broader version of liberalism, would encourage both voice through membership as well as respecting the multiplicity of our allegiances. For Shklar, the law was the medium through which this balance was to be attained.

Exile, then, has several dimensions: it can be a form of religious and spiritual homelessness that may or may not accompany actual political and legal exile; it can refer to the political and legal condition of individuals and groups who have fled from or have been forced out of their homelands. Exiles are often, though not always, stateless.[5] Arendt and Shklar were quite attentive to the membership status of exiles. In fact, Arendt's contribution is unique in that she focuses upon the condition of statelessness that had hitherto been of interest to international lawyers alone (see chapter 6). Partly under her influence in contemporary political thought, the condition of exile, refugee, and statelessness have become the prism through which to reflect upon the dysfunctionalities of the nation-state system.

*Legality and Legitimacy in Liberal Democracies.* Max Weber's sociology of modernity and his account of the philosophical dilemmas of value pluralism have deeply affected nearly all the thinkers considered in this volume. Although his 1931 essay on "The Actuality of Philosophy" is atypical of Adorno's later work in the tradition of Critical Theory—a tradition referred to even as "Weberian Marxism"[6]—Adorno, in this essay, criticizes the subjectivism of neo-Kantian epistemology, which Weber saw as the only plausible response to the demise of the two world-metaphysics of Plato and Kant (see chapter 3 above). Adorno, however, believed that to assume that the object of knowledge was constituted by the subjective assumptions of the knower, be they epistemological or value-axioms, was equivalent to indulging the conceit of "constitutive subjectivity" that denied our imbrication in the otherness of external nature and our inner nature, that is, our embedded existence and emotional, affective dispositions. Adorno's attempt to recoup otherness from the imperialism of modern subjectivity—a theme that never left his work—takes the form of a defense of essay-writing as opposed to philosophical system-building. The philosopher becomes like a miniature artist who tries to capture the dignity of the particular through disclosing crystalline elements and configurations. This early essay, which is still key to understanding Adorno's mature work, left many of his colleagues baffled and certainly seemed to be a very elusive, not to say, rather obscure response to Weber's challenge.

overlapping

Kelsen, Schmitt, Strauss, and Shklar as well as Berlin were haunted by Weber's questions, which I have named the "Weimar syndrome": how to defend, intellectually and institutionally, modern constitutional republics and liberal societies in an age of value pluralism as well as class conflict? Liberalism seemed incapable of providing a strong justification in its own defense. Kelsen admitted that the bases of the legal system rested on a *Grundnorm* for which no further justification was possible. For Schmitt, this was a clear recognition of the fact that every legal system rested on presuppositions that it could neither fully clarify nor justify. The existential decision between "friend" and "foe" is constitutive of the political, and Schmitt in his *Concept of the Political* presents this view as being nothing more than an application of Weber's theory of value-differentiation to the political realm.[7] Strauss was the one who saw the potentially nihilist consequences of Weber's challenge and who wrote one of the most penetrating critiques of Weber and Schmitt (see chapter 2 above). For Strauss, liberalism could be defended only if a strong conception of human value, ultimately leading to a form of natural law, could also be accepted. Far from having solved the politico-theological problem, liberalism only exacerbated it.

Shklar, who was a keen student of Weber, reformulated his challenge not through metaphysics or value theory but as the question of whether the authority of legal norms could be accepted independently of moral and political considerations. Shklar's response to legal decisionism and legal formalism was a form of contextualism: a legal system was viewed as legitimate because it was embedded in the historical context of other practices and institutions. Shklar thought that the philosophy and sociology of law were inseparable. In that sense for her it was not the philosophical question of justification that was primary but the more empirical question of why people accepted a legal system to be legitimate at all. Legalism, in the manner of Kelsen and his student, H.L.A. Hart, was unsatisfactory because it attempted to create a universe of self-contained legal norms that was illusory. Nevertheless, legalism, understood as the core of the rule of law, was fundamental to liberal politics: liberal equality required, much as Weber had taught, the procedurally correct formulation and application of publicly promulgated general norms. Shklar was too shrewd a social analyst not to note that, thus formulated, legalism would be compatible with certain forms of authoritarian regimes, as well. Where did the democratic element come in?

The pursuit of a wider concept of legitimacy led Shklar as well as Arendt to the paradoxes of revolutionary foundings. On the one hand, the law framed the political and thus had to stand outside it; on the other hand, the law was made possible by the political acts of humans joining together in contract, association, and promise. Whereas Shklar is convinced that legalism and liberalism need to be reconnected in a disenchanted universe that has demystified the sources of law, Arendt searches for some element in the Western tradition, for some aspect of political experience that would give law stability without ontologizing it. Arendt rereads the Founding Fathers of the American Revolution and discovers the Montesquieuan concept of the "principle." The "abyss of freedom" (Arendt, *The Life of the Mind*, vol. 2, *Willing*, 207) encountered in the project of the "new," i.e. in the founding of republics and the formation of democratic sovereignties, cannot be avoided, but the will of the sovereign can be bound through principles. Such beginnings "rupture the linear continuity of time"[8] and initiate a new political practice requiring the founding of new rules and institutions; they bring forth a new world. The indeterminacy of new beginnings cannot be avoided any more than the "tragedy of the political" can through which hopeful and emancipatory beginnings turn into tyranny or terror. The "revolution can devour its own children." Precisely because she had faith in human natality and the capacity to create new beginnings, Arendt insisted on the republican vigilance of the citizenry in liberal democracies. Liberalism presupposed a more active and vigorous concept of politics than "negative liberty" permitted. Arendt, who wrote one of the first and most brilliant dissections of twentieth-century totalitarianism, was just as alert as Berlin to the perversions of politics through totalizing ideologies that denied plurality. In her much-misunderstood conclusion to *On Revolution*,[9] she predicted the transformation of democratic republics into consumerist paradises in which citizens were duped by technocrats on the one hand and self-advertising politicians on the other. Only vigilant citizens' involvement could prevent this. I, for one, am not ready to say that she was wrong.

*Pluralism and the Problem of Judgment.* Berlin's concept of value pluralism can be brought into relation fruitfully with Arendt's concept of perspectival plurality. Such perspectival plurality for Arendt could only be differentiated from sheer relativism through the faculties of narrative and judgment. Arendt went back to Kant's doctrine of judgment and in particular to his doctrine of the "enlarged mentality" in her attempts to avoid perspectival relativism; whereas Berlin, who had placed Kant at the beginning of the slippery slope that would lead to the advocacy of a doomed project of freedom as self-realization, never explored the problem of judgment as a way out of the *aporias* of his value relativism.

Recall that for Kant reflective judgment, as distinguished from determinative judgment, involved the search for the general rule or principle where none was at hand (chapter 3 above). Determinative judgment, by contrast, meant the application of known principles to particularities. It is interesting to note that in his discussion of "The Burdens of Judgment" Rawls weakens this distinction by showing that even when evidence, general concepts, and rules are at hand, interpretation and, yes, some exercise of judgment are also called for. To decide *which* general concept or rule to bring to bear on the particular is not a mere mechanical act: even the activity of determinative judgment requires reflective judgment in that it involves a decision to choose which general concepts or rules could apply to particulars.[10] The exercise of judgment, in Barbara Herman's perspicacious words, always entails some "rules of salience,"[11] which may or may not be easily articulable.

Perspicacious judgment must be communicable. It is not the isolated thinker or citizen alone who can absolve fully the burdens of judgment. Such burdens must be shareable with others in order for tolerance, openness of mind, and spirit to be cultivated, in order, that is, for an enlarged mentality to become a *habitus*. Arendt, as well as Rawls, who each knew Kant's teaching of public reason, realized that in liberal democracies the fact that citizens would fail to share judgments about particulars was just as dangerous as their fundamental disagreement about principles. Unless the universal and the particular could be mediated via a third term, and unless identity in difference could transcend imprisonment within the walls of one's particularity such as to enable communication across divides, the public culture of free societies would collapse. Rawls believed that liberal democracies could remain stable over time only insofar as citizens supported the rationality as well as reasonableness of their terms of cooperation in a just society. Such terms of cooperation were needed to guarantee a sense of fairness and equality among citizens and residents. Arendt agreed, but, for her, the vigilance required for the preservation of such free societies meant that citizens had to exercise judgment about constitutional essentials by learning to act by them and as their interpreters. In acts of civil disobedience, the citizens once again become the legislator and permit themselves to judge the terms of the original social contract and of constitutional essentials.[12]

———

We live in a time when the crises of our republic, in the United States, are approaching Weimar-like dimensions. Growing socioeconomic inequality in the last twenty years has resulted in a negative redistribution of wealth from the bottom to the top; loss of homes and ways of life as a result of corrupt and risky financial practices perpetuated by Wall Street are legion; faith in the fairness of American democracy has been deeply shaken by globalization, which has outsourced jobs as well as subjecting the population to brutal competition, without government or other public and civic institutions coming to the help of those who have lost their jobs in the way of retraining or reskilling programs. Along with the erosion of socioeconomic equality, political equality and reciprocal respect has also eroded. Partisanship today comes close to the dimensions of the Schmittian "friend" versus "foe" distinction.

The fragmentation resulting from the rise of the new social media as well as the spread of some of the more insular forms of identity politics have done serious damage to the cultivation of enlarged mentality among the citizens and to their capacity and willingness to take the standpoint of the others. Such fragmentation is not wholly negative, in that it has also given rise to "counter-publics" by oppositional groups that had not enjoyed their own public voices and media. Yet the more the *interlocking* of these counter-publics fails, and the more individuals withdraw into the cocoons of their own epistemological universes, the more we will lose a sense of a shared political world. Today such loss is accompanied by another epistemological predicament: we are said to be living in "post-truth" or "post-fact" societies.

Such loss of truth has made it easy, particularly since the events of September 11, 2001, to transform legitimate security concerns into intense paranoia and public lies. A significant portion of the American public still believes that the attacks of September 11 were caused by Iraqi nationals. The inconclusive wars against Iraq and Afghanistan, started by the George W. Bush administration, have set into motion an unravelling process in the Middle East. For the first time since the Sykes-Picot accords of 1915, the map of this region is being redrawn. But the United States is busy closing its borders to refugees.

The global refugee crisis reveals not only Europe's clay feet but also the withdrawal of the United States into an isolationist posture seeking to absolve itself of its human rights obligations and commitments. The refugee becomes the enemy, the other, and the criminal. Continuing a trend that had already started under the Obama administration, the Immigration and Customs Enforcement Agency is supplied with personnel and resources, while refugee camps in the United States' southern border are becoming internment camps for mothers and children. The Federal government is declaring that activities by its own citizens to solidarize with refugees in sanctuary cities are illegal and is penalizing them.

Against this worrisome panorama, recalling the work and lives of the émigré intellectuals discussed in this book summons both hope and fear: hope, because their reflections on politics shows that catastrophes can be overcome, that new beginnings are possible, and that wise and lasting institutions can be built on the ruins of old ones; fear, because the one country that opened its arms to many, even if not all, of these great thinkers (Berlin was British, and Levinas French) is now turning away from its own best and unique legacies.

Their lives, work, and example show us that hope must triumph over fear and that the courage for telling it as it is can cut through the deluge of propaganda, fake news, and the illusions of a post-truth society.

# NOTES

## Preface

1. http://gmdac.iom.int/global-migration-trends-factsheet. Accessed on March 3, 2017.

2. http://www.unhcr.org/en-us/news/latest/2016/6/5763b65a4/global-forced-displace ment-hits-record-high.html. Accessed November 14, 2017.

3. As Ned Curthoys writes, "The legacies of the liberal Jewish tradition in ethics, philosophy, history, and literature are many and varied. Indeed, they are too diverse and profuse to be definitely accounted for here, since 'post-Zionism' is now a rubric for a variety of scholarly tendencies encompassing revisionist Israeli historiography, denationalized versions of Jewish history, Mizrahi critiques of Zionist Eurocentrism and Ashkenazi hegemony in Israel, sociological analyses of post-national tendencies in Israel, and a growing interest in the cultural Zionism of Martin Buber and Judah Magnes." In *The Legacy of Liberal Judaism. Ernst Cassirer and Hannah Arendt's Hidden Conversation* (New York and Oxford: Berghahn Books, 2013), 213.

## Chapter 1. The Intertwined Lives and Themes among Jewish Exiles

1. See Detlev Schottker and Erdmut Wizisla, "Hannah Arendt und Walter Benjamin. Konstellationen, Debatten, Vermittlungen," in *Arendt und Benjamin. Texte, Briefe, Dokumente*, ed. Detlev Schottker and Erdmut Wizisla (Frankfurt: Suhrkamp, 2006), 13*ff*. [Referred to hereafter as *Arendt und Benjamin*]. See Arendt's letter to Gershom Scholem of October 17, 1941, recounting her meeting with "Benji" (Walter Benjamin) in Lourdes, after she escapes from the camps in Gurs, reprinted in *Arendt und Benjamin*, 153. This episode will be discussed extensively in chapter 3.

2. Heinrich Blücher to Arendt from Paris on September 15, 1937, and Arendt to Blücher on September 16, 1937, from Geneva, in *Within Four Walls: The Correspondence between Hannah Arendt and Heinrich Blücher, 1936–1968*, ed. Lotte Kohler (New York: Harcourt, 2000), 39–40. On Benjamin in Paris, see Hannah Arendt, "Walter Benjamin: 1892–1940," in Walter Benjamin. *Illuminations. Essays and Reflections*, ed. and with an introduction by Arendt (New York: Schocken Books, 1968), 21*ff*.; on Blücher and herself, Hannah Arendt to Walter Benjamin on July 16, 1937, reprinted in *Arendt und Benjamin*, 127; cf. Elisabeth Young-Bruehl, *For Love of the World: A Biography of Hannah Arendt* (New Haven, CT: Yale University Press, 1984), 122.

3. Yuri Slezkine, *The Jewish Century* (Princeton and Oxford: Princeton University Press, 2004), 61.

4. Bettina Stangneth, *Eichmann vor Jerusalem. Das unbehelligte Leben eines Massenmörders* (Zurich-Hamburg: Rowohlt Taschenbuch , 2014 [2011]), trans. as *Eichmann before Jerusalem. The Unexamined Life of a Mass Murderer* (New York: Alfred Knopf, 2014).

5. On Trotta's movie, see Hannah Arendt (2012)—IMDb; see also *Vita Activa, The Spirit of Hannah Arendt* by Ada Ushpiz, https://zeitgeistfilms.com/film/vitaactivathespiritofhannah arendt.

6. Martin Jay, *Forcefields. Between Intellectual History and Cultural Critique* (London and New York: Routledge, 1993).

## Chapter 2. Equality and Difference: Human Dignity and Popular Sovereignty in the Mirror of Political Modernity

1. Jacques Derrida's oddly named, but significant, autobiographical reflections set me on this path a while ago; see Jacques Derrida, *Monolingualism of the Other: or, The Prosthesis of Origin*, trans. Patrick Mensah, *Cultural Memory in the Present* (Stanford: Stanford University Press, 1998).

2. Marjorie Lehman, *The En Yaaqov. Jacob Ibn Habib's Search for Faith in the Talmudic Corpus* (Detroit: Wayne State University Press, 2012). Cecil Roth in his *History of the Marranos* (London: George Routledge and Sons, Ltd., 1932; printed at the Hebrew press of the Jewish Publication Society in Philadelphia) refers to a "Levi ben Habib, subsequently spiritual leader of the community of Jerusalem," as being "amongst those who were compelled by sheer force to accept Catholicism" (61). I am unable to establish the connection of Levi ben Habib to Jacob Ibn Habib and my family has had no memory of any kind of conversion. Most likely, these are relatives within large families who adapted the Arabic (Ibn) or the Hebrew (ben) or who dropped it altogether and simply retained "Habib." Cf. Roth, discussing "Juan Rodrigo, alias Amatus Lusitanus, of the old family of Habib" in ibid., 297. Thanks to Samuel Zeitlin for bringing Cecil Roth's classic to my attention.

3. Yirmiyahu Yovel, *The Other Within. The Marranos. Split Identity and Emerging Modernity* (Princeton, NJ: Princeton University Press, 2009), 3.

4. Immanuel Kant, "Zum Ewigen Frieden" [1795], in Suhrkamp *Werkausgabe*, vol. 11 (Frankfurt am Main: Suhrkamp, 1977), 213; English trans.: Kant, "Perpetual Peace: A Philosophical Sketch," trans. H. B. Nisbet, in Kant, *Political Writings*, ed. Hans Reiss, Cambridge Texts in the History of Political Thought (Cambridge: Cambridge University Press, 1994, 2nd and enlarged edn.), 105–8.

5. Jacques Derrida, *On Cosmopolitanism and Forgiveness*, trans. Mark Dooley and Michael Hughes (New York: Routledge, 2001), xx.

6. For the historical origins of the concept of the *dhimmi* in the Ummayad dynasty in Spain from the eighth century to the end of the first millennium, see Yovel, *The Other Within*, 11ff.

7. Discrepancies abound in the spelling of the name of Sabbatai Zevi. Scholem himself spells it as "Şevi," with a cedilla. Except when directly referencing Scholem's text, I will use the English spelling Zevi, and in German Zwi. See Gershom Scholem, *Sabbatai Şevi. The Mystical Messiah* (Princeton, NJ: Princeton University Press, 1973).

8. Scholem, *Sabbatai Şevi*, 674–81. In the years following Zevi's apostasy, many of the details

of this encounter with the sultan assumed mythical proportions and bore little relation to historical fact. I am following Scholem's account here, who clarifies that Zevi was heard by the privy council and not the sultan himself, and that the sultan followed the proceedings through a gated window (*kafes*). Zevi appeared before the sultan only to accept his new name and to be appointed "kapici," gatekeeper in the palace. Although Scholem does not comment on this, it is interesting that an individual accused of stirring up the Jewish subjects of the sultan with claims that he was their king, and who was considered by other Jews as their messiah, would nonetheless be accepted into such a confidential place in the palace without much fuss. The facility of the conversion to Islam by a circumcised Jew should also be noted. All he needed to do was recite the "Reis-ul-Allah" prayer, acknowledging Mohammed as the sole and unique prophet of God. Such conversions into Islam or Christianity were common among Jews, with the beginning of the Inquisition in Spain and even before. The Ottoman Empire relied on Christian and Jewish converts to Islam to build and sustain its power in the Balkans. Yovel analyzes how the multiple ethnic and religious identities created in this period can be seen as the beginnings of modern concepts of individuality, in that the individual now fashions a self for him- or herself through a new identity that can no longer be easily confined within the traditional definitions of the community. See Yovel, *The Other Within*, 287ff.

9. After the expulsion from Spain, Salonica became home to many Jewish *conversos* who had converted to Christianity, as well as being inhabited by other Jews who had accepted Islam at earlier times. Salonica was one of the cosmopolitan centers of Europe from the fifteenth to the nineteenth centuries, and these various Jewish groups competed with one another not only for influence and wealth in the Ottoman Empire, but also for the proper understanding of the Jewish Bible and law. For a lively account, see Mark Mazower, *Salonica, City of Ghosts. Christians, Muslims and Jews 1430–1950* (New York: Vintage Books, 2006). Jacob Ibn Habib wrote *En Yaakov* (*The Story of Jacob*) because he felt that the Jews of Salonica were forgetting their traditions rooted in the Old Testament.

10. This episode still has not been widely discussed in Turkish historiography, but there have been a number of studies devoted to it. See Rifat N. Bali, *The "Varlik Vergisi" Affair. A Study of Its Legacy with Selected Documents* (Istanbul: Gorgias Press and Isis Press, 2005); Ayhan Aktar, *Varlik Vergisi ve "Türklestirme" Politikalari* [The Capital Tax and the Politics of Turkification] (Istanbul: Iletisim Yayinları, 2000); Ridvan Akar, *Askale Yolculari: Varlik Vergisi ve Çalisma Kamplari* [The Passengers of Ashkale: The Capital Tax and Labor Camps] (Istanbul: Belge Yayinlari: 2006); Sait Çetinoglu, "The Mechanisms for Terrorizing Minorities: The Capital Tax and Work Battalions in Turkey during the Second World War," *Mediterranean Quarterly* 23, no. 2 (2012): 14–29. I thank Onur Bakiner for helping me with bibliographical references around this issue. In her well-documented work, Corry Guttstadt dates these events to the period between May 1941 and July 1942, during Hitler's march to the Balkans. See Corry Guttstadt, *Die Türkei, die Juden und der Holocaust* (Berlin and Hamburg: Assoziation A Verlag, 2008), 198–201, trans. as *Turkey, the Jews and the Holocaust* (New York: Cambridge University Press, 2013).

11. Certainly, the Jewish encounter with the New World in North and Latin America cannot be ignored. But these experiences, at least for the first generations of European migrants, remained umbilically tied to European modernity, even while uncovering and rediscovering different aspects of the Hebrew faith as in the case of the Jewish encounter with the Puritans of

New England in particular. As Jim Sleeper writes: "But history presented Jews with an arresting irony: Even when they have abjured their ancient, revolutionary, and cosmopolitan faith, it still has driven their historical fate. They are passionate about America not only because they are relieved to have escaped a long nightmare in Europe but also because the old Hebrew faith has figured so decisively in the building of the republic itself. Free of Christian preoccupations with personal salvation—free also, largely, of specific rabbinic constraints—yet still driven by elements of the ancient faith as well as their more recent historical fate, many Jews embraced a new civic covenant that entwined personal renewal with public progress. While a minority of these new Americans let historical scars do the work of fresh wounds—driving them to militarism of one stripe or another—most Jews become poster children for the old civic-republican balance of public obligation and inner integrity." James A. Sleeper, "American Brethren. Hebrews and Puritans," *World Affairs. A Journal of Ideas and Debate* (Fall 2009), 46–60, here 57–58.

12. Steven Aschheim, *Beyond the Borders. The German-Jewish Legacy Abroad* (Princeton, NJ: Princeton University Press, 2007), 20–22. For an informed account of the history of the Jews of Baghdad, whose presence in Mesopotamia reaches back to the Babylonian captivity of 586 BC, and their political as well as cultural influence on the formation of modern Iraq, see the autobiographical account by Nissim Rejwan, *The Last Jews in Baghdad. Remembering a Lost Homeland* (Austin: University of Texas Press, 2004).

13. These intentions may not be as far from certain historical sources in the Jewish tradition as may appear at first sight. The Maskilim, a group of German and Central European Jewish reformers, who were profoundly affected by the emancipation of the Jews from the ghetto and by increasing contact with the secular and humanistic ideals of the Enlightenment, rediscovered the Sephardic tradition of Iberian Jews and their descendants in seventeenth-century Holland. Ned Curthoys writes: "The Maskilim were deeply skeptical of the power of rabbinical authority in ghettoized Jewish communities and wanted to curb an over-emphasis in Jewish education on the study of the Talmud, the textual codification of an oral rabbinical tradition . . . Drawing upon Sephardic models . . . meant widening the past of German Jews, evoking historical figures very different from the prominent rabbinical authorities of recent tradition, promoting an elastic conception of historical Judaism populated by figures that combined religious, philosophical and worldly virtues, proud defenders of Judaism but also skilled community advocates who encouraged dialogue with the non-Jewish world." In *The Legacy of Liberal Judaism*, 46–47. Heinrich Heine is probably the most familiar figure of this orientation. The tragic poem by Heinrich Heine, *Almansor*, is set in Sephardic Spain. See Heine, *Almansor. Eine Tragödie*, ed. Karl-Maria Guth. Deutsche Nationalbibliothek (Berlin: Contumax GmbH and Co: 2015 [1821]).

14. Leopold Lucas, "Die Wissenschaft des Judentums und die Wege zu ihrer Förderung," in Lucas, *Schriften der Gesellschaft zur Förderung der Wissenschaft des Judentums* (Berlin, 1906). All page references are to this edition and will be cited as Lucas, followed by page number.

15. Moritz Goldstein, "Deutsch-Jüdischer Parnass," in *Der Kunstwart* 25, no. 11 (März 1912). All page numbers in the text are to this edition.

16. Margret Heitmann, " 'Sie wirken in einer Gemeinde, die einen historischen Namen besitzt.' Zu Leben und Werk des letzten Glogauer Rabbiners Leopold Lucas (1872–1943)," *Silesiographia. Festschrift für Norbert Conrad* (Carsten Rabe und Matthias Weber: Würzburg, 1998), 105–17.

17. Ibid., 111. All translations from the German in the text are mine in consultation with Stefan Eich. A scholarly and cultural movement called *Wissenschaft des Judentums* (The Science of Judaism) had already been started in 1819 by such luminaries as Leopold Zunz, the Hegelian scholar Eduard Gans, and Heinrich Heine. See Amos Elon, *The Pity of It All. A Portrait of the German-Jewish Epoch. 1743–1933* (New York: A Metropolitan Book, 2002), 110–14, and Curthoys, *The Legacy of Liberal Judaism*, 51. Rabbi Lucas revived this movement rather than establishing it anew. For a lively account of Heine's role in this movement, see Shlomo Avineri, "Where They Have Burned Books, They Will End Up Burning People," *Jewish Review of Books* 8, no. 3 (Fall 2017): 39–41.

18. Heitmann, "Sie wirken in einer Gemeinde," 111.

19. Lucas, "Die Wissenschaft des Judentums," 18.

20. See Yosef Hayim Yerushalmi's masterful account of biblical and secular time, *Zakhor. Jewish Memory and Jewish History*, the Samuel and Althea Stroum Lectures in Jewish Studies (Seattle and London: University of Washington Press, 1982). Cf. also Arendt's very interesting reflections on Herder's significance for the Jews after the Enlightenment. She credits Herder with rendering Jewish history visible in Germany "as history defined essentially by their possession of the Old Testament." Arendt, "The Enlightenment and the Jewish Question," in Arendt, *The Jewish Writings*, ed. Jerome Kohn and Ron H. Feldman (New York: Schocken Books, 2007), 12. At the same time, insofar as this history is theological history and not history connected to that of the world at large, for Herder, writes Arendt, "the Jews have become a people without history within history. Herder's understanding of history deprives them of their past" (16).

21. Lucas, *Geschichte der Stadt Tyrus zur Zeit der Kreuzzüge* (Marburg: Joh. Hamel, 1895).

22. For the concept of "redemptive" historical writing, see Walter Benjamin, "Theses on the Philosophy of History," [1941] in Benjamin, *Illuminations. Essays and Reflections*, ed. Arendt, 253–64.

23. Goldstein, "Deutsch-Jüdischer Parnass," in *Der Kunstwart*, 282. Referred to in the text as Goldstein, followed by page number. All translations are mine with the assistance of Stefan Eich. See the discussion of this essay by Yuri Slezkine, *The Jewish Century*, 69–71.

24. See Amos Elon's moving history of German Jewry from Mendelssohn to the Holocaust: Elon, *The Pity of It All. A Portrait of the German-Jewish Epoch. 1743–1933*.

25. Hannah Arendt quotes Moritz Goldstein's "Deutsch-Jüdischer Parnass" in her essay on Walter Benjamin in "Walter Benjamin: 1892–1940," *Men in Dark Times* (New York: Harcourt, Brace, 1968), 183–84. Cf. Seyla Benhabib, *The Reluctant Modernism of Hannah Arendt*, new edn. (Lanham, New York: Rowman and Littlefield Publishers, Inc., 2003), 36–37 for further discussion.

26. Goldstein, "German Jewry's Dilemma. The Story of a Provocative Essay," in *Leo Baeck Institute Yearbook* (New York, 1957), 236–54.

27. See Homi Bhabha, "Dissemi/Nation: Time, Narrative and the Margins of the Modern Nation" in Bhabha, *The Location of Culture* (New York: Routledge Press, 1994), 139–71.

28. George Steiner, *Errata. An Examined Life* (New Haven, CT: Yale University Press 1998 [1997]), 62.

29. Ibid., 57.

30. Assaf Sagiv, "George Steiner's Jewish Problem," *Azure* 5763 (Summer 2003), 130–54.

31. Ibid., 140–41.

32. Hans Kelsen, *Das Problem der Souveränität und die Theorie des Völkerrechts. Beitrag zu einer reinen Rechtslehre* (Tübingen: J.C.B. Mohr [Paul Siebeck], 1920), 320. See further Judith Shklar on Kelsen, see p. 130 above.

33. Arendt, "The Jew as Pariah: A Hidden Tradition," in Arendt, *The Jewish Writings*, 275–98. See Bernard Lazare, *Job's Dungheap. Essays on Jewish Nationalism and Social Revolution*, with a "Portrait of Bernard Lazare" by Charles Peguy, trans. Harry Lorin Binsse and with a preface by Arendt (New York: Shocken Books, 1948), 65, 84–86.

34. G.W.F. Hegel, "Independence and Dependence of Self-Consciousness: Lordship and Bondage," in *Hegel's Phenomenology of Spirit* [1807], trans. A. V. Miller (Oxford: Clarendon Press, 1977), 111ff.

35. These observations lead Raz-Krakotzkin to a sensitive and illuminating account of the interwovenness of the Jewish and Palestinian experiences, in Amnon Raz-Krakotzkin, *Exil und Binationalismus: Von Gershom Scholem und Hannah Arendt bis zu Edward Said und Mahmoud Darwish* (Berlin: Berlin-Brandenburgische Akademie der Wissenschaften, 2011), 118.

36. On the Brith-Shalom movement, see Shalom Ratzabi, *Between Zionism and Judaism: The Radical Circles in Brith Shalom, 1925–1933* (Leiden: Brill, 2002); Joseph Heller, *From Brith Shalom to Ichud: Judah Leib Magnes and the Struggle for a Binational State in Palestine* (Jerusalem: Magnes Press of Hebrew University, 2003). For a discussion of the transformation of Scholem's views from his anticolonialist critique of Zionism in the 1930s to an affirmation of the Zionist state, see Raz-Krakotzkin, *Exil und Binationalismus*, 97–108.

37. The Israeli citizens of Palestinian origin, whether Muslim, Christian, or Druze, possess all nominal rights, which are, of course, often curtailed for security reasons—such as the right of family unification with members from the Occupied Territories who marry Israeli-Arabs. They are also discriminated against in employment and schooling. It is the Palestinian refugees, whether in Jordan, Lebanon, or Egypt, who have lost their right to have rights with the founding of the State of Israel. While some of these refugees are now citizens of Jordan, Syria, Egypt, and other Arab countries of the Gulf, seventy years after the 1948 war, there are more than half a million Palestinian refugees still living in camps. Their situation has become "the new normal" in the Middle East.

38. Arendt, "Zionism Reconsidered," originally in the *Menorah Journal* 32, no. 2 (October–December 1945): 162–96, in Arendt, *The Jewish Writings*, 343–75, and Arendt, "To Save the Jewish Homeland. There is Still Time," 388–402. For the influence of Arendt's writings on Zionism upon the generation of historians calling themselves "post-Zionists," see Moshe Zimmermann, "Hannah Arendt, the Early 'Post-Zionist,'" in *Hannah Arendt in Jerusalem*, ed. Steven E. Aschheim (Berkeley and Los Angeles: University of California Press, 2001), 181–94.

39. See her concluding and somewhat surprising statements about the establishment of the State of Israel, *The Origins of Totalitarianism*, 299, and my commentary, Benhabib, *The Rights of Others. Aliens, Citizens and Residents. John Seeley Lectures* (Cambridge: Cambridge University Press, 2004), 61–65; cf. Benhabib, "International Law and Human Plurality in the Shadow of Totalitarianism: Hannah Arendt and Raphael Lemkin," in *Politics in Dark Times. Encounters with Hannah Arendt* (Cambridge and Malden, MA: Polity Press, 2011), 219–47.

40. Hans Kelsen, "The Preamble of the Charter—A Critical Analysis," *Journal of Politics* 8 (1946), 134–59; Hersch Lauterpacht, *International Law and Human Rights*, with an introduction by Isodore Silver, The Garland Library of War and Peace (New York: Garland Publishing, Inc., 1973). Lauterpacht writes: "Moreover, irrespective of the question of enforcement, there ought to be no doubt that the provisions of the Charter in the matter of fundamental human rights impose upon the Members of the United Nations a *legal* duty to respect them." 34.

41. Hans Kelsen, "Sovereignty and International Law," vol. 48, no. 5 *Georgetown Law Journal* 627 (Summer 1960), 627–40.

42. See Dan Diner and Michael Stolleis (eds.), *Hans Kelsen and Carl Schmitt. A Juxtaposition* (Gerlingen: Bleicher, 1999).

43. For an illuminating discussion of Schmitt's rejection of what he considered "the Jewish" concept of *Gesetz* as emanating from an act of will in favor of a concept of *nomos* that reveals the "order of the earth," see Raphael Gross, "Jewish Law and Christian Grace—Carl Schmitt's Critique of Kelsen," in Diner and Stolleis, 101–13, here: 106, and Benhabib, "Carl Schmitt's Critique of Kant. Sovereignty and International Law," *Political Theory* 40, no. 6 (December 2012): 688–713. For Schmitt's remarks about Hersch Lauterpacht, "the teacher of public international law at the University of London," cf. Carl Schmitt, "The Turn to the Discriminating Concept of War," in Schmitt, *Writings on War*, ed. Timothy Nunan (Cambridge: Polity Press, 2011[1938]), 37, 40, 48–53. Thanks to Samuel Zeitlin for bringing this reference to my attention.

44. In 1932 Leo Strauss published a commentary on Carl Schmitt's *Der Begriff des Politischen. Mit einer Rede über das Zeitalter der Neutralisierungen und Entpolitisierungen* (Munich and Leipzig, 1932), called "Anmerkungen zu Carl Schmitt, Der Begriff des Politischen," (*Archiv für Sozialwissenschaft und Sozialpolitik* 67, no. 6, 732–49). Highly regarded by Schmitt himself, this essay is included in the English translation of Schmitt's *The Concept of the Political*, expanded edn., trans. George Schwab, with introduction and notes (Chicago: University of Chicago Press, 2007 [1996]). For the discussion of Weber, see Schmitt, *The Concept of the Political*, 20ff. and for Strauss's commentary, see "Notes on Carl Schmitt, *The Concept of the Political*," 81–109, here 103ff. and on whether man is by nature "good" or "evil," 110–11.

45. Leo Strauss, *The Political Philosophy of Hobbes. Its Basis and Its Genesis*, trans. Elsa M. Sinclair [first published in 1936 by Clarendon Press: Oxford] American edn., (Chicago: University of Chicago Press, 1952); Schmitt, *The Leviathan in the State Theory of Thomas Hobbes. Meaning and Failure of a Political Symbol*, trans. George Schwab and Erna Hilfstein (Chicago: University of Chicago Press, 1996) [originally published in 1938 as *Der Leviathan in der Staatslehre des Thomas Hobbes: Sinn und Fehlschlag eines politischen Symbols*].

46. Strauss, *Natural Right and History* (Chicago and London: University of Chicago Press, 1968 [1953]). All references in the text are to this edition.

47. In his compelling account based on Leo Strauss's unpublished lecture notes of Grotius, Kant, and international law, Robert Howse shows the degree to which Strauss was preoccupied by legal questions as well. See Robert Howse, *Leo. Strauss. Man of Peace* (Cambridge: Cambridge University Press, 2014) and my review, *Political Theory*. 45, no. 2 (April 2017): 273–77.

48. Strauss, "Jerusalem and Athens," in Strauss, *Jewish Philosophy and the Crisis of Modernity*, ed. and with an introduction by Kenneth Hart Green (Albany: SUNY Press at Albany, 1997), 377–409. For an exploration of how reflections on theology and cosmology were always guided

by the moral quest for the "good life" for Strauss, see Heinrich Meier, *Das theologisch-politische Problem. Zum Thema von Leo Strauss* (Stuttgart and Weimar: J. B. Metzler Verlag, 2003), 53*ff.* See also Steven B. Smith, *Reading Leo Strauss: Politics, Philosophy, Judaism* (Chicago: University of Chicago Press, 2006).

49. Jürgen Habermas, "The European Nation-State: On the Past and Future of Sovereignty and Citizenship," in *The Inclusion of the Other: Studies in Political Theory*, ed. Ciaran Cronin and Pablo De Greiff (Cambridge, MA: MIT Press, 1998), 105–29, here 115.

50. Benhabib, "Democratic Exclusions and Democratic Iterations: Dilemmas of Just Membership and Prospects of Cosmopolitan Federalism," in Benhabib, *Dignity in Adversity*, 138–66.

51. I first suggested this formulation in Benhabib, *The Rights of Others*, 219.

52. Kant, "Die Metaphysik der Sitten in zwei Teilen" [1797], in *Immanuel Kants Werke*, 121; *The Metaphysics of Morals*, trans. and ed. Mary Gregor (Cambridge: Cambridge University Press, 1996), 140.

53. William Pencak writes: "My main conclusions are that a strain of popular anti-Semitism appeared intermittently before the American Revolution, largely derived from traditional European prejudices . . . the revolutionary era witnessed increased anti-Semitism, along with increased popular participation in civic life, as the Jews were linked with local elites even though they, too, sought privileges they had lacked (except in New York), during the colonial era. Political anti-Semitism exploited popular anti-Semitism as the status of the Jews in a republic, a predominantly Christian republic, became an item of debate far out of proportion to the minuscule number of Jews (about three thousand) in the new nation as of 1790." In William Pencak, *Jews and Gentiles in Early America. 1654–1800* (Ann Arbor: University of Michigan Press, 2005), v-vi. Thanks to Jim Sleeper for helping out with this reference.

54. See Jon Elster, *Ulysses Unbound. Studies in Rationality, Precommitment, and Constraints* (Cambridge: Cambridge University Press, 2000), 88–177; Stephen Holmes, *Passions and Constraint. On the Theory of Liberal Democracy* (Chicago: University of Chicago Press, 1995).

55. Jürgen Habermas has argued for the "cooriginality" [*Gleichursprünglichkeit*] of human rights and sovereignty in an attempt to resolve the paradoxes that so preoccupied Arendt and Kelsen. See Habermas, *Between Facts and Norms. Contributions to a Discourse Theory of Law and Democracy*, trans. William Regh (Cambridge: Polity Press, 1996), 84–104.

56. See Robert Cover, "Foreword: Nomos and Narrative," The Supreme Court 1982 Term, *Harvard Law Review* 97, no. 4 (1983/84): 4–68; reprinted in Robert Cover, *Narrative, Violence and the Law. The essays of Robert Cover*, ed. Martha Minow, Michael Ryan, and Austin Sarat (Ann Arbor: University of Michigan Press, 1993), 95–172. All references are to this edition and cited as Cover, followed by page number.

57. These formulations are relevant not only on the social creation of meaning but for the more specialized question of legal hermeneutics as well. See Cover's comments on Hans Georg Gadamer's *Truth and Method*, trans. G. Barden and J. Cumming (New York: Continuum, 1975): "The entire discussion of legal hermeneutics in *Truth and Method* is disappointingly provincial in several ways." Cover, 98.

58. Jacques Derrida, "The Force of Law: The "Mystical Foundation of Authority," in *Cardozo Law Review*, vol. 11: 919 (1989–1990), 920–1046, bilingual text, trans. Mary Quaintance.

59. There is also a narrower sense of "imperial" in Cover's work (see 106), which resonates deeply with what Judith Shklar has called "legalism." See chapter 7 below.

60. Kant, *Critique of Judgment*, trans. Werner S. Pluhar, with a foreword by Mary J. Gregor (Indianapolis/Cambridge: Hackett Publishing Company, 1987 [1790]), Section 40, "On Taste as a Kind of *Sensus Communis*," 161.

61. Some of these issues are discussed in the collective volume based on 9 years of Istanbul Seminars, dedicated to the Dialogue of Civilizations and conducted by the RESET Foundation on whose Executive Council I serve. See, *Toward New Democratic Imaginaries. Istanbul Seminars on Islam, Culture and Politics*, ed. Seyla Benhabib and Volker Kaul (Zurich: Springer Press, 2016).

62. Derrida, *On Cosmopolitanism and Forgiveness*, xx.

63. A colloquialism in contemporary German to refer to the language and style of young Germans of plural migrant backgrounds.

64. See Salman Rushdie, in particular, *The Moor's Last Sigh* (New York: Vintage Books, 1997); Tahar Ben-Jelloun, *Leaving Tangier: A Novel*, trans. Linda Coverdale (Penguin Books, 2009); Zafer Şenocak, *Atlas of a Tropical Germany. Essays on Politics and Culture. 1990–1998*, trans. and ed. Leslie Adelson (2000); Orhan Pamuk's best-known novel in the West is *Snow* (Faber and Faber Fiction, 2014) but the themes of otherness and the intermingling of Ottoman and Western identities are masterfully explored first in his early work, *Beyaz Kale* (*The White Castle*), trans. Victoria Holbrook (New York: Vintage International, 1998); Deniz Utlu is a young German-Turkish writer and the editor of the journal *freitext* and the author of *Die Ungehaltenen* (Ullstein Buchverlag: Berlin, 2014). Cf. also the interesting work by Ruth Mandel, *Cosmopolitan Anxieties. Turkish Challenges to Citizenship and Belonging in Germany* (Chapel Hill: Duke University Press, 2008).

65. Arendt, *Lectures on Kant's Political Philosophy*, ed. and with an interpretive essay by Ronald Beiner (Chicago: University of Chicago Press, 1982).

66. In "The Hyphenate Writer and American Letters," in Daniel Aaron, *American Notes. Selected Essays* (Boston: Northeastern University Press, 1994), 69–85, here 72–73. While I don't want to suggest that the same process would be or ought to be recapitulated by the hyphenated writers of contemporary Europe, I believe that all those whose work is cited in note 64 above, as well as Moritz Goldstein, would agree with Aaron's observations about this "double vision."

## Chapter 3. The Elusiveness of the Particular: Hannah Arendt, Walter Benjamin, and Theodor Adorno

1. Benjamin, "Theses on the Philosophy of History," in Benjamin, *Illuminations. Essays and Reflections*, ed. and with an introduction by Arendt, 253–65, here 253. For the history of the invention of this automaton by a Hungarian civil servant with the name of Wolfgang von Kempelen in the service of Empress Maria Theresa, and its eventful sale and purchase by others, see Tom Standage, *The Turk. The Life and Times of the Famous Eighteenth-Century Chess-Playing Machine* (New York: Berkeley Books, 2002).

2. Arendt, "Walter Benjamin: 1892–1940," in Benjamin, *Illuminations. Essays and Reflections*, 1–55. There were apparently two versions of the "Theses," one that was published in the

*Zeitschrift für Sozialforschung* in the commemorative issue on Walter Benjamin (Los Angeles, 1942) and another version that Arendt had in her possession and that she subsequently published. I am grateful to Asaf Angermann for clarifying this point for me. For discussion regarding the "Theses," see Theodor Adorno and Gershom Scholem, *Briefwechsel 1939–1969*, ed. Asaf Angermann (Frankfurt: Suhrkamp, 2015), 36. Referred to in the text as *Adorno-Scholem Correspondence*. All translations from the German are mine.

3. Benjamin, "Theses on the Philosophy of History," in Benjamin, *Illuminations*, 255.

4. See Benhabib, "Hannah Arendt and the Redemptive Power of Narrative," in *Social Research* 57, no. 1 (1990): 167–96. The idea of redemptive critique and narrative is indebted to Jürgen Habermas's essay, "Bewußtmachende oder rettende Kritik—die Aktualität Walter Benjamins," in *Philosophisch-politische Profile* (Frankfurt: Suhrkamp, 1981), 336–76 [trans. as Habermas, "Consciousness-Raising or Redemptive Criticism," in *New German Critique*, Special Walter Benjamin issue, no. 17 (Spring 1979): 3–59].

5. For an original and subtle account of the themes of exile and metaphysics in Adorno's work, see Asaf Angermann, "Exile and Metaphysics. Adorno and the Language of Political Experience," *Naharaim* 9, no. 1–2 (2015): 179–94.

6. See *Arendt und Adorno*, ed. Dirk Auer, Lars Rensmann, and Julia Schulze Wessel (Frankfurt: Suhrkamp, 2003); referred to hereafter as *Arendt und Adorno*. See in particular the introduction by the three editors, "Einleitung: Affinität und Aversion. Zum theoretischen Dialog zwischen Arendt und Adorno," 8*ff.*

7. For this whole episode, see Young-Bruehl, *For Love of the World*, 80.

8. For Arendt's reference to Adorno and Horkheimer as a "Schweinebande," (a bunch of pigs) for not wanting to publish Benjamin's "Theses on the Philosophy of History," referred to in this letter as "Über den Begriff der Geschichte," see Hannah Arendt to Heinrich Blücher on August 2, 1941, reprinted in *Arendt und Benjamin*, 146; also, *Within Four Walls*, 72–73. For further correspondence on the edition of the "Theses," which Arendt was preparing for the English publication in *Illuminations*, see Arendt's letter to Adorno of January 20, 1967, in *Arendt und Benjamin*, 175; Adorno's answer of February 3, 1967, 176–77; and their further exchange, again in *Arendt und Benjamin*, 178–81. The patient politesse was at least the public face that Adorno portrayed in his dealings with Hannah Arendt, but in private he revealed that the dislike was mutual. In a letter to Scholem, dated February 17, 1960, concerning a posthumous edition of Benjamin's writings on which they were collaborating at the time, Adorno writes: "the choice of what is to be included is to be decided by you and me; under no circumstances should Mrs. Hannah Arendt in some fashion or another be involved." *Adorno-Scholem Correspondence*, 191. And he continues. "By the way, on the matter of Hannah Arendt, I am intransigent, not only because of my own low esteem of this lady, whom I consider a laundress (*eine Waschweib*), rather, and primarily because, I know what Benjamin thought about her and her earlier husband." 191–92. Adorno means here "Gunther Anders," who was Benjamin's cousin. See also Young-Bruehl, *For Love of the World*, 167.

9. See Theodor Adorno, *Jargon der Eigentlichkeit* (Frankfurt: Suhrkamp, 1964), trans. Knut Tarnowski and Frederic Will as *The Jargon of Authenticity* (Evanston: Northwestern University Press, 1973). On April 18, 1966, Arendt writes to Jaspers concerning a new publication on Hei-

degger by Alexander Schwan, *Politische Philosophie im Denken Heideggers* (Verl: Köln-Opladen, 1965), that "the attacks on him are coming only from that quarter and no other . . . Then too, I can't prove it, but I'm quite convinced that the real people behind the scenes are the Wiesengrund-Adorno crowd in Frankfurt. And that is grotesque, all the more so because it has been revealed (students found this out) that Wiesengrund (a half-Jew and one of the most repulsive human beings I know) tried to go along with the Nazis. For years now he and Horkheimer have accused or threatened to accuse anyone in Germany who was against them of being anti-Semitic. A really distinguished bunch, and yet Wiesengrund is not untalented." *Hannah Arendt and Karl Jaspers. Correspondence. 1926–1969*, ed. Lotte Kohler and Hans Saner (New York: Harcourt, Brace, Jovanovich, 1992), 634. Arendt is referring to an article by Adorno in 1934 in a Frankfurt student newspaper called *Diskus*, discussing a poetry collection by the "Reichsjugendführer" (Youth Leader of the Reich), Baldur von Schirah. See *Arendt und Adorno*, 8. Given how extensive Adorno's critique of Jaspers is in this book, it is unclear to me whether Arendt actually was familiar with this text or was referring to general reviews of it in the German press. Otherwise, it is hard to account for the fact that she leaves Adorno's critique of Jaspers uncommented upon. See Adorno, *The Jargon of Authenticity*, 8–9, 22–23, 28. Ironically, Adorno's critique of Heidegger's "jargon" is quite akin to the objections to Heidegger that Jaspers himself had raised in his "Letter to the Freiburg University Denazification Committee," on December 22, 1945, in Richard Wolin, ed., *The Heidegger Controversy: A Critical Reader* (Cambridge, MA: MIT Press, 1993), 147–51. Jaspers writes of "the torrent" of Heidegger's language and that his "manner of thinking to me seems in its essence unfree, dictatorial, and incapable of communication . . . today in its pedagogical effects [it would] be disastrous." 149.

10. This is a complex phrase that captures multiple epistemological, methodological, and even psychoanalytical dimensions for Adorno to which I shall return. See his statement from the preface to *Negative Dialectics*: "To use the strength of the subject to break through the fallacy of constitutive subjectivity—this is what the author felt to be his task ever since he came to trust his own mental impulses," in Adorno, *Negative Dialektik* (Frankfurt: Suhrkamp, 1973); trans. E. B. Ashton as *Negative Dialectics* (New York: Seabury Press, 1973), xx. Referred to in the text as *ND*.

11. Cf. Samir Gandesha's statement: "Mit anderen Worten, wenn für beide die Moderne die Unterordnung des 'Neuen' unter das immergleiche beinhaltet dann wurde das 'Neue' gerade im ästhetischen Urteil als Problem behandelt." ("In other words, when for both modernity means the subsumption of the 'new' under repetitive sameness, then precisely in aesthetic judgment 'the new' is treated as a problem.") Gandesha names "das Auffressen oder Verschlingen des Partikularen durch das Universelle" (the devouring or swallowing whole of the particular through the universal) as one of the central features of the development of modernity, in "Schreiben und Urteilen. Adorno, Arendt und der Chiasmus der Naturgeschichte," in *Arendt und Adorno*, 199–233, here 227.

12. Adorno, "Zur Aktualität der Philosophie," in *Philosophische Frühschriften. Gesammelte Schriften*, vol. 1 (Frankfurt: Suhrkamp, 1973), 325*ff.*; this lecture was not published until after Adorno's death. English translation by Benjamin Snow (a pseudonym for Susan Buck-Morss) as "The Actuality of Philosophy," with an introduction in *Telos* (Spring 1977), 120–33. All page

references in the text are to this English translation. Professor Buck-Morss personally clarified that she had used Benjamin Snow as a pseudonym during an Adorno Conference at Bogazici University held in Istanbul on June 2–4, 2016. Adorno's text is abbreviated as *AP*.

13. Hegel, *Grundlinien der Philosophie des Rechts* [1821], in *Werke*, vol. 7, ed. Eva Moldenhauer and Karl Markus Michel (Frankfurt: Suhrkamp-Taschenbuch Wissenschaft, 1970), 24; English edn., *Elements of the Philosophy of Right*, ed. Allen W. Wood, *Cambridge Texts in the History of Political Thought* (New York: Cambridge University Press, 1991), 20.

14. See Martin Heidegger, *Sein und Zeit*, 10th edn. (Tübingen: Max Niemeyer Verlag, 1963) [1927]); English edn., *Being and Time*, trans. John Macquarrie and Edward Robinson (New York: Harper and Row, 1962 [1927]). For a masterful discussion of Kierkegaard, Husserl, and Heidegger in Adorno's thought, see Peter E. Gordon, *Adorno and Existence* (Cambridge, MA, and London, UK: Harvard University Press, 2016).

15. Georg Lukács, "Reification and the Consciousness of the Proletariat," in *History and Class Consciousness*, trans. Rodney Livingstone (Cambridge, MA: MIT Press, 1971), 110–31.

16. Referring to Lukács's solution of the "thing-in-itself problem" through an analysis of the "commodity structure," Adorno writes that "the truth content of a problem is in principle different from the historical and psychological conditions out of which it grows" ("Actuality of Philosophy," 128). This is a reductionist reading of Lukács, because for Lukács "the commodity structure" is a category that shapes the form of a world as well as of consciousness; it is not merely a psychological or historical "fact." Adorno does not so much reject the analysis of the commodity structure as much as he substitutes his Benjaminian materialism for Lukács's ontology of social labor, and writes that "Like a source of light, the historical figure of commodity and of exchange value may free the form of a reality, the hidden meaning of which remained closed to investigation of the thing-in-itself problem" (128). Of course, the Marxian theory of the emancipation of humans from the forces of nature through the transformative activity of labor is subject to a devastating critique in the *Dialectic of Enlightenment*. Quite to the contrary: the process of social labor is now seen as subjecting not only nature but the nature within humans themselves to domination, such that the price of civilization is the repression of the nature within us. This, of course, is the well-known argument of the *Dialectic of Enlightenment*. Cf. Theodor Adorno and Max Horkheimer, *Dialektik der Aufklärung*, 7th edn. (Frankfurt: Fischer Verlag, 1980); trans. John Cumming, *Dialectic of Enlightenment* (New York: Herder and Herder, 1972); cf. Benhabib, *Critique, Norm and Utopia. A Study of the Foundations of Critical Theory* (New York: Columbia University Press, 1986), 164–71. As Deborah Cook observes, "The affinity between mind and nature should not be understood as positive, it does not authorize a foundational conception of nature because the human mind partially extricated itself from nature in its attempts to dominate it. The mind becomes 'something else,' something other than instinct by virtue of 'reflecting existence' with a view to ensuring its survival . . . Consequently, reflection on nature in ourselves involves both acknowledging our resemblance to nature as instinctual, embodied beings, and respecting nature's heterogeneity." Deborah Cook, "The One and the Many: Revisioning Adorno's Critique of Western Reason," in *Studies in Social and Political Thought* 18 (Winter 2010), 69–80, here 74.

17. See Benjamin, *The Origin of German Tragic Drama*, trans. John Osbourne (London: New

Left Review, 1977). See Susan Buck-Morss's exploration of the terms "configuration" and "crystallization of elements" as methodological dimensions of Benjamin's work in *The Origin of Negative Dialectics: Theodor W. Adorno, Walter Benjamin and the Frankfurt Institute* (New York: Free Press, 1977), 96–111.

18. Cf. Max Horkheimer, "Traditional and Critical Theory," in *Critical Theory*, trans. M. J. O'Connell et al., (New York: Herder and Herder, 1972), 188–244. "It is easy," writes Detlev Claussen, "to imagine Horkheimer also having been irritated by the lecture Adorno gave on the occasion of the *Habilitation*, with the challenging title, 'The Actuality of Philosophy' . . . Horkheimer, who according to Adorno thought that people were like animals, tends to derive his thinking from the French materialism of the Enlightenment, while Adorno does the reverse: feeling that animals are like humans, he aspires to go beyond German idealism." *Theodor W. Adorno. One Last Genius*, trans. Rodney Livingstone (Cambridge, MA: Harvard University Press, 2008), 228.

19. Susan Buck-Morss (alias Benjamin Snow), "Introduction to Adorno's 'The Actuality of Philosophy,'" 116.

20. Hegel, *Die Phänomenologie des Geistes*, ed. J. Hoffmeister. *Philosophische Bibliothek* (Hamburg: Felix Meiner, 1952 [1807]), 69; English edn., *Phenomenology of Spirit*, trans. A. V. Miller, with an analysis and foreword by John Findlay (Oxford: Clarendon Press, 1977), 138.

21. Although it has not been much discussed in the literature on Adorno, careful commentators have noted the significance of this early essay in anticipating central themes of Adorno's *Negative Dialectics*; cf. Detlev Claussen, *Theodor W. Adorno. One Last Genius*, 321. Thus, Adorno returns to Husserl many times throughout his life. His discussion of Husserl in *Against Epistemology: A Metacritique. Studies in Husserl and the Phenomenological Antinomies* [trans. Willis Domingo (Oxford: Basil Blackwell 1982], first composed in Oxford during 1934–37, in preparation for a second dissertation that never came to fruition, is much more critical. Siding with Hegel's critique of epistemology in the *Phenomenology of Spirit*, Adorno criticizes the Husserlian search for an "absolutely first," unmediated beginning, as illusory. "The first and immediate," he writes, "is always, as a concept, mediated and thus not first" (7).

22. For an extensive discussion see Benhabib, *The Reluctant Modernism of Hannah Arendt*, 63ff.

23. Arendt, "A Reply," exchange with Eric Voegelin about his review of *The Origins of Totalitarianism*, in *Review of Politics* 15 (January 1953), 78.

24. See Arendt, "What Is Existenz Philosophy?," *Partisan Review* 18, no. 1(1946): 35–56. The essay was published in German as "Was ist Existenz Philosophie?" in *Hannah Arendt. Sechs Essays* (Heidelberg: Schneider, 1948). It has been reprinted as Arendt, "What Is Existential Philosophy?," trans. Robert and Rita Kimber, in Arendt, *Essays in Understanding. 1930–1954*, ed. Jerome Kohn (Harcourt, Brace, and Company: New York, 1994), 163–87. Referred to in the text as *EP*. As I explain in *The Reluctant Modernism of Hannah Arendt* (56–60, fn. 35) because the term *Existenzphilosophie* in German connotes a much-wider philosophical movement—including Dilthey's *Lebensphilosophie* for example—than do the terms existentialism or existential philosophy in English, I will retain the original title. All references in the text are to the Kohn edition, unless otherwise noted. I have consulted the original and used my own translations as

indicated when necessary. For Arendt's shyness that Jaspers may not have appreciated what she had to say about his philosophy, see Letter 42 in *Hannah Arendt and Karl Jaspers. Correspondence. 1926–1969*, 47.

25. Arendt, *Between Past and Future. Eight Exercises in Political Thought* (New York: The Viking Press, 1961). Referred to in the text as *BPF*.

26. Arendt, *The Human Condition*, 8th edn. (Chicago: University of Chicago Press, 1973 [1958]). Referred to in the text as *HC*.

27. See Adorno, *Negative Dialectics*, 295ff.; cf. also Benhabib, *Critique, Norm and Utopia*, 209–11.

28. See Letters 40 and 42 in *Hannah Arendt and Karl Jaspers. Correspondence. 1926–1969* on their exchange concerning the circular issued by the Nazi Ministry of Education, which Heidegger had also signed, prohibiting Husserl from using the university library (42–49); on Jaspers's own version of these events and Arendt's insistence that Heidegger can be regarded "as a potential murderer" for having done this to Husserl, see p. 48. For similar concerns about the education of the German youth in the post-World War II period, see Adorno, "Education after Auschwitz," in *Critical Models: Interventions and Catchwords*, ed. Henry Pickford (New York: Columbia University Press, 2005), 191–204.

29. Richard Rorty, "The World Well Lost," originally in *Journal of Philosophy* (1972) reprinted in *Consequences of Pragmatism* (Minneapolis: University of Minnesota Press, 1982), 3–18.

30. See Benhabib, "Appendix: The Personal Is Not the Political," in *The Reluctant Modernism of Hannah Arendt*, 221–35. Not much of philosophical import has been added in the last decade to understanding the Arendt-Heidegger nexus better, but ever-new biographical accounts of this fascinating story abound. Most recently, cf. Daniel Maier-Katkin, *Stranger from Abroad. Hannah Arendt, Martin Heidegger, Friendship and Forgiveness* (New York and London: W.W. Norton and Company, 2010). Their love affair remains at the center of Margarete von Trotta's much-acclaimed biopic on Hannah Arendt (http://www.imdb.com/title/tt1674773). Ada Ushpiz's *Vita Activa. The Spirit of Hannah Arendt* focuses on her Jewishness and her theory of totalitarianism. (https://zeitgeistfilms.com/film/vitaactivathespiritofhannaharendt.).

31. Heidegger, "Letter on Humanism," in *Basic Writings*, ed. David Farrell Krell (New York: Harper and Collins, 1993), 213–67, here 234; also Heidegger, "Überwindung der Metaphysik," in *Vorträge und Aufsätze* (Pfüllingen: Günther Neske, 1978 [1954]), 67–97. These notes were originally composed between 1936 and 1946.

32. Again, there are remarkable parallels between Arendt's and Adorno's assessment of these aspects of Heidegger's thought. See Adorno, *The Jargon of Authenticity*, 71, 136, 147ff., 151, where Adorno writes: "For Heidegger the They become a cloudy mixture of elements which are merely ideological products of the exchange relationship."

33. For an early diagnosis of this aspect of Heidegger's thought much before the Heidegger scandals of the 1970s erupted, see Karsten Harries, who writes: "*Being and Time* invites a resolve to be resolved, a readiness to commit oneself without prior assurance that there is a cause worthy of our commitment. To insist on such assurance would be a mark of inauthenticity. But what is to distinguish the readiness to be resolved from a readiness to be seized?" "Heidegger as a Political Thinker," *Review of Metaphysics* (June 1976): 648.

34. Heidegger, *Being and Time*, English edn., 155; German edn., 118; emphasis in the German original.

35. See Benhabib, *The Reluctant Modernism of Hannah Arendt*, 135.

36. See Adorno, Else Frenkel-Brunswik, Daniel J. Levinson, and R. Nevitt Sanford, "'The Authoritarian Personality," abridged edn., *Studies in Prejudice*, ed. Max Horkheimer and Samuel H. Flowerman (New York and London: W. W. Norton, 1982 [1950]), particularly part 3 called "Qualitative Studies of Ideology," authored by Adorno, 295ff. Adorno writes of the "mental rigidity" of those who score high on the various scales designated to study prejudice and anti-Semitism (299), and that "the object must possess features, or at least be capable of being perceived and interpreted in terms of features which harmonize with the destructive tendencies of the prejudiced subject" (300). For further discussion of parallelisms and divergences between Arendt's and Adorno and Horkheimer's analyses of anti-Semitism, see my essay, "From 'The Dialectic of Enlightenment' to 'The Origins of Totalitarianism' and the Genocide Convention: Adorno and Horkheimer in the Company of Arendt and Lemkin," in *The Modernist Imagination. Intellectual History and Critical Theory. Essays in Honor of Martin Jay*, ed. Warren Breckman, Peter E. Gordon, A. Dirk Moses, Samuel Moyn, and Elliot Neaman (New York and Oxford: Berghahn Books, 2009), 299–331.

37. Adorno and Horkheimer, *Dialektik der Aufklärung*, 167.

38. Arendt, "Thinking and Moral Considerations: A Lecture," (1971), reprinted in *Social Research*, 50th anniversary issue (Spring/Summer 1984).

39. Ibid., 5. See also, Benhabib, *The Reluctant Modernism of Hannah Arendt*, 172–99.

40. Arendt, *Lectures of Kant's Political Philosophy*, ed. and with an interpretive essay by Ronald Beiner (Chicago: University of Chicago Press, 1982); and Arendt, "Preface," *Thinking*, vol. 1., *The Life of the Mind* (New York: Harcourt, Brace, and Jovanovich, 1978 [1977]), 3ff.; Kant, *Critique of Judgment*, trans. and with an introduction by Werner S. Pluhar (Indianapolis and Cambridge: Hackett Publishing Company, 1987). Abbreviated in the text as *CJ*.

41. Richard Bernstein, "Judging—the Actor and the Spectator," in *Philosophical Profiles* (Philadelphia: University of Pennsylvania Press, 1986), 232–33.

42. Arendt, "Introduction," *Thinking*, vol. 1., *The Life of the Mind*, 5 and Arendt, "Thinking and Moral Considerations," 8.

43. Arendt's reflections on judgment continue to fascinate scholars. In an extremely interesting article, David L. Marshall discusses Arendt's view in the light of her reading of Hegel's doctrine of judgment in his Logic. See David L. Marshall, "The Origin and Character of Hannah Arendt's Theory of Judgment," in *Political Theory* 38, no. 3 (April 2010): 367–93.

44. Arendt, "Crisis in Culture," in *Between Past and Future. Six Exercises in Political Thought*, 220–21.

45. I have dealt with these themes in great length in my *Critique, Norm and Utopia*; for Hegel's critique of Kant, cf. 70–84 and for Adorno's critique of Kant, 205–13.

46. Adorno, *Ästhetische Theorie*, in *Gesammelte Schriften*, ed. Rolf Tiedemann (Frankfurt: Suhrkamp, 1970), vol. 7, 111. Abbreviated in the text as *AT*.

47. Susan Buck-Morss investigates this search for the "cipher" in relation to Benjamin's method of building constellations in *The Origins of Negative Dialectics*, 96ff.

48. Albrecht Wellmer, "Truth, Semblance, Reconciliation," in *The Persistence of Modernity*.

*Essays on Aesthetics, Ethics and Postmodernism*, trans. David Midgley (Cambridge: Polity Press, 1991), 7–8.

49. Ibid., 6–7.

50. Wellmer, "Modernism and Postmodernism: The Critique of Reason since Adorno," in *The Persistence of Modernity*, 71.

51. Habermas, "Urgeschichte der Subjektivität und verwilderte Selbstbehauptung," in *Philosophisch-politische Profile*, 167–79; English trans., "Theodor Adorno—The Primal History of Subjectivity—Self-Affirmation Gone Wild," in *Philosophical-Political Profiles*, trans. Frederick Lawrence (Cambridge, MA: MIT Press, 1983), 99–111, here 107.

## Chapter 4. Whose Trial? Adolf Eichmann's or Hannah Arendt's? The Eichmann Controversy Revisited

1. Arendt, *Eichmann in Jerusalem. A Report on the Banality of Evil* (New York: Penguin Books, 1994 [1963]), revised and enlarged edn. Referred to in the text as *EiJ*.

2. "Nearly every major literary and philosophical figure in New York chose sides in what the writer Irving Howe called a 'civil war' among New York intellectuals—a war, he later predicted, that might 'die down, simmer' but will perennially 'erupt again.' So it has." Roger Berkowitz, "Misreading 'Eichmann in Jerusalem,'" *New York Times Opinionator*, July 7, 2013. See Irving Howe, "The New Yorker and Hannah Arendt," *Commentary* (October 1963): 318–19, 322. Also, Anson Rabinbach, "Eichmann in New York: The New York Intellectuals and the Hannah Arendt Controversy," *October* 108 (Spring 2004): 97–111.

3. Some parts of this essay have previously appeared in Benhabib, "Arendt's *Eichmann in Jerusalem*," in *The Cambridge Companion to Hannah Arendt*, ed. Dana Villa (Cambridge: Cambridge University Press, 2000), 65–86.

4. Gershom Scholem, "'Eichmann in Jerusalem': An Exchange of Letters between Gershom Scholem and Hannah Arendt," *Encounter* 22 (January 1964), 51–56; reprinted in Arendt, *The Jew as Pariah: Jewish Identity and Politics in the Modern Age*, ed. Ron H. Feldman (New York: Grove Press, 1978), 241. The new and expanded edition of this volume, Arendt, *The Jewish Writings*, contains Arendt's reply to Scholem and other documents in the controversy but not Scholem's letter (see 465*ff.*).

5. Arendt, "A Letter to Gershom Scholem," in Arendt, *The Jewish Writings*, 466.

6. Ibid.

7. Judith Butler, "I Merely Belong to Them," *London Review of Books* 29, no. 9–10 (May 2007): 26–28.

8. Cf. Arendt, "Zionism Reconsidered" (1941), in Arendt, *The Jewish Writings*, 343–75, here 372. Also my discussion of Arendt's politics in this period in Benhabib, *The Reluctant Modernism of Hannah Arendt*, 35–47.

9. Tom Segev, *The 7th Million. The Israelis and the Holocaust*, trans. Haim Watzman (New York: Henry Holt and Company, 1991); Leora Bilsky gives an excellent analysis of the broader political as well as jurisprudential issues involved in the Eichmann trial, in *Transformative Justice. Israeli Identity on Trial* (Ann Arbor: University of Michigan Press, 2004). See also Idith Zertal,

*Israel's Holocaust and the Politics of Nationhood* (New York and Cambridge: Cambridge University Press, 2005).

10. See Michael R. Marrus, *The Holocaust in History* (Toronto: Lester and Orpen Dennys, 1987), 4–5: "Up to the time of the Eichmann trial in Jerusalem, in 1961, there was relatively little discussion of the massacre of European Jewry . . . Since then scholarship has proceeded apace . . . Hannah Arendt's *Eichmann in Jerusalem*, originally an assessment of the trial for *The New Yorker*, prompted a debate in the historical literature that echoes to our own times." Lucy S. Dawidowicz's immensely popular, *The War against the Jews. 1933–1945*, special tenth anniversary edn. (New York: Bantam Books, 1986 [1975]) was written nearly a decade after *Eichmann in Jerusalem* and engaged, of course, in the ritual diatribe of Jewish historians against Hannah Arendt for having misrepresented the behavior of the Judenräte and their leaders; see Dawidowicz, *The War against the Jews*, 435–36, fn. 7.

11. David Cesarani, *Becoming Eichmann. Rethinking the Life, Crimes and Trial of a "Desk Murderer,"* (Raleigh, Essex: Da Capo Press: 2007 [2006]); Deborah Lipstadt, *The Eichmann Trial, Jewish Encounters* (New York: Schocken Books, 2011).

12. Ralph Ellison, "The World and the Jug," in *Shadow and Act* (New York: Random House, 1964), 108.

13. Cf. Arendt: "Psychology, depth psychology or psychoanalysis, discovers no more than the ever-changing moods, the ups and downs of our psychic life, and its results and discoveries are neither particularly appealing nor very meaningful in themselves." Arendt, *Thinking*, vol. 1, *The Life of the Mind*, 35. I thank my student Clara Picker's research paper, "Arendt, Eichmann and the Problem of Thinking under Modern Conditions," for calling my attention to this quote.

14. Léon Poliakov's *Harvest of Hate. The Nazi Program for the Destruction of the Jews of Europe*, foreword by Reinhold Niebuhr (New York: Syracuse University Press, 1954), was one of the first works to report more or less accurately the extent of the destruction of European Jewry.

15. David Cesarani's discussion of Stanley Milgram's experiments on "obedience" and his attempt to present them as consonant with Arendt's analysis is helpful; cf. Cesarani, *Becoming Eichmann*, 352–54.

16. Christopher Browning, *Ordinary Men. Reserve Police Battalion 101 and the Final Solution in Poland* (New York: Harper Collins, 1993[1992]); Daniel Jonah Goldhagen, *Hitler's Willing Executioners. Ordinary Germans and the Holocaust* (New York: Alfred Knopf, 1996).

17. See Mommsen's introduction to the 1986 German revised edition of *Eichmann in Jerusalem*, reprinted as: "Hannah Arendt and the Eichmann Trial," in Hans Mommsen, *From Weimar to Auschwitz: Essays in German Historiography* (Princeton, NJ: Princeton University Press, 1991), 254–78.

18. Saul Friedlander, *Nazi Germany and the Jews. 1933–1945*, abridged edn. by Orna Kennan (New York: Harper Collins Publishers, 2009).

19. Cf. Richard Wolin, "The Banality of Evil. The Demise of a Legend," *Jewish Review of Books*, (September 4, 2014) at http://jewishreviewofbooks.com/articles/1106/the-banality-of-evil-the-demise-of-a-legend/ (accessed on September 14, 2014).

20. While *OT* is more intentionalist, *EiJ* contains "functionalist" elements that stress the

bureaucracy and impersonal machinery of death that made the Holocaust possible, but Arendt never disputes the centrality of anti-Semitism for understanding the Third Reich as a whole. See the important chapter in *The Origins of Totalitarianism* called "Ideology and Terror," (1976 [1951]), 460–79.

21. Bettina Stangneth, *Eichmann vor Jerusalem. Das unbehelligte Leben eines Massenmörders* (Zurich-Hamburg: Rowohlt Taschenbuch , 2014 [2011]), trans. as *Eichmann before Jerusalem. The Unexamined Life of a Mass Murderer* (New York: Alfred Knopf, 2014). Referred to in the text as *EvJ*. I have used the German edition; all translations are mine. There is a double meaning in Stangneth's title: on the one hand the title can be read to mean that Eichmann stands *before* [the judges of] Jerusalem and on the other, it can also be read to mean Eichmann *anterior* to Jerusalem. See also my intervention in this debate, criticizing Richard Wolin and Deborah Lipstadt, "Who's on Trial? Eichmann or Arendt?," http://opinionator.blogs.nytimes.com /2014/09/21/whos-on-trial-eichmann-or-anrendt/?_php=true&_type=blogs&_r=0.

22. Note that Arendt herself thought that "according to well-informed circles" in Europe "it was the Russian Intelligence service that spilled the news" (*EiJ*, 238). Stangneth's research shows that in addition to Fritz Bauer, Simon Wiesenthal and his colleagues were on Eichmann's trail as well.

23. See Theodor Adorno's pedagogical efforts to raise public consciousness in postwar Germany about this issue in his *Erziehung zur Mündigkeit: Vorträge und Gespräche mit Helmut Becker 1959–1969*, ed. Gerd Kadelbach (Suhrkamp: Frankfurt, 1970).

24. Quoted in Jennifer Schuessler, "Book Portrays Genocidal Nazi as Evil, but Not Banal," *New York Times*, Sept. 3, 2014, C5.

25. Wolin, "The Banality of Evil. The Demise of a Legend."

26. As evidence mounted that Eichmann, "the specialist for Jewish affairs," had provided the first hypothetical numbers of the Jews murdered, and after Robert Jackson, the American chief prosecutor in the Nuremberg trials, named Eichmann "this dark figure, who was in charge of the extermination program," Eichmann and his cohort were alarmed and dismayed. According to Bettina Stangneth, in 1949 Léon Poliakov also published the first more or less accurate estimate of the Holocaust's figures under the title "A. Eichmann ou le rêve de Caligulas" (*Adolf Eichmann or Caligula's Dream*), cited in Stangneth (*EvJ*, English trans., 97). Increasing mentions of his name as well as the undeniable facts of the Holocaust that began to appear all over the world press convinced Eichmann and his circle of neo-Nazi buddies to counter this Jewish "propaganda" by telling their story. Arendt believed that Eichmann himself "had made many efforts to break out of his anonymity" (*EiJ*, 238).

27. There were many attempts to understand this syndrome by famous psychologists such as Bruno Bettelheim and members of the Frankfurt School who worked on the "authoritarian personality." Cf. Bruno Bettelheim, "Individual and Mass Behavior in Extreme Situations." *Journal of Abnormal and Social Psychology* 38 (1943): 417–52; Adorno, et al. "The Authoritarian Personality."

28. Kant, *Critique of Judgment*, par. 40, "On Taste as a Kind of Sensus Communis," 160.

29. Arendt, "The Crisis in Culture. Its Social and Political Significance," in *BPF*, 197–226.

30. Arendt, *Denktagebuch 1950–1973. Erster Band,* ed. Ursula Ludz and Ingeborg Nordmann (Munich and Zurich: Piper Verlag, 2002), Notebook 22, pp. 571–84.

31. Arendt, "The Crisis in Culture," in *Between Past and Future*, 220.

32. Ibid., 221.

33. Richard Wolin, "Thoughtlessness Revisited. A Response to Seyla Benhabib," *Jewish Review of Books*, September 30, 2014, http://jewishreviewofbooks.com/articles/1287/in-still-not -banal-a-response-to-seyla-benhabib/?utm_source=Jewish+Review+of+Books&utm _campaign=4142abc423-Fall_2014-Wolin&utm medium=email&utm_term=0_538f7810ff -4142abc423-.

34. Heidegger, "Was heisst Denken?," in *Vorträge und Aufsätze* (Pfullingen: Verlag Gunther Neske, 1954 [1978]), 123–39, here 125. This text is based on a brief radio lecture which Heidegger gave in May 1952 in the Bayrischer Rundfunk and published in the journal *Merkur* in 1952. The English translation is based on the lectures that Heidegger gave in the winter semester of 1951–52 at the University of Freiburg and that were published as: Heidegger, "Was heisst Denken," in *Gesamtausgabe. I. Abteilung. Veröffentlichte Schriften 1910–76*, vol. 8 (Frankfurt: Vittorio Klostermann, [1954] 2002), 1–26. Cf. Heidegger, "What Is Called Thinking?," trans. J. Glenn Gray, (New York: Harper Perennial, [1968] 1976), 5–12, here 5–6. I have compared the two editions of "Was heisst Denken?" and noted discrepancies.

35. Heidegger, "Was heisst Denken?," in *Vorträge und Aufsätze*, 126. There are some sentences included in this essay that are neither in the lecture version of the German nor in the English translation. Heidegger writes that the claim that "in our thought-provoking time we are still not thinking," means that "what is worth thinking about (*das Bedenkliche*) shows itself in this assertion. The assertion should by no means be interpreted to mean, therefore, in the prejorative sense that everywhere only thoughtlessness (*Gedankenlosigkeit*) prevails" (125–26). These sentences are not contained in the corresponding German lectures on p. 7 nor in the Gray translation on pp. 5–6.

36. Heidegger, "Was heisst Denken?," 127; English trans. of the lectures, 7.

37. In the introduction to *The Life of the Mind*, the first volume on *Thinking*, Arendt explains again how the puzzles of the Eichmann trial led her to focus on thinking and moral concerns. In this work, however, as opposed to *The Human Condition* in which she was concerned with the *vita activa* (the life of activity), she turns to the *vita contemplativa* (the life of the mind). Yet rather than just following Heidegger, she situates herself between Kant and Heidegger. She interprets Kant's distinction between "reason" (*Vernunft*) and "intellect" (*Verstand*) to correspond to the distinction between thinking and knowing. Whereas thinking aims at generating meaning; intellect is concerned with truth. "The need of reason is not inspired by the quest for truth but by the quest for meaning. And truth and meaning are not the same," she writes. (15) The basic metaphysical fallacy is to interpret "meaning on the model of truth." This then leads her to the striking claim that "The latest and in some respects most striking instance of this occurs in Heidegger's *Being and Time*, which starts out by raising 'anew the question of the meaning of Being.' Heidegger himself, in a later interpretation of his own initial question, says explicitly: 'Meaning of Being' and 'Truth of Being' say the same." (15) It would be beyond the scope of this chapter to follow all the epistemological questions that Arendt's claims raise but we see again that thinking for Arendt is not the same as thinking for Heidegger.

38. Stangneth discusses Eichmann referring to himself as "eine kleine Zahnrädchen im Getriebe," that is, a "small cog in the machinery" of the Nazi high command (282). Neither Arendt

nor Stangneth accepted this account of Eichmann's actions, and in fact, Stangneth shows that it was Willem Sassen who first came up with this phraseology (487).

39. Arendt, *The Life of the Mind, Thinking*, 5.

40. Arendt, "Thinking and Moral Considerations: A Lecture," *Social Research* 38, no. 3 (Autumn 1971), reprinted in *Social Research*. 50th anniversary issue (Spring/Summer, 1984), 8.

41. Arendt, "Thinking and Moral Considerations," 180–89.

42. Mary McCarthy writes to Arendt on August 10, 1945, and Arendt responds in *Between Friends. The Correspondence of Hannah Arendt and Mary McCarthy, 1949–1975*, ed. Carol Brightman (New York: Harcourt, Brace, Jovanovich), 19.

43. Ibid., 22.

44. Ibid., 27.

45. Cf. the heart-wrenching story of Mr. Storfer, a member of the Jewish community of Vienna, who writes to Eichmann upon being deported to Auschwitz. When Eichmann informs him that he cannot be released, Storfer requests that he be given less heavy work. His assignment will now be to keep the gravel paths in order with the broom but he will also have the right to sit down on one of those benches along the path to rest. Arendt quotes Eichmann: "Whereupon he was very pleased, and we shook hands, and then he was given the broom and sat down on his bench. It was a great inner joy to me that I could at least see the man with whom I had worked for so many long years, and that we could speak to each other." Six weeks after this normal human encounter, Storfer was dead—not gassed, apparently, but shot. Arendt asks: "[Is] this a textbook case of bad faith, of lying self-deception combined with outrageous stupidity? Or is it simply the case of the eternally unrepentant criminal . . . who cannot afford to face reality because his crime has become part and parcel of it?" (*EiJ*, 51–52).

46. Irving Howe, "Banality and Brilliance: Irving Howe on Hannah Arendt," reprinted in *Dissent Magazine* (June 5, 2013), http://www.dissentmagazine.org/online_articles/banality -and-brilliance-irving-howe-on-hannah-arendt.

47. For earlier account of the controversy between Richard Wolin and myself, see Corey Robin, http://coreyrobin.com/2014/10/01/the-arendt-wars-continue-richard-wolin-v-seyla -benhabib/ and http://coreyrobin.com/2014/10/02/did-hannah-arendt-ever-see-eichmann -testify-a-second-reply-to-richard-wolin/.

48. Corey Robin, "The Trials of Hannah Arendt," *Nation*, May 12, 2015, 12–25, here 14. Online at https://www.thenation.com/article/trials-hannah-arendt/.

49. Ibid., 20 and 21*ff.*

50. Ibid., 22.

51. Ibid., 23.

52. Ibid., 25.

53. Arendt, "A Letter to Gershom Scholem," July 24, 1963, in Arendt, *The Jewish Writings*, 467. The editors note that this "personality" was none other than Golda Meir, then foreign minister of Israel and that Arendt deleted her name and changed the pronouns at Scholem's urging.

54. Curthoys, *The Legacy of Liberal Judaism*, 187.

55. Ibid., 188. The early 1960s are not only dominated by the Eichmann controversy; this is the period when Arendt immerses herself in a study of the American Founding Fathers and the civic republican tradition, the end result of which is her book *On Revolution* (New York: Viking

Compass 1963 [1965]). Her liberalism was never of the Lockean kind, though Lockean liberalism as well as Jeffersonian civic republicanism belong to the Enlightenment tradition. For a masterful account of the evolution of Arendt's thought in her encounter with America, see Richard King, *Arendt and America* (Chicago: University of Chicago Press, 2015), 217*ff.*; 223–24, and my discussion of Kings's book and Arendt's *On Revolution* in http://s-usih.org/2016/66/arendts-american-republicanism.html.

56. George Kateb even argued that Arendt's thought was "amoral" when not "immoral," see George Kateb, *Hannah Arendt: Politics, Conscience, Evil* (Totowa, NJ: Rowman and Allenheld, 1984). On Nietzsche's influence on Arendt, see Dana Villa, "Beyond Good and Evil: Arendt, Nietzsche, and the Aestheticization of Political Action," *Political Theory* 20, no. 2 (1992): 274–309.

57. Despite the fact that Arendt possessed copies of Cohen's work in her library, there is no extensive discussion of Hermann Cohen in her hitherto published writings, but just brief references. See chapter 5, note 31 on this issue. In "Interpretations at War: Kant, the Jews, the German," Jacques Derrida subjects Cohen's attempted synthesis of Germanness and Judaism in his famous essay "Deutschtum und Jedentum" (1915) to a devastating critique. Derrida not only criticizes the "hypernationalism" of this essay, addressed primarily to American Jews, in order to persuade them to put pressure on the American government not to enter the war against Germany, but also because of Cohen's naïve philosophical methodology, which proceeds through centuries of history via an identitarian logic that assumes that "the Christian logos ... will serve as mediator between Judaism and Germanity, between the Jewish spirit and the German spirit." Derrida, "Interpretations at War: Kant, the Jews, the German," trans. Moshe Ron, *New Literary History* 22, no. 1 (Winter 1991): 39–95, here 50. Despite Curthoy's valiant efforts to defend Cohen, Arendt, following Moritz Goldstein, stands in the tradition of Jewish half-otherness and pariahdom and not of German nationalism. See Curthoys, *The Legacy of Liberal Judaism*, 84–91.

58. I have tried to show how Hannah Arendt's concept of "the right to have rights" needs to be grounded via a universalist ethics in "Another Universalism: On the Unity and Diversity of Human Rights," in Benhabib, *Dignity in Adversity*, 57–77; and Benhabib, "Reason-Giving and Rights-Bearing. Concerning the Subject of Rights," in *Constellations* 20, no. 1 (2013): 38–51, revised version in Benhabib, *Kosmopolitismus ohne Illusionen. Menschenrechte in turbulenten Zeiten* (an enlarged and revised collection of my essays from *Dignity in Adversity* [Berlin: Suhrkamp, 2017], see 77–97.

59. I am referring here to Hegel's famous discussion of "lordship" and "bondage" in *Hegel's Phenomenology of Spirit*, 228–40.

## Chapter 5. Ethics without Normativity and Politics without Historicity: On Judith Butler's *Parting Ways. Jewishness and the Critique of Zionism*

1. All page numbers in the text refer to this edition as *PW*.

2. My original article contained the following footnote: "A web search with the keywords of 'Judith Butler and Palestine' produced nearly 13,400 results. The video of a teach-in at Berkeley in 2006 in which Butler, in answer to a question from students, acknowledges that Hamas

and Hezbollah can be considered as social movements within the Global Left, is also followed by her remark that this does not imply that those interested in non-violent movements cannot also engage in a critique of their tactics. (Cf. http://cifwatch.com/2012/10/18/judith -butler-more-palestinian-than-the-palestinians/.) Butler's remarks occur toward the end, around the tenth minute of the video. I should point out that some of the material on the web is posted by hate groups from the Jewish side who wish to forget that Hamas was in part brought into existence by Israel in the aftermath of the First Lebanon War (1982 onwards) as a counterweight to the secular, third-worldist liberation ideologies that dominated at the time among the Palestinian Liberation Movements. This does not resolve the issue whether we want to call Hamas and Hezbollah resistance movements today, more than thirty years later. I do not think so, but this is a separate matter." A new search has revealed that this video has now been removed from the internet. Enter the URL, https://ukmediawatch.org/2012/10/18/judith-butler-more -palestinian-than-the-palestinians/, click on the video link, and you will be directed to a screen that informs the viewer that the video in question has been removed: https://www.youtube .com/watch?v=zFp_6J0e92Q. Accessed on March 15, 2017. Many thanks to Samuel Zeitlin for helping track down this information.

3. See *Antigone's Claim. Kinship between Life and Death.* Wellek Library Lectures (New York: Columbia University Press, 2000); *Precarious Life. The Powers of Mourning and Violence* (London: Verso, 2004); *Giving an Account of Oneself* (New York: Fordham University Press, 2005); *Frames of War. When Is Life Grievable?* (London: Verso, 2009).

4. I am aware that this is a controversial claim for those who have argued that deconstruction always already had an ethical-political core. Gayatri Spivak discusses this ethical turn in Derrida's work in *A Critique of Postcolonial Reason. Toward a History of the Vanishing Present* (Cambridge: Harvard University Press, 1999), 426. For a careful account of the evolution in Derrida's thought, cf. Richard Bernstein, "Serious Play. The Ethical-Political Horizon of Derrida," in his *The New Constellation: The Ethical-Political Horizon of Modernity* (Cambridge: Polity Press, 1991), 172–98. For explorations of the ethical implications of Derrida's work for feminist theory in particular, see Drucilla Cornell, *Beyond Accommodation. Ethical Feminism, Deconstruction, and the Law* (New York and Oxford: Routledge Books, 1991) and Drucilla Cornell, Michel Rosenfeld, and David Grey Carlson, eds., *Deconstruction and the Possibility of Justice* (New York and London: Routledge, 1992). Somewhat more polemically on Derrida's turn to law, cf. John McCormick, "Derrida on Law. Poststructuralism Gets Serious," *Political Theory* 29, no. 3 (June 2001): 395–423. Butler has written about free speech and democracy in *Excitable Speech. A Politics of the Performative* (New York: Routledge, 1997), and most recently on freedom of assembly and protest, Butler, *Notes toward a Performative Theory of Assembly* (Cambridge, MA: Harvard University Press, 2015); Judith Butler and Athena Athanasiou, *Dispossession: The Performative in the Political* (Cambridge and Malden, MA: Polity, 2013).

5. Arendt, "The Promise of Politics," in *Responsibility and Judgment*, ed. Jerome Kohn (New York: Schocken Books, 2003), 37.

6. For a lucid account of Levinas's claim in relation to the phenomenological tradition, see Bernhard Waldenfels, "Levinas and the Face of the Other," in *The Cambridge Companion to Levinas*, ed. Simon Critchley and Robert Bernasconi (Cambridge: Cambridge University Press, 2004), 63–81.

7. Benhabib, "The Generalized and the Concrete Other. The Kohlberg-Gilligan Controversy and Moral Theory," in Benhabib, *Situating the Self. Gender, Community and Postmodernism in Contemporary Ethics* (New York and London: Routledge and Polity, 1992), 148–78.

8. Waldenfels places Levinas's work among "phenomenologically oriented ethics," in "Levinas and the Face of the Other," in *The Cambridge Companion to Levinas*, 64.

9. I am very briefly recalling accounts of the moral development of the child in the Kolbergian tradition, which I have discussed in Benhabib, "The Generalized and the Concrete Other." Controversies about these accounts begin at a different stage, and my claim is not that normativity can be naturalized, but that "the self-other" dyad needs to be interrupted in the course of ordinary human development with the introduction of what George Herbert Mead had called the perspective of the "generalized other." These were some of the central issues in the feminist debates and contentions of the mid-1990s. Cf. *Feminist Contentions: A Philosophical Exchange* with Seyla Benhabib, Judith Butler, Nancy Fraser, and Drucilla Cornell (New York: Routledge, Kegan, and Paul, 1996). Revised and expanded English edition of *Der Streit um Differenz* (Frankfurt: Fischer Verlag, 1993).

10. For a recent discussion concerning the necessity as well as limitations of universalism in ethics, see my exchange with Rainer Forst, in Benhabib, "The Uses and Abuses of Kantian Rigorism. On Rainer Forst's Moral and Political Philosophy," in *Political Theory* 43, no. 6 (2015): 777–92, and Rainer Forst's reply, "Moral and Political, Transcendental and Historical. Reply to Seyla Benhabib, Jeffrey Flynn and Matthias Fritsch," in *Political Theory* 43, no. 6 (2015), 822–37.

11. Hilary Putnam, "Levinas and Judaism," in *The Cambridge Companion to Levinas*, 33–62, here 34. Abbreviated in the text as *LJ*.

12. Emanuel Levinas, *Difficile Liberté* [(Livre de Poche, 1984), trans as *Difficult Freedom. Essays on Judaism* by Sean Hand (Baltimore: Johns Hopkins University Press, 1997 [1990]), 225. In his important contribution to this debate, Michael L. Morgan disagrees with this reading of Levinas and offers the following alternative reading. "The persecution that he takes to be the ultimate essence of Judaism and the Jewish people is the central teaching of interpersonal responsibility, and while he may think that the long history of persecutions of the Jews as the target of anti-Jewish and anti-Semitic hatred is part of what warrants calling attention to this feature of the Jewish experience ... [There] are surely psychological and personal reasons why Levinas privileges Judaism and the Jewish people in his illustrations, examples, and even choice of terminology and expression." Michael L. Morgan, *Levinas's Ethical Politics* (Bloomington and Indianapolis: Indiana University Press, 2016), 332. But Morgan insists that "even if he does take responsibility to others to be the essence of Judaism, it need not be exclusive, and it hardly means that unless one is a Jew in the cultural, historical sense, one cannot be a just and humane person" (333). Butler is pointing to a confusion of "ontological" and "pre-ontological" levels in Levinas's work (Butler, *Giving an Account of Oneself*, 94, cited by Morgan, 393, fn. 54) from which Morgan radically dissents and sees this to be a consequence of Butler's own confusion (Morgan, 342).

13. Levinas, "Ethics and Politics," in *The Levinas Reader*, ed. Sean Hand (Oxford and Cambridge, MA: Basil Blackwell, 1989), 289–97, here 292–93. All page references in parentheses are to this edition.

14. Ibid., 293. There is significant controversy about this interview as well as Butler's interpretation of it among Levinas scholars. In a helpful overview of the issues, Eisenstadt and Elise Katz conclude that "the thrust of the interview as a whole, the idea that Levinas opens with and closes with, is that there is responsibility even when there is no guilt, that this is, as he says at the beginning, a Jewish idea, and as he says at the end, a talmudic idea . . . Levinas's statements in the interview rely on the idea that ethics precedes ontology, and thus precedes the political, but do little to clarify the potential application of the idea. If we add a volatile political situation in which everyone is assumed to have chosen a side . . . Second, and more simply [if we add] that Levinas does not issue an unequivocal denunciation of Israel's hand in the massacre . . ." then the potential for explosive misinterpretations of Levinas abound. Oona Eisenstadt and Claire Elise Katz, "The Faceless Palestinian: A History of an Error," *Telos* 174 (Spring 2016): 9–32; 18–19. I will leave aside the thought that the distinction between "guilt" and "responsibility" is a Talmudic one alone; Greek ethics certainly has a similar distinction. However, Eisenstadt and Elise Katz like Morgan discussed above (note 12), and William Simmons's views explained below (note 16), have recourse to the distinction, not to say, the disjunction between ethics and politics and ontology. It is the absence of clear mediations among these domains that is the difficulty in Levinas's work, and Butler, rather than rejecting Levinas's mapping of these domains, introduces an ontology that she believes will be more amenable to the politics she wants to defend. I am unconvinced about replacing normative ethics by an ontology. My thanks to Samuel Zeitlin for bringing this article to my attention.

15. Levinas, "Ethics and Politics," 294.

16. William Paul Simmons interprets Levinas here as "saying that his philosophical definition of the Other does not rest on any nationality or kinship of the Other. Yes, the Palestinian can be the Other, but so too can the Israeli, Saudi, or Iraqi." In W. Paul Simmons, *Human Rights Law and the Marginalized Other* (Cambridge: Cambridge University Press, 2011), 101–2. This is certainly correct, but it does not solve the question of how to mediate between the abstract ethical injunctions of Levinas's philosophy of the face and his politics.

17. Commenting on Levinas's claim that whereas the proximity to the other's face is the source of justice, the relationship to the third is a condition in which the asymmetry of proximity is ef-faced, Waldenfels writes: "However, we must admit that political, juridical, linguistic or cultural orders are neither created by the other's demand nor by its correction. They require a sort of creative response to the other. Because Levinas simply presupposes such orders without questioning their origin a hole seems to open in Levinas's ethics of the other which should not be papered over." Waldenfels, "Levinas and the Face of the Other," 78. Butler is not "papering over this hole" but evading it. And this is where historicity may be essential. She notes Levinas's position on the Palestinian people and claims that "in some ways he gave us the very principle that he betrayed. And this means that we are not only free, but obligated to extend that principle to the Palestinian people, precisely because he could not" (*PW*, 23). But is it that Levinas could not or that he would not? Maybe the very aloofness of the injunction "in the face of the other" from any normative ethics and politics permitted Levinas to fill this injunction with an ethical and political content that was highly particularist rather than universalist? Maybe ethical formalism is not so easy to avoid after all?

18. Butler, "I Merely Belong to Them," 26–28. According to Jewish religious law, any child born of a Jewish mother is considered Jewish.

19. See the important volume, Steven E. Aschheim, ed., *Hannah Arendt in Jerusalem.*

20. For a discussion of this passage in the context of Arendt's understanding of genocide, see my essay, "International Law and Human Plurality in the Shadow of Totalitarianism. Hannah Arendt and Raphael Lemkin," in *Politics in Dark Times,* 219–47, especially 239–42. On Arendt's lack of differentiation between genocide and crimes against humanity, see David Luban, "Hannah Arendt as a Theorist of International Criminal Law," *International Criminal Law Review* 11 (2011): 621–41, here 627–31.

21. See Elisabeth Young-Bruehl, *For Love of the World,* "Cura Posterior: Eichmann in Jerusalem. (1961–1965)," 328ff. *Cura posterior* refers to Arendt's own complex sense of relief from the past, as expressed in her statement to Mary McCarthy, "You are the only reader to understand that I wrote this book in a curious state of euphoria. And ever since I did it I feel—after twenty years—light-hearted about the whole matter. Don't tell anybody: is it not proof-positive that I have no 'soul'?," as cited in Young-Bruehl, 337. For further discussions of the linguistic infelicities of the Eichmann book as well as the issues of "ethnic stereotyping," see also Benhabib, "Arendt's *Eichmann in Jerusalem,*" 65–86..

22. As the underlined sentence suggest, Butler is still trying to derive norms from "the unchosen character of modes of cohabitation." There is a parallel problem about the normativity of ontology in Arendt's work, but this is why Arendt turns repeatedly to Kant—a move that Butler finds objectionable.

23. Arendt, "The Promise of Politics," in *The Promise of Politics,* 175.

24. Patricia Owens, *Between War and Politics. International Relations and the Thought of Hannah Arendt* (Oxford: Oxford University Press, 2007), 110.

25. Butler accuses Arendt of equivocating between "world" and "earth" in her verdict on Eichmann, but this is puzzling (*PW,* 166). The distinction between these two categories is quite crucial in Arendt's thought and marks the point of her divergence from Heidegger. *The Human Condition* distinguishes sharply between "earth alienation" and "world alienation" (*HC,* 248–57). Arendt's own parsing out of the concept of the world with respect to the plurality of action and speech with others marks her true point of departure from Heidegger.

26. For Butler's appropriation of this phrase from Nietzsche, see Butler, *Gender Trouble. Feminism and the Subversion of Identity* (New York and London: Routledge, 1990), 25, and my critical remarks, "Feminism and the Question of Postmodernism," in *Feminist Contentions,* 21ff.

27. For a strong defense of the significance of individual reflection and judgment and the limitations of the "dialogic" model of judgment, see Bryan Garsten, "The Elusiveness of Arendtian Judgment," in Benhabib, ed., *Politics in Dark Times. Encounters with Hannah Arendt,* 316–42.

28. In his illuminating essay, "Pseudology. Derrida on Arendt and Lying in Politics," Martin Jay discusses the relationship between lying and freedom, which would seem at first quite counterintuitive. Freedom, as a positive value, can hardly be associated with deception it would seem. Jay, *Essays from the Edge. Parerga and Paralipomena* (Charlottesville and London: University of Virginia Press, 2011), 132–49. But both freedom and narration, whether truthful or not, for

Arendt contain a moment of unpredictable spontaneity. Freedom is not obeying a law one has given oneself as it was in Kant but rather acting in such a way that a "principle" is manifested through one's action. And this capacity to embed a principle in one's action is closely related to the capacity to tell the story of who we are and what we are doing—which is also the origin of the capacity to lie, to fabulate—in a more positive light. See chapter 6 below for a discussion of Arendt's account of "principle."

29. On Arendt's first meeting with Blumenfeld, see Elisabeth Young-Bruehl, *For Love of the World*, 70ff. On the correspondence between Hannah Arendt and Kurt Blumenfeld, see *In keinem Besitz verwurzelt. Die Korrespondenz*, ed. Ingeborg Nordmann and Iris Philling (Noerdlingen: Rotbuch, 1995), 257–65 and Ingeborg Nordmann, "Nachwort. Eine Freundschaft auf des Messers Schneide," in *In keinem Besitz verwurzelt. Die Korrespondenz*, 349ff.

30. For more details on the family background, see Young-Bruehl, *For Love of the World*, 8ff.

31. In a letter to Heinrich Blücher, who is here playfully referred to as "the Golem," Arendt writes: "The Golem is wrong when he argues that the Jews are a people, or a people which, like others, is in the process of realizing itself. In the East they are already a people without a territory. And in the West, God knows what they are (including myself)." In *Hannah Arendt-Heinrich Blücher, Briefe. 1936–1968*, ed. Lotte Koehler, 58 (my translation).

32. Hermann Cohen shows up twice in Arendt's *Jewish Writings*. In her essay "Antisemitism," where she gives a historical overview of modern Jewish history, Cohen is quoted in passing: "In the hands of the assimilationists Jewish history was turned into a history of the injustice inflicted on us, that lasted until the end of the eighteenth century, when—with no transition and by the grace of God and/or the French Revolution—it merged into world history, to whose 'creeping pace,' as Hermann Cohen put it, we have cheerfully entrusted ourselves." Arendt, "Antisemitism," in Arendt, *The Jewish Writings*, 48. In the same essay, Arendt seems to use Cohen as someone who stands for a specific historical *Zeitgeist*. Cohen writes: "We feel that we have become persons of culture (following the Emancipation Edict of 1812). What sense of gratitude can have deeper roots than that which lifts us up to become a moral personality . . . All the injustice we must endure should not mislead us into doubting *progress over time*" (Hermann Cohen, *Jüdische Schriften* [*Jewish Writings*], vol. 2, *Emancipation* (1912), 223–24; cited by Arendt, *Jewish Writings*, 112, fn. 3. Emphasis in the text). "He continues: "Let us make confident use here as well of *world history* and its creeping pace . . . One consequence that arises for us . . . out of this edict is that our *patriotism* is deeper than before and still not exhausted." Arendt quotes Cohen ironically: Truly: "World history follows meandering paths" (Cohen, 227, as cited by Arendt, "Antisemitism," 112. Emphases in the original). Arendt is being ironical by quoting Cohen here, since she never endorsed the kind of "patriotism" and historical teleology that Cohen adumbrated. My thanks to Carmen Dege for helping out with this reference.

33. Discussing Arendt, Butler writes, "She wrote and spoke some clearly racist beliefs and she is no model for a broader politics of understanding across cultural difference" (*PW*, 234, fn. 6). And most problematically, Butler accuses Arendt of accusing "those who are stateless" of being "a threat to the human." Among the stateless Arendt is said to include the Palestinians as well as the Pakistanis (*PW*, 236–237, fn. 30). See Arendt, *OT* [1951] 1979, 290. As I will argue in the next chapter this is a very dismissive treatment of the stateless in Arendt's writings. She was one of the first to put this issue on the map of political philosophy.

34. For an early critique that romantically combines third-world revolutionary aspirations with the critique of Eurocentrism, see Jacques Derrida, "The Ends of Man," in *After Philosophy. End or Transformation*, ed. Kenneth Baynes, James Bohman, and Thomas McCarthy (Cambridge, MA, and London, UK: MIT Press, 1986), 125–58.

35. Said writes with reference to the Oslo I Accord between Israel and the Palestinian Liberation Organization, officially called the "Declaration of Principles on Interim Self-Government," and signed after the First Gulf War in 1993: "After all the hoopla celebrating 'the first step towards a Palestinian state,' we should remind ourselves that much more important than having a state is the kind of state it is. The history of the post-colonial world is disfigured by one-party tyrannies, rapacious oligarchies, social dislocation caused by Western 'investments,' and large scale pauperization brought about by famine, civil war or outright robbery. Any more than religious fundamentalism, mere nationalism is not, and can never be, 'the answer' to the problems of new secular societies. Alas one can already see in Palestine's potential statehood the lineaments of a marriage between the chaos of Lebanon and the tyranny of Iraq." Edward Said, "The Morning After," *London Review of Books* 15, no. 20–21 (October 1993); accessed through http://www.lrb .co.uk/v15/n20/edward-said/the-morning-after. My thanks to Andrew Arato for his comments alerting me to the precise historical context of these remarks.

36. See Hegel, "Über die wissenschaftlichen Behandlungsarten des Naturrechts, seine Stelle in der praktischen Philosophie, und sein Verhaltnis zu den positiven Rechtswissenschaften," in *Werke in Zwanzig Banden*, vol. 2, 434–533. English trans., T. M. Knox, *Natural Law* (Philadelphia: University of Pennsylvania Press, 1975). In the English translation, the discussion of the "tragedy" and "comedy" in ethical life occurs on 104–8.

37. The phrase, "the land without a people—for the people without a land" is attributed to the journalist Bernard (Israel) Zangwill. See Amos Elon, *The Israelis. Founders and Sons* (New York: Holt, Rinehart, and Winston, 1971). (I discuss Zangwill's actual phraseology and Arendt's paraphrasing of it in *The Reluctant Modernism of Hannah Arendt*, 59, fn. 26.) There is a tragic blindness in this phrase and even more so in Zangwill's own version, "Palestine is a ruined country; and the Jews are a broken people. But neither is beyond recuperation. Palestine needs a people; Israel needs a country." In Israel Zangwill, "Zion, Whence Cometh My Help?," in *Speeches, Articles and Letters of Israel Zangwill*, ed. Maurice Simon, with a foreword by Edith Aryton Zangwill (London: Soncino, 1937). Of course, there were "people" in Palestine and in old Jerusalem! The crux of the struggle between cultural Zionists such as Martin Buber and political Zionists such as Ben-Gurion was about how to deal with these other "peoples," namely the Palestinian Arabs, Armenians, Druze, and others who were Ottoman subjects but who then were subject to the British Protectorate at the end of World War I. Arendt, as Butler also notes (*PW*, 120ff.), belonged to the Judah Magnes group that advocated a binational federation in Palestine.

38. Cf. Benhabib on the "Mavi Marmara" affair, "Israel's Stalemate," http://www.resetdoc .org/story/00000021248 (posted June 2, 2010). For my recent reflections on the situation in the Middle East and for some deeply illuminating essays by a number of contributors on Islam and democracy see Benhabib, "Introduction," in Seyla Benhabib and Volker Kaul, eds., *Toward New Democratic Imaginaries. Istanbul Seminars on Politics, Culture and Islam* (Zurich: Springer Verlag, 2016), xxix-xlviii.

39. For Arendt, extensive local democracy, in which Jews and Arabs participated equally, and a federative state structure, integrated into a larger community of Mediterranean nations, were the only viable political structures for Israel/Palestine. Cf. Arendt, "Zionism Reconsidered," *Menorah Journal* 32, no. 2 (October–December, 1945): 162–96; now in Arendt, *The Jewish Writings*, 343–74. On the idea of federalism in interwar Europe, see below the chapter on Albert Hirschman.

## Chapter 6. From the "Right to Have Rights" to the "Critique of Humanitarian Reason"

1. This is a reference to a migrant and refugee camp in the vicinity of the French town of Calais, where those hoping to make the transit to the United Kingdom via the Port of Calais or the Eurotunnel gathered for months. Starting in October 2016, the French government evacuated more than six thousand refugees to different regions of France.

2. In the complex architecture of the European Union, the movement of refugees seeking asylum is governed by the various Dublin agreements. The Dublin regulation was first put into force in 1997 and revised several times since then in 2003 and 2008. It seeks to determine most rapidly the member state responsible for processing an asylum claim. All EU member states, except Denmark, as well as non-member states such as Norway, Iceland, and Switzerland, participate in this system. Originally designed to prevent refugees from placing multiple applications in different countries of the European Union, the Dublin regulations by now have created a system of unfair burdens on first countries of entry such as Greece, Italy, and Spain, which are reached by refugees traveling across the Mediterranean. For a recent account of the refugees' harrowing stories, see Jason DeParle, "The Sea Swallows People," *New York Review of Books* 64, no. 3 (February 23, 2017): 31–36. For a more in-depth analysis of the historical and economic factors of colonialism at the origins of the migration from African countries into Europe, see Hauke Brunkhorst, "Europa, die Flucht und das koloniale Erbe," ("Europe, the Flight and the Colonial Legacy"), in *Blätter für deutsche und international Politik* 61, no. 9 (September 2016): 63–75.

3. See http://www.unhcr.org/en-us/news/latest/2016/6/5763b65a4/global-forced-displacement-hits-record-high.html.

4. See *Escape from Violence: Conflict and the Refugee Crisis in the Developing World*, ed. by Aristide R. Zolberg, Astri Suhrke and Sergio Aguayo (Oxford: Oxford University Press, 1989).

5. Arendt, "Es gibt nur ein einziges Menschenrecht," *Die Wandlung* (1949), 754–70, here 755. "Die Nachkriegsbezeichnung 'displaced persons' ist ausdrücklich erfunden worden, um diese störende 'Staatenlosigkeit' ein für allemal einfach durch ignorieren aus der Welt zu schaffen." My translation.

6. Giorgio Agamben, *Homo Sacer. Sovereign Power and Bare Life*, trans. Daniel Heller-Roazen (Stanford: CA: University of Stanford Press, 1998); Butler, *Precarious Life. The Powers of Mourning and Violence*; Jacques Rancière, "Who Is the Subject of the Rights of Man?," in *The South Atlantic Quarterly* 203, no. 2/3 (Spring/Summer 2004), 297–310. Wendy Brown has discussed the transformations of state sovereignty with reference to control their borders in Wendy Brown, *Walled States, Waning Sovereignty* (New York: Zone Books, 2010).

7. For a discussion of these historical episodes I am much indebted to Elisabeth Young-Bruehl, *For Love of the World*, 113; see also Jeremy Adelman, "Pariah: Can Hannah Arendt Help Us Rethink Our Global Refugee Crisis?," *Wilson Quarterly* 40, no. 2 (Spring 2016), http://wilson quarterly.com/quarterly/looking-back-moving-forward/pariah-can-hannah-arendt-help-us -rethink-our-global-refugee-crisis/.

8. For a lively account of organized groups of European socialists and communists who helped Jewish refugees escape across the Pyrénées into Spain and Portugal, see the autobiography by Lisa Flittko, *Escape through the Pyrenées*, trans. David Koblick (Evanston, Illinois: Northwestern University Press, 1991 [1985]). Many thanks to Jürgen Habermas for bringing this book to my attention. Albert Hirschman was working with Varian Fry from the Friend Services Committee in Marseilles at the time to help settle refugees like Arendt in the United States. See chapter 8 above for a discussion of his role.

9. Arendt, "Es gibt nur ein einziges Menschenrecht," *Die Wandlung* (1949), 754–70; Cf. also *OT*, 296–97.

10. "Karl Marx and the Tradition of Political Thought," first and second drafts (1953), container 71 in the Hannah Arendt Papers in the Library of Congress. Arendt had applied for a Guggenheim fellowship with the title, "Totalitarian Elements of Marxism," which she was awarded in 1952. See also Arendt, "The Concept of History: Ancient and Modern," in *BPF*, 41–91; especially on Marx, cf. *BPF*, 77–82; also Arendt, "From Hegel to Marx," in *The Promise of Politics*, ed. and with an introduction by Jerome Kohn (New York: Schocken Books, 2005), 70–81.

11. See Benjamin, "Theses on the Philosophy of History," in Benjamin, *Illuminations*, 253–65.

12. The passage reads: "There is no document of civilization which is not at the same time a document of barbarism. And just as such a document is not free of barbarism, barbarism taints also the manner in which it was transmitted from one owner to another. A historical materialist therefore dissociates himself from it as far as possible. He regards it as his task to brush history against the grain." In Benjamin, *Illuminations*, ed. Arendt, 248.

13. I have criticized the lack of normative foundations in Arendt's political thought in several writings in the last decade and have sought to reconcile her right to have rights with a concept of "communicative freedom." See Benhabib, *The Rights of Others*, 49–71; Benhabib, *Dignity in Adversity*, 41–57; and most recently, Benhabib, *Kosmopolitismus ohne Illusionen. Menschenrechte in unruhigen Zeiten*, 46–77. My revisiting this particular issue in Arendt's work is motivated not only by the continuing relevance of her observations to our times but also by the publication of several very important reinterpretations by contemporary scholars, and in particular by Ayten Gündogdu, *Rightlessness in an Age of Rights. Hannah Arendt and the Contemporary Struggles of Migrants* (Oxford: Oxford University Press, 2015), and Alison Kesby, *The Right to Have Rights. Citizenship, Humanity, and International Law* (Oxford: Oxford University Press, 2012).

14. Christoph Menke, "The 'Aporias of Human Rights' and the 'One Human Right': Regarding the Coherence of Hannah Arendt's Argument," in *Social Research: An International Quarterly* 74, no. 3 (Fall 2007): 739–62, here 742.

15. Cf Menke's insistence that Arendt agreed that rights not posited by law are "nonsense upon stilts." Ibid., 755; cf. Jeremy Bentham, *The Works of Jeremy Bentham*, ed. John Bowring, 11 vols. (Edinburgh and London: W. Tait, 1843), vol. 2, 501; Alasdair MacIntyre, *After Virtue*.

*A Study in Moral Theory,* 3rd edn. (Notre Dame: University of Notre Dame Press, 2007 [1981]), 67.

16. Arendt, " 'The Rights of Man': What Are They?" *Modern Review* 3, no. 1 (1949), 24–37.

17. Menke, "Aporias of Human Rights," 752.

18. Ibid., 756.

19. Gündogdu, *Rightlessness in an Age of Rights,* 166.

20. Ibid.

21. Ibid., 172.

22. On "principles" of action, see Arendt, "What Is Freedom?," in *BPF,* 152–53; Arendt, "Montesquieu's Revision of the Tradition," in *The Promise of Politics,* 63–70.

23. Cf. Balibar's discussion of the "Declaration of the Rights of Man and Citizen": "If one really wants to read it literally, the Declaration in fact says that equality is identical to freedom, is equal to freedom and vice versa. Each is the exact measure of the other. This is what I propose to call, with a deliberately baroque phrase, the proposition of equaliberty—a portmanteau term, impossible and yet possible only as a play on words, that nevertheless alone addresses the central proposition." Étienne Balibar, *Equaliberty. Political Essays,* trans. James Ingram (Durham and London: Duke University Press, 2014), 46.

24. Gündogdu, *Rightlessness in an Age of Rights,* 183.

25. Ibid., 185.

26. Ibid., 186. Democratic iteration and jurisgenerativity are discussed in chapter 1 above.

27. The ongoing dispute between Habermasian-inspired universal pragmatics and discourse ethics on the one hand and varieties of French theory (Foucaultian, Derridean, and inspired by Rancière) on the other, rests on whether speech-acts, which are always interlaced by force, persuasion, or rhetoric, can ever be so clearly isolated from speech-acts aiming at validity claims. Put in other words, theorists of performativity doubt that the "illocutionary" and "perlocutionary" dimensions of speech acts can be so neatly separated. In McCarthy's felicitous phrase, "reason remains impure," see Thomas A. McCarthy, "The Critique of Impure Reason. Foucault and the Frankfurt School," in *Political Theory* 18, no. 3 (1990): 437–69. Matheson Russell and Andrew Montin recently give a good overview of the issues involved, in "The Rationality of Political Disagreement: Rancière's Critique of Habermas," in *Constellations* 22, no. 4 (2015): 543–54.

28. This phrase comes from Hannah Arendt's interview with the journalist Gunther Gauss, "Hannah Arendt im Gespräch mit Günter Gauss," https://www.youtube.com/watch?v=dsoImQfVsO4. Conducted on October 28, 1964. A shortened version in English is available in Arendt, *Essays in Understanding,* 1–24. Cf. also her designation of concentration camps as "the appearance of some radical evil, previously unknown to us . . . the realization that something seems to be involved in modern politics that actually should never be involved in politics as we used to understand it" (*OT,* 443).

29. See my essay, Benhabib, "In the Shadow of Aristotle and Hegel. Communicative Ethics and Current Controversies in Practical Philosophy," in *Situating the Self. Gender, Community and Postmodernism in Contemporary Ethics,* 23–67. Despite minor disagreements, my position is closest to Rainer Forst, *The Right to Justification. Elements of a Constructivist Theory of Justice,* trans. Jeffrey Flynn (New York: Columbia University Press, 2007), 203–67.

30. Kesby writes: " 'Place' is a particularly rich concept for examining the right to have rights for it not only raises the question of the site or sphere of right-holding, but crucially also a person's status or means of recognition as rights-bearer within it, and the resulting level of protection of human rights afforded. With these layered meanings in mind, a recurring question . . . is 'what does it mean to be "in place" within the international legal system' and 'who is out of place.' " Kesby, *The Right to Have Rights. Citizenship, Humanity, and International Law*, 6–7.

31. Quoting Aristotle, Arendt writes, "for what appears to all, this we call being" (*HC*, 199). I explore the relationship of being as appearing to Heidegger's doctrine of "alethia," and Arendt's indebtedness to Aristotle and Heidegger in *The Reluctant Modernism of Hannah Arendt*, 114–17.

32. Bruno Bettelheim, "Individual and Mass Behavior in Extreme Situations," *Journal of Abnormal and Social Psychology* 38 (1943); Eli Wiesel, *Night*, trans. Marion Wiesel (New York: Hill and Wang, 2006 [1972]), first published in France as *La Nuit* (Paris: Les Editions de Minuit, 1958); Primo Levi, *Survival in Auschwitz: If This Is a Man*, trans. Stuart Woolf (New York: Touchstone, 1996), Italian original as *Se questo è un Uomo* (Torino: Giulio Enuadi, 1947); Imre Kertész, *Fatelessness*, trans. Tom Wilkinson (New York: Vintage International, 2004 [first Hungarian publication, 1975]).

33. In *The Origins of Totalitarianism*, Arendt refers to David Rousset, *Les Jours de Notre Mort* (Paris: Pavois, 1947) and Bruno Bettelheim, "On Dachau and Buchenwald," in *Nazi Conspiracy and Aggression*, vol. 7 (May 1938 to April 1939) as her sources. See *OT*, 439.

34. See http://www.un.org/en/documents/udhr/.

35. The most precise analyses of the implications of these legal developments—not all of which are salutary—for Arendt's right to have rights is found in Kesby, *The Rights to Have Rights*, 39–66; 92–111.

36. Benhabib, *The Rights of Others*, 134–42. Kesby's analysis has made me see that in parsing the right to have rights as a "right to political membership" in this work I was bringing together the right to nationality and the right to citizenship under one heading (Benhabib, *The Rights of Others*, 3). Kesby cites Paul Weiss from *Nationality and Statelessness in International Law* [(Alphaen aan den Rijn: Sijthoff and Noordhoff, 1979), 2nd edn., 4–5] to the effect that "nationality pertains to the external aspects of state membership and citizenship to the inter relationship between the individual and the state, which under the law of most states connotes 'full membership' (including political rights)." Kesby, *The Rights to Have Rights*, 43. It is important to retain this distinction because *not* all nationals have full citizenship rights: they may be disenfranchised on the basis of race, ethnicity, language community, or civil status such as felons and prisoners are. Full citizenship rights are always the subject of political contestation.

37. Arendt, "Es gibt nur ein einziges Menschenrecht," 768. The German reads: ". . . hat es nur mit Gesetzen und Abkommen zu tun, welch in Frieden und Krieg den Verkehr souveräner Nationen regeln." My translation.

38. Ibid., 768.

39. See http://www.unhcr.org/3b66c2aa10.html.

40. Tania Inlaender, "Status Quo or Sixth Ground? Adjudicating Gender Asylum Claims," in *Migrations and Mobilities. Citizenship, Borders and Gender*, ed. Seyla Benhabib and Judith Resnik (New York and London: New York University Press, 2009), 356–80.

41. See http://www.achpr.org/instruments/refugee-convention.

42. See www.oas.org/dil/1984_Cartagena_Declaration_on_Refugees.pdf, art. 3.

43. Didier Fassin, *Humanitarian Reason. A Moral History of the Present* (Berkeley and Los Angeles: University of California Press, 2012), 4.

44. Ibid., 246. This cautious assessment is to be contrasted with the words of Samuel Moyn, whose much-acclaimed book, *The Last Utopia: Human Rights in History*, best illustrates the jaundiced sense about human rights that gripped the progressive community in the early decade of the twenty-first century. Some sought to achieve, Moyn writes, "through a moral critique of politics the sense of pure cause that had once been sought in politics itself" in *The Last Utopia*: (Cambridge, MA: Harvard University Press, 2010), 171; further, human rights substituted a "plausible morality for failed politics" (175). And using a more cutting formula, he asserts that human rights were born in "antipolitics" and that they survived as a "moral utopia when political utopias died" (214). These claims are not only provocative, but presuppose binarisms that are never clarified. Morality is juxtaposed to politics, utopianism to realism, and liberal internationalism and cosmopolitanism are said to be antagonistic to democratic sovereigntism. Ironically, Hannah Arendt, the most trenchant critic of national sovereigntist delusions, is summoned by Moyn to his side with the claim that the history of human rights reveals "the persistence of the nation-state as the aspirational forum for humanity" (*The Last Utopia*, 212). Moyn's work is part of an *amoral* turn in our understanding of the political, one that blends together old-fashioned, nation-state centered political realism with postmodern skepticism toward normativity. See our exchange: Benhabib, "Moving beyond False Binarisms. On Samuel Moyn's *The Last Utopia*," in *Qui Parle* 22, no. 1 (Fall–Winter 2013): 81–93; and Moyn's response, "The Continuing Perplexities of Human Rights," in the same issue, 95–115, his response to myself and other critics.

45. Jacques Rancière, "Who Is the Subject of the Rights of Man?," 297–310. Rancière discusses Arendt's work in other contexts as well but to engage with them is beyond the purposes of this chapter: See *Disagreement: Politics and Philosophy,* trans. J. Rose (Minneapolis: University of Minnesota Press, 1999); *Dissensus: On Politics and Aesthetics,* trans. S. Corcoran (London: Continuum, 2010); *On the Shores of Politics,* trans. L. Heron (London: Verso, 1995).

46. Rancière, "Who Is the Subject of the Rights of Man?," 298.

47. Biopolitical sovereignty, which is understood as the power to make decisions over life, perpetrates in different forms the metaphysical divide between *bios* (politically qualified life) and zoē (natural life). Refugees are caught in this dangerous divide between bios and zoē, law and violence, becoming *homines sacri*. See Giorgio Agamben, *Homo Sacer. Sovereign Power and Bare Life*, 127–28. Cf. Gündogdu's astute remarks on Agamben in *Rightlessness in an Age of Rights,* 51–52. This eschatological approach to human history, based on a synthesis of Foucault and Heidegger, is not useful for understanding Arendt for whom political thinking is always about the art of making distinctions.

48. Rancière, "Who Is the Subject of the Rights of Man?," 301.

49. See Hegel, *Hegel's Phenomenology of Spirit*, preface, 79.

50. Rancière, "Who Is the Subject?," 298.

51. Ibid., 298.

52. "Yet in light of recent events it is possible to say that even slaves still belonged to some

sort of human community; their labor was needed, used, and exploited, and this kept them within the pale of humanity." Arendt, *OT*, 297.

53. Rancière, "Who Is the Subject?," 299. Gündogdu rightly points to misreadings of "Arendt's attentiveness to the equivocal and contingent effects of the Rights of Man as a discourse pervaded by perplexities" by Julia Kristeva and others. In *Rightlessness in an Age of Rights*, 217, fn. 11. See Arendt's remarkable discussion of the democratic potential of the labor movement in *The Human Condition* where she writes: "From the revolution of 1848 to the Hungarian revolution of 1956, the European working class, by virtue of being the only organized and hence the leading section of the people, has written one of the most glorious and probably the most promising chapter of recent history" (*HC*, 215–16). See also Gündogdu for a critique of Rancière, *Rightlessness in an Age of Rights*, 85–86.

54. Hanna Pitkin, *The Attack of the Blob. Hannah Arendt's Concept of the Social* (Chicago: University of Chicago Press, 1998); Bonnie Honig, *Feminist Interpretations of Hannah Arendt* (University Park: Pennsylvania University Press, 1995). For a contemporary critique of Rancière's assumptions concerning political subjectivation, see Ayten Gündogdu, "Disagreeing with Rancière: Speech, Violence and the Ambiguous Subjects of Politics," *Polity* 49, no. 2 (April 2017): 188–219.

55. Rancière, "Who Is the Subject?," 302.

56. Joan Scott, *Only Paradoxes to Offer: French Feminists and the Rights of Man* (Cambridge, MA: Harvard University Press, 1996); Linda Kerber, *Women of the Republic. Intellect and Ideology in Revolutionary America* (Chapel Hill: University of North Carolina Press, 1980).

57. Arendt, "We Refugees," in Arendt, *The Jewish Writings*, 264–74, here 264.

58. Article 25 on the right to equal conditions of work; Article 26 on the right to join a trade union; Article 30 on the rights of children of migrants to receive an education; Article 18 on the right to legal counsel in a language intelligible to the migrant; Article 28 on the right to health care of the *International Convention on the Protection of the Rights of All Migrant Workers (ICPRMW)*, though the ambiguity about the status of the undocumented or those of "irregular status" affects these rights as well. https://treaties.un.org/doc/Publication/UNTS/Volume%202220/v2220.pdf.

It is also remarkable that out of the 195 states and state parties, only thirty-eight are signatories and fifty are state parties to this Convention; these are mainly countries from the Global South and East who are sender countries. See https://treaties.un.org/Pages/ViewDetails.aspx?src=IND&mtdsg_no=IV-13&chapter=4&clang=_en.

59. The rights of refugees are governed by the Geneva Convention of 1951 and their Protocols of 1967; the rights of stateless persons by the Geneva Convention of 1954 and the 1961 Convention for the Reduction of Statelessness. See https://treaties.un.org/Pages/Treaties.aspx?id=5&subid=A&clang=_en.

60. Kesby, *The Rights to Have Rights*, 132–33.

61. See Benhabib, "The New Sovereigntism and Transnational Law: Legal Utopianism, Democratic Scepticism and Statist Realism," in *Global Constitutionalism* 5, no. 1 (March 2016): 109–44, where I discuss the prisoner disenfranchisement case. Some Tory politicians such as the former justice minister, Michael Gove, who voiced some of the most vociferous objections to the judgments of the ECtHR (European Court of Human Rights) were subsequently quite

active in the Brexit campaign as well. See Michael Watt and Owen Bowcott, "Tories Plan to Withdraw UK from European Convention on Human Rights," *Guardian* (online), October 3, 2014. Available at http://www.theguardian.com/politics/2014/oct/03/tories-plan-uk-with drawal-european-convention-on-human-rights, accessed August 10, 2015.

62. Kesby, *The Right to Have Rights*, first quote is on p. 98 and the second one on p. 99.

63. Ibid., 99. Gündogdu also points out that the *ICPRMW* does not impose on states an obligation to regularize undocumented immigrants. Gündogdu, *Rightlessness in an Age of Rights*, 190. See *ICPRMW*, art. 35.

64. Gündogdu, *Rightlessness in an Age of Rights*, 117.

65. Judith Resnik, "'Within Its Jurisdiction': Moving Boundaries, People and the Law of Migration," *Proceedings of the American Philosophical Society* 160, no. 2 (June 2016): 117–58, here 118.

66. See Itamar Mann's powerful analysis in *Humanity at Sea: Maritime Migration and the Foundations of International Law* (Cambridge: Cambridge University Press, 2016).

67. Julia Schulze Wessel, "On Border Subjects: Rethinking the Figure of the Refugee and the Undocumented Migrant," in *Constellations* 23, no. 1 (2016): 46–57.

68. Ibid., 52. See also Matthew Longo, *The Politics of Borders. Sovereignty, Security, and the Citizen after 9/11* (Cambridge: Cambridge University Press, 2017).

69. Benhabib, *The Reluctant Modernism of Hannah Arendt*, 135.

## Chapter 7. Legalism and Its Paradoxes in Judith Shklar's Work

1. Judith N. Shklar, *Legalism. An Essay on Law, Morals and Politics* (Cambridge, MA: Harvard University Press, 1964). All references in the text are to this edition.

2. See Samuel Moyn, "Judith Shklar versus the International Criminal Court," in *Humanity* 4, no. 3 (Winter 2013): 473–500, who observes how few reviews had appeared in legal journals and contrasts this with increasing references to her work in recent years (500, fn. 43). In this comprehensive review essay, Moyn is mainly concerned with the politics of international criminal courts and takes Shklar to be one of the first voices to emphasize "the ineliminable politics of law" (474). Early reviews of Shklar's book were: H. A. Bedau, "Review," *Philosophical Review* 76 (1967): 129–30; Brendan F. Brown, "Review," *University of Toronto Law Journal* 17 (1967): 218–25; Francis R. Aumann, "Review," *Journal of Politics* 27 (1965): 703–5.

3. Shklar, "A Life of Learning," in *Liberalism without Illuisons. Essays on Liberal Theory and the Political Vision of Judith N. Shklar*, ed. Bernard Yack (Chicago: University of Chicago Press, 1996), 263–81. [Originally delivered as the Charles Homer Haskins Lecture, American Council of Learned Societies, Washington, DC, April 1989 and published as ACLS Occasional Paper No. 9]. Shklar writes: "By 1939, I already understood that books, even scary ones, would be my best refuge from a world that was far more terrible than anything they might reveal. And that is how I became a bookworm. It was also the end of my childhood." "A Life of Learning," 264. For further discussion of Shklar's life, see Andreas Hess, *The Political Theory of Judith N. Shklar* (New York: Palgrave Macmillan, 2014), 23–39. Hess draws upon the remarkable autobiographical conversation that Judith Shklar carried out with Judith B. Walzer in 1981, and which is housed in the Murray Research Archive of Harvard University, located in Radcliffe College. See Judith

B. Walzer, "Oral History of Tenured Women in the Faculty of Arts and Sciences at Harvard University." (1988). Hadl. 1902.1/00709. Murray Research Archive. I had a chance to visit these archives and listen to this conversation, which, if it could be published, would be invaluable not only for understanding Shklar better but would illuminate the history of the development of political theory in the 1950s in the United States. Of particular importance is the role of Carl Friedrich in bringing certain Weimar problems and concerns to American academe and their influence upon Zbigniew Brzezinski as well as Henry Kissinger and many others who had been his students.

4. Parts of this discussion have previously appeared in Benhabib, "Judith Shklar's Dystopic Liberalism," in *Social Research. An International Quarterly* 61, no. 2 (Summer 1994): 477–88.

5. W. A. Galston, "Realism in Political Theory," *European Journal of Political Theory* 9, no. 4 (2010): 385–411. See the important article by Katrina Forrester, "Judith Shklar, Bernard Williams and Political Realism," in *European Journal of Political Theory* 11, no. 3 (2012): 247–72. Forrester argues that Shklar had more in common with the "high liberalism" of John Rawls, in particular, than has been acknowledged.

6. Shklar, *Legalism*, 125. For a more differentiated account of the midcentury realist position, and particularly that of Hans Morgenthau, see the illuminating article by William Scheuerman, "The Realist Revival in Political Philosophy, or: Why New Is Not Always Improved," *International Politics* 50, no. 6 (2013): 798–814. Tiphaine Dickson also focuses on the importance of Shklar's work for international relations and international law, claiming that Morgenthau shared Shklar's critique of legalism in the domain of international law. See Tiphaine Dickson, "Shklar's Legalism and the Liberal Paradox," *Constellations* 22, no. 2 (2015): 188–98. For Shklar's early critique of international realism as falling into a species of political decisionism, see her claim: "Realism is not a descriptive approach to international relations. It is extremely didactic. Politics should be a matter of decisions, taken by those who have the power to make them stick." Shklar, "Decisionism," in *Nomos 7: Rational Decision*, ed. Carl Friedrich (New York: Atherton Press, 1964), 3–17, here 11.

7. Judith Shklar, "The Liberalism of Fear," first published in *Liberalism and the Moral Life* (1989), ed. Nancy Rosenblum and reproduced in Shklar, *Political Thought and Political Thinkers*, ed. Stanley Hoffmann, with a preface by George Kateb (Chicago: University of Chicago Press, 1998), 5–20.

8. Cf. Habermas, *Between Facts and Norms* (1996 [1992]).

9. See Horkheimer and Adorno, *Dialektik der Aufklärung* (1944), "Preface." English trans. John Cumming, *The Dialectic of Enlightenment*, xi–xvii.

10. Shklar, *Freedom and Independence: A Study of the Political Ideas of Hegel's Phenomenology of Mind* (Cambridge: Cambridge University Press, 1976). In her interview with Judith Walzer, Shklar states that this book was one she was least satisfied with. See interview with Judith B. Walzer "Oral History of Tenured Women in the Faculty of Arts and Sciences at Harvard University" (1988). Hadl. 1902.1/00709. Murray Research Archive.

11. G.W.F. Hegel, *Phänomenologie des Geistes* (1807), English trans. A. V. Miller, *Hegel's Phenomenology of Spirit*, 252–62. See also my discussion, Benhabib, *Critique, Norm and Utopia*, 72–87.

12. Hegel's interpretation of the Categorical Imperative as a principle of non-contradiction

alone is by no means accepted by all scholars of Kant's moral philosophy. For a classical critique, see H. J. Paton, *The Categorical Imperative: A Study in Kant's Moral Philosophy* (Philadelphia: University of Pennsylvania Press, 1971). See also Bernard Williams's trenchant rearticulation of the Hegelian critique in his: *Ethics and the Limits of Philosophy* (London and New York: Routledge, 2006 [1985]).

13. She writes: "The 'thereness' of legal systems as historical institutions is . . . far from self-evident. Nothing in human history is self-evident. Formalism creates this 'thereness' because its promoters think that a legal system *ought* to be 'there' in order to function properly." *Legalism*, 35.

14. Steven White, *Political Theory and Postmodernism* (New York: Cambridge University Press, 1991).

15. Moyn, "Judith Shklar versus the International Criminal Court," 474; Shklar raised these observations about her own work in the preface to the new edition of *Legalism: Law, Morals and Political Trials* (Cambridge: MA: Harvard University Press, 1986), xi–xii, commenting that "*Legalism*, which is my favorite of the books that I have written, went quickly from being a radical outrage to being a conventional commonplace, when compared to the 'assaults' of the Critical Legal Studies Movement." Shklar, "A Life of Learning," 274–75. In a careful consideration of Shklar's theses, Robin West argues that, "In the forty years since Shklar's book was published, not all, but much of it has stood the test of time." Robin West, "Reconsidering Legalism," *Minnesota Law Review* 88 (2003): 119–58, here 122. West points out that Shklar did not accept the far more "thorough-going critique of legalism," put forward by the critical legal studies movement, which she describes as the contention "that the core aspirations of legalism—the control of both individual and state conduct through rules—is impossible to achieve . . . because of the inherent indeterminacy of rules—any rules." West, "Reconsidering Legalism," 127. Thanks to Blake Emerson for commenting on differences between "legal realism" and "critical legal studies," which I am unable to develop further here. Shklar writes about legal realism in "Decisionism," 8–10.

16. Shklar, "In Defense of Legalism," *Journal of Legal Education* 19, no. 1 (1966): 51–58, here 53.

17. See also her statement that "Kelsen does not define the 'basic' norm. What legitimizes authority is ultimately a moral one." Judith Shklar Archives in Widener Library at Harvard, Box 18 on "Law and Morality," (1963), card 14. Shklar made notes for her lectures via index cards, which are now contained in these boxes. For a more positive assessment of Kelsen's legacy and theory, cf. "Editor's Introduction," in Hans Kelsen, *The Essence and Value of Democracy*, Nadia Urbinati and Carlo Invernizzi Accetti, eds. and Brian Graff, trans. (New York and Toronto: Rowman and Littlefield Publishers, Inc., 2013): 1–25.

18. Allan Janik and Stephen Toulmin, *Wittgenstein's Vienna*, first published in 1973 as "Elephant Paperbacks" by Simon and Schuster, New York, and reissued in 1996 by Ivan R. Dee Publisher: Chicago.

19. Shklar, "In Defense of Legalism," 53.

20. Ibid., 53, fn. 5. The Weber quote comes from: Max Weber, *On Law in Economy and Society*, ed. Max Rheinstein (Cambridge, MA: Touchstone, 1954), 4–5.

21. In "Authoritarian Populism and the Rule of Law," William E. Scheuerman carefully dis-

tinguishes between "the rule of law" and "legalism." The defense of the rule of law is crucial to all phases of Shklar's political theory; legalism is a narrow interpretation of what the rule of law amounts to. This is an important distinction and shows the subtleties of Shklar's position. Forthcoming in *Judith N. Shklar: A Political Companion*, ed. Sam Ashenden and Andreas Hess (Philadelphia: University of Pennsylvania Press.)

22. Moyn, "Judith Shklar versus the International Criminal Court," 494

23. Ibid.

24. Ibid., 495.

25. Shklar, "In Defense of Legalism," 58.

26. Nearly two decades later, in a comprehensive essay discussing models of the rule of law in Aristotle, Montesquieu, A. V. Dicey, Lon Fuller, Ronald Dworkin, and Roberto Unger, Shklar defends the rule of law against legalistic distortions and too much over-idealization on the one hand, and critical legal studies-style debunking on the other. She concludes that there is not much point in discussing the rule of law if rules governing courts were understood analogously to those regulating football games or free market transactions. But "[If] one begins with the fear of violence, the insecurity of arbitrary government, and the discriminations of injustice, one may work one's way up to finding a significant place for the Rule of Law." Shklar, "Political Theory and the Rule of Law," in Shklar, *Political Thought and Political Thinkers*, 21–38, here, 38. This essay was originally published in *The Rule of Law*, ed. A. Hutchinson and P. Monahan (Toronto: Carswell, 1987).

27. In *Ordinary Vices* (Cambridge, MA: Belknap Press of Harvard University Press, 1984), Shklar explores the relationship between vices such as hypocrisy, snobbery, betrayal, and misanthropy and liberal democracies. Legalism may be a form of hypocrisy endemic to democratic liberalism since the basic norm of liberal democracy is the consent of the governed, "and consent is not easily won or preserved. The means to achieve it are bound to heighten governmental hypocrisy" (70). Also, the democracy of everyday life "is based on the pretense that we must speak to each other as if social standing were a matter of indifference in our views of each other" (77). I thank Andrea Sangiovanni for his suggestion to think of legalism as a form of hypocrisy. But given how morally objectionable the concept of "hypocrisy" tends to be in ordinary moral understanding, to call legalism a form of hypocrisy does not help. Shklar's thought continues to dance at the edge of a form of debunking criticism from which she wants to distance herself.

28. Shklar's observations about the conceptual absurdities of the Tokyo trials, and her sardonic comments on the work of the chief prosecutor, Joseph Keenan, anticipate many postcolonial critiques of international law in our times (*Legalism*, 181ff.). Commenting on Mr. Keenan's claim that the "Christian-Judaic absolutes of good and evil" had universal validity, Shklar exclaims: "What on earth could the Judeo-Christian ethic mean to the Japanese?" (183). For a postcolonial critique of international law, cf. Anthony Anghie, *Imperialism, Sovereignty and the Making of International Law* (Cambridge: Cambridge University Press, 2007). But was Shklar objecting to the obtuseness of the American prosecutor alone, or did she have a more radical objection in mind, such as the legitimacy of holding a trial for war criminals across such vast cultural divides at all? Why couldn't one see the Tokyo trials as a form of "creative policy" much the same way as she did Nuremberg? After all, Japan was not as removed from and as unin-

formed about Western conceptions of legality as Shklar may have assumed. For a recent judicious account of the controversies concerning the legitimacy of the Tokyo War Crimes Trial in the light of new historical evidence, see Yuma Totani, *The Tokyo War Crimes Trial. The Pursuit of Justice in the Wake of WW II*. Harvard East Asian Monograph, 299 (Cambridge, MA, and London: Harvard University Press, 2008).

29. Tiphaine Dickson and Robin West give a more nuanced account of Shklar's assessment of the legitimacy of international law and international tribunals than Samuel Moyn in "Judith Shklar versus the International Criminal Court," See Dickson, "Shklar's Legalism and the Liberal Paradox," 193–94; West, "Reconsidering Legalism," 122–24.

30. See my discussion, "International Law and Human Plurality in the Shadow of Totalitarianism: Hannah Arendt and Raphael Lemkin," in Benhabib, *Dignity in Adversity*, 41–57.

31. This question was quite central to the Hart-Fuller debate that so provoked Shklar. Hart discusses the case of a woman who in 1944, wishing to be rid of her husband, had denounced him to the authorities for insulting remarks he had made about Hitler. The husband was arrested and sentenced to death, though he was not executed but sent to the front instead. In 1949, the woman was prosecuted in a West German court for "illegally depriving a person of his freedom." She pleaded that under Nazi laws, she had committed no crime. The court of appeal held that the wife was guilty because the Nazi statute was "contrary to the sound conscience and sense of justice of all decent human beings." Hart observes that "the unqualified satisfaction with this result seems to me to be hysteria." H.L.A. Hart, "Positivism and the Separation of Law and Morals," *Harvard Law Review* 71, no. 4 (February 1958): 593–629; the phrases in quotation marks are from Hart's discussion, here 618–19; see the rejoinder by Lon L. Fuller, "Positivism and the Fidelity to Law—A Reply to Professor Hart," *Harvard Law Review* 71, no. 4 (February, 1958): 630–72. Fuller writes: "First, Professor Hart seems to assume that evil aims may have as much coherence and inner logic as good ones. I, for one, refuse to accept that assumption" (636).

32. Shklar, "Review Essay" of *Between Past and Future* by Hannah Arendt, in *History and Theory* 2, no. 3 (1963): 286–92; "Hannah Arendt's Triumph," *The New Republic* 173, no. 26 (December 27, 1975): 8–10; "Rethinking the Past," in Shklar, *Political Thought and Political Thinkers*, ed. Stanley Hoffmann, 352–61 [originally published in *Social Research* 44 (1977): 80–90]; "Hannah Arendt as Pariah," in *Political Thought and Political Thinkers*, 362–75, [originally published in *Partisan Review* 50, no. 1 (1983): 64–77]. This last essay appears to be a critical piece occasioned by the publication of Young-Bruehl's biography of Arendt, *For Love of the World* (1983); Shklar, Review of Hannah Arendt, *Lectures on Kant's Political Philosophy*, ed. and with an interpretive essay by Ronald Beiner. (Brighton: Harvester Press, 1982), in *The Bulletin of the Hegel Society of Great Britain* 9 (Spring–Summer 1984): 42–44.

33. Shklar, "Hannah Arendt's Triumph," 8.

34. Shklar, "Hannah Arendt as Pariah," 363.

35. Ibid., 364.

36. Ibid., 375.

37. Shklar's review of Arendt's *Between Past and Future* of 1963 does not deal with the Eichmann book; there is also no mention of this controversy in her last review of Arendt's *Lectures on Kant's Political Philosophy* in 1984. Most interestingly, Shklar does not even refer to Eichmann in her 1975 encomium to Arendt ("Hannah Arendt's Triumph"), restricting herself to a discus-

sion of *The Origins of Totalitarianism*; *The Human Condition*; and *On Revolution*. Nor is *Eichmann in Jerusalem* discussed in "Rethinking the Past."

38. Shklar, "Hannah Arendt as Pariah," 372.

39. For a critique of Arendt's use of historical sources and documents, see Hans Mommsen's introduction to the 1986 German edition of the *Eichmann in Jerusalem*; English trans. published as "Hannah Arendt and the Eichmann Trial," in Hans Mommsen, *From Weimar to Auschwitz: Essays in German History*, trans. by Philip O'Connor (Princeton, NJ: Princeton University Press, 1991): 254–78. Raul Hilberg, *The Destruction of the European Jews* (New York: Holmes and Meier, 1986 [1961]); Raoul Hilberg, *Perpetrators, Victims, Bystanders: The Jewish Catastrophe, 1933–1945* (New York: Harper Collins, 1992).

40. Shklar, "Hannah Arendt as Pariah," 373.

41. Shklar, *Ordinary Vices*, 2.

42. My strong suspicion is that Shklar, like most of us, first found out about the Arendt-Heidegger affair through Young-Bruehl's account and may have been quite shocked by it and unwilling to indulge Arendt's weakness vis-à-vis Heidegger, for whom Shklar expressed the deepest contempt. "Eventually she found it easy to forgive Heidegger," writes Shklar of Arendt. "She had always seen through the cult that surrounded him, knowing perfectly well that none of his admirers had a clue about what he was saying. That, in fact, is still the condition of the thriving Heidegger industry. Arendt, however, not only understood him, she was and remained under his philosophical spell." In "Hannah Arendt as Pariah," 365.

43. Shklar, "Rethinking the Past," 353.

44. Ibid., 358.

45. Cf. Jon Elster, *Ulysses Unbound. Studies in Rationality, Precommitment, and Constraints* (Cambridge: Cambridge University Press, 2000). See also chapter 1 above for a discussion of precommitments in the bounding of the demos.

46. For a discussion of Arendt's views of the French Revolution in relation to Hegel, Burke, and de Tocqueville, see my *Reluctant Modernism of Hannah Arendt*, 161–63.

47. See Richard King, *Hannah Arendt and America* (Chicago and London: University of Chicago Press, 2015) for a consideration of these theses in the light of recent histories of the American Revolution and in particular the "republican revival," 245–71.

48. Shklar, *The Quest for Inclusion. The Tanner Lectures on Human Values* (Cambridge, MA: Harvard University Press, 1991). After naming *On Revolution* "a valentine presented to America," (Shklar, "Hannah Arendt's Triumph," 9) in keeping up with the acid tone of "Hannah Arendt as Pariah," Shklar writes: "The only really interesting thing about this *embarrassing book* is that it is a new version of Friedrich Gentz's comparison of the two revolutions" (Shklar, "Hannah Arendt as Pariah," 371. My emphasis). Friedrich Gentz (1764–1832) was a well-known Prussian statesman and influential diplomat, whose opposition to the French Revolution led him to translate Edmund Burke's *Reflections on the Revolution in France* into German (1794). He was for many years Metternich's right-hand man and one of the architects of the Vienna Congress (1814–15). He had a liaison with Rahel Varnhagen (von Ense), on whom Arendt had written an early book; see Arendt, *Rahel Varnhagen. The Life of a Jewish Woman*, revised edn., and trans. into English by Richard and Clara Winston (New York: Harcourt, Brace, Jovanovich, 1974 [1957]).

49. Shklar, *American Citizenship. The Quest for Inclusion*, ch. 2, "Earning," 63–101.

50. In an original essay, Anna Jurkevics has unearthed Arendt's critique of Carl Schmitt in these pages. See Anna Jurkevics, "Hannah Arendt Reads Carl Schmitt's *The Nomos of the Earth: A Dialogue on Law and Geo-Politics from the Margins*," *European Journal of Political Theory* (February 2015). Jurkevics deciphers the marginalia in Arendt's edition of Schmitt's *Nomos der Erde* (held at the Bard College Library), and translates Arendt's very difficult handwriting from the German. Arendt denies the naturalistic origins of law that Schmitt tries to establish via the etymological shorthands of "nemein" (to take, to possess) and "nomos." Arendt is quite clear that Schmitt's "pseudo-ontological derivation" of law from terrestriality serves as a justification of dominion over the earth, as in imperialist conquest of the earth, the so-called "Besitznahme." Etymologically, "Arendt agrees with Schmitt that *nomos* comes from the word *nemein* and contains within it two moments: acquisition (*nemein* as *nehmen*—to take) and division (*nemein* as *teilen*—to divide)," but the act of taking possession seems itself to give rise to the law rather than the law justifying or legitimizing taking possession. As Jurkevics explains: "Arendt accuses Schmitt, in his answer to the question 'what is the source of law?,' of not understanding the relationship between law and politics because he does not understand the nature of the political. Plurality, the primary condition of politics for Arendt, is absent from Schmitt's *nomos*" (5). For Arendt, the origins of law are in the human community itself: law defines the polis and is presupposed by it; there is no polis without *nomos* and vice versa. See also Benhabib, "Carl Schmitt's Critique of Kant. Sovereignty and International Law," *Political Theory* 40, no. 6 (December 2012): 688–713.

51. For feminist considerations and critiques of Hannah Arendt, see Bonnie Honig, *Feminist Interpretations of Hannah Arendt* and Benhabib, *The Reluctant Modernism of Hannah Arendt*, 134–46.

52. See Shklar's comments on Arendt's interpretation of the Romans, which according to Shklar, downplays the Roman "pragmatism in politics . . . Constitutional engineering, the emphasis on techniques for achieving political success at home and abroad." Shklar, "Review Essay" of *Between Past and Future*, 291.

53. Jurkevics, "Hannah Arendt Reads Carl Schmitt," 12. For further reflections on the distinction between *Nomos* and *Lex*, see Keith Breen, "Law beyond Command? An Evaluation of Arendt's Understanding of Law," in *Hannah Arendt and the Law*, ed. Marco Goldoni and Christopher McCorkindale (Oxford and Portland: Hart Publishing, 2012), 20–24.

54. Although never directly interested in matters of distributive justice, Shklar's thinking became increasingly radicalized over the years. She continued to dismiss free-market ideologies and even questioned the line between so-called "natural" and "man-made" misfortunes. See the remarkable discussion, Shklar, *The Faces of Injustice*, Storrs Lectures on Jurisprudence, Yale Law School, 1988 (New Haven, CT: Yale University Press, 1990), 65–71. Also Scheuerman, "Authoritarian Populism and the Rule of Law," (Forthcoming).

55. See Bonnie Honig, "Declarations of Independence: Arendt and Derrida on the Problem of Founding a Republic," *American Political Science Review* 85, no. 1 (1991): 97–113, for a provocative interpretation of founding in Arendt's work with reference to Jacques Derrida's novel reading of the Declaration of Independence in terms of a theory of the performative in Jacques Derrida, "Declarations of Independence," *New Political Science* 7, no. 1 (1986): 7–15.

56. John Rawls, *Political Liberalism* (New York: Columbia University Press, 1993). Forrester gives a nuanced account of Shklar's defense of "Rawls's achievements," when contrasted with Bernard Williams's more thoroughgoing critique of Rawls. She writes: "Thus her sympathy with Rawls sits uncomfortably alongside her antiformalist realism," but Forrester concludes that it was Shklar's "moral preference for liberal reformist politics and . . . some kind of welfare state," that led her to rally for Rawls. Forrester, "Judith Shklar, Bernard Williams and Political Realism," 261–62.

57. Robert Post, "Theorizing Disagreement: Re-Conceiving the Relationship between Law and Politics," *California Law Review* 98, no. 4 (2010): 1319–50. See also the concept of "democratic constitutionalism" developed by Robert Post and Reva B. Siegel in "Roe Rage: Democratic Constitutionalism and Backlash," *Harvard Civil Rights and Civil Liberties Review* 42, no. 2 (2007): 373–434.

58. For further discussion of this course and the archival materials on it, see Andreas Hess, *The Political Theory of Judith N. Shklar*, 178–87.

59. See Shklar, "Obligation, Loyalty, and Exile," in *Political Thought and Political Thinkers*, 21–38 [first published in *Political Theory* 21, no. 2 (May 1993): 181–97]. Referred to in the text as "OLE"; Shklar, "The Bonds of Exile," in *Political Thought and Political Thinkers*, 56–75. Previously unpublished. The note appended to this second text says that it was written in 1993, which is obviously a mistake since she passed away in 1992.

60. See http://www.unhcr.org/en-us/1951-refugee-convention.html. Accessed March 30, 2017.

61. "Pieds noirs," literally "black feet," refers to Europeans (both Muslim and Jewish) who lived in Algeria during French rule and who returned to Europe after Algeria won its independence in 1962. Cf. https://en.wikipedia.org/wiki/Pied-Noir. Accessed May 2, 2017.

62. Shklar's Harvard colleague, Michael Walzer, had discussed questions of political membership and belonging extensively in his *Spheres of Justice. A Defense of Pluralism and Equality* (New York: Basic Books, 1983).

63. Hess, *The Political Theory of Judith N. Shklar*, 189.

## Chapter 8. Exile and Social Science: On Albert Hirschman

1. I am much indebted to Jeremy Adelman's excellent biography of Albert Hirschman, *Worldly Philosopher. The Odyssey of Albert O. Hirschman* (Princeton, NJ: Princeton University Press, 2013), 465.

2. Albert O Hirschman, *Exit, Voice, and Loyalty. Responses to Decline in Firms, Organizations, and States* (Cambridge, MA, and London: Harvard University Press, 1970), 2. Abbreviated in this chapter as *EVL*.

3. Hirschman, "Preface," in his *Crossing Boundaries. Selected Writings* (Zone Books: New York, 1998), 8.

4. Adelman, *Worldly Philosopher*, 32. See also Anna Barbara Sum, "Widerspruch als Prinzip: Nachruf auf Albert Hirschman (April 7, 1915–10. Dezember, 2012)," *Geschichte und Gesellschaft* 39 (January–March 2013): 125–38 for further biographical details about Hirschman's life. This article appeared the same year in which Adelman's biography was about to be published. The

author uses the term "Widerspruch," which can be translated as "contradiction" or "resistance" with reference to the title of the German translation of *EVL* as "Abwanderung und Widerspruch." See note 42 below.

5. Adelman, *Worldly Philosopher*, 573.

6. Amos Elon, *The Pity of It All. A History of the Jews in Germany 1743–1933*.

7. This phrase comes from Hannah Arendt's interview with the journalist Gunther Gauss, "Hannah Arendt im Gespräch mit Günter Gauss," https://www.youtube.com/watch?v =dsoImQfVsO4. Conducted on October 28, 1964. The conversation around language occurs around the thirty-seventh minute, and this phrase occurs at thirty-eighth minute. A shortened version in English is available in Arendt, *Essays in Understanding*, 1–24.

8. Adelman, *Worldly Philosopher*, 60.

9. In an insightful tribute to Hirschman, Nadia Urbinati writes: "The way in which a person expatriates reveals a great deal about him- or herself. Hirschman chose to leave Germany in April 1933—only four months after Adolf Hitler took power. In making that wise decision he was guided by what I regard as his primary mental habit, doubt—doubt concerning the new regime. Doubting, questioning, and a disinclination to trust the status quo—this led Albert and Ursula to take a vacation in Paris. This was the best decision of their lives." Nadia Urbinati, " 'Proving Hamlet Wrong': The Creative Role of Doubt in Albert Hirschman's Social Thought," in "Albert Hirschman and the Social Sciences: A Memorial Roundtable," *Humanity: An International Journal of Human Rights, Humanitarianism, and Development* 6, no. 2 (Summer 2015): 267–71, here 268.

10. Adelman, *Worldly Philosopher*, 119.

11. Ibid., 135. Cf. also Arthur Koestler, *Darkness at Noon* (New York: Vintage, 2010 [1941]); Manès Sperber, *Wie eine Träne im Ozean. Romantrilogie* (Munich: Deutsche Taschenbuch Verlag, 1980 [1976]).

12. For a brief personal tribute to Varian Fry, see Hirschman, "With Varian Fry in Marseilles, 1936–1938," in Hirschman, *A Propensity to Self-Subversion* (Cambridge, MA: Harvard University Press, 1995), 120–23. This was an introduction to Varian Fry's autobiography, *Assignment: Rescue—An Autobiography* (New York: Scholastic, 1993 [1968]).

13. Hirschman, *World Politics* 22, no. 3 (March 1970): 329–43, here 334.

14. Dipesh Chakrabarty, *Provincializing Europe. Postcolonial Thought and Historical Difference*.

15. Adelman, *Worldly Philosopher*, 32.

16. Hirschman, *National Power and the Structure of Foreign Trade* (Berkeley and Los Angeles: University of California Press, 1945); reprinted in 1969 and 1980.

17. Ibid., quoted in Adelman, *Worldly Philosopher*, 209.

18. Hirschman, *National Power and the Structure of Foreign Trade*, quoted by Adelman, 213.

19. Ibid., 213.

20. At the time of the composition of this report projecting the idea of a federated Europe, Hirschman was working for the Economic Cooperation Administration (ECA), together with Richard Bissell from the Office of Strategic Services to plan strategies for European recovery. See Adelman, *Worldly Philosopher*, 261ff. The quote comes from *Worldly Philosopher*, 271.

21. The Manifesto is made available online through the Union of European Federalists at

http://www.federalists.eu/uef/library/books/the-ventotene-manifesto/. Accessed on May 6, 2017. All citations in the text are from this document.

22. This refers to the concept of "Lebensraum" developed by Nazi theorists to justify the expansion of the German Reich into territories mainly in Central and Eastern Europe. Cf. Schmitt, *Der Nomos der Erde im Völkerrecht des Jus Publicum Europaeum*, 4th edn. (Berlin: Duncker and Humblot, 1997 [1950]); English trans. by G. L. Ulmen, *The Nomos of the Earth in International Law of the Jus Publicum Europeum* (New York: Telos Press Publishing, 2003); Schmitt, *Land and Sea. A World-Historical Meditation*, trans. Samuel Garrett Zeitlin, ed. and with an introduction by Russell A. Berman (Candor, NY: Telos Press Publishing, 2015 [1942]); Samuel Garrett Zeitlin, "Propaganda and Critique: An Introduction to Land and Sea," in *Spatiality, Sovereignty and Carl Schmitt*, xxxi-lxix; *Spatiality, Sovereignty and Carl Schmitt. Geographies of the Nomos*, ed. Stephen Legg (London and New York: Routledge, 2001). For Hannah Arendt's critique of Schmitt's derivation of law from terrestriality, cf. above chapter 7.

23. As discussed briefly in chapter 2, this was an ideal articulated by Kant in all its philosophical clarity in "Perpetual Peace." See Kant, "Perpetual Peace: A Philosophical Sketch," trans. H. B. Nisbet, in Kant, *Political Writings*.

24. This is an odd expression and I wonder if the authors meant "flexible," rather than "plastic."

25. Among the prolific literature on the European Union's constitutional revolutions and characteristics, see Joseph H. Weiler, *The Constitution of Europe* (Cambridge: Cambridge University Press, 1999); Alec Stone Sweet, *Governing with Judges. Constitutional Politics in Europe* (Oxford: Oxford University Press, 2000); Sweet, *The Judicial Construction of Europe* (Oxford: Oxford University Press, 2004); Habermas, "Why Europe Needs a Constitution," *New Left Review* 11, no. 5 (2001); Habermas, *Europe. The Faltering Project*, trans. C. Cronin (Malden, MA, and Cambridge: Polity Press, 2009); Habermas, *The Crisis of the European Union: A Response*, trans. C. Cronin (Malden, MA, and Cambridge: Polity Press, 2012); for an excellent analysis of the contradictory ideals of European constitutionalism, see Turkuler Isiksel, *Europe's Functional Constitution. A Theory of Constitutionalism beyond the State* (Oxford: Oxford University Press, 2016).

26. For an analysis of the complexities of historical memory in postwar Europe and the impulse toward reconstruction among Protestants and Catholics, see Peter Verovsek, *The European Rupture: A Critical Theory of Memory and Integration in the Wake of Total War* (Forthcoming).

27. Adelman, *Worldly Philosopher*, 331.

28. Hirschman, *The Strategy of Economic Development*. Third printing. (New Haven, CT: Yale University Press, 1960 [1958]), 26.

29. Hirschman, *Development Projects Observed* (Washington, DC: Brooking, 1967; reprinted in 1994). The new preface to the 1994 edition, titled "A Hidden Ambition," is reprinted in Hirschman, *A Propensity to Self-Subversion*, 128–31, here 128.

30. Hirschman, "A Hidden Ambition," 129.

31. Hirschman, "The Rise and Decline of Development Economics," in Hirschman, *Essays in Trespassing. Economics to Politics and Beyond* (Cambridge: Cambridge University Press, 1981), 3ff.

32. Ibid., 4.

33. For an early compilation of Marx's contradictory attitudes toward the impact of imperialism on so-called "underdeveloped" societies and their path to modernization, see Shlomo Avineri, *Karl Marx on Colonialism and Modernization*, ed. and with an introduction by Shlomo Avineri (New York: Doubleday Anchor Book, 1969); George Lichtheim discusses the Asiatic Mode of Production under the heading "Oriental Despotism," in Lichtheim, "Marx and the Asiatic Mode of Production," *St. Anthony's Papers*, no. 14 (1963): 82–112, and most recently, Gareth Stedman Jones, *Karl Marx. Greatness and Illusion* (London: Allen Lane of Penguin Books, 2016), 568–86.

34. Hirschman, "The Rise and Decline of Development Economics," 9.

35. Ibid., 24.

36. Amartya Sen, "Foreword to the Twentieth Anniversary Edition," in *The Passions and the Interests* (Princeton, NJ: Princeton University Press, 1997 [1977]), xvii.

37. Hirschman, *Development Projects Observed*, 146–47; discussed in *EVL*, 44–45. The outbreak of the Nigerian Civil War (also known as the Biafran War) in 1967 to 1970 between Ibos and the Igbo people was not explicitly thematized in this work, although Hirschman had made field notes about simmering unrest. See Jeremy Adelman, "Unfinished Work: Albert Hirschman's Exit, Voice and Loyalty," in "Albert Hirschman and the Social Sciences: A Memorial Roundtable," *Humanity: An International Journal of Human Rights and Humanitarianism and Development* 6, no. 2 (Summer 2015): 277–80, here 278.

38. Hirschman, *The Rhetoric of Reaction. Perversity, Futility, Jeopardy* (Cambridge, MA: Belknap Press of Harvard University Press, 1991), 38–19. Abbreviated in the text as *RR*.

39. Hirschman noted how his early book, *National Power and the Structure of Foreign Trade* (1945) would be considered the "unacknowledged founding grandfather" of "dependency theories," which focused on the structural and exploitative imbalances between center and periphery, in Hirschman, "Beyond Asymmetry: Critical Notes on Myself as a Young Man and on Some Other Old Friends," *International Organization* 32, no. 1 (Winter 1978, special issue on *Dependence and Dependency in the Global System*): 45–50, here 45. In characteristic fashion, he made the quite unexpected observation that: "if the efforts of a country to lessen its dependence are to prosper, there is no substitute for that 'wise and salutary neglect' on the part of the imperial power which Burke long ago recognized as a basic cause of the growing strength of England's North American colonies. And it is my contention that the likelihood of such neglect—and of correspondingly concentrated attention on the part of the dependent country—is inscribed in the asymmetrical trade percentages just as much as the facts of dependence and domination themselves" (48).

40. See the collection of essays by Hirschman called *A Propensity to Self-Subversion.*

41. Hirschman, "Exit, Voice and the Fate of the German Democratic Republic. An Essay in Conceptual History," in *World Politics* 45 (January 1993): 173–202, here 202.

42. This reference is to an article published by Henning Ritter in the *Frankfurter Allgemeine Zeitung* on November 9, 1989, as "Abwandern, Widersprechen: Zur aktuellen Bedeutung einer Theorie von A.O. Hirschman," ("To Exit, to Voice: On the Current Relevance of a Theory of A. O. Hirschman). "Abwanderung und Widerspruch," literally "outmigration" and "contradict-

ing," was a very loose translation of *Exit, Voice, and Loyalty!* See Hirschman for a discussion of this article, "Exit, Voice and the Fate of the German Democratic Republic," 174.

43. Hirschman, "Exit, Voice, and the State," *World Politics* 31, no. 1 (1978), 90–107.

44. Stephen D. Krasner, *Sovereignty. Organized Hypocrisy* (Princeton, NJ: Princeton University Press, 1999).

45. Hirschman, "Exit, Voice, and the State," 90, fn. 2.

46. Ibid., 93.

47. Jonathan W. Moses uses Hirschman's exit, voice, and loyalty model to understand the political effects of globalization on labor. While it is generally agreed that labor is hampered by increased globalization, he claims that "a modified Hirschman approach suggests that the problem facing labor is not globalization, per se. In a world characterized by relatively free mobility of other factors of production (and their owners), labor appears to be handicapped by being a prisoner of territory." Jonathan W. Moses, "Exit, Vote and Sovereignty: Migration, States and Globalization, *Review of International Political Economy* 12, no. 1 (February 2005): 53–77. Moses observes that "loyalty" complicates labor's mobility and increases exit costs, not only because citizens of liberal democracies enjoy voice but also because of the basic human costs—familial, linguistic, psychological—of exit, caused by emigration/immigration (67). In that sense, the analogy between citizens and consumers is simplistic since as a member of a human community, the citizen is motivated by more than the search for economic gain and livelihood. It is striking that contemporary migratory movements mostly flow from the Global South and East to the North and the West. This may suggest that the absence of democratic voice in many regimes of Africa, South Asia, and the Middle East, coupled with dire economic conditions, reduces the ties of loyalty to such a point that despite the enormously high personal cost of exit, today's migrants and refugees often risk death but still undertake to leave.

48. Hirschman, *The Passions and the Interests. Political Arguments for Capitalism before Its Triumph* (Princeton, NJ: Princeton University Press, 1977). Abbreviated in the text as *PI*.

49. Hirschman, *The Rhetoric of Reaction*.

## Chapter 9. Isaiah Berlin: A Judaism between Decisionism and Pluralism

1. Leon Wieseltier, "When a Sage Dies, All Are His Kin," *The New Republic,* December 1, 1997, 27–31.

2. Ibid., 31*ff.*

3. See "Isaiah Berlin in Conversation with Steven Lukes," in *Salmagundi,* no. 120 (Fall 1998): 52–135; George Crowder, "Pluralism and Liberalism," *Political Studies* 42(1994): 293–305; Isaiah Berlin and Bernard Williams, "Pluralism and Liberalism: A Reply," *Political Studies,* 42 (1994), 306–9; Peter Lassman, *Pluralism* (Malden, MA, and Cambridge: Polity Press, 2011).

4. Wieseltier, "When a Sage Dies," 31.

5. Shklar, "Review of Isaiah Berlin's *Against the Current: Essays in the History of Ideas* (New York: Viking, 1979)," in *The New Republic,* April 5, 1980, 32–35, here 35.

6. Since Berlin was trained in analytical philosophy as practiced in Oxford in the 1930s within

a group that included Stuart Hampshire, A. J. Ayer, J. L. Austin, and others, his decision to leave philosophy for the "field of the history of ideas" was more significant for him intellectually than for Shklar, who practiced political philosophy without paying much attention to methodological issues. Berlin reports that as a result of a conversation with Professor H. M. Sheffer of Harvard, who told him that only in logic and psychology could one hope for an increase in knowledge, he asked himself "whether I wished to devote the rest of my life to a study, however fascinating and important in itself, which, transforming as its achievements undoubtedly were, would not any more than criticism or poetry, add to the store of positive human knowledge. I gradually came to the conclusion that I should prefer a field in which one could hope to know more at the end of one's life than when one had begun; and so I left philosophy for the field of the history of ideas." Isaiah Berlin, "Author's Preface," in Berlin, *Concepts and Categories*, ed. Henry Hardy and with a foreword by Alasdair MacIntyre (Princeton, NJ: Princeton University Press, 2013), xxvii. Both Alasdair MacIntyre in his foreword to this volume (xi–xvii) and Bernard Williams in his introduction (xxix–xxxix) emphasize the critique of logical positivism implicit in Berlin's abandonment of the Oxford program of the 1930s and of linguistic philosophy of the 1940s.

7. Berlin's aversion to Hannah Arendt is deep and has been documented by the publication of his letters and other sources. The most detailed examination can be found in David Caute: *Isaac and Isaiah. The Covert Punishment of a Cold War Heretic* (New Haven, CT: Yale University Press, 2013), 262–75. Caute points out that Berlin had met Arendt in 1941, and again in the early 1950s. Berlin appears to have assiduously prevented the publication of *The Human Condition* in the United Kingdom (264). In February 1959, after the publication of *The Human Condition*, Berlin encouraged his friend Morton White to "up and rout her." As quoted by Kei Hiruta, "The Meaning and Value of Freedom: Berlin contra Arendt," *The European Legacy* 19, no. 7 (2014): 854. See also Berlin, *Enlightening Letters 1946–60*, ed. Henry Hardy and Jennifer Homes (London: Chatto and Windus, 2009), 676 on Arendt.

Berlin shared Gershom Scholem's judgment that she suffered a "terrible lack of heart," in Michael Ignatieff, *Isaiah Berlin. A Life* (New York: Metropolitan Books, 1998), 253. He most certainly helped plant a hostile and anonymous review in the *Times Literary Supplement* of April 30, 1964, of *Eichmann in Jerusalem*. The author was John Sparrow, warden of All Souls College, and Berlin's close friend (Caute, 269–72). Even after the Eichmann controversy, Berlin claimed about Arendt's work that there was "no evidence of serious philosophical or historical thought. It is all a stream of metaphysical free association." Quoted by Ramin Jahanbegloo, *Conversations with Isaiah Berlin* (London: Phoenix Press, 2000), 82.

It is the great merit of Kei Hiruta's recent articles to move beyond the level of personal animosities to a serious philosophical consideration of the different paradigms of political freedom in Berlin's and Arendt's works. See his, "An 'Anti-Utopian Age? Isaiah Berlin's England, Hannah Arendt's America, and Utopian Thinking in Dark Times," in *Journal of Political Ideologies* 22, no. 1 (2017): 12–29.

8. Berlin, "Isaiah Berlin in Conversation with Steven Lukes," 102.

9. Peter Lassman, *Pluralism*, 57. See also John Gray, *Isaiah Berlin* (Princeton: Princeton University Press, 1996), 58. Gray underscores the role of Weber for Berlin's thought but criticizes

Weber for not basing his value pluralism on moral psychology or philosophical anthropology, etc. The source of Weber's value pluralism is his interpretation of the condition of modernity.

10. Berlin, *Four Essays on Liberty* (Oxford: Oxford University Press, 1969), 48. Quoted by Lassman, *Pluralism*, 173, fn. 80. Berlin also refers to Weber's three types of legitimate authority in his "Does Political Theory Still Exist?," in Berlin, *Concepts and Categories*, 187–226, here 207. This essay was first published in 1961 in French as "La Théorie politique existe-t-elle?" in *Review française de science politique* 11 (1961), and then in English in Pater Laslett and W. G. Runciman, eds., *Philosophy, Politics and Society*, 2nd series (Oxford: Blackwell, 1962). See Berlin, editor's note, *Concepts and Categories*, xxii.

11. Stefan Eich and Adam Tooze, "The Allure of Dark Times: Max Weber, Politics and the Crisis of Historicism," in *History and Theory* 56, no. 2 (June 2017): 197–215, here 201.

12. Eich and Tooze, "The Allure of Dark Times." The authors carefully document how Weber misquotes Leon Trotsky's statement on state violence from the peace negotiations at Brest Litovsk in January 1918 and they dissect the political as well as theoretical implications of this, 199ff.

13. See Peter E. Gordon, "Critical Theory between the Sacred and the Profane," *Constellations* 23, no. 4 (2016): 466–81 on *Entzauberung*.

14. As a cognitive attitude, formal rationality means the attempt to comprehend reality by means of "increasingly precise and abstract concepts," enabling prediction and the instrumental control and organization of phenomena. Max Weber, "The Social Psychology of World Religions," in Weber, *Essays in Sociology*, ed. and trans. H. H. Gerth and C. W. Mills (New York: Oxford University Press, 1974), 293. This text is based on the 1920 introduction to Weber's *Gesammelte Aufsätze zur Religionssoziologie*, published the same year. This cognitive attitude is accompanied by a practical-instrumental attitude according to which social action is increasingly oriented to the attainment of given ends by "means of an increasingly precise calculation of adequate means" (ibid.) on the basis of "universally applied rules, laws or regulations." Stephen Kahlberg, "Max Weber's Types of Rationality: Cornerstone for the Analysis of Rationalization Processes in History," *American Journal of Sociology* 85, no. 5 (1980): 1158. This mode of action is characterized by Weber as "purposive-rational" (*Zweckrational*).

15. I am indebted to Jürgen Habermas's magisterial analysis and reconstruction of Weber's theory of modernity in his *The Theory of Communicative Action*, vols. 1 and 2, trans. Thomas A. McCarthy (Boston: Beacon Press, 1973); for an extensive discussion of Weber's place in the theories of the Frankfurt School, see Benhabib, *Critique, Norm and Utopia*, 182–85 and for a discussion of "the paradox of rationalization" in Habermas's work, *Critique, Norm and Utopia*, 228–55. See also Niklas Luhmann, *The Differentiation of Society*, trans. Stephen Holmes and Charles Larrmore. European Perspectives: A Series in Social Thought and Cultural Criticism. (New York: Columbia University Press, 1984).

16. This is Karl Polanyi's famous phrase to describe the relation of economy and society. See his *The Great Transformation. The Political and Economic Origins of Our Times*, foreword by Joseph Stieglitz, second paperback edn. (Boston: Beacon Press, 2001 [1957]); first publication (New York: Farrar and Rinehart, 1944).

17. Max Weber, *The Theory of Social and Economic Organization*, ed. and with an introduction

by Talcott Parsons (New York: The Free Press, 1964 [1947]), 124–43; Max Weber, *Economy and Society*, trans. Guenther Roth and Claus Wittich (Berkeley and Los Angeles: University of California Press, 1978).

18. For an explanation of the "ideal type," see Weber: "Understanding (*Verstehen*) may be of two kinds: the first is the direct observational understanding (*aktuelles Verstehen*) of the subjective meaning of a given act as such, including verbal utterances . . . Understanding, may, however, be of another sort, namely explanatory understanding (*erklärendes Verstehen*). Thus we understand in terms of motive the meaning an actor attaches to a proposition . . . in that we understand what makes him do this at precisely this moment in these circumstances." Weber, *The Theory of Social and Economic Organization*, 94–95. Ideal types are constructions by the social scientist of configurations of the motives and goals of social action that possess both "subjective meaning" and "causal likelihood." Ibid, 9–99.

19. Such considerations have given rise to the "multiple" and "alternative modernities" approach among Weber's late followers. See Shmuel Eisenstadt, ed., *Multiple Modernities* (New York: Routledge, 2002) and Domenic Sachsenmeier and Jens Riedel, eds., *Reflections on Multiple Modernities*, with Shmuel Eisenstadt (Brill Publishers, 2002).

20. See the following comment by Weber: "All the analysis of the infinite reality which the finite human mind can conduct rests on the tacit assumption that only a finite portion of this reality constitutes the object of scientific investigation, and that only it is 'important' in the sense of being 'worthy of being known.'" Weber, "Objectivity in Social Science and Social Policy," in Max Weber, *The Methodology of the Social Sciences*, trans and ed. Edward A. Shils and Henry Finch (New York: The Free Press, 1949 [1904]). I discuss the epistemological dimensions of Max Weber's writings in Benhabib, "Rationality and Social Action: Critical Reflections on Max Weber's Methodological Writings," *Philosophical Forum* 12, no. 4 (1981): 356–75.

21. Weber, "The Meaning of 'Ethical Neutrality' in Sociology and Economics," in *The Methodology of the Social Sciences*, 14.

22. For Weber, *Verstehen* or "explanatory understanding" is exercised not through an act of imagination or empathy but through the construction of ideal types that are adequate both to explain the subjective meaning that individual actors attach to their behavior and that also have causally predictive power. See note 18 above.

23. Weber, "Objectivity in Social Science and Social Policy," 76.

24. Max Weber, "Science as a Vocation," in *Max Weber: Essays in Sociology*, 149. Originally published as "Wissenschaft als Beruf" (1919).

25. Weber, "The Meaning of 'Ethical Neutrality,'" 17.

26. Hirschman, quoted in Adelman, *Worldly Philosopher*, 573.

27. Weber, "Science as a Vocation," 158; on the rationalist and enlightenment functions of social science, see Weber, "The Meaning of 'Ethical Neutrality,'" 20–23.

28. For an account of the tensions in Weber's politics and the uses to which his thought was put in the postwar period in Germany, see Wolfgang J. Mommsen, *Max Weber und die deutsche Politik, 1890–1920* (Tübingen: J.C.B. Mohr, 1974).

29. Berlin, "The Pursuit of the Ideal," in *The Proper Study of Mankind. An Anthology of Essays*, ed. Henry Hardy and Roger Hausheer (New York: Farrar, Strauss, and Giroux, 1997), 1–17, here 7.

30. See Hegel's unforgettable discussion of Antigone in *The Phenomenology of Spirit*, 266–78. Hegel's analysis shows that as incompatible as these values may be, they also need to be harmonized, and both the gods of *the oikos* and those of *the polis* need to appeased. The ancient world, even if no stranger to the clash of values, was still "monistic" in Berlin's terms and searched for reconciliation in a harmonious whole. For a lucid account, see Berlin, "The Apotheosis of the Romantic Will. The Revolt against the Myth of an Ideal World," in *The Crooked Timber of Humanity. Chapters in the History of Ideas*, ed. Henry Hardy (Princeton, NJ: Princeton University Press, 1990), 207–38, here, 209.

31. Lassman gives a compelling account of the question of modernity in Berlin's thought and emphasizes the significance for him of the romantic critique of liberalism and the rise of the counter-Enlightenment with Vico, Hamann, Herder, and de Maistre. See Lassman, *Pluralism*, 54–59.

32. Stefan Eich and Adam Tooze, "The Allure of Dark Times: Max Weber, Politics and the Crisis of Historicism."

33. Rousseau, bk. 1, sec. 7.

34. Karl Popper, *The Open Society and Its Enemies*, in one volume, introduction by Alan Ryan, (Princeton, NJ: Princeton University Press, 1994 [1944]); Raymond Aron, *The Opium of the Intellectuals* (New York: W. W. Norton and Company, 1962 [1955]); Friedrich Hayek, *The Road to Serfdom*. 50th anniversary edn., with Milton Friedman (London and New York: Routledge, 1994 [1944]); Jean-François Lyotard, *The Post-Modern Condition: A Report on Knowledge*, trans. Geoffrey Bennington and Brian Massumi (Minneapolis: University of Minnesota Press, 1984). Mark Lilla has deployed the temptation of intellectuals by their search for totality as a new weapon of critique in *The Reckless Mind: Intellectuals in Politics* (New York: New York Review of Books, 2001).

35. See chapter 2, note 44 for further references. For the discussion of Weber, see Schmitt, *The Concept of the Political*, 20*ff.*; for Strauss's commentary, "On Schmitt's Concept of the Political," 103*ff.* and on whether man is by nature "good" or "evil," 110–11. Leo Strauss criticizes Berlin along similar lines as well in Strauss, "Relativism," in H. Schoeck, ed. *Relativism and the Study of Man* (Princeton, NJ: Van Nostrand, 1961), 138–40.

36. Berlin, "The Rationality of Value Judgments," in *Concept and Categories*, 315–17, here 316; originally published in *Nomos 7, Rational Decision*, ed. Carl Friedrich (New York: Atherton Press, 1964).

37. Berlin, "The Pursuit of the Ideal," 9.

38. Berlin, "Does Political Theory Still Exist?," in *Concepts and Categories*, 187–225, here 217.

39. Berlin, "The Pursuit of the Ideal," 15.

40. Caute, *Isaac and Isaiah*, 251.

41. Ibid. See also Michael Ignatieff, *Isaiah Berlin. A Life*, 118.

42. For a discussion of this period in Arendt's life and her political activities, see Benhabib, *The Reluctant Modernism of Hannah Arendt*, 39–47. Arendt, "Zionism Reconsidered," first published in the *Menorah Journal* 32, no. 2 (October–December 1945): 162–96; reprinted in Arendt, *The Jewish Writings*, 343–75.

43. George Crowder gives an incisive analysis of this issue in "Pluralism and Liberalism," 293–305. The joint response by Berlin and Bernard Williams focuses on the absence of a "lexical

priority rule" for solving value conflicts and insists that "choices among incommensurable values" contain an element of "rational indeterminacy." In Berlin and Williams, "Pluralism and Liberalism: A Reply," in the same issue, 306–9. They conclude that "neither of the present writers believes that this formal style is the most illuminating way in which to discuss these matters. *There are indeed well known and very important issues about the social and political stability of liberalism and of the outlooks historically associated with it.* It is from concrete discussion of those issues, rather than from debate about logical possibilities, that the weaknesses of liberalism and the problems of self-conscious pluralism, are likely to emerge." Berlin and Williams, 309. It is left tantalizingly unclear what form such more "concrete discussions" would take (emphasis added).

44. Young-Bruehl, *For Love of the World*, 70ff.

45. John Rawls, "The Priority of Right and the Ideas of the Good," in *Collected Papers*, ed. Samuel Freeman (Cambridge, MA, and London, England: Harvard University Press, 1999), 462–63.

46. Rawls, "The Priority of the Right and the Ideas of the Good," 462–63, fn. 24.

47. Rawls, "The Burdens of Judgment," in *Political Liberalism*, 56. This aspect of Rawls's work is missed by John Gray, who identifies Rawls's work with a vision of rule-bound liberalism as opposed to Berlin's "agonistic conception" and tragic sense of politics. A more nuanced reading of Rawls is required. See Gray, *Isaiah Berlin*, 8–9.

48. Ibid., 16.

49. For well-known early critiques, see Michael Sandel, *Liberalism and the Limits of Justice* (Cambridge: Cambridge University Press, 1982); Sheldon Wolin, *Politics and Vision. Continuity and Innovation in Western Political Thought*, with a new foreword by Wendy Brown (Princeton, NY: Princeton University Press, 2016 [1960]), ch. 15; Bonnie Honig, *Political Theory and the Displacement of Politics* (Ithaca, Cornell: Cornell University Press, 1993).

50. Lassman, *Pluralism*, 98–99.

51. See Benhabib, *Situating the Self; Dignity in Adversity;* and *Kosmopolitismus ohne Illusionen* for my defense of a program of communicative ethics, deliberative democracy, and transnational human rights.

## Conclusion: The Universal and the Particular. Then and Now

1. Shklar, "Hannah Arendt as Pariah," *The New Republic*, 364.

2. See Benhabib, *The Claims of Culture. Equality and Diversity in the Global Era* (Princeton, NJ: Princeton University Press, 2002).

3. http://www.jewishvirtuallibrary.org/galut

4. We must not forget Edward Said's poignant words: "Exile is a jealous state. What you achieve is precisely what you have no wish to share . . . What could be more intransigent than the conflict between Zionist Jews and Palestinian Arabs? Palestinians feel that they have been turned into exiles by the proverbial people of exile, the Jews." Said, "Reflections on Exile," in *Reflections on Exile and Other Essays* (Cambridge, Mass.: Harvard University Press, 2000), 173–87, here 178.

5. Commenting on the connection between these two dimensions of exile, Said argues that "exile cannot be made to serve notions of humanism. On the twentieth-century scale, exile is neither aesthetically nor humanistically comprehensible." I beg to differ and have attempted to show in many of these essays how these dimensions are interlaced with one another. "Reflections on Exile," 174.

6. Habermas, *The Theory of Communicative Action*, vols. 1 and 2

7. Schmitt, *The Concept of the Political*, 26.

8. Gündogdu, *Rightlessness in an Age of Rights*, 166.

9. I say "much misunderstood" because it was thought that Arendt called for the "self-appointment of a new revolutionary elite," whereas I believe that she was saying that for most people, to paraphrase Oscar Wilde, "politics would take too many evenings." And only those who really cared for the res publica should choose to engage in politics. In that sense, it is possible to respect the negative liberty of some to abstain from politics and the desire of others to dedicate themselves to it. But there needs to be a balance between them, and when that balance is lost, republics perish. See Arendt, *On Revolution*, 275–77, 279–80.

10. Already aware of the difficulty of subsuming empirical objects under general concepts, Kant discussed this problem in *The Critique of Pure Reason* under the heading of the "schemata of the concept." He conceded that "the schema is in itself always a product of the imagination." See Kant, *Critique of Pure Reason*, unabridged edn. trans. Norman Kemp Smith (St. Martin's Press: New York, 1965 [1781]), 182ff.

11. Barbara Herman, *The Practice of Moral Judgment* (Cambridge, MA: Harvard University Press, 1996).

12. See Arendt, "Civil Disobedience," in *Crises of the Republic* (New York: Harcourt, Brace, and Jovanovich: 1972), 49–103.

# REFERENCES

## Primary Sources Cited in the Text

### Works by Theodor Adorno

Adorno, Theodor. *Against Epistemology: A Metacritique. Studies in Husserl and the Phenomenological Antinomies.* Translated by Willis Domingo. Oxford: Basil Blackwell, 1982.

Adorno, Theodor. *Ästhetische Theorie.* In *Gesammelte Schriften.* Edited by Rolf Tiedemann. Frankfurt: Suhrkamp, 1970.

Adorno, Theodor. "Education after Auschwitz." In *Critical Models: Interventions and Catchwords.* Edited by Henry Pickford, 191–204. New York: Columbia University Press, 2005.

Adorno, Theodor. *Erziehung zur Mündigkeit: Vorträge und Gespräche mit Helmut Becker 1959–1969.* Edited by Gerd Kadelbach. Frankfurt: Suhrkamp, 1970.

Adorno, Theodor. *Jargon der Eigentlichkeit.* Frankfurt: Suhrkamp, 1964. Translated by Knut Tarnowski and Frederic Will as *The Jargon of Authenticity.* Evanston: Northwestern University Press, 1973.

Adorno, Theodor. *Negative Dialektik.* Frankfurt: Suhrkamp, 1973. Translated by E. B. Ashton as *Negative Dialectics.* New York: Seabury Press, 1973.

Adorno, Theodor. "Zur Aktualität der Philosophie." In *Philosophische Frühschriften. Gesammelte Schriften,* vol. 1. Frankfurt: Suhrkamp, 1973. Translated by Susan Buck-Morss (alias Benjamin Snow) as "The Actuality of Philosophy," with an introduction in *Telos* (Spring 1977): 120–33.

Adorno, Theodor, Else Frenkel-Brunswik, Daniel J. Levinson, and R. Nevitt Sanford. "The Authoritarian Personality." In *Studies in Prejudice.* Edited by Max Horkheimer and Samuel H. Flowerman. New York and London: W. W. Norton, 1982.

Adorno, Theodor, and Max Horkheimer. *Dialektik der Aufklärung.* 7th edition. Frankfurt: Fischer Verlag, 1980. Translated by John Cumming as *Dialectic of Enlightenment.* New York: Herder and Herder, 1972.

Adorno, Theodor, and Gershom Scholem. *Briefwechsel 1939–1969.* Edited by Asaf Angermann. Frankfurt: Suhrkamp, 2015.

### Works by Hannah Arendt

Arendt, Hannah. *Between Past and Future. Six Exercises in Political Thought.* New York: Viking, 1961.

Arendt, Hannah. "Civil Disobedience." In *Crises of the Republic*. New York: Harcourt, Brace, and Jovanovich, 1972: 49–103.

Arendt, Hannah. *Denktagebuch 1950–1973*. Edited by Ursula Ludz and Ingeborg Nordmann. Munich and Zurich: Piper Verlag, 2002.

Arendt, Hannah. *Eichmann in Jerusalem. A Report on the Banality of Evil*. New York: Penguin Books, [1963] 1994.

Arendt, Hannah. "Es gibt nur ein einziges Menschenrecht." *Die Wandlung*, 754–70. 1949.

Arendt, Hannah. *The Human Condition*. 8th edition. Chicago: University of Chicago Press, 1973 [1958].

Arendt, Hannah. "Introduction." In Walter Benjamin, *Illuminations. Essays and Reflections*. Edited by Hannah Arendt. New York: Schocken Books, 1968.

Arendt, Hannah. *The Jewish Writings*. Edited by Jerome Kohn and Ron H. Feldman. New York: Schocken Books, 2007.

Arendt, Hannah. "Karl Marx and the Tradition of Political Thought." First and second drafts. Container 71 in the Hannah Arendt Papers in the Library of Congress, 1953.

Arendt, Hannah. *Lectures on Kant's Political Philosophy*. Edited by Ronald Beiner. Chicago: University of Chicago Press, 1982.

Arendt, Hannah. *The Life of the Mind*. New York: Harcourt, Brace, and Jovanovich, 1978.

Arendt, Hannah. *On Revolution*. New York: Viking Compass, 1963 [1965].

Arendt, Hannah. *The Origins of Totalitarianism*. 3rd edition. New York: Harcourt, Brace, and Jovanovich, 1979. Originally published as Arendt, Hannah. *The Burden of Our Time*. London: Secker and Warburg, 1951.

Arendt, Hannah. *Rahel Varnhagen. The Life of a Jewish Woman*. 1957. Translated by Richard and Clara Winston. New York: Harcourt, Brace, Jovanovich, 1974.

Arendt, Hannah. "A Reply." *Review of Politics* 15, no. 1 (January 1953): 76–84.

Arendt, Hannah. *Responsibility and Judgment*. Edited by Jerome Kohn. New York: Schocken Books, 2003.

Arendt, Hannah. " 'The Rights of Man': What Are They?". *Modern Review* 3, no. 1 (1949): 25–37.

Arendt, Hannah. "Thinking and Moral Considerations: A Lecture." (1971). Reprinted in *Social Research*. 50th anniversary issue (Spring/Summer 1984).

Arendt, Hannah. "Walter Benjamin: 1892–1940." In *Men in Dark Times*. New York: Harcourt, Brace, 1968: 153–207.

Arendt, Hannah. "What Is Existenz Philosophy?" *Partisan Review* 18, no. 1 (1946): 35–56. Reprinted as "What Is Existential Philosophy?", translated by Robert and Rita Kimber, in Arendt, *Essays in Understanding. 1930–1954*, ed. Jerome Kohn. New York: Harcourt, Brace, and Company, 1994: 163–87.

Arendt, Hannah. "Zionism Reconsidered." *Menorah Journal* 32, no. 2 (October–December 1945): 162–96.

Arendt, Hannah, and Heinrich Blücher. *Hannah Arendt-Heinrich Blücher, Briefe. 1936–1968*. Edited by Lotte Koehler. Munich: R. Piper Verlag, 1996.

Arendt, Hannah and Kurt Blumenfeld. *In keinem Besitz verwurzelt. Die Korrespondenz. Hannah Arendt und Kurt Blumenfeld*. Edited by Ingeborg Nordmann and Iris Philling. Noerdlingen: Rotbuch, 1995.

Arendt, Hannah, and Mary McCarthy. *Between Friends: The Correspondence of Hannah Arendt and Mary McCarthy: 1949–1975*. Edited by Carol Brightman. New York: Harcourt, Brace, Jovanovich, 1996.

Arendt, Hannah, and Karl Jaspers. *Hannah Arendt and Karl Jaspers. Correspondence. 1926–1969.* Edited by Lotte Kohler and Hans Saner. New York: Harcourt, Brace, Jovanovich, 1992.

"Hannah Arendt im Gespräch mit Günter Gauss," https://www.youtube.com/watch?v =dsoImQfVsO4. Conducted on October 28, 1964. Shortened English version in Hannah Arendt, *Essays in Understanding. 1930–1954. Formation, Exile, and Totalitarianism.* Edited by Jerome Kohn. New York: Schocken Books, 1994: 1–24.

## Works by Walter Benjamin

Benjamin, Walter. *Illuminations. Essays and Reflections.* Edited by Hannah Arendt. New York: Harcourt, Brace, and Jovanovich, 1968.

Benjamin, Walter. *The Origin of German Tragic Drama.* Translated by John Osbourne. London: New Left Review, 1977.

## Works by Isaiah Berlin

Berlin, Isaiah. "The Apotheosis of the Romantic Will. The Revolt against the Myth of an Ideal World." In *The Crooked Timber of Humanity. Chapters in the History of Ideas.* Edited by Henry Hardy, 207–38. Princeton, NJ: Princeton University Press, 1990.

Berlin, Isaiah. *Concepts and Categories.* Edited by Henry Hardy and with a foreword by Alasdair MacIntyre. Princeton, NJ: Princeton University Press, 2013.

Berlin, Isaiah. "Does Political Theory Still Exist?" In *Philosophy, Politics and Society.* 2nd series. Edited by Peter Laslett and W. G. Runciman. Oxford: Blackwell, 1962.

Berlin, Isaiah. *Enlightening Letters 1946–60.* Edited by Henry Hardy and Jennifer Homes. London: Chatto and Windus, 2009.

Berlin, Isaiah. *Four Essays on Liberty.* Oxford: Oxford University Press, 1969.

Berlin, Isaiah. "The Pursuit of the Ideal." In *The Proper Study of Mankind. An Anthology of Essays.* Edited by Henry Hardy and Roger Hausheer, 1–17. New York: Farrar, Strauss, and Giroux, 1997.

Berlin, Isaiah. "The Rationality of Value Judgments." In *Concept and Categories*, 315–17; Originally published in *Nomos 7, Rational Decision*, ed. Carl Friedrich. New York: Atherton Press, 1964.

Berlin, Isaiah. "La Théorie politique existe-t-elle?" *Review française de science politique* 11 (1961): 309–37.

Berlin, Isaiah and Bernard Williams. "Pluralism and Liberalism: A Reply." *Political Studies* 42 (1994): 306–9.

"Isaiah Berlin in Conversation with Steven Lukes." *Salmagundi*, no. 120 (Fall 1998): 52–135.

## Works by Judith Butler

Butler, Judith. *Antigone's Claim. Kinship Between Life and Death.* Wellek Library Lectures. New York: Columbia University Press, 2000.

Butler, Judith. *Excitable Speech. A Politics of the Performative.* New York: Routledge, 1997.

Butler, Judith. *Frames of War. When Is Life Grievable?* London: Verso, 2009.

Butler, Judith. *Gender Trouble. Feminism and the Subversion of Identity.* New York and London: Routledge, 1990.

Butler, Judith. *Giving an Account of Oneself.* New York: Fordham University Press, 2005.

Butler, Judith. "I Merely Belong to Them." *London Review of Books* 29, no. 9–10 (May 2007): 26–28.

Butler, Judith. *Notes toward a Performative Theory of Assembly.* Cambridge, MA: Harvard University Press, 2015.

Butler, Judith. *Parting Ways. Jewishness and the Critique of Zionism.* New York: Columbia University Press, 2012.

Butler, Judith. *Precarious Life. The Powers of Mourning and Violence.* London: Verso, 2004.

Butler, Judith and Athena Athanasiou. *Dispossession: The Performative in the Political.* Cambridge and Malden, MA: 2013.

## Works by Moritz Goldstein

Goldstein, Moritz. "Deutsch-Jüdischer Parnass." *Der Kunstwart* 25, no. 11 (März 1912).

Goldstein, Moritz. "German Jewry's Dilemma. The Story of a Provocative Essay." In *Leo Baeck Institute Yearbook.* New York, 1957.

## Works by Jürgen Habermas

Habermas, Jürgen. *Between Facts and Norms. Contributions to a Discourse Theory of Law and Democracy.* Translated by William Regh. Cambridge: Polity Press, 1996.

Habermas, Jürgen. "Bewußtmachende oder rettende Kritik—die Aktualität Walter Benjamins." In *Philosophisch-politische Profile,* 336–76. Frankfurt: Suhrkamp, 1981.

Habermas, Jürgen. *The Crisis of the European Union: A Response.* Translated by C. Cronin. Malden, MA, and Cambridge: Polity Press, 2012.

Habermas, Jürgen. *Europe. The Faltering Project.* Translated by C. Cronin. Malden, MA, and Cambridge: Polity Press, 2009.

Habermas, Jürgen. "The European Nation-State: On the Past and Future of Sovereignty and Citizenship." In *The Inclusion of the Other: Studies in Political Theory.* Edited by Ciaran Cronin and Pablo De Greiff, 105–29. Cambridge, MA: MIT Press, 1998.

Habermas, Jürgen. *The Theory of Communicative Action.* Translated by Thomas A. McCarthy. Boston: Beacon Press, 1973.

Habermas, Jürgen. "Urgeschichte der Subjektivität und verwilderte Selbstbehauptung." In *Philosophisch-politische Profile,* 167–79. English translation, "Theodor Adorno—The Primal History of Subjectivity—Self-Affirmation Gone Wild." In *Philosophical-Political Profiles.* Translated by Frederick Lawrence, 99–111. Cambridge, MA: MIT Press, 1983.

Habermas, Jürgen. "Why Europe Needs a Constitution." *New Left Review* 11, no. 5 (2001).

## Works by G.W.F. Hegel

Hegel, G.W.F. *Grundlinien der Philosophie des Rechts 1821.* In *Werke,* vol. 7. Edited by Eva Moldenhauer and Karl Markus Michel. Frankfurt: Suhrkamp-Taschenbuch Wissenschaft, 1970. English edition, *Elements of the Philosophy of Right.* Edited by Allen W. Wood. New York: Cambridge, 1991.

Hegel, G.W.F. *Die Phänomenologie des Geistes.* Edited by J. Hoffmeister. *Philosophische Bibliothek.* Hamburg: Felix Meiner, 1952 [1807]. English translation by A.V. Miller, *Hegel's Phenomenology of Spirit.* With an analysis and foreword by John Findlay. Oxford: Oxford University Press, 1977.

Hegel, G.W.F. "Über die wissenschaftlichen Behandlungsarten des Naturrechts, seine Stelle in der praktischen Philosophie, und sein Verhältnis zu den positiven Rechtswissenschaften." In *Werke in Zwanzig Bänden,* vol. 2, 434–533. English translation by T. M. Knox, *Natural Law.* Philadelphia: University of Pennsylvania Press, 1975.

## Works by Martin Heidegger

Heidegger, Martin, "Letter on Humanism." In *Basic Writings.* Edited by David Farrell Krell, 213–67. New York: Harper and Collins, 1993.

Heidegger, Martin. *Sein und Zeit.* 10th edition. Tübingen: Max Niemeyer Verlag, 1963 [1927]. English translation, *Being and Time.* Translated by John Macquarrie and Edward Robinson. New York: Harper and Row, 1962 [1927].

Heidegger, Martin. "Überwindung der Metaphysik." In *Vorträge und Aufsätze,* 67–97, Pfüllingen: Günther Neske, 1978 [1954].

Heidegger, Martin. "Was heisst Denken?" In *Vorträge und Aufsätze,* 123–39. Pfüllingen: Verlag Günther Neske, 1954 [1978].

Heidegger, Martin. "Was heisst Denken?" In *Gesamtausgabe. I. Abteilung. Veröffentlichte Schriften 1910–1976,* vol. 8, 1–266. Frankfurt: Vittorio Klostermann, [1954] 2002. English translation, "What Is Called Thinking?" Translated by J. Glenn Gray. New York: Harper Perennial, 1968.

## Works by Albert Hirschman

Hirschman, Albert O. "Beyond Asymmetry: Critical Notes on Myself as a Young Man and on Some Other Old Friends." Special issue on "Dependence and Dependency in the Global System." *International Organization* 32, no. 1 (Winter 1978): 45–50.

Hirschman, Albert O. *Crossing Boundaries. Selected Writings.* New York: Zone Books, 1998.

Hirschman, Albert O. *Development Projects Observed.* Washington, DC: Brooking, 1967.

Hirschman, Albert O. *Essays in Trespassing. Economics to Politics and Beyond.* Cambridge: Cambridge University Press, 1981.

Hirschman, Albert O. *Exit, Voice, and Loyalty. Responses to Decline in Firms, Organizations, and States.* Cambridge, MA, and London: Harvard University Press, 1970.

Hirschman, Albert O. "Exit, Voice and the Fate of the German Democratic Republic. An Essay in Conceptual History." *World Politics* 45 (January 1993): 173–202.

Hirschman, Albert O. "Exit, Voice, and the State." *World Politics* 31, no. 1 (1978): 90–107.

Hirschman, Albert O. *National Power and the Structure of Foreign Trade*. Berkeley and Los Angeles: University of California Press, 1945.

Hirschman, Albert O. *The Passions and the Interests. Political Arguments for Capitalism before Its Triumph*. Princeton, NJ: Princeton University Press, 1977.

Hirschman, Albert O. *A Propensity to Self-Subversion*. Cambridge, MA: Harvard University Press, 1995.

Hirschman, Albert O. *The Rhetoric of Reaction. Perversity, Futility, Jeopardy*. Cambridge, MA: Belknap Press of Harvard University Press, 1991.

Hirschman, Albert O. "The Search for Paradigms as a Hindrance to Understanding." *World Politics* 22, no. 3 (March 1970): 329–34.

Hirschman, Albert O. *The Strategy of Economic Development*. 3rd printing. New Haven, CT: Yale University Press, 1960 [1958].

## Works by Immanuel Kant

Kant, Immanuel. *Critique of Pure Reason*, unabridged edn. Translated by Norman Kemp Smith. St. Martin's Press: New York, 1965 [1781].

Kant, Immanuel. *Kritik der Urteilskraft*. 1790. Translated by Werner S. Pluhar as *Critique of Judgment*. Indianapolis and Cambridge: Hackett Publishing Company, 1987.

Kant, Immanuel. "Die Metaphysik der Sitten in zwei Teilen." 1797. In *Immanuel Kants Werke, The Metaphysics of Morals*. Translated and edited by Mary Gregor. Cambridge: Cambridge University Press, 1996.

Kant, Immanuel. "Zum Ewigen Frieden." 1795. In *Suhrkamp Werkausgabe*, vol. 11. Frankfurt am Main: Suhrkamp, 1977. English translation: "Perpetual Peace: A Philosophical Sketch." Translated. by H. B. Nisbet, in *Political Writings*. 2nd edition. Edited by Hans Reiss. Cambridge: Cambridge University Press, 1994.

## Works by Emmanuel Levinas

Levinas, Emmanuel. *Difficile Liberté*. Livre de Poche, 1984. Translated by Sean Had as *Difficult Freedom. Essays on Judaism*. 1990. Baltimore: Johns Hopkins University Press, 1997.

Levinas, Emmanuel. "Ethics and Politics." In *The Levinas Reader*. Edited Sean Hand, 289–97. Oxford and Cambridge, MA: Basil Blackwell, 1989.

## Works by Leopold Lucas

Lucas, Leopold. *Geschichte der Stadt Tyrus zur Zeit der Kreuzzüge*. Marburg: Joh. Hamel, 1895.

Lucas, Leopold. "Die Wissenschaft des Judentums und die Wege zu ihrer Förderung." In *Schriften der Gesellschaft zur Förderung der Wissenschaft des Judentums*. Berlin: Druck von Carl Flemming, A. G. Glogau, 1906.

## Works by Carl Schmitt

Schmitt, Carl. *Der Begriff des Politischen. Mit einer Rede über das Zeitalter der Neutralisierungen und Entpolitisierungen.* Munich and Leipzig, 1932.

Schmitt, Carl. *The Concept of the Political.* Expanded edition. Translated by George Schwab. Chicago: University of Chicago Press, 2007 [1996].

Schmitt, Carl. *Land and Sea. A World-Historical Meditation.* Translated by Samuel Garrett Zeitlin. Edited with an introduction by Russell A. Berman. Candor, NY: Telos Press Publishing, 2015 [1942].

Schmitt, Carl. *The Leviathan in the State Theory of Thomas Hobbes. Meaning and Failure of a Political Symbol.* Translated by George Schwab and Erna Hilfstein. Chicago: University of Chicago Press, 1996. Originally *Der Leviathan in der Staatslehre des Thomas Hobbes: Sinn und Fehlschlag eines politischen Symbols* (1938).

Schmitt, Carl. *Der Nomos der Erde im Völkerrecht des Jus Publicum Europaeum.* 4th edition. Berlin: Duncker and Humblot, 1997 [1950]. English translation by G. L. Ulmen. *The Nomos of the Earth in International Law of the Jus Publicum Europeum.* New York: Telos Press Publishing, 2003.

Schmitt, Carl. "The Turn to the Discriminating Concept of War." 1938. In *Writings on War.* Edited by Timothy Nunan. Cambridge: Polity Press, 2011.

## Works by Judith Shklar

Shklar, Judith. *American Citizenship. The Quest for Inclusion.* Cambridge, MA: Harvard University Press, 2001.

Shklar, Judith. "Decisionism." In *Nomos 7: Rational Decision.* Edited by Carl Friedrich, 3–17. New York: Atherton Press, 1964.

Shklar, Judith. *The Faces of Injustice.* Storrs Lectures on Jurisprudence at Yale Law School, 1988. New Haven, CT: Yale University Press, 1990.

Shklar, Judith. *Freedom and Independence: A Study of the Political Ideas of Hegel's Phenomenology of Mind.* Cambridge: Cambridge University Press, 1976.

Shklar, Judith. "Hannah Arendt as Pariah." In *Political Thought and Political Thinkers,* 362–75. Originally published in *Partisan Review* 50, no. 1 (1983): 64–77.

Shklar, Judith. "Hannah Arendt's Triumph." *The New Republic* 173, no. 26 (December 27, 1975): 8–10.

Shklar, Judith. *Legalism. An Essay on Law, Morals and Politics.* Cambridge, MA: Harvard University Press, 1964.

Shklar, Judith. "The Liberalism of Fear." In *Liberalism and the Moral Life.* Edited by Nancy Rosenblum. Cambridge, MA: Harvard University Press, 1996.

Shklar, Judith. "A Life of Learning." In *Liberalism without Illusions. Essays on Liberal Theory and the Political Vision of Judith N. Shklar.* Edited by Bernard Yack, 263–81. Chicago: University of Chicago Press, 1996.

Shklar. Judith. *Ordinary Vices.* Cambridge, MA: Belknap Press of Harvard University Press, 1984.

Shklar, Judith. "Political Theory and the Rule of Law." In *Political Thought and Political Thinkers*. Originally published in Allan C. Hutchinson and Patrick J. Monahan, ed., *The Rule of Law. Ideal or Ideology*. Toronto: Carswell, 1987: 21–38.

Shklar, Judith. *Political Thought and Political Thinkers*. Edited by Stanley Hoffmann. Chicago: University of Chicago Press, 1998.

Shklar, Judith. *The Quest for Inclusion*. *The Tanner Lectures on Human Values*. Cambridge, MA: Harvard University Press, 1991.

Shklar, Judith. "Rethinking the Past." In Shklar, *Political Thought and Political Thinkers*, ed. by Stanley Hoffmann, 352–61. Originally published in *Social Research* 44 (1977): 80–90.

Shklar, Judith. "Review Essay" of *Between Past and Future* by Hannah Arendt, in *History and Theory* 2, no. 3 (1963): 286–92.

Shklar, Judith. "Review of Isaiah Berlin's *Against the Current: Essays in the History of Ideas* (New York: Viking, 1979)." *The New Republic*, April 5, 1980: 32–35.

Shklar, Judith. Review of Hannah Arendt, *Lectures on Kant's Political Philosophy* (ed. with an interpretive essay by Ronald Beiner. Brighton: Harvester Press, 1982), in *The Bulletin of the Hegel Society of Great Britain* 9 (Spring–Summer 1984): 42–44.

## Works by Leo Strauss

Strauss, Leo. "Anmerkungen zu Carl Schmitt, Der Begriff des Politischen." *Archiv für Sozialwissenschaft und Sozialpolitik* 67, no. 6 (1932): 732–49.

Strauss, Leo. "Jerusalem and Athens." In *Jewish Philosophy and the Crisis of Modernity*. Edited by Kenneth Hart Green. Albany: SUNY Press at Albany, 1997.

Strauss, Leo. *Natural Right and History*. 1953. Chicago and London: University of Chicago Press, 1968.

Strauss, Leo. "Notes on Carl Schmitt's *The Concept of the Political*," in Carl Schmitt, *The Concept of the Political*, translation by George Schwab: 82–109.

Strauss, Leo. *The Political Philosophy of Hobbes. Its Basis and Its Genesis*. Translated by Elsa M. Sinclair. Oxford: Clarendon Press, 1936. American edition, Chicago: University of Chicago Press, 1952.

Strauss, Leo. "Relativism." In H. Schoeck, ed. *Relativism and the Study of Man*. Princeton, NJ: Van Nostrand, 1961: 138–40.

## Secondary Works

Aaron, Daniel. "The Hyphenate Writer and American Letters." In *American Notes. Selected Essays*, 69–85. Boston: Northeastern University Press, 1994.

Adelman, Jeremy. "Pariah: Can Hannah Arendt Help Us Rethink Our Global Refugee Crisis?" *Wilson Quarterly* 40, no. 2 (Spring 2016). https://wilsonquarterly.com/quarterly/looking -back-moving-forward/pariah-can-hannah-arendt-help-us-rethink-our-global-refugee -crisis/.

Adelman, Jeremy. "Unfinished Work: Albert Hirschman's *Exit, Voice and Loyalty*." In "Albert Hirschman and the Social Sciences: A Memorial Roundtable." *Humanity: An International*

*Journal of Human Rights and Humanitarianism and Development* 6, no. 2 (Summer 2015): 277–80.

Adelman, Jeremy. *The Worldly Philosopher. The Odyssey of Albert O. Hirschman.* Princeton, NY: Princeton University Press, 2013.

Agamben, Giorgio. *Homo Sacer. Sovereign Power and Bare Life.* Translated by Daniel Heller-Roazen. Stanford: University of Stanford Press, 1998.

Akar, Ridvan. *Aşkale Yolculari: Varlik Vergisi ve Çalisma Kamplari.* Istanbul: Belge Yayinları: 2006.

Aktar, Ayhan. *Varlik Vergisi ve "Türkleştirme" Politikalari.* Istanbul: Iletisim Yayinları, 2000.

Angermann, Asaf. "Exile and Metaphysics. Adorno and the Language of Political Experience." *Naharaim* 9, no. 1–2 (2015): 179–94.

Anghie, Anthony. *Imperialism, Sovereignty and the Making of International Law.* Cambridge: Cambridge University Press, 2007.

Aron, Raymond. *The Opium of the Intellectuals.* New York: W. W. Norton and Company, 1962 [1955].

Ashheim, Steven. *Beyond the Borders. The German-Jewish Legacy Abroad.* Princeton: Princeton University Press, 2007.

Aumann, Francis R. "Review." *Journal of Politics* 27 (1965): 703–5.

Avineri, Shlomo. *Karl Marx on Colonialism and Modernization,* edited by and with an introduction by Shlomo Avineri. New York: Doubleday Anchor Book, 1969.

Avineri, Shlomo. "Where They Have Burned Books, They Will End Up Burning People," *Jewish Review of Books* 8, no. 3 (Fall 2017): 39–41.

Bali, Rifat N. *The "Varlik Vergisi" Affair. A Study of Its Legacy with Selected Documents.* Istanbul: Gorgias Press and The Isis Press, 2005.

Balibar, Etienne. *Equaliberty. Political Essays.* Translated by James Ingram. Durham and London: Duke University Press, 2014.

Bedau, H. A. "Review." *Philosophical Review* 76 (1967): 129–30.

Benhabib, Seyla. "Arendt's American Republicanism." *US Intellectual History Blog of Society for U.S. Intellectual History,* June 29, 2016. http://s-usih.org/2016/06/arendts-american-republicanism.html.

Benhabib, Seyla. "Arendt's *Eichmann in Jerusalem*," in *The Cambridge Companion to Hannah Arendt,* ed. Dana Villa. Cambridge: Cambridge University Press, 2000: 65–86

Benhabib, Seyla. "Carl Schmitt's Critique of Kant. Sovereignty and International Law." *Political Theory* 40, no. 6 (December 2012): 688–713.

Benhabib, Seyla. *The Claims of Culture. Equality and Diversity in the Global Era.* Princeton, NJ: Princeton University Press, 2002.

Benhabib, Seyla. *Critique, Norm and Utopia. A Study of the Foundations of Critical Theory.* New York: Columbia University Press, 1986.

Benhabib, Seyla. *Dignity in Adversity. Human Rights in Troubled Times.* Malden, MA and London: Polity Press, 2011.

Benhabib, Seyla. "From 'The Dialectic of Enlightenment' to 'The Origins of Totalitarianism' and the Genocide Convention: Adorno and Horkheimer in the Company of Arendt and Lemkin," in *The Modernist Imagination. Intellectual History and Critical Theory. Essays in*

*Honor of Martin Jay.* Edited by Warren Breckman, Peter E. Gordon, A. Dirk Moses, Samuel Moyn, and Elliot Neaman. New York and Oxford: Berghahn Books, 2009: 299–331.

Benhabib, Seyla. "The Generalized and the Concrete Other. The Kohlberg-Gilligan Controversy and Moral Theory." In Benhabib, *Situating the Self. Gender, Community and Postmodernism in Contemporary Ethics.* New York and London: Routledge and Polity, 1992: 148–78.

Benhabib, Seyla. "Hannah Arendt and the Redemptive Power of Narrative." *Social Research* 57, no. 1 (1990): 167–96.

Benhabib, Seyla. "International Law and Human Plurality in the Shadow of Totalitarianism: Hannah Arendt and Raphael Lemkin." In *Politics in Dark Times. Encounters with Hannah Arendt,* Seyla Benhabib ed. with the assistance of Roy Tsao and Peter Verovsek. Cambridge and Malden, MA: Polity Press, 2011: 219–47. Revised version in Benhabib, *Dignity in Adversity,* 41–57.

Benhabib, Seyla. "Introduction." In Seyla Benhabib and Volker Kaul, eds., *Toward New Democratic Imaginaries. Istanbul Seminars on Politics, Culture and Islam.* Zurich: Springer Verlag, 2016, xxix-xlviii.

Benhabib, Seyla. "Israel's Stalemate." *ResetDOC,* June 26, 2010. http://www.resetdoc.org /story/00000021248.

Benhabib, Seyla. "Judith Shklar's Dystopic Liberalism." *Social Research. An International Quarterly* 61, no. 2 (Summer 1994): 477–88.

Benhabib, Seyla. *Kosmopolitismus ohne Illusionen. Menschenrechte in turbulenten Zeiten.* Berlin: Suhrkamp, 2017.

Benhabib, Seyla. "Moving beyond False Binarisms. On Samuel Moyn's *The Last Utopia.*" *Qui Parle* 22, no. 1 (Fall–Winter 2013): 81–89.

Benhabib, Seyla. "The New Sovereigntism and Transnational Law: Legal Utopianism, Democratic Scepticism and Statist Realism." *Global Constitutionalism* 5, no. 1 (March 2016): 109–44.

Benhabib, Seyla. "Rationality and Social Action: Critical Reflections on Max Weber's Methodological Writings." *Philosophical Forum* 12, no. 4 (1981): 356–75.

Benhabib, Seyla. "Reason-Giving and Rights-Bearing. Concerning the Subject of Rights." *Constellations* 20, no. 1 (2013): 38–51.

Benhabib, Seyla. *The Reluctant Modernism of Hannah Arendt.* California: Sage Publications, 1996. Reprinted with a new introduction and afterword. Rowman and Littlefield, New Jersey, 2003.

Benhabib, Seyla. "Review of Robert Howse, *Leo Strauss. Man of Peace.*" *Political Theory* 45, no. 2 (April 2017): 273–77.

Benhabib, Seyla. "The Uses and Abuses of Kantian Rigorism. On Rainer Forst's Moral and Political Philosophy." *Political Theory* 43, no. 6 (2015): 777–92.

Benhabib, Seyla. "Who's on Trial? Eichmann or Arendt?" *Opinionator* (blog), *New York Times,* September 21, 2014. https://opinionator.blogs.nytimes.com/2014/09/21/whos-on-trial -eichmann-or-anrendt/?_r=0.

Benhabib, Seyla, Judith Butler, Nancy Fraser, and Drucilla Cornell. *Feminist Contentions: A Philosophical Exchange.* New York: Routledge, Kegan, and Paul, 1996. Originally *Der Streit um Differenz.* Frankfurt: Fischer Verlag, 1993.

Ben Jelloun, Tahar. *Leaving Tangier: A Novel.* Translated by Linda Coverdale. Penguin Books, 2009.

Bentham, Jeremy. *The Works of Jeremy Bentham.* Vol. 2. Edited By John Bowring. Edinburgh and London: W. Tait, 1843.

Berkowitz, Roger. "Misreading 'Eichmann in Jerusalem.'" *Opinionator* (blog), *New York Times,* July 7, 2013.

Bernstein, Richard. "Judging—the Actor and the Spectator." In *Philosophical Profiles.* 232–33. Philadelphia: University of Pennsylvania Press, 1986.

Bernstein, Richard. "Serious Play. The Ethical-Political Horizon of Derrida." In *The New Constellation: The Ethical-Political Horizon of Modernity,* 172–98. Cambridge: Polity Press, 1991.

Bettelheim, Bruno. "Individual and Mass Behavior in Extreme Situations." *Journal of Abnormal and Social Psychology* 38 (1943): 417–52.

Bettelheim, Bruno. "On Dachau and Buchenwald." In *Nazi Conspiracy and Aggression,* vol. 7 (May 1938 to April 1939). Washington, DC: United States Government Printing Office, 1946.

Bhabha, Homi. "Dissemi/Nation: Time, Narrative and the Margins of the Modern Nation." In *The Location of Culture.* New York: Routledge Press, 1994.

Bilsky, Leora. *Transformative Justice. Israeli Identity on Trial.* Ann Arbor: University of Michigan Press, 2004.

Breen, Keith. "Law beyond Command? An Evaluation of Arendt's Understanding of Law." In *Hannah Arendt and the Law.* Edited by Marco Goldoni and Christopher McCorkindale, 20–24. Oxford and Portland: Hart Publishing, 2012.

Brown, Brendan F. "Review." *University of Toronto Law Journal* 17 (1967): 218–25.

Brown, Wendy. *Walled States, Waning Sovereignty.* New York: Zone Books, 2010.

Browning, Christopher. *Ordinary Men. Reserve Police Battalion 101 and the Final Solution in Poland.* New York: Harper Collins, 1993.

Brunkhorst, Hauke. "Europa, die Flucht und das koloniale Erbe." *Blätter für deutsche und international Politik* 61, no. 9 (September 2016): 63–75.

Buck-Morss, Susan. Alias Benjamin Snow. "Introduction to Adorno's 'The Actuality of Philosophy.'" *Telos* (Spring 1977): 120–33.

Buck-Morss, Susan. *The Origin of Negative Dialectics: Theodor W. Adorno, Walter Benjamin and the Frankfurt Institute.* New York: Free Press, 1977.

Caute, David. *Isaac and Isaiah. The Covert Punishment of a Cold War Heretic.* New Haven, CT: Yale University Press, 2013.

Cesarani, David. *Becoming Eichmann. Rethinking the Life, Crimes and Trial of a "Desk Murderer."* Raleigh, Essex: Da Capo Press: 2007.

Çetinoglu, Sait. "The Mechanisms for Terrorizing Minorities: The Capital Tax and Work Battalions in Turkey during the Second World War." *Mediterranean Quarterly* 23, no. 2 (2012): 14–29.

Chakrabarty, Dipesh. *Provincializing Europe. Postcolonial Thought and Historical Difference.* Princeton, NJ: Princeton University Press, 2000.

Claussen, Detlev. *Theodor W. Adorno. One Last Genius.* Translated by Rodney Livingstone. Cambridge, MA: Harvard University Press, 2008.

Cohen, Hermann. *Jüdische Schriften [Jewish Writings].* Volume 2, *Emanzipation.* 1912.

Cook, Deborah. "The One and the Many: Revisioning Adorno's Critique of Western Reason." *Studies in Social and Political Thought* 18 (Winter 2010): 69–80.

Cornell, Drucilla. *Beyond Accommodation: Ethical Feminism, Deconstruction, and the Law.* New York and Oxford: Routledge Books, 1991.

Cornell, Drucilla, Michel Rosenfeld, and David Grey Carlson, eds., *Deconstruction and the Possibility of Justice.* New York and London: Routledge, 1992.

Cover, Robert. "Foreword: Nomos and Narrative." *Harvard Law Review* 97, no. 4 (1983/84): 4–68.

Cover, Robert. *Narrative, Violence and the Law. The Essays of Robert Cover.* Edited by Martha Minow, Michael Ryan, and Austin Sarat, 95–172. Ann Arbor: University of Michigan Press, 1993.

Crowder, George. "Pluralism and Liberalism." *Political Studies* 42 (1994): 293–305.

Curthoys, Ned. *The Legacy of Liberal Judaism. Ernst Cassirer and Hannah Arendt's Hidden Conversation.* New York and Oxford: Berghahn Books, 2013.

Dawidowicz, Lucy S. *The War against the Jews: 1933–1945.* Special tenth anniversary edition. New York: Bantam Books, 1986.

DeParle, Jason. "The Sea Swallows People." *New York Review of Books* 64, no. 3 (February 23, 2017): 31–36.

Derrida, Jacques. "Declarations of Independence." *New Political Science* 7, no. 1 (1986): 7–15.

Derrida, Jacques. "The Ends of Man." In *After Philosophy. End or Transformation,* edited by Kenneth Baynes, James Bohman, and Thomas McCarthy, 125–58. Cambridge, MA, and London: MIT Press, 1986.

Derrida, Jacques. "The Force of Law: The 'Mystical Foundation of Authority.'" Translated by Mary Quaintance. *Cardozo Law Review* 11, no. 919 (1989–90): 920–1046.

Derrida, Jacques. "Interpretations at War: Kant, the Jews, the German." Translated by Moshe Ron. *New Literary History* 22, no. 1 (Winter 1991): 39–95.

Derrida, Jacques. *Monolingualism of the Other: or, The Prosthesis of Origin.* Translated by Patrick Mensah. Stanford: Stanford University Press, 1998.

Derrida, Jacques. *On Cosmopolitanism and Forgiveness.* Translated by Mark Dooley and Michael Hughes. New York: Routledge, 2001.

Dickson, Tiphaine. "Shklar's Legalism and the Liberal Paradox." *Constellations* 22, no. 2 (2015): 188–98.

Diner, Dan and Michael Stolleis, eds. *Hans Kelsen and Carl Schmitt. A Juxtaposition.* Gerlingen: Bleicher, 1999.

Eich, Stefan and Adam Tooze. "The Allure of Dark Times: Max Weber, Politics and the Crisis of Historicism." *History and Theory* 56, no. 2 (June 2017): 197–215.

Eisenstadt, Oona and Claire Elise Katz. "The Faceless Palestinian: A History of an Error." *Telos* 174 (Spring 2016): 9–32.

Eisenstadt, Shmuel, ed. *Multiple Modernities.* New York: Routledge, 2002.

Ellison, Ralph. "The World and the Jug." In *Shadow and Act.* New York: Random House, 1964.

Elon, Amos. *The Israelis. Founders and Sons.* New York: Holt, Rinehart, and Winston, 1971.

Elon, Amos. *The Pity of It All. A History of the Jews in Germany 1743–1933.* New York: A Metropolitan Book, 2002.

Elster, Jon. *Ulysses Unbound: Studies in Rationality, Precommitment, and Constraints*. Cambridge: Cambridge University Press, 2000.

Fassin, Didier. *Humanitarian Reason. A Moral History of the Present*. Berkeley and Los Angeles: University of California Press, 2012.

Flittko, Lisa. *Escape through the Pyrenées*. 1985. Translated by David Koblick. Evanston, Illinois: Northwestern University Press, 1991.

Forrester, Katrina. "Judith Shklar, Bernard Williams and Political Realism." *European Journal of Political Theory* 11, no. 3 (2012): 247–72.

Forst, Rainer. "Moral and Political, Transcendental and Historical. Reply to Seyla Benhabib, Jeffrey Flynn and Matthias Fritsch." *Political Theory* 43, no. 6 (2015), 822–37.

Forst, Rainer. *The Right to Justification. Elements of a Constructivist Theory of Justice*. Translated by Jeffrey Flynn. New York: Columbia University Press, 2007.

Friedländer, Saul. *Nazi Germany and the Jews. 1933–1945*. Abridged edition by Orna Kennan. New York: Harper Collins Publishers, 2009.

Fry, Varian. *Assignment: Rescue. An Autobiography*. New York: Scholastic, 1993 [1968].

Fuller, Lon L. "Positivism and the Fidelity to Law—A Reply to Professor Hart." *Harvard Law Review* 71, no. 4 (February 1958): 630–72.

Gadamer, Hans Georg. *Truth and Method*. Translated by Garrett Barden and John Cumming. New York: Continuum, 1975.

Galston, W. A. "Realism in Political Theory." *European Journal of Political Theory* 9, no. 4 (2010): 385–411.

Garsten, Bryan. "The Elusiveness of Arendtian Judgment." In *Politics in Dark Times. Encounters with Hannah Arendt*. Edited by Seyla Benhabib, 316–42. New York: Cambridge University Press, 2010.

Goldhagen, Daniel Jonah. *Hitler's Willing Executioners. Ordinary Germans and the Holocaust*. New York: Alfred Knopf, 1996.

Goldstein, Moritz. "Deutsch-Jüdischer Parnass." *Der Kunstwart* 25, no. 11 (März 1912): 281–94.

Gordon, Peter E. *Adorno and Existence*. Cambridge, MA, and London: Harvard University Press, 2016.

Gordon, Peter E. "Critical Theory between the Sacred and the Profane." *Constellations* 23, no. 4 (2016): 466–81.

Gray, John. *Isaiah Berlin*. Princeton: Princeton Univesity Press, 1996.

Gross, Raphael. "Jewish Law and Christian Grace—Carl Schmitt's Critique of Kelsen." In *Hans Kelsen and Carl Schmitt, a Juxtaposition*. Edited by Daniel Diner and Michael Stolleis, 101–11. Gerlingen: Bleicher, 1999.

Gündogdu, Ayten. "Disagreeing with Rancière: Speech, Violence and the Ambiguous Subjects of Politics," *Polity* 49, no. 2 (April 2017): 188–219.

Gündogdu, Ayten. *Rightlessness in an Age of Rights. Hannah Arendt and the Contemporary Struggles of Migrants*. Oxford: Oxford University Press, 2015.

Guttstadt, Corry. *Die Türkei, die Juden und der Holocaust*. Berlin and Hamburg: Assoziation Verlag, 2008. Translated by Kathleen Dell'Orto, Sabine Bartel, and Michelle Milesas as *Turkey, the Jews and the Holocaust*. New York: Cambridge University Press, 2013.

Harries, Karsten. "Heidegger as a Political Thinker," *Review of Metaphysics* 29, no. 4 (June 1976): 642–69.

Hart, H.L.A. "Positivism and the Separation of Law and Morals." *Harvard Law Review* 71, no. 4 (February 1958): 593–629.

Hayek, Friedrich. *The Road to Serfdom.* 50th anniversary edition, with Milton Friedman. London and New York: Routledge, 1994 [1944].

Hayim, Yosef. *Zakhor. Jewish Memory and Jewish History.* Samuel and Althea Stroum Lectures in Jewish Studies. Seattle and London: University of Washington Press, 1982.

Heine, Heinrich. *Almansor. Eine Tragödie.* Edited by Karl-Maria Guth. Deutsche Nationalbibliothek. Berlin: 2015 [1821].

Heitmann, Margret. " 'Sie wirken in einer Gemeinde, die einen historischen Namen besitzt.' Zu Leben und Werk des letzten Glogauer Rabbiners Leopold Lucas (1872–1943)." In *Silesiographia. Festschrift für Norbert Conrad.* Carsten Rabe und Matthias Weber: Würzburg, 1998.

Heller, Joseph. *From Brith Shalom to Ichud: Judah Leib Magnes and the Struggle for a Binational State in Palestine.* Jerusalem: Magnes Press, Hebrew University, 2003.

Herman, Barbara. *The Practice of Moral Judgment.* Cambridge, MA: Harvard University Press, 1996.

Hess, Andreas. *The Political Theory of Judith N. Shklar.* New York: Palgrave Macmillan, 2014.

Hilberg, Raul. *The Destruction of the European Jews.* 1961. New York: Holmes and Meier, 1986.

Hilberg, Raul. *Perpetrators, Victims, Bystanders: The Jewish Catastrophe, 1933–1945.* New York: Harper Collins, 1992.

Hiruta, Kei. "An 'Anti-Utopian Age?' Isaiah Berlin's England, Hannah Arendt's America, and Utopian Thinking in Dark Times." *Journal of Political Ideologies* 22, no. 1 (2017): 12–29.

Hiruta, Kei. "The Meaning and Value of Freedom: Berlin Contra Arendt." *European Legacy* 19, no. 7 (2014): 854–68.

Holmes, Stephen. *Passions and Constraint. On the Theory of Liberal Democracy.* Chicago: University of Chicago Press, 1995.

Honig, Bonnie. "Declarations of Independence: Arendt and Derrida on the Problem of Founding a Republic." *American Political Science Review* 85, no. 1 (1991): 97–113.

Honig, Bonnie. *Feminist Interpretations of Hannah Arendt.* University Park: Pennsylvania University Press, 1995.

Honig, Bonnie. *Political Theory and the Displacement of Politics.* Ithaca, NY: Cornell University Press, 1993.

Horkheimer, Max. "Traditional and Critical Theory." In *Critical Theory.* Translated by M. J. O'Connell et al., 188–244. New York: Herder and Herder, 1972.

Howe, Irving. "Banality and Brilliance: Irving Howe on Hannah Arendt." *Dissent Magazine,* June 5, 2013.

Howe, Irving. "The New Yorker and Hannah Arendt." *Commentary,* October 1963.

Howse, Robert. *Leo. Strauss. Man of Peace.* Cambridge: Cambridge University Press, 2014.

Ignatieff, Michael. *Isaiah Berlin. A Life.* New York: Metropolitan Books, 1998.

Inlaender, Tania. "Status Quo or Sixth Ground? Adjudicating Gender Asylum Claims." In *Migrations and Mobilities. Citizenship, Borders and Gender.* Edited by Seyla Benhabib and Judith Resnik, 356–80. New York and London: New York University Press, 2009.

Işiksel Türküler. *Europe's Functional Constitution. A Theory of Constitutionalism beyond the State.* Oxford: Oxford University Press, 2016.

Jahanbegloo, Ramin. *Conversations with Isaiah Berlin.* London: Phoenix Press, 2000.

Janik, Allan and Stephen Toulmin. *Wittgenstein's Vienna.* Chicago: Ivan R. Dee Publisher, 1996.

Jaspers, Karl. "Letter to the Freiburg University Denazification Committee," on December 22, 1945. In *The Heidegger Controversy: A Critical Reader.* Edited by Richard Wolin. Cambridge, MA: MIT Press, 1993.

Jay, Martin. *Essays from the Edge. Parerga and Paralipomena.* Charlottesville and London: University of Virginia Press, 2011.

Jay, Martin. *Forcefields. Between Intellectual History and Cultural Critique.* London and New York: Routledge, 1993.

Jones, Gareth Stedman. *Karl Marx. Greatness and Illusion.* London: Allen Lane of Penguin Books, 2016.

Jurkevics, Anna. "Hannah Arendt Reads Carl Schmitt's *The Nomos of the Earth:* A Dialogue on Law and Geo-Politics from the Margins." *European Journal of Political Theory* (February 2015). http://journals.sagepub.com/doi/abs/10.1177/1474885115572837.

Kahlberg, Stephen. "Max Weber's Types of Rationality: Cornerstone for the Analysis of Rationalization Processes in History." *American Journal of Sociology* 85, no. 5 (1980): 1145–79.

Kateb, George. *Hannah Arendt: Politics, Conscience, Evil.* Totowa, NJ: Rowman and Allenheld, 1984.

Kelsen, Hans. *The Essence and Value of Democracy.* Edited by Nadia Urbinati and Carlo Invernizzi Accetti and translated by Brian Graff. New York and Toronto: Rowman and Littlefield Publishers, Inc., 2013: 1–25.

Kelsen, Hans. "The Preamble of the Charter—A Critical Analysis." *Journal of Politics* 8 (1946): 134–59.

Kelsen, Hans. *Das Problem der Souveränität und die Theorie des Völkerrechts. Beitrag zu einer reinen Rechtslehre.* Tübingen: J.C.B. Mohr [Paul Siebeck], 1920.

Kelsen, Hans. "Sovereignty and International Law." *Georgetown Law Journal* 48, no. 4 (Summer 1960): 627–40.

Kerber, Linda. *Women and the Republic. Intellect and Ideology in Revolutionary America.* Carolina: University of North Carolina Press, 1980.

Kertész, Imre. *Fatelessness.* 1975. Translated by Tom Wilkinson. New York: Vintage International, 2004.

Kesby, Alison. *The Right to Have Rights. Citizenship, Humanity, and International Law.* Oxford: Oxford University Press, 2012.

King, Richard. *Arendt and America.* Chicago: University of Chicago Press, 2015.

Koestler, Arthur. *Darkness at Noon.* New York: Vintage, 2010 [1941].

Krasner, Stephen D. *Sovereignty. Organized Hypocrisy.* Princeton, NJ: Princeton University Press, 1999.

Lassman, Peter. *Pluralism.* Malden, MA, and Cambridge: Polity Press, 2011.

Lauterpacht, Hersch. *International Law and Human Rights.* The Garland Library of War and Peace. New York: Garland Publishing, Inc., 1973.

Lazare, Bernard. *Job's Dungheap. Essays on Jewish Nationalism and Social Revolution.* New York: Schocken Books, 1948.

Lehman, Marjorie. *The En Yaaqov. Jacob Ibn Habib's Search for Faith in the Talmudic Corpus.* Detroit: Wayne State University Press, 2012.

Levi, Primo. *Survival in Auschwitz: If This Is a Man.* Translated by Stuart Woolf. New York: Touchstone, 1996. In Italian as *Se questo è un Uomo.* Torino: Giulio Enuadi, 1947.

Lichtheim, George. "Marx and the Asiatic Mode of Production." *St. Anthony's Papers,* no. 14 (1963): 82–112.

Lilla, Mark. *The Reckless Mind: Intellectuals in Politics.* New York: New York Review of Books, 2001.

Lipstadt, Deborah. *The Eichmann Trial, Jewish Encounters.* New York: Schocken Books, 2011.

Longo, Matthew. *The Politics of Borders. Sovereignty, Security, and the Citizen after 9/11.* Cambridge: Cambridge University Press, 2017.

Luban, David. "Hannah Arendt as a Theorist of International Criminal Law." *International Criminal Law Review* 11 (2011): 621–41.

Lucas, Leopold. "Silesiographia. Festschrift für Norbert Conrad." Carsten Rabe und Matthias Weber: Würzburg, 1998.

Luhmann, Niklas. *The Differentiation of Society.* Translated by Stephen Holmes and Charles Larmore. European Perspectives: A Series in Social Thought and Cultural Criticism. New York: Columbia University Press, 1984.

Lukács, Georg. "Reification and the Consciousness of the Proletariat." In *History and Class Consciousness.* Translated by Rodney Livingstone, 110–31. Cambridge, MA: MIT Press, 1971.

Lyotard, Jean-François. *The Post-Modern Condition. A Report on Knowledge.* Minnesota: University of Minnesota Press, 1984.

MacIntyre, Alasdair C. *After Virtue. A Study in Moral Theory.* Notre Dame: University of Notre Dame Press, 2007 [1981].

Maier-Katkin, Daniel. *Stranger from Abroad. Hannah Arendt, Martin Heidegger, Friendship and Forgiveness.* New York and London: W. W. Norton and Company, 2010.

Mandel, Ruth. *Cosmopolitan Anxieties. Turkish Challenges to Citizenship and Belonging in Germany.* Chapel Hill: Duke University Press, 2008.

Mann, Itamar. *Humanity at Sea: Maritime Migration and the Foundations of International Law.* Cambridge: Cambridge University Press, 2016.

Marrus, Michael R. *The Holocaust in History.* Toronto: Lester and Orpen Dennys, 1987.

Marshall, David L. "The Origins and Character of Hannah Arendt's Theory of Judgment." *Political Theory* 38, no. 3 (April 2010): 1–27.

Mazower, Mark. *Salonica, City of Ghosts: Christians, Muslims and Jews 1430–1950.* New York: Vintage Books, 2006.

McCarthy, Thomas A. "The Critique of Impure Reason. Foucault and the Frankfurt School." *Political Theory* 18, no. 3 (1990): 437–69.

McCormick, John. "Derrida on Law. Poststructuralism Gets Serious." *Political Theory* 29, no. 3 (June 2001): 395–423.

Meier, Heinrich. *Das theologisch-politische Problem. Zum Thema von Leo Strauss.* Stuttgart and Weimar: J. B. Metzler Verlag, 2003.

Menke, Christoph. "The 'Aporias of Human Rights' and the 'One Human Right': Regarding the Coherence of Hannah Arendt's Argument." *Social Research: An International Quarterly* 74, no. 3 (Fall 2007): 739–62.

Mommsen, Hans. *From Weimar to Auschwitz: Essays in German Historiography.* Princeton, NJ: Princeton University Press, 1991.

Mommsen, Wolfgang J. *Max Weber und die deutsche Politik, 1890–1920.* Tübingen: J.C.B. Mohr, 1974.

Morgan, Michael L. *Levinas's Ethical Politics.* Bloomington and Indianapolis: Indiana University Press, 2016.

Moses, Jonathan W. "Exit, Vote and Sovereignty: Migration, States and Globalization." *Review of International Political Economy* 12, no. 1 (February 2005): 53–77.

Moyn, Samuel. "The Continuing Perplexities of Human Rights." *Qui Parle* 22, no. 1 (Fall–Winter 2013): 95–115.

Moyn, Samuel. "Judith Shklar versus the International Criminal Court." *Humanity* 4, no. 3. (Winter 2013): 473–500.

Moyn, Samuel. *The Last Utopia.* Cambridge, MA: Harvard University Press, 2010.

Owens, Patricia. *Between War and Politics. International Relations and the Thought of Hannah Arendt.* Oxford: Oxford University Press, 2007.

Pamuk, Orhan. *Beyaz Kale (The White Castle).* Translated by Victoria Holbrook. New York: Vintage International, 1998.

Pamuk, Orhan. *Snow.* Faber and Faber Fiction, 2014.

Paton, H. J. *The Categorical Imperative: A Study in Kant's Moral Philosophy.* Philadelphia: University of Pennsylvania Press, 1971.

Peguy, Charles. "Portrait of Bernard Lazare." In Bernard Lazarre, *Job's Dungheap.* Translated by Harry Lorin Binsse. New York: Schocken Books, 1948.

Pitkin, Hanna. *The Attack of the Blob. Hannah Arendt's Concept of the Social.* Chicago: University of Chicago Press, 1998.

Polanyi, Karl. *The Great Transformation. The Political and Economic Origins of Our Times.* Foreword by Joseph Stiglitz. Boston: Beacon Press, 2001 [1957].

Poliakov, Léon. *Harvest of Hate. The Nazi Program for the Destruction of the Jews of Europe.* New York: Syracuse University Press, 1954.

Popper, Karl. *The Open Society and Its Enemies.* Princeton, NJ: Princeton University Press, 1994 [1944].

Post, Robert. "Theorizing Disagreement: Re-Conceiving the Relationship between Law and Politics." *California Law Review* 98, no. 4 (2010): 1319–50.

Post, Robert and Reva B. Siegel. "Roe Rage: Democratic Constitutionalism and Backlash." *Harvard Civil Rights and Civil Liberties Review* 42, no. 2 (2007): 373–434.

Putnam, Hilary. "Levinas and Judaism." In *The Cambridge Companion to Levinas.* Edited by Simon Critchley and Robert Bernasconi, 33–62. Cambridge: Cambridge University Press, 2002.

Rabinbach, Anson. "Eichmann in New York: The New York Intellectuals and the Hannah Arendt Controversy." *October* 108 (Spring 2004): 97–111.

Rancière, Jacques. *Disagreement: Politics and Philosophy.* Translated by J. Rose. Minneapolis: University of Minnesota Press, 1999.

Rancière, Jacques. *Dissensus: On Politics and Aesthetics.* Translated by S. Corcoran. London: Continuum, 2010.

Rancière, Jacques. *On the Shores of Politics.* Translated by L. Heron. London: Verso, 1995.

Rancière, Jacques. "Who Is the Subject of the Rights of Man?" *South Atlantic Quarterly* 203, no. 2/3 (Spring/Summer 2004): 297–310.

Ratzabi, Shalom. *Between Zionism and Judaism: The Radical Circles in Brith Shalom, 1925–1933.* Leiden: Brill, 2002.

Rawls, John. *Political Liberalism.* New York: Columbia University Press, 1993.

Rawls, John. "The Priority of Right and the Ideas of the Good," in *Collected Papers,* ed. Samuel Freeman. Cambridge, MA, and London, England: Harvard University Press, 1999: 462–63.

Raz-Krakotzkin, Amnon. *Exil und Binationalismus: Von Gershom Scholem und Hannah Arendt bis zu Edward Said and Mahmoud Darwish.* Berlin: Berlin- Brandenburgische Akademie der Wissenschaften, 2011.

Rejwan, Nissim. *The Last Jews in Baghdad. Remembering a Lost Homeland.* Austin: University of Texas Press, 2004.

Resnik, Judith. "'Within Its Jurisdiction': Moving Boundaries, People and the Law of Migration." *Proceedings of the American Philosophical Society* 160, no. 2 (June 2016): 117–58.

Ritter, Henning. "Abwandern, Widersprechen: Zur aktuellen Bedeutung einer Theorie von A. O. Hirschman." *Frankfurter Allgemeine Zeitung,* November 9, 1989.

Robin, Corey. "The Arendt Wars Continue. Richard Wolin v. Seyla Benhabib." *Corey Robin* (blog). October 1, 2014. http://coreyrobin.com/2014/10/01/the-arendt-wars-continue -richard-wolin-v-seyla-benhabib/.

Robin, Corey. "Did Hannah Arendt Ever See Eichmann Testify? A Second Reply to Richard Wolin." *Corey Robin* (blog). October 2, 2014. http://coreyrobin.com/2014/10/02/did -hannah-arendt-ever-see-eichmann-testify-a-second-reply-to-richard-wolin/.

Robin, Corey. "The Trials of Hannah Arendt." *Nation,* May 12, 2015: 12–25. https://www .thenation.com/article/trials-hannah-arendt/.

Rorty, Richard. "The World Well Lost." In *Consequences of Pragmatism.* 3–18. Minneapolis: University of Minnesota Press, 1982. Originally in *Journal of Philosophy* 69, no. 19 (1972): 649–65.

Roth, Cecil. *History of the Marranos.* London: George Routledge and Sons, Ltd., 1932.

Rousset, David. *Les Jours de Notre Mort.* Paris: Pavois, 1947.

Rushdie, Salman. *The Moor's Last Sigh.* New York: Vintage Books, 1997.

Russell, Matheson and Andrew Montin. "The Rationality of Political Disagreement: Rancière's Critique of Habermas." *Constellations* 22, no. 4 (2015): 543–54.

Sachsenmeier, Domenic and Jens Riedel, with Shmuel Eisenstadt, eds. *Reflections on Multiple Modernities.* Brill Publishers, 2002.

Sagiv, Assaf. "George Steiner's Jewish Problem." *Azure* 5763 (Summer 2003): 130–54.

Said, Edward. "The Morning After." *London Review of Books* 15, no. 20–21 (October 1993). https://www.lrb.co.uk/v15/n20/edward-said/the-morning-after.

Said, Edward. "Reflections on Exile." In *Reflections on Exile and Other Essays*. New York: Harvard University Press, 2000: 173–86.

Sandel, Michael. *Liberalism and the Limits of Justice*. Cambridge: Cambridge University Press, 1982.

Scheuerman, William E. "Authoritarian Populism and the Rule of Law." Forthcoming in *Judith N. Shklar: A Political Companion*. Edited by Sam Ashenden and Andreas Hess. Philadelphia: University of Pennsylvania Press.

Scheuerman, William. "The Realist Revival in Political Philosophy, or: Why New Is Not Always Improved." *International Politics* 50, no. 6 (2013): 798–814.

Scholem, Gershom. "'Eichmann in Jerusalem': An Exchange of Letters between Gershom Scholem and Hannah Arendt." *Encounter* 22 (January 1964): 51–56.

Scholem, Gershom. *Sabbatai Ṣevi. The Mystical Messiah*. Princeton, NJ: Princeton University Press, 1973.

Schottker, Detlev and Erdmut Wizisla. "Hannah Arendt und Walter Benjamin. Konstellationen, Debatten, Vermittlungen." In *Arendt und Benjamin. Texte, Briefe, Dokumente*. Edited by Detlev Schottker and Erdmut Wizisla. Frankfurt: Suhrkamp, 2006.

Schuessler, Jennifer. "Book Portrays Genocidal Nazi as Evil, but Not Banal." *New York Times*, September 3, 2014.

Schwan, Alexander. *Politische Philosophie im Denken Heideggers*. Westdt. Verl: Köln- Opladen, 1965.

Scott, Joan. *Only Paradoxes to Offer: French Feminists and the Rights of Man*. Cambridge, MA: Harvard University Press, 1996.

Segev, Tom. *The 7th Million. The Israelis and the Holocaust*. Translated by Haim Watzman. New York: Henry Holt and Company, 1991.

Sen, Amartya. "Foreword to the Twentieth Anniversary Edition." In *The Passions and the Interests*. Princeton, NJ: Princeton University Press, 1997 [1977].

Şenocak, Zafer. *Atlas of a Tropical Germany. Essays on Politics and Culture. 1990–1998*. Translated and edited by Leslie Adelson. Lincoln and London: University of Nebraska Press, 2000.

Simmons, W. Paul. *Human Rights Law and the Marginalized Other*. Cambridge: Cambridge University Press, 2011.

Sleeper, James A. "American Brethren. Hebrews and Puritans." *World Affairs. A Journal of Ideas and Debate* 172, no. 2 (Fall 2009): 46–60.

Slezkine, Yuri. *The Jewish Century*. Princeton, NJ: Princeton University Press, 2006.

Sperber, Manès. *Wie eine Träne im Ozean. Romantrilogie*. Munich: Deutsche Taschenbuch Verlag, 1980 [1976].

Spivak, Gayatri. *A Critique of Postcolonial Reason. Toward a History of the Vanishing Present*. Cambridge, MA: Harvard University Press, 1999.

Standage, Tom. *The Turk. The Life and Times of the Famous Eighteenth-Century Chess-Playing Machine*. New York: Berkeley Books, 2002.

Stangneth, Bettina. *Eichmann vor Jerusalem. Das unbehelligte Leben eines Massenmörders*. 2011. Zurich-Hamburg: Rowohlt Taschenbuch, 2014. Translated by Ruth Martin as *Eichmann before Jerusalem. The Unexamined Life of a Mass Murderer*. New York: Alfred Knopf, 2014.

Steiner, George. *Errata. An Examined Life*. New Haven, CT: Yale University Press, 1998 [1997].

Suhrke, Astri and Sergio Aguayo. *Escape from Violence: Conflict and the Refugee Crisis in the Developing World*. Edited by Aristide R. Zolberg. Oxford: Oxford University Press, 1989.

Sum, Anna Barbara. "Widerspruch als Prinzip: Nachruf auf Albert Hirschman." *Geschichte und Gesellschaft* 39 (January–March 2013): 125–38.

Sweet, Alec Stone. *Governing with Judges. Constitutional Politics in Europe*. Oxford: Oxford University Press, 2000.

Sweet, Alec Stone. *The Judicial Construction of Europe*. Oxford: Oxford University Press, 2004.

Totani, Yuma. *The Tokyo War Crimes Trial. The Pursuit of Justice in the Wake of World War II*. Harvard East Asian Monograph, 299. Cambridge, MA, and London: Harvard University Press, 2008.

Urbinati, Nadia. " 'Proving Hamlet Wrong': The Creative Role of Doubt in Albert Hirschman's Social Thought." In "Albert Hirschman and the Social Sciences: A Memorial Roundtable." *Humanity: An International Journal of Human Rights, Humanitarianism, and Development* 6, no. 2 (Summer 2015): 267–27.

Utlu, Deniz. *Die Ungehaltenen*. Ullstein Buchverlag: Berlin, 2014.

The Ventotene Manifesto of the Union of European Federalists at http://www.federalists.eu/uef/library/books/the-ventotene-manifesto/. Accessed on May 6, 2017.

Verovšek, Peter. *The European Rupture: A Critical Theory of Memory and Integration in the Wake of Total War*. Forthcoming.

Villa, Dana. "Beyond Good and Evil: Arendt, Nietzsche, and the Aestheticization of Political Action." *Political Theory* 20, no. 2 (1992): 274–30.

Waldenfels, Bernhard. "Levinas and the Face of the Other." In *The Cambridge Companion to Levinas*. Edited by Simon Critchley and Robert Bernasconi. Cambridge: Cambridge University Press, 2004.

Walzer, Judith B. "Oral History of Tenured Women in the Faculty of Arts and Sciences at Harvard University." (1988). Hadl. 1902.1/00709. Murray Research Archive.

Walzer, Michael. *Spheres of Justice. A Defense of Pluralism and Equality*. New York: Basic Books, 1983.

Watt, Michael and Owen Bowcott. "Tories Plan to Withdraw UK from European Convention on Human Rights." *Guardian*, October 3, 2014. https://www.theguardian.com/politics/2014/oct/03/tories-plan-uk-withdrawal-european-convention-on-human-rights.

Weber, Max. *Economy and Society*. Translated by Guenther Roth and Claus Wittich. Berkeley and Los Angeles: University of California Press, 1978.

Weber, Max. *Gesammelte Aufsätze zur Religionssoziologie*. Tübingen: J.C.B. Mohr, 1920.

Weber, Max. "The Meaning of 'Ethical Neutrality' in Sociology and Economics." In *The Methodology of the Social Sciences*. Edited by Henry A. Finch. London and New Brunswick: Transaction Publishers: 2011.

Weber, Max. "Objectivity in Social Science and Social Policy." In *The Methodology of the Social Sciences*. Translated and edited by Edward A. Shils and Henry Finch. New York: The Free Press, 1949 [1904].

Weber, Max. *On Law in Economy and Society*. Edited by Max Rheinstein. Cambridge, MA: Touchstone, 1954.

Weber, Max. "Science as a Vocation." In *Max Weber: Essays in Sociology*. Originally published as "Wissenschaft als Beruf." In *Gesammlte Aufsaetze zur Wissenschaftslehre*, 524–55. Tübingen, 1922.

Weber, Max. "The Social Psychology of World Religions." In Max Weber. *Essays in Sociology*. Edited and translated by H. H. Gerth and C. W. Mills. New York: Oxford University Press, 1974.

Weber, Max. *The Theory of Social and Economic Organization*. Edited and with an introduction by Talcott Parsons. New York: The Free Press, 1964 [1947].

Weiler, Joseph H. *The Constitution of Europe*. Cambridge: Cambridge University Press, 1999.

Weiss, Paul. *Nationality and Statelessness in International Law*. 2nd edition. Alphaen aan den Rijn: Sijthoff and Noordhoff, 1979.

Wellmer, Albrecht. *The Persistence of Modernity. Essays on Aesthetics, Ethics and Postmodernism*. Translated by David Midgley. Cambridge: Polity Press, 1991.

Wessel, Julia Schulze. "On Border Subjects: Rethinking the Figure of the Refugee and the Undocumented Migrant." *Constellations* 23, no. 1 (2016): 46–57.

West, Robin. "Reconsidering Legalism." *Minnesota Law Review* 88 (2003): 119–58.

White, Steven. *Political Theory and Postmodernism*. New York: Cambridge University Press, 1991.

Wiesel, Eli. *Night*. 1972. Translated by Marion Wiesel. New York: Hill and Wang, 2006. Originally as *La Nuit*. Paris: Les Editions de Minuit, 1958.

Wieseltier, Leon. "When a Sage Dies, All Are His Kin." *The New Republic*, December 1, 1997: 27–31.

Williams, Bernard. *Ethics and the Limits of Philosophy*. 1985. London and New York: Routledge, 2006.

Wolin, Richard. "The Banality of Evil. The Demise of a Legend." *Jewish Review of Books*, September 4, 2014.

Wolin, Richard, ed. *The Heidegger Controversy*. Cambridge, MA: MIT Press, 1993.

Wolin, Richard. "Thoughtlessness Revisited. A Response to Seyla Benhabib." *Jewish Review of Books*. September 30, 2014.

Wolin, Sheldon. *Politics and Vision. Continuity and Innovation in Western Political Thought*. New foreword by Wendy Brown. Princeton, NJ: Princeton University Press, 2016 [1960].

Yerushalmi, Yosef Hayim. *Zakhor. Jewish Memory and Jewish History*. The Samuel and Althea Stroum Lectures in Jewish Studies. Seattle and London: University of Washington Press, 1982.

Young-Bruehl, Elisabeth. *For Love of the World: A Biography of Hannah Arendt*. New Haven, CT: Yale University Press, 1982.

Yovel, Yirmiyahu. *The Other Within. The Marranos. Split Identity and Emerging Modernity*. Princeton, NJ: Princeton University Press, 2009.

Zangwill, Israel. "Zion, Whence Cometh My Help?" In *Speeches, Articles and Letters of Israel Zangwill*. Edited by Maurice Simon, London: Soncino, 1937.

Zeitlin, Samuel Garrett. "Propaganda and Critique: An Introduction to Land and Sea." In *Spatiality, Sovereignty and Carl Schmitt. Geographies of the Nomos*. Edited by Stephen Legg, xxxi–lxix. London and New York: Routledge, 2001.

Zertal, Idith. *Israel's Holocaust and the Politics of Nationhood*. New York and Cambridge: Cambridge University Press, 2005.

Zimmermann, Moshe. "Hannah Arendt, the Early 'Post-Zionist.'" In *Hannah Arendt in Jerusalem*. Edited by Steven E. Aschheim, 181–94. Berkeley and Los Angeles: University of California Press, 2001.

Zollberg, Aristide, Astri Suhrke, and Sergio Aguayo. *Escape from Violence: Conflict and the Refugee Crisis in the Developing World*. Oxford: Oxford University Press, 1989.

# INDEX

## A NOTE ON THE TYPE

This book has been composed in Arno, an Old-style serif typeface in the classic Venetian tradition, designed by Robert Slimbach at Adobe.